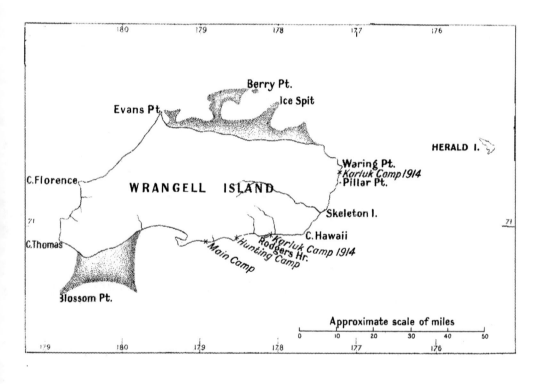

Ada Blackjack

ADA
BLACKJACK

A TRUE STORY OF SURVIVAL IN THE ARCTIC

JENNIFER NIVEN

NEW YORK

The author makes grateful acknowledgment to the following for
permission to reprint photographs:

Billy Blackjack Johnson, Bill Lawless, Marian Reiss:
Photos (Section 1): 1; 2; 3; 4; 5; 7; 8; 9; 11; 12; 21; 23; 24; 25; 26; 27; 29
Photos (Section 2): 1; 5; 6; 7; 9; 10; 11; 12; 13; 14; 15; 16; 17; 19; 20; 21; 23; 24; 25; 26; 27
Photo of Expedition Team, page 4

Dartmouth College Library:
Photos (Section 1): 13; 14; 15; 16; 17; 18; 19; 20; 22; 28; 30
Photos (Section 2): 2; 3; 4; 8; 18
Map

Copyright © 2003 by Jennifer Niven

For information address
Hyperion
77 West 66th Street
New York, New York 10023-6298.

Excerpt from *Northern Tales* by Howard Norman,
copyright © 1990 by Howard Norman. Used by permission of
Pantheon Books, a division of Random House, Inc.

Library of Congress Cataloging-in-Publication Data

Niven, Jennifer.
    Ada Blackjack : a true story of survival in the Arctic / by Jennifer Niven.
        p.   cm.
    ISBN: 0-7868-6863-5
    1. Blackjack, Ada, 1898 or -9—   2. Inuit women—Biography.   3. Women explorers—
Arctic regions—Biography.   4. Arctic regions—Discovery and exploration.   5. Wrangel
Island (Russia)—Discovery and exploration.   I. Title.

E99.E7B6563 2003
915.7'7—dc21
[B]   2003050826

Hyperion books are available for special promotions and premiums.
For details contact
Michael Rentas, Manager, Inventory and Premium Sales
Hyperion
77 West 66th Street, 11th floor
New York, New York 10023,
or call 212-456-0133.

FIRST EDITION

1 3 5 7 9 10 8 6 4 2

Contents

Part IV: Relief

Part V: Fallout

Part VI: Remembrance

As she looked back, the trail behind
her faded away and she was way up
in the air, with no man behind her
and only the smooth trail
leading into the sky.

—ADA BLACKJACK
"The Lady in the Moon"

Preface

IN SEPTEMBER 1923, a diminutive twenty-five-year-old Eskimo woman named Ada Blackjack emerged as the heroic survivor of an ambitious polar expedition. In the annals of Arctic exploration, many men have been hailed as heroes, but a hero like Ada was unheard of at the time. She was a young and unskilled woman who headed into the Arctic in search of money and a husband. What she found instead was a nightmare rivaling even the most horrific folktales she had grown up hearing from the storytellers in her village.

After Ada's triumphant return to civilization, the international press called her the female Robinson Crusoe. But all reports came from the imaginations of reporters. Ada Blackjack refused to talk to anyone about her two years in the Arctic. Only on one occasion did she speak up for herself.

Ada Blackjack never considered herself a hero. As far as she was concerned, she did what she *had* to do when she found herself in a life and death situation. Faced with responsibilities and challenges she had never known existed, she survived.

In later years, when people called her brave, she would tilt her head to one side and gaze at them, unblinking, with dark brown eyes. After some time, she would answer simply: "Brave? I don't know about that. But I would never give up hope while I'm still alive."

*　　*　　*

I first heard of Ada when I was researching my first book, *The Ice Master*. I discovered that one of the men I was writing about, Fred Maurer, had miraculously survived the ill-fated Canadian Arctic Expedition of 1913–1914 only to return to Wrangel Island years later with three other men and one woman—Ada Blackjack. I was mystified as to why Maurer would go back to the island, after all he had suffered there. But even more than that, I was intrigued by the woman's story. Who was Ada Blackjack?

Searching for answers, I discovered numerous materials housed in archives in Canada, Alaska, New Hampshire, and North Carolina. First and foremost, there was Ada's own diary, one of the most important resources of all. The rest of the story is filled in by her collection of papers; other records and firsthand accounts, including the detailed, two-volume diary of her comrade Lorne Knight, in which Ada figures prominently; and the memories and knowledge of Billy Blackjack Johnson, Ada's surviving son, who was enthusiastic about my telling the story of his mother's experience in the Arctic and who gave me full access to his own materials and information. Tragically, Billy died on June 22, 2003, at age seventy-eight—and thus did not live to see this book published.

In addition, I received from the nephew of Milton Galle—the youngest member of the expedition—a treasure box filled with papers, letters, telegrams, photographs, and a partial journal. Until Milton Galle's nephew, Bill Lawless, generously entrusted them to my care, these papers had never been read or seen by anyone outside of the Galle family—even though expedition organizer Vilhjalmur Stefansson had been anxious to obtain them.

As Mrs. Rudolph Martin Anderson once wrote to the mother of Allan Crawford, the young Canadian placed in charge of the party, "Real history is made up from the documents that were not meant to be published." Perhaps my most valuable resources have been the letters written between the families of the four young men on the expedition—to each other and also to Vilhjalmur Stefansson. All impressions expressed by the characters herein come from these letters, journals, and other firsthand materials, as does any quoted dialogue. Also in keeping with the language of the time, I use the term "Eskimo" instead of the present-day preferred "Inuit." Because the four men called each other by their last names, I refer to them as Crawford, Knight, Maurer, and Galle. The only exceptions come in regard to their families and loved ones, who knew them as Allan, Lorne, Fred, and Milton. Ada Blackjack, however, was only known to the men and to Stefansson as Ada, and that is what she is called herein.

Loss and survival quickly emerged as the two main themes in this book, made all the more resonant and ironic by my own unexpected journey of loss and survival throughout the writing of it. Four days after I finished the first draft of the manuscript, my father passed away after a gallant battle with cancer. As I wrote about Lorne Knight's own deterioration from scurvy and Ada's struggle to live in spite of all that she endured, the parallels to my father's last days became all too real.

This book is the story of Ada Blackjack—during her ordeal and after. It is also the story of four young men—Lorne Knight, Fred Maurer, Allan Crawford, and Milton Galle—and their families.

Finally, it is very much the story of an enormous spirit that could outlast anything. As one of Ada's great-nephews remembers, "I recall her as a small, sweet woman whose faith was as big as the sky."

Members of the 1921 Wrangel Island Expedition

Allan Crawford—*commander; Toronto, Canada (age 20)*
Lorne Knight—*second in command; McMinnville, Oregon (age 28)*
Fred Maurer—*third in command; New Philadelphia, Ohio (age 28)*
Milton Galle—*assistant; New Braunfels, Texas (age 19)*
Ada Blackjack—*seamstress; Nome, Alaska (age 23)*
Victoria ("Vic")—*expedition cat*

PART I

THE FIVE

There, with only a dead man as companion,
surrounded by seas of ice, Ada Blackjack
wrote the real epic of the North.

—*THE WORLD MAGAZINE*
October 30, 1927

One

HER FATHER WAS DYING. He had eaten meat that was too old and afterward he had eaten fresh meat, which turned his stomach, and now he was sick from poison. Eight-year-old Ada Delutuk and one of her younger sisters dressed him in pants and skin boots and his "parkie," as Ada called it, and then they wrapped him up in skins to keep him warm.

Together, they somehow managed to tie their father to a sled, hitch the dogs up, and set out to drive to Nome. The town was thirty miles east of their remote village of Spruce Creek, Alaska, but the little girls had no choice. They needed to get help and, with their mother away, Ada was the oldest and the one left in charge.

It was difficult to say how many miles they had traveled before Ada and her sister realized that their father was dead. And so, defeated and brokenhearted, they simply turned back and took him home.

*   *   *

Their home was the Eskimo settlement of Spruce Creek, Alaska, eight miles east of the tiny, rustic village of Solomon. Ada Delutuk was born in 1898, the year of the Alaskan Gold Rush. In 1899 and 1900, thousands of people converged upon Solomon in search of gold. By 1904, the Gold Rush had brought seven saloons and a post office to the town, and soon after there was phone and mail service and a daily boat to Nome. But in 1913, tidal storms with 60-mile-per-hour winds and 40-foot breakers washed away the railroad tracks and most of the town, and the once thriving village of one thousand people became a quiet Eskimo community of three hundred. In 1918 the flu epidemic swept through the area, extinguishing almost the entire population of Spruce Creek.

Ada Delutuk was spared, however. Shortly after her father's death she had been sent by her mother to Nome, where she was taken in by Methodist missionaries, who taught her to read and write English at a third-grade level. At the mission school she learned mathematics, composition, and handwriting. She also learned to cook "white people's food" and to wash, iron, clean, and sew. Sewing was especially vital in the education of an Eskimo girl because the skill was so crucial to surviving in the cold, frozen North. In addition, the missionaries taught her many things at the school that she would never have known otherwise—how to sing hymns, to bathe, to comb her hair, to brush her teeth, to avoid tobacco and alcohol, to handle money, and to honor the American flag.

While there, she also discovered the Bible. She was educated about God and she learned to pray. The school was a welcome relief from the dinginess and depression of the Solomon region. Even though Solomon was barely large enough to be considered a village, and Spruce Creek was even more rural, Ada had essentially been raised as a city Eskimo. She wasn't required to hunt or trap or build shelters, and therefore did not have the experience of tribal living. She knew how to sew furs and she could do this pretty well, eventually earning a part-time living in Nome making clothing for the miners there.

Ada was a full-blooded Eskimo, with delicate features and a guarded smile. She was small—not even five feet tall—poker-faced, pretty, and unassuming. Her olive complexion was clear with a flush of underlying red; her hair a straight blue-black. Ada liked nice clothes and hats, and dressed as smartly as she was able on her skimpy earnings as a seamstress and housekeeper. She displayed a particular fondness for dark blue suits, which she often bought in the children's sections of the Nome stores.

She had a dignified, graceful air about her and she could be charming. She said little, though, because she was extremely shy and private. One of her friends described her dark brown eyes as being "habitually enigmatic—closed windows." Her voice was low and soft, and she had a habit of sitting still as a statue, listening to someone talk with her head cocked to one side. She was accustomed to long silences and was distrustful of strangers. Yet her natural instinct was to be cheerful and there was often a lightheartedness about her that she didn't allow many people to see.

She had been nourished on the legends passed down by the storytellers—among them her grandmother—who would weave their tales around the cramped light of the oil lamps. The stories were sometimes poetic, sometimes wise, sometimes blood-curdling. As a young girl, Ada learned to read the sky through stories. She knew that the Milky Way was a trail of old women wandering across the heavens. She knew that the Big Dipper was a caribou because her mother always said, "Ada, look at it a long time and see if you can't see a caribou." She knew that when the handle of the Big Dipper was clear and straight there would be good hunting and reindeer would be plentiful.

She also knew that the polar bear, the greatest mythical figure of her people, was to be feared more than death. Eskimo legends were filled with images of "the great lonely roamer," as they called the fiercest of bears. Nanook, the polar bear, was a wise and powerful creature which possessed eerily humanlike qualities. Many of the legends merged bears with men into a kind of polar-man hybrid who walked upright and lived in igloos. Eskimos believed readily in animism, in which each living thing and object possesses a malevolent or benevolent spirit. The Eskimo's life was often governed by a need to appease these spirits and keep them happy. They believed that Nanook shed his skin in private, that he was able to talk, and that he allowed himself to be killed to capture the souls of the tools that did the killing so that he might take them with him into the afterlife. Bred on these convictions, Ada was haunted by the idea of being eaten alive by a polar bear and trapped in its stomach.

When Ada was sixteen, she married a notorious hunter and musher named Jack Blackjack, but in 1921, by the time she was twenty-two, she was already divorced. Early in her marriage to Blackjack she knew it was no good. She had three children by him, two of whom died. He treated her brutally—beating her and starving her, and eventually deserting her on the Seward Peninsula, where they were living.

In Eskimo tradition most men and women chose each other as husband and wife without a legal marriage ceremony. There was no minister or official document; the couple would simply move in together. The practice made getting divorced much easier. If you tired of someone or liked another man's wife, you would just leave or trade spouses and that meant you were divorced.

After her marriage ended, Ada found herself abandoned by her husband, "bone poor, almost naked for lack of clothes and with no money." There was nothing to do but go home to her mother, who now lived in Nome, some forty miles away. Ada and five-year-old Bennett, her only surviving child, had to walk the entire distance from the Seward Peninsula to Nome, and when Bennett grew too tired, she carried him.

There was an orphanage in Nome which looked after children who had no parents or whose parents couldn't take care of them, and this was where Ada took Bennett. He was tubercular and fragile, and because she could not afford to keep him any longer on her meager and sporadic earnings from sewing clothes and cleaning houses, and because he needed the full-time attention of doctors and nurses, she brought him to a home where others could care for him and try to make him well.

Nome in 1921 was violent, turbulent, and grim. There were no sewers, no ditches, no safe drinking water, and crime was rampant.

Inhabitants feared for their lives as people were frequently shot to death or stabbed in the middle of town. The miners had built the city around themselves and their greed in 1899, just a year after Ada was born in Spruce Creek. Since then, the population of Nome had ebbed and flowed, according to the climate of gold. In 1900, there had been an influx of 12,488 inhabitants arriving by steamship from Seattle and San Francisco ports, while thousands more converged upon the town from other points in Alaska. Nome was barren and treeless and ran smack against the water. The beaches were covered with prospectors and their tents, while the town took shape hastily in slapdash wooden buildings and shanties.

Still, even with its crime and streets of mud, it was the fanciest, most sophisticated place Ada had ever seen. And there were white men everywhere, making money from their discoveries on the beach. They seemed to Ada more cultured than the Eskimo men she was used to—better educated and smarter, as if they knew how to take care of themselves and their money.

With Bennett safely housed in the orphanage, Ada tried to find work as a seamstress. She had never heard the word *igloo*, and did not know the first thing about hunting, fishing, trapping, or living on the land. She eventually was able to find work sewing for the miners in town. But it was sporadic work with little pay, and she needed the money for herself and for Bennett.

If she was ever going to be able to bring Bennett home again, she would have to save as much money as she could. It was not easy for a mother to be away from her only child, to know that she wasn't able to care for him or heal him or give him what he needed. Ada hoped that it would only be a matter of time before she and Bennett were reunited and living together again, under the same roof.

Here was a chance to gratify a longing
of my heart that was with me at all times—
it was the wanderlust calling from the lands
of the aurora, the midnight sun, and wastes
of ice and snow.

—FRED MAURER

Two

ON FEBRUARY 18, 1921, Americans heard the voice of their president—Warren G. Harding—booming across the radio airwaves for the first time. That same day, French aviator Etienne Oehmichen successfully made the world's first helicopter flight. On February 22, the first day-night transcontinental flight delivered mail from New York to San Francisco, and several days later the first Thompson submachine gun was manufactured.

In spite of the postwar boom, 3.5 million people were unemployed. There were over nine million automobiles on America's roads. Charlie Chaplin brought moving picture audiences to tears with *The Kid*, and Rudolph Valentino made women swoon in the World War I epic *The Four Horsemen of the Apocalypse*. In Pennsylvania, police, alarmed by the shrinking hems of women's skirts, issued a decree that required all skirts to fall at least four inches below the knee.

And in towns across America, Chautauqua week became the most important week of the whole year. Flyers were pasted to store fronts, shop windows, and lampposts. Banners waved proudly from automobiles and buggies.

Called "the most American thing in America" by Teddy Roosevelt, the Chautauqua circuit was a touring college of sorts, bringing art, education, and issues to people who might never have been exposed to them otherwise. Seven days in one place, five days in another, it always took place in small towns in the heartland, where people were, for the most part, cut off from the outside world. Four-tent circuits traveled one route, and seven-tent circuits traveled another. Lively programs offered variety in morning, afternoon, and evening shows for each day of the tour; then the entertainers packed up and moved on to the next place and started over again. To the performers, the routine often became tedious, but to the audiences of each town they visited, Chautauqua was magic every time.

Photography was still a novelty in many small towns; movies and radio were in the infant stage; and there was no television. For those who never left home, Chautauqua exposed them to art, literature, political thought and theory, social issues, and geographical wonders. For the very first time, they might see a photograph or lantern slide of the North Pole, the African desert, or the pyramids of Egypt.

It was the seven-tent Chautauqua that pulled into New Braunfels, Texas, in April 1921. *Seven days filled with splendid attractions! Twelve concerts! Ten lectures! A big play production!* The air was filled with the noise of people and automobiles and equipment as the smart, perfumed women and handsome, mustached men stepped off the train or out of sleekly lined motor cars and had the look of Somewhere Else.

The residents of New Braunfels greeted the visitors with a parade, which was how they had celebrated the start of each Chautauqua since April of 1917, the first year the tour had come to town. People from neighboring cities which weren't lucky enough to have been chosen as stopping points traveled in for the show.

Local boys lined up for a chance to set out folding chairs or pound nails into platforms or raise the gigantic brown tents that were Chautauqua's trademark. Under those tents—each of which could hold two thousand people—presidents and politicians, opera singers and musicians, actors, humorists, contortionists, adventurers, authors, and orators would perform or speak to the people who had worked hard to set aside extra money to purchase a ticket—75 cents for a day or $2.50 for the whole week.

On opening night, audiences were treated to music, dancing, and speeches. The following afternoon they might see barbershop quartets, magicians, gymnasts, acrobats, and bands. Children rushed out of school at three o'clock and ran to catch the matinees. In the evening, after most of the young people had been put to bed, there was a melodrama, with a cast of six or so, and music again. Then there was the backbone of the Chautauqua circuit—the inspirational and informational lecture, a different one every evening, on topics ranging from women's suffrage to the environment. On the third night the keynote speaker—the star of the tour—would appear.

That spring of 1921, when the highly anticipated third night arrived, the audience in New Braunfels, Texas, enjoyed a musical prelude. Then it was Fred Maurer's difficult mission to warm up the crowd. The twenty-eight-year-old had given up his job filling orders and overseeing inventory at the Goodyear Tire and Rubber Company in Akron, Ohio, to take on the thankless position of being the opening act for noted explorer and anthropologist Vilhjalmur Stefansson, who, as a headliner, commanded $1,000 each week for his speeches.

Maurer had not always been an office worker sitting behind a desk. Seven years earlier he had returned from the Arctic a hero. In spite of his piercing blue eyes and chiseled jaw, his thick blond hair, broad shoulders, and stocky, football player physique, Maurer didn't look like an adventurer. The beloved and pampered youngest of ten, he was introverted, soft-spoken, stoic, reserved, and cool. He was a kind man who hated conflict and raised voices, and he didn't frequent beer halls or chase women. He was an upstanding member of his small Ohio community. He belonged to the Masonic Lodge of New Philadelphia, the Delta Upsilon Fraternity of Marietta College, and the Geographical Society, and was a devout congregant of the First Church of the Reformed.

He had left home at age eighteen to pursue his dreams of adventure. In San Francisco he signed up as deckhand on a whaling ship named the *Belvedere*. In March of 1906 at Herschel Island, just off the northern coast of Canada, Maurer met Vilhjalmur Stefansson for the first time when the explorer came aboard as the honored guest of the ship's captain. A noted explorer, ethnologist, anthropologist, author, and orator, Stefansson was a man who inspired awe in young boys who dreamed of the North. Maurer was no exception, having read about him in the papers and heard his name for years.

It was not until 1912, when Stefansson was planning his highly ambitious 1913 Canadian Arctic Expedition, that Maurer was to meet up with him again. In addition to scientific and geographic work, the primary goal of the expedition was to discover new lands. Stefansson staunchly believed there was an uncharted, undiscovered continent at the top of the world, and he intended to find it. The *Belvedere*'s skipper recommended Maurer to Stefansson for work on the expedition's crew. Impressed by Maurer's poise and intelligence, Vilhjalmur Stefansson hired him as fireman.

But the 1913 expedition proved a disaster. After the expedition ship *Karluk* became trapped in an ice floe just a month after setting sail, Stefansson abandoned most of his company to continue his journey on foot, crossing over the ice to the Alaskan mainland. For months, the ship drifted to the northwest until, five months later, the *Karluk* sank, stranding scientists and seamen far out in the polar ice. Maurer joined his fellow crewmen in cursing their absent leader. After the ship's captain led the abandoned group one hundred miles across treacherous ice to formidable, desolate Wrangel Island, Maurer and the others again cursed Stefansson while they struggled to eke out an existence. Many of the men died—eleven of the original twenty-five— but Maurer survived somehow and spent six months on Wrangel

Island, two hundred miles northeast of Siberia and four hundred miles northwest of Alaska, before he was rescued.

"It seemed like entering into another world," Maurer wrote when he returned home to Ohio afterward. "The daily mail, the roar and rumble of traffic . . . seemed so new. The great silent north was far behind." After he set foot once more on American soil, he found that everything seemed novel and interesting. He became fascinated with billboards and signs, and had a strange desire to purchase everything he saw. For two years, he had lived like a prisoner of the ice, the cold, and a barren and unfriendly island, and once home he reveled in his newfound freedom. He let himself buy what he wanted and eat what he wanted and he slowly began to feel like himself again. But not completely.

After returning from Wrangel Island, Maurer felt partially lost, partially empty, and increasingly restless. There was a void inside him which he tried to fill by joining the army during World War I and through speaking and writing about the *Karluk* expedition. None of it helped to heal the old wounds or ease the restlessness Maurer felt deep down, in a place so private he rarely revealed it to anyone.

Gradually, he began to forget his resentment toward Stefansson and his gratitude at being home and safe, warm, and well fed. He began to yearn for adventure again, just as he had when he was a teenager and longing to go to sea, and he became obsessed with study, spending his spare hours schooling himself on the Arctic. It was Stefansson who suggested he join the Chautauqua tour.

"Can you give me definite information as to prospects of going north, anxious to . . . but should know soon before close of Chautauqua season so can make plans accordingly," Maurer had telegraphed Stefansson before joining him in Texas.

"Sorry no chance to go north this year but think there will be next year if you still want to go," Stefansson had replied.

Actually, it was a privilege and an honor to be a part of Chautauqua and to speak to people about his polar adventures, and Maurer also liked to help out in any other ways he could, whether running the projector or setting up and taking down tents. He had signed with Chautauqua to spend the summer lecturing on the Fours, as they called the four-day circuit, which was something to be proud of. No warm-up act—just Maurer himself as a main attraction.

But here on the spring tour, as the opening act to Stefansson, it was disheartening to see the restless looks on the faces in the audience, the glances at wristwatches to check the time, the yawns behind the paper fans that fluttered constantly under the oppressive heat of the tent. Maurer always drew a quarter of the crowd that Stefansson attracted with his famous name and reputation, and although a good many of that number were admiring young ladies, eager for a glimpse of Maurer's intense blue eyes, golden hair, dimpled chin, and matinee idol looks, it only served as a frustrating reminder to the want-to-be explorer of just how far he needed to go to grow into his hero's shoes.

Why should any one want to explore the Arctic?

Vilhjalmur Stefansson knew how to work an audience, and no audience was more willing to listen to his promise of the Great White North than the ones he found in the small, dusty, uncultured towns on the Chautauqua tour.

The land up there is all covered with eternal ice; there is everlasting winter with intense cold. The country, whether land or sea, is a lifeless waste of eternal silence. The stars look down with a cruel glitter, and the depressing effect of the winter darkness upon the spirit of man is heavy beyond words. This . . . is the current picture of the Arctic, and this is . . . what we have to unlearn before we can read in a true light any story of Arctic exploration.

His words packed a punch. It was as if he knew what people wanted to believe, at their deepest level, and he gave it to them forcefully, assuredly, conclusively. He created dreams and ideas, and, some would argue, had even created himself. Born William Stephenson in 1879 in Manitoba, Canada, he had changed his name to Vilhjalmur Stefansson in college because he thought it sounded more in keeping with his Icelandic heritage and because it seemed a more fitting name for a future explorer.

In order to understand the Arctic explorer and his work we must understand the Arctic as it really is.

At forty-one, Stefansson was effortlessly elegant, polished, articulate, and brilliant. With his fair, wavy hair, delicate features, and slight build, he did not look the part of explorer. But he possessed great charisma born out of enormous confidence, and it took little for him to capture an audience as he spoke of his years in the distant, exotic North. Stefansson believed in a concept he called the Friendly Arctic and it served as the message of his speeches and the foundation of his career. He portrayed the North as an hospitable, habitable place for anyone with good sense. "Given a healthy body and a cheerful disposition," he was fond of declaring, "a family can now live at the North Pole as comfortably as it can in Hawaii." And, "I think that anyone with good eyesight and a rifle can live anywhere in the Polar regions indefinitely."

When he spoke about the Arctic and when he showed his lantern slides from various expeditions, the audience was enraptured. There was a great, convincing power in his words because Stefansson himself believed in them so completely and resolutely. He was a man concerned with glory and power, a man of deep, steadfast conviction, and a man whose passion could be infectious to those who admired him. "In one way or another," he once said, "the idea of greatness formed part of all my visions."

The Arctic as pictured in . . . the minds of our contemporaries, does not exist. It may be a pity to destroy the illusion, for the world is getting daily poorer in romance. Elves and fairies no longer dance in the woods, and it appears a sort of vandalism to destroy the glamorous and heroic North by too intimate knowledge.

Each time Stefansson took to the podium, his Chautauqua traveling companions hung on his words, just like the rugged pioneers from the American heartland, or the unschooled farmers from down south. He gave them all something grand to believe in and they grasped at it willingly. After all, here was a man who had commanded the longest expedition in polar history and who had discovered the last unmapped islands in the world, claiming them for Canada.

In addition to Fred Maurer, Stefansson's travel companions of that 1921 spring Chautauqua circuit included the outspoken Lorne Knight. After his lectures, Stefansson would answer questions from the platform where he stood, and the taciturn Maurer and the forthright Knight sometimes sat up there with him, working the lantern slides or film projector, and adding their viewpoints as former Arctic travelers who had served with Stefansson. The two Stefansson alumni, despite their divergent personalities, had become fast friends on the Chautauqua circuit. But because they were so different in character and taste, Maurer and Knight often disagreed with each other, which meant Stefansson himself stepped in as mediator.

Twenty-seven-year-old Errol Lorne Knight had lucked into becoming the chief feature of the Ellison-White Chautauqua four-tent circuit of 1920 when Stefansson was unable to free himself from a messy contractual situation. Chautauqua used the explorer's famous name to advertise Knight as well as the motion pictures Stefansson had taken while in the Arctic: "Famous Stefansson films with lecture by E. Lorne Knight. It is the first presentation on any Chautauqua program of the famous Stefansson films. E. Lorne Knight, one of the members of the memorable five-years expedition, will tell the thrilling story."

Adventure, Knight enjoyed telling people, "must have been born in me." As outgoing and carefree as Maurer was reserved and serious, Knight was loud, cheerful, and direct, his racy conversation spiced with slang and American idioms. He was coarse and unrefined, but he had a good heart and decent values and came from solid, humble parents. He loved his family—above all, his mother—more than anything on earth. His wide, smiling face was more pleasant than handsome, and his cheeks were round and red as a cherub's. He wore his light brown hair parted carelessly over his broad forehead and his blue eyes usually shone with a satisfied twinkle, as if he were enjoying a good joke. At over six feet tall and 230 pounds, Knight was a robust, boisterous bear, with big paws and trunklike legs and arms. His bulk, he boasted, protected him from the cold.

He had the chance to test this theory at age twenty-one when a neighbor, Captain Louis Lane, invited Knight to leave his Seattle home and join an expedition into the Arctic. In late 1915, Lane's ship, the *Polar Bear*, was anchored just a few miles off the shore of Canada's Cape Kellett when a man was spotted on the icy beach. Knight and the others assumed he was an Eskimo since that particular part of the globe was supposed to be uninhabited, but he was clearly trying to get their attention. Lane gave the orders to land, and Knight was chosen for the shore-going party. As they approached the beach, Knight could see the man wasn't an Eskimo at all, but a white man with a shaggy mane of blond hair—Vilhjalmur Stefansson.

After leaving the members of his Canadian Arctic Expedition aboard the ice-ensnared ship *Karluk* in 1913, Stefansson had continued his quest for undiscovered land, crossing by foot to Alaska's mainland where he hired additional ships and men. He then disappeared into the high Canadian Arctic for two years; government officials, colleagues, and newspapermen had long given him up for dead.

Knight would never forget his first sight of the man. Stefansson didn't look like anyone who had just spent two years in the Arctic living off the land. He was not a masculine man in appearance— indeed, he leaned toward the effeminate. But it struck Knight that there was something about the man that seemed to be made of steel. Due to his knowledge of the polar regions, Stefansson had survived years in the Arctic wilderness. "It's just as easy to live up here as it is down home if you know how," he had said firmly and Knight was heartily impressed. He made up his mind at that moment to learn how to conquer the North.

For the next four years, Knight received a crash course in Arctic survival under Stefansson's leadership. The plan was to journey two hundred miles north of Alaska's northern coast where they would then set themselves adrift on an ice floe for a year's time and sustain themselves by hunting. Stefansson hoped eventually to float up near Wrangel Island or the Siberian coast and then travel south from there.

Knight learned to build a snow house; to drive the dogs; to cut a trail through ice ridges; to trap and to shoot; to travel in a blizzard; and to measure the depth of the sea. He also learned firsthand about scurvy. He first noticed the stiffening of his joints and the tenderness in his gums after accidentally freezing his ankle on a midwinter hike. He would never forget the helplessness; the pain; the thick, black gloom; the eventual relief of fresh, raw meat, which cured him; and the gratitude he felt to God when he was at last on the mend.

At the close of his journey, Knight felt the greatest sense of accomplishment of his young life. He was barely twenty-six years old and he believed that the North had made a man out of him. "Would you do it again, Knight?" Stefansson asked him before their parting on August 26, 1919, four years to the day after he had joined the explorer's expedition.

"Just try me," was Knight's answer. "But wait a couple of years if you don't mind. I want to get thoroughly warm and thoroughly clean again before I start out."

In the spring of 1921 Knight entered into a contract for Chautauqua's four-day circuit, where he would lecture and show the Stefansson films. He had been working as chief of police, traffic officer, and motorcycle policeman in tiny McMinnville, Oregon, when Stefansson invited him to join the tour. He was also engaged, and his young and earnest fiancée, Miss Doris Jones, traveled to visit him from Oregon whenever she could.

Enough time had passed to make Knight take the comfort of good health and food for granted, and he was itchy once more for the North, anxious now to use his years in the Arctic to lead others and teach them that it was indeed, as Stefansson claimed, a friendly place. A trip to the Arctic would be a homecoming for Knight. It was the one place he never tired of, and the place that he always came back to in his mind. What's more, he believed in Stefansson and was just as willing to put his faith in him now as he had been all those years ago when he was young and green and just starting out.

The explorer, said Stefansson, *is the scientist urged by a thirst for knowledge who struggles on through the Arctic night with the same spirit that keeps the astronomer at his telescope, neither of them thinking of material profit or necessarily of glory.*

During Chautauqua's visit to New Braunfels the year before, enterprising and rebellious young Milton Harvey Robert Galle had earned the envy of all his friends when he landed a job running the projector for Stefansson. Afterward, he joined the tour and traveled from April until August on the circuit, making sure to send his mother flowers for Mother's Day from Pomona, California, an event that was reported excitedly in the New Braunfels paper. The tour took Galle through all the western states, and he tapped out vivid and observant notes on his prized Corona typewriter.

Now, after a brief, unsatisfying stint as a traveling salesman for the Brown Rawhide Whip Company—which, at the very least, had kept him from having to attend college—nineteen-year-old Galle was resuming his career with Chautauqua. At the start of the 1921 spring Chautauqua tour, he had been on the road only a week, operating the projector as he had before, when he received orders to return to New Braunfels and take the position of Stefansson's secretary. It was an exciting step forward for him. "Purpose—plus punch—plus persistence equals most anything your heart desires," read the thought for the week of March 18 in the Chautauqua weekly newsletter. Galle had plenty of persistence and now he had a purpose. To him, Chautauqua and Stefansson meant a chance to fulfill his dreams of exploration and adventure.

With his father's tall, high-cheekboned leanness and his mother's infectious, quickfire grin, Milton Galle was irresistible to everyone—parents adored him, boys admired him, girls developed wild, fervent crushes on him, swooning over the angular lines of his face, his straight nose, his firm chin, his strong hands, and his tousled brown hair. He won people over instantly with his raw and reckless good looks, his wicked sense of humor, his easy charm, his quick and active mind, and his confidence. The oldest of three, Galle was nicknamed Sohnie—"little boy" in German—by his mother, and had been encouraged by his parents to think freely, to learn, to explore, and to appreciate life. Because of that, he grew up filled with faith in himself and others and believing he could do anything he set his mind to.

So at age nineteen he was set on going north. Maurer and Knight welcomed him into their elite circle; in his eyes, they had been privileged to have gone north with Stefansson and he meant to have his chance, too. The front page of the newspaper ran a list every week of the local young men who had been lucky enough to be called to fight in World War I and the places they served: Britain, France, Germany, Austria. Although he and his family had lived for a few years in nearby Mexico, the only other place Galle had been—until meeting up with Chautauqua—was Texas. Yet he had grown up in a house where Spanish and German were spoken along with English, and he was fluent in all three.

His ancestors had founded New Braunfels, the poor and dusty German-settled Texas town where he was raised. Founding fathers were on both sides—his mother's and his father's people had established the town, which lay in the heart of cow country, thirty miles northeast of San Antonio and forty-five miles southwest of Austin. One hundred years of Galles had lived and died on Academy Street. But Galle was determined that he wasn't going to live in New Braunfels forever.

Maurer and Knight took an immediate liking to Milton Galle when they met him on the 1921 tour. They told Stefansson that if they did have the chance to go north again, they wanted him to come along. The three young men talked backstage at the Chautauqua events and were unable to stop conversing about the hoped-for journey. It wouldn't cost much to go, they reasoned, because it didn't take a lot of money to live up north. They could dress in the skins of the animals they hunted and eat off the land.

There was something about the Arctic once you had experienced it, Maurer and Knight told young Galle, something indescribable that nagged at you, even if you had seen and nearly tasted death and vowed never to return. Something about having gone there once—just once— that made you unfit for anything, or anywhere, else on earth.

For Maurer, it would mean not staying in Ohio and working at the Goodyear Tire Company or at his father's tailoring shop. For Knight, it meant not keeping on as chief of police of McMinnville, Oregon. And for Milton Galle, it would mean not selling rawhide whips or hanging about in the drawing rooms of New Braunfels, flirting with the local girls. But it was more than not wanting to do those things temporarily, and more than not wanting to do them forever.

Wrangel Island had claimed a part of Fred Maurer while he was there. Eight years ago he had scraped seal oil off the tops of his boots to nourish himself when there was no other food. Eight years ago he helped to bury three of his friends there. Eight years ago he prayed on his mother's Bible for salvation, and hoped never to see his comrades—or that island—again. Now, going back was all he could think of. He wanted to make sense of what had happened, to try to justify the deaths of his friends and companions, and to prove, once and for all, that he could master that place.

Maurer's life was good now—he had a supportive family, a decent job, and a sweet-smelling, smartly dressed girlfriend named Delphine Jones, who seemed to love him fiercely. But he believed that he would never be able to live happily until he returned to the Arctic. There was only one man who could offer Maurer that opportunity— Stefansson.

Knight also made it clear to Stefansson that he needed to go north again. As always, he was more forthcoming about it than the more reticent Maurer, telling Stefansson repeatedly that he wanted the chance to go and trying to persuade him to send out an expedition.

Young and clever Galle was quiet because he had no right to assume that he, of all the wide-eyed boys who worked at Chautauqua and who hung about after Stefansson's lectures to ask questions and steal an autograph, would be chosen to go on such a journey.

When the world was once known to be round, there was no difficulty in finding many navigators to sail around it, Stefansson told his audience. *When the polar regions are once understood to be friendly and fruitful, men will quickly and easily penetrate their deepest recesses.*

They continually approached Stefansson about the possibility of a new expedition north. He seemed interested but noncommittal. Consumed with his writing and his lectures on the Chautauqua circuit, he told them he had no plans to return to the Arctic in 1921. The time wasn't right, he said. It was too late in the year to get up an expedition, and, as always, there was the issue of funding.

But in private, Stefansson was actually planning and had been planning in earnest since the fall of 1920 when he had approached Canada's Prime Minister, Arthur Meighen, and various members of the government about his desire to send out another expedition to Wrangel Island. As far as Stefansson could see, the ownership of the island was debatable. Some believed the Russians had rights to Wrangel because Baron Ferdinand Petrovich von Wrangell had been the first to search for it—albeit unsuccessfully—between 1822 and 1824; the island was named for him by the American captain Thomas Long in 1867. More substantially, the Soviets occupied the island for a brief period of time in 1834, and in 1911 erected a navigation beacon there. But others believed that Americans had held it ever since Captain Calvin L. Hooper made the first official landing on the island in 1881 and took formal possession for the United States.

Stefansson felt otherwise, however. In his view, any claim that might have belonged to the Russians or the Americans had lapsed. Captain Henry Kellett had discovered the island in 1849 for England far before Captain Long claimed it for America and renamed it after Baron Wrangell. When Maurer and other members of Stefansson's own ill-fated 1913-1914 Canadian Arctic Expedition landed there after their ship *Karluk* had been crushed in ice, and lived there six months before the survivors were rescued, it was the longest occupation of the island by anyone. Thus Stefansson felt Great Britain—through its dominion Canada—had just as much right to the island as the Russians or Americans.

Stefansson had never set foot on Wrangel himself, but its primary attraction for him was its far northern location, which promised a future air base. No flights yet ventured across the Arctic, but Stefansson, who considered himself a visionary, believed it was only a matter of time before the world would be flying by that route from America or Eastern Asia to Europe. When they did, his Wrangel Island could be one of the primary embarkation points.

"During your stay on Wrangel Island did you ever go any considerable distance inland?" Just the previous year Stefansson had questioned Maurer about the game conditions, livability of the island, vegetation, and topography. "Did you see lichens, mosses or grasses? Were flowers common? On what parts of the island did you find the most driftwood and what kind of wood was it?"

Stefansson was particularly interested in the British-Canadian flag hoisted on Wrangel's soil, July 1, 1914. Maurer and two of the other *Karluk* men had raised it in honor of Dominion Day without any other motive. But Stefansson thought it could mean something more, possibly even that they had, by doing so, claimed official possession of the island. He had interrogated Maurer about it, asking him about the particulars of the flag-raising ceremony with such intensity and frequency that Maurer told Knight he had a strong feeling Stefansson was interested in Wrangel. If this was true and their hero was really planning some sort of expedition to the island, both Maurer and Knight—and now Galle—wanted a part of it.

Stefansson had not yet been able to convince the Canadian government to back such a politically tenuous and ambitious venture, but he hoped, with enough substantiation that the island was indeed an invaluable asset, that they would forget the disastrous results of his previous expedition. There was the fact of the eleven lost lives, the matter that he may have abandoned his ship, and the condemnation by his peers in the government and elsewhere.

He knew they would need a British or Canadian citizen on the expedition in order officially to claim the island—someone who, if not the actual leader, could at least act as one in name. He hadn't yet told Maurer, Knight, and Galle that he was actually planning on sending them on the expedition they so desired. And so it was entirely unknown to them that he had already sent out a letter, dated March 13, 1921, to the University of Toronto, advertising for a recent graduate who might be interested in lending his nationality to the cause.

Ottawa, Ontario
13th March, 1921.

Dear Sir Robert,

I am planning a three-year polar expedition. This year I want to send north to a point within the Arctic Circle an advance party, consisting of a Topographer, a Botanist, a Zoologist, a Geologist, and one or two other men.

My experience has been that generally the younger the man the more readily he adapts himself to northern conditions. For that reason I should prefer to get men just out of college. The chief qualification is temperamental. There should be no tendency to imagine that you are a hero or that it constitutes remarkable hardships to be away from movies and operas for a year or two. Moderately good health is desirable. The man should be especially a good walker; his circulation should be at least so good that there is no marked tendency to numbness of hands or feet, and the eyesight should be above the average. No man is useful in mid-winter work in the far north who is not able to get along without glasses. . . . The wages would be nominal—$1,800 a year. The man should at the very least have specialized as an undergraduate in Botany, Zoology or Geology; preferably he should have had at least a year's post-graduate work.

This letter is confidential in so far that I should not like to get any mention of the undertaking into the public press.

Yours sincerely,
V. STEFANSSON.

SIR ROBERT FALCONER, PRESIDENT,
University of Toronto,
Toronto, Ontario.

Three

I AM PLANNING *a three-year polar expedition.*

Allan Rudyard Crawford had never been north of his native Toronto, Canada, but, like most boys his age, he had grown up hero-worshipping the explorers and adventurers who were reshaping the world.

The younger the man the more readily he adapts himself to northern conditions. For that reason I should prefer to get men just out of college.

Crawford was twenty years old and taking his third-year exams at the University of Toronto. He had not yet received his degree, but he had a solid grounding in mathematics and science, and had been awarded the first Edward Blake Scholarship in Science at the honor matriculation examination in 1918. As far as he was concerned, that was close enough.

The chief qualification is temperamental.

Crawford was known for his extreme patience, his even temper, and his warm sense of humor. His parents were highly educated, his father a popular professor at the university. Crawford had grown up in Toronto, a sophisticated city, and those who knew him found in him a quiet strength and a sharp, well-nurtured intelligence that made him seem capable and dependable.

Moderately good health is desirable.

He was in excellent physical condition. His five-foot-ten-inch, 150-pound frame was lanky but athletic and he never suffered from poor circulation, stomach trouble, irregular heart action, or any serious illness.

And the eyesight should be above the average. No man is useful in mid-winter work in the far north who is not able to get along without glasses.

His eyes were a clear green, and his vision was definitely above-average.

The man should at the very least have specialized as an undergraduate in Botany, Zoology or Geology; preferably he should have had at least a year's post-graduate work.

Crawford was studying geology, paleontology, chemistry, and mineralogy at the University of Toronto when one of his professors, Dr. W. A. Parks, gave him the letter, marked confidential, which had originally been directed to Sir Robert Falconer, the university president. Crawford was desperate to be chosen by Stefansson, and his father, Professor J. T. Crawford, backed his son's enthusiasm wholeheartedly. He knew how capable Allan was, how quietly passionate and determined, and he knew his son could make good at whatever he put his mind to, be it teaching or exploring.

For young Crawford it was impossible to think of anything else. "If you are disposed to consider me we might arrange an interview either in New York or wherever would be convenient to you," he wrote to Stefansson in his introductory letter of April 11, 1921. It was a difficult letter to write, having to advertise himself like that, trying to convince Stefansson that he was just the man to join his expedition. Crawford's name would be forwarded to Stefansson by the university, as a possible candidate for the position, but he felt the situation called for going above and beyond, and that he should provide additional information that might help his cause.

"I was under age to go overseas but I was in the Officers' Training Corps in Canada," he continued. "I was employed by the Geological

Survey of Canada last summer in Algoma and so have some practical experience in Pre-Cambrian geology."

At age twenty, Crawford was an attractive, dapper young man, with a trim mustache and dark hair, which he wore slicked back in a neat, precise part. His skin was pale and his eyes, a deepset green, were framed expressively by arched brows. He was shy by nature, but he wasn't afraid to speak up if he wanted something—his parents had taught him that—and he felt confident that he had stumbled onto a tremendous opportunity.

"Although I have not written for my degree, I find in my course I am up against men much older and more experienced than myself. I feel I could acquit myself much more creditably if I had the opportunity such as you offer."

Crawford lived with his family at 168 Walmer Road in Toronto. The oldest of three, he was close to his parents, and to his siblings, Marjorie and Johnnie. His mother, Helen, he considered a good friend, although perhaps a tad domineering and smothering at times. His father, a handsome, small-boned man, even more dapper and polished than his son, was a great favorite among his students.

John Thomas Crawford had been a mathematics professor for seventeen years before he accepted, in 1910, the appointment to lecturer in mathematics at the University of Toronto, as well as the role of chief instructor of mathematics of the university schools. He was the author of arithmetic and algebra textbooks, and a frequent contributor to *The School*, the monthly magazine of the Ontario College of Education.

Allan Crawford did his best to emulate his father's academic and personal success. Allan had been an avid Boy Scout as a youth and was now circulation manager of *The Goblin*, the University of Toronto's comic newspaper, which he had helped to found. He was a good, humorous writer and a rugby player on his college team. He was studious and inquisitive, and had formed a makeshift laboratory

THE FIVE / 33

in the cellar of his house, with liquids and powders, vials and bottles that he used to conduct scientific experiments.

He sent off his letter to Stefansson on April 11 and waited, trying to concentrate on his friends, the latest issue of *The Goblin*, his schoolwork, and the upcoming summer vacation to a resort in Muskoka. More than a week passed and he heard nothing.

The return telegram from Stefansson arrived, at last, on April 24: "Your qualifications look good. You should hear from me again inside two weeks."

*   *   *

Wrangel Island's appeal was not only as a future airstrip for trans-Arctic aviation. Stefansson viewed the island as a possible radio station and meteorological station as well. He believed a meteorological station on Wrangel would be invaluable in forecasting the weather of northwestern Canada and Alaska. He also knew that the island would be a prime spot for walrus hunting and fur trapping, both of which would be immensely profitable, and he calculated that it would be a useful place for reindeer breeding.

Stefansson's biggest worry was the Japanese. There was Japanese penetration in Siberia, and there were rumors that the Japanese were trying to seize land from Russia. He was certain that it was only a matter of a year or two before Japan realized the importance of Wrangel Island and sent its own team to occupy it.

Knowing how daunting and formidable the ice conditions could be as far north as Wrangel, Stefansson was anxious to sail by summer. Members of the Canadian government had placed the matter under discussion and he was told to do nothing further until they decided whether to grant their support. In reality, however, they had already made up their minds. The government was wary about the reputation Stefansson had earned on his disastrous Canadian Arctic Expedition. He was resented by some for his ego, his insolence, and his unreliability. No one wanted to give him the responsibility of another expedition under the Canadian flag because they didn't trust him. His patriotism, in this case, seemed suspiciously self-serving, and, as J.B. Harkin, Commissioner of Dominion Parks, noted skeptically, "Stefansson is a Canadian in the sense that he was born in Canada but that is all."

With the summer fast approaching, Stefansson decided to take matters into his own hands.

While Stefansson, with Galle as his secretary, continued on the Chautauqua seven-day circuit, Fred Maurer and Lorne Knight were both now traveling on a separate four-day tour. Stefansson knew Maurer and Knight were waiting anxiously in the wings, eager to serve him and to return to the North. "Of course you must realize that I am very anxious to go," Knight, typically direct, had written him recently, "and am awaiting eagerly that opportunity. Last night Maurer lectured in Amity and I brought him home in a car. We were together all day and he continually talked about the North. I think (if possible) he wants to get back up there as bad as I do."

Stefansson had been vague about any plans, except to say that they should stand by and wait for information, but on June 6, he sent a confidential telegram to both Knight and Maurer regarding a mission that would combine exploration with commercial development. "Would you go some Arctic island via Nome for hundred dollars month and small share in proceeds of operation?" he wanted to know. "Would you become Canadian subject if that is necessary to give you command of this enterprise which I believe has a future?"

Both Knight and Maurer answered immediately, yes.

By the end of June 1921, Stefansson was back in touch to let them know that everything was coming together, and he asked Knight and Maurer to be ready to leave just as soon as they received word. Rumors of a supposed expedition had already leaked to the papers, and everyone in McMinnville, Oregon, was bombarding Knight with questions about where he was going and what he would be doing there.

Knight himself had no idea, but he talked it over privately with his young fiancée, Doris Jones, and she was anxious to go with him. Even though Knight did not know where they were headed or what the nature of the work would be, and even though he knew his father would not approve—Mr. Knight was none too fond of the simple and scatterbrained Miss Jones—Knight wrote to Stefansson to tell him that he would like to bring Doris, if possible. But he also made it clear that if it came down to a choice between his betrothed and the North, the North would win.

* * *

Stefansson enlisted his old friend, Alfred J. T. Taylor of Vancouver, to organize the expedition. Because Stefansson didn't want to risk confiding in the unsympathetic Canadian government, he and Taylor agreed to keep their plans secret. When an attorney informed them that an application for Canadian citizenship would not make Knight and Maurer British enough to claim the island, Stefansson once again contacted young Canadian Allan Crawford.

It was the end of June, and Stefansson was still lecturing on the Chautauqua circuit. To his great satisfaction, the University of Michigan offered him an honorary doctorate, but there was one stipulation—Stefansson must be present on commencement day to receive it. Although reluctant to shift his lecture schedule, Stefansson was eager to collect the doctorate, and also saw it as the perfect opportunity to talk with Sir Auckland Geddes, British Ambassador to the United States, who would be receiving an honorary doctorate at the same ceremony.

After rearranging his schedule with Chautauqua, Stefansson wired an invitation to Crawford: "I am not sure I can offer you this year anything attractive in the way of northern exploration, but can you meet me at Ann Arbor, Michigan, June 30. It will be a brief conversation. But on the chance of its coming to something I shall pay your expenses if you will risk the time."

Crawford was in Muskoka, Canada, with some of his friends from

The Goblin, when he received the letter. He had been waiting for further word from Stefansson since April. The highly anticipated two weeks had stretched into seven weeks, and he had almost given up hope of ever hearing from Stefansson again. He replied immediately. He would be there.

While awaiting Crawford's arrival in Ann Arbor, Stefansson discussed his ideas about Wrangel Island with Sir Auckland Geddes, who listened diplomatically and noncommittally. Stefansson sensed enthusiasm, but Geddes could make no promise of support. Geddes did caution him strongly to keep word of his proposal as quiet as possible, as both Russia and Japan, in his estimation, were likely to find Wrangel Island an appealing acquisition as well.

Allan Crawford, meanwhile, arrived in Michigan, not knowing what to expect. He and Stefansson spent the better part of a day together, discussing Canadian politics and the upcoming election, and Stefansson was greatly impressed with the boy's maturity, sensitivity, and shrewdness.

That evening, Stefansson confided his plan for Wrangel Island to Crawford, after swearing the boy to secrecy and forbidding him to mention the plot even to his own parents. Crawford would have agreed to just about anything at that point, and listened with bright interest as Stefansson talked to him of the island and the claim that needed to be made. Stefansson himself would not be able to go to the island until the following year, and so Crawford would need to be in command. There might not be any pay, Crawford was warned, if the government decided not to participate. At the most, Stefansson could pay him $150 a month, which seemed a great deal to the boy. But regardless of money, Crawford felt he wanted to be a part of this noble cause, and told Stefansson he was willing to take any chances in order to go.

Stefansson sent him back to Toronto to wait and see, and then rejoined the Chautauqua circuit. He was still waiting for word from the Canadian government and promised to wire Crawford as soon as he heard anything. Very quickly, the government responded, letting Stefansson know that they would not support his expedition. He decided to move forward anyway, with the thought that he might be able to sway the government—particularly if a new regime moved into office after the upcoming election—in the months to come.

* * *

In early July, Allan Crawford received a formal invitation to come to Vancouver, where he would receive his orders for the Wrangel Island Expedition of 1921. In a whirlwind, he packed his bag, said farewell to his faithful college friends, and then dashed to Mary Lake, where his family was summering. He bid a hasty good-bye to his mother, father, Marjorie, and Johnnie, and then caught the Trans-Canada train, arriving in Vancouver on July 5. He met with Alfred J. T. Taylor, Stefansson's business partner, who issued him a contract of employment and handed him three Canadian and three British flags, which were to be planted in the soil of Wrangel Island.

From there, Crawford headed down to Seattle, where he was introduced to the two veterans, Lorne Knight and Fred Maurer. Knight and Maurer were already good friends by now, and they found it hard not to like the bright, well-spoken young Canadian who seemed older than his years. Crawford's quiet disposition meshed well with Maurer's more retiring, contemplative personality, while his smart sense of humor blended nicely with Knight's boisterous good nature.

Because he was a Canadian citizen, and therefore a British subject, twenty-year-old Crawford would be in official command of the expedition. But Knight, having the greatest length of experience in the North, would be the unofficial voice of authority and officially second in charge. Crawford was given geological and meteorological instruments and various books on collecting and identifying birds and animals on the coast of Siberia so that he could document life on the island accurately.

First, the young men would head to Nome, Alaska, where they

would purchase dogs and hire Eskimos, and then they would continue on to Wrangel. Tension ran high because the last boat sailing to Nome that year would leave August 5, and if they weren't on it, they would be forced to delay the expedition until the following summer. Stefansson had resumed his lecture tour and said the men—including his assistant, Galle—might as well join him and see the American northwest as hang around in Seattle waiting for word on a ship. They would be telegraphed just as soon as a boat became available. Until then, they would travel through Washington, Oregon, and Idaho.

Galle was still employed by Chautauqua, helping to set up tents, fulfilling secretarial duties, and running the projector for Stefansson. He liked the travel and meeting new people; he had made good friends and seen a part of the country he'd never expected to see. But when he overheard Knight, Maurer, and the new fellow, Crawford, talking over the Arctic with Stefansson in hushed, conspiratorial tones, he knew he had to figure out the best way to convince Stefansson to let him go along. Crawford, after all, was only a year older than Galle.

Knight and Maurer, for their part, went directly to Stefansson on Galle's behalf. Galle was a strong, smart fellow, they argued, and he had already proven what a hard worker he was. He might not have the experience that they had, or the education and pedigree of Crawford, but he had heart and a quick, sharp mind.

Stefansson was agreeable but dismissive. It was fine if they wanted Galle, he said, but he still wasn't convinced. If Galle did go, Stefansson couldn't afford to pay the boy a salary. Galle would earn a percentage from any furs he managed to bring back from the island, but that was all. The arrangement suited Milton Galle perfectly.

*   *   *

After the team was formed, Georgia Knight worked all day in her kitchen to prepare a celebratory meal for her husband, sons Lorne and Joseph, Milton Galle, Vilhjalmur Stefansson, Allan Crawford, and several of the Chautauqua performers. The young men were preparing to leave for Seattle, where they would spend the weeks preceding their departure outfitting and organizing the expedition, and the Knights had graciously welcomed all of them into their home in the agricultural town of McMinnville, Oregon, thirty miles outside of Portland in Yamhill County.

This dinner would mark the first time the Knights had met Allan Crawford, and it was exciting for them to have everyone—excepting Maurer, who was fulfilling his Chautauqua obligation—at the same table. There was much to celebrate—Lorne's return to the Arctic, the introduction to Crawford, the expedition's future success, the presence at their table of a man as famous as Stefansson. In John Irvine Knight's work as an insurance man and bill collector, there had been little opportunity to brush shoulders with people such as Stefansson.

"Milton's knowledge of Spanish won't be of much use to him in the North," Mr. Knight remarked to Stefansson over the meal. It was meant to be a casual, lighthearted comment, but when he saw the crestfallen look on young Galle's face he instantly regretted saying it.

There was a weighty, collective silence as Stefansson turned thoughtfully to Galle and asked him if he wouldn't rather go to South America with Teddy Roosevelt.

Galle had never wanted anything more in his life than to go to the Arctic. But he wasn't going to argue the point with Stefansson. Maurer and Knight, he knew, had already argued for him, and finally it appeared they had convinced Stefansson to take him. Whatever Stefansson thought best for him was what he would do, he said aloud, although it took an effort to form the words. But he did want to go north. This last was said softly but firmly, and there was no mistaking the great rush of feeling behind it.

A few days later, Galle received a telegram from Stefansson saying that Roosevelt reported unfavorable conditions in South America and Stefansson was unable to procure a position for Galle there. If he still wanted to go north, Stefansson would pay his expenses.

Galle had to read the words over again to believe them. He had never been so relieved. To think he could have been sent to South America with Teddy Roosevelt, when his heart was so set on the frozen Arctic with Stefansson.

As far as Galle was concerned, he was the luckiest boy in America. It was what Stefansson wanted him to believe. He counted on the kind of enthusiasm that bred great loyalty, and wanted each of his four young expedition members to appreciate the importance and honor of what they were setting out to do. Although he did not advertise his expedition or invite any men other than the four he had chosen, Stefansson told Galle that he had beaten out ten thousand other fellows for his spot on the Wrangel Island team, even the chief engineer of the highway department of Kansas and some college professors. Galle couldn't believe his good fortune. He, Milton Galle, nineteen-year-old son of a house painter and a piano teacher, with the dust of New Braunfels, Texas, barely swept from his skin, had beaten out all of them. "I am simply overjoyed, yes tickeled [*sic*] to death. Out of this whole bunch Stef had to choose me," he wrote his parents elatedly. "Is this not enough as yet to show you that there is something besides just lollypopping around, if it isn't, GOOD NIGHT!"

The more Galle saw of the rest of the country, the more embarrassed he was by the provincialism of New Braunfels. Things were different out here in the big world. People traveled and went places. They worked during the summer so that they could save their money and then head off to the beach for a vacation. Nothing like that ever seemed to get into the heads of the people in his hometown, who did the same old thing day after day and never seemed to have any ambition. There was also a spirit in Seattle, in Oregon, and in the other cities and states he had visited, that New Braunfels lacked. People seemed more adventurous, more exuberant, more alive. They weren't just waiting to die in some dead-end little town at the bottom of the map where no one ever dreamed of going, and where no one ever left.

Ever since Galle had landed in Seattle, he had been befriended by many of the prominent local businessmen. The girls of McMinnville had thrown him a party upon his arrival and had been ardent and dedicated followers ever since. The Knight family had welcomed him into their home and into their hearts as one of their own. He enjoyed the stimulating camaraderie of Knight, Maurer, and Crawford. Suddenly, there were people who shared his beliefs and his ambitions, who didn't pressure him to be sensible, to go to school, to come home and settle down.

"Stef has chosen me amongst all those men and it is up to me now to make good[;] whether or not I am to receive your blessing is still a real puzzle and I feel as tho I should leave thinking that you have given them to me," he wrote to his mother. "You should feel real proud of the fact that I can have the chance of going to work for such a man as Stef, doing other things than living in Drawing Rooms and the like. My frank opinion is that I really do not care to live in Texas any more. I have seen how they are in other places besides Oregon too. This trip will very likely be of almost any length. I really hope that it will last about five years as I know of nothing I would rather do than go north for Stef."

For his mother, it was heartbreaking. Alma Galle hadn't seen her son since April, and now she would not see him again until he came back in a year or two years or five years. *If* he came back. "To my thinking," his latest telegram said, "it is about time I leave the apron behind."

*   *   *

Crawford, Knight, Maurer, and Galle would head for Wrangel Island while Stefansson footed the bill for the voyage and remained in Canada, campaigning their cause to the government. On June 23, 1921, to protect the expedition as a private venture, Stefansson incorporated the Stefansson Arctic Exploration and Development Company.

Stefansson had essentially ended his active exploring career in 1919 and was living largely off the income he made from his books and lectures. He saw this expedition as an investment for his future. Perhaps the governments of Canada or of Britain would reward him for capturing the island. Perhaps, as he hoped, they would grant him a lease on the island out of gratitude. A fifty-year lease would suit him, and after he secured it, he would stock the island with reindeer, which he could raise and farm for profit. Or, if the government was unwilling, perhaps he could simply maintain possession of the island himself, subletting it "to some fur company for enough to get a handsome annual return on the money so far invested."

Stefansson and his business partners pooled what money they had so that Crawford, Knight, Maurer, and Galle could buy the equipment and supplies they needed for the expedition before they sailed for Nome. Maurer was surprised when Stefansson approached him privately to let him know he was short of ready cash to cover the expense of the equipment. Were he in New York, he told Maurer, he could have access to all the money he needed, but not so here on the west coast. Maurer wrote his older brother immediately to ask for a loan, which John Maurer initially rejected. When Fred appealed to him again, his brother relented and sent him one thousand dollars. Stefansson accepted the money with the agreement that he would pay Maurer back with interest at the end of one year, or he could choose to put it toward shares of stock in the Stefansson Arctic Exploration and Development Company.

Additionally, Stefansson gave the men signed checks from his New York account, not to exceed a total of $2,500—nearly $26,000 by today's standards—to complete the outfitting of the expedition. While Crawford handled all communication with Stefansson, and took special effort with all records of expenditures, the polar-experienced Maurer and Knight were in charge of the purchasing. Galle's only instruction was to assist the others when needed.

Buy two tons of groceries, Stefansson advised them, but no canned goods or preserves kept in glass. They should limit their purchase of bacon and butter because those could be replaced by seal and bear fat. Likewise, they shouldn't buy much meat because they could catch their own game on the island. Stefansson also suggested they limit the number of rifles, shotguns, and ammunition, and that they should take four tents, two big and two small, instead of eight, as previously discussed, because they could build driftwood houses instead.

They focused primarily on the purchase of hunting equipment because they planned to take supplies for only six months. After that, they could hunt and kill their own food and prove that they could live off the land. That, after all, was one more important component of the expedition—to prove Stefansson's theory that anyone with sense could thrive in the Arctic. Stefansson had also instructed them to spend their time on the island trapping, and to save the furs and skins to bring back with them.

They chose five thousand pounds of groceries, and purchased guns, ammunition, traps, harpoons, fish nets, fishhooks, photographic supplies, thermometers, flashlights, batteries, lanterns, stoves, shovels, ice picks, cooking gear, canvas, and assorted other hardware. For each man, there were twelve pairs of socks, eleven pairs of pants, skin mitts, blanket mitts, skin shirts, towels, water boots, canvas boots, belts, handkerchiefs, undershirts, one pair of drawers, and one suit of underwear. Once they were on the island, the rest of their clothing would be sewn from furs and skins by the Eskimos they planned to hire. They also bought chewing gum, tobacco, and chocolate, as well as twenty-six boxes of candy, Galle's lone request.

The choices were left to Maurer and Knight because they were the only ones with Arctic experience, although neither had ever outfitted an expedition. The only thing Stefansson stressed was that they must buy an umiak, a skin boat, for hunting in the water off the island. Made of driftwood and covered in seal or walrus skins, an umiak usually spanned from twenty-five to thirty-five feet in length. It was light enough for men to carry, yet it was able to transport a load of two or three tons. The other thing they must do was to hire Eskimo families to hunt, to cook, and to sew their winter clothing. Both the umiak and the Eskimos would be imperative for their livelihood and their survival.

There would be a $1,250 line of credit waiting for them in Nome, which they could use for any additional supplies and for buying dogs if there was money left over. Before they left Seattle, all four men stopped in at the Old Book Store to browse their secondhand stock. They shared a love of reading and knew the books would help to ease the long solitude that lay ahead. They bought a hundred dollars' worth of the best books by authors from Thomas Carlyle to Rabelais.

The ship would need to be of British registry if it was to be operated in British or Canadian waters by a Canadian expedition. Crawford, Knight, and Maurer struggled for weeks to find a vessel that was appropriate and that met the criteria, as well as one that was already heading for Nome. At last they located the passenger ship *Victoria*.

Back in Oregon, Ohio, Texas, and Canada, the parents, at first, were kept in the dark about their destination, given only some vague sketch of mysterious northern lands. They knew they must send any letters to their sons in cloth-lined envelopes and write them in such a way that moisture would not blur the words. Mail was to be addressed in care of the Stefansson Company in Vancouver, and would be forwarded to the boys from there.

Although both the Galles and the Crawfords were given the impression that Stefansson would be joining their young sons on the expedition, he had no such plan. Had they known he had no intention of accompanying their sons, neither the Galles nor the Crawfords would have allowed them to go. All four men expected that Stefansson would join them on the island in one year's time with a larger expedition. But whether he joined them or not, the plan was for a supply ship to be sent in the summer of 1922 with a relief party aboard to join them or to take back any of them who cared to go home.

They were told they were to represent the front line of a grand Arctic expedition. Young, green Crawford and Galle, and the older and more seasoned Maurer and Knight were thrilled with the responsibility, as well as the enormity of their mission, and all were anxious to prove themselves worthy of Stefansson's trust and confidence. There were several nations that wanted this island, Stefansson had told them, and who would only covet it more if news leaked out that Stefansson and his four explorers were taking it for Britain. They must not breathe a word of their mission to anyone.

There were whispers—false ones that Stefansson led them to believe—of governmental support from the British. Perhaps, he hinted, the government was secretly behind the expedition after all. And there were whispers—actual ones that he kept from them—of danger from the Russians. If the Russians had known of the political nature of the expedition, of the fact that another country was approaching a Russian-owned island to claim it and take possession, there was a very good chance of trouble and of peril to anyone found on their territory.

While Crawford and Knight were busy outfitting and readying the expedition, Maurer had taken a brief sojourn to Montana with Delphine Jones. He had met twenty-four-year-old Delphine on the Chautauqua circuit and become immediately smitten. She was fashionable and smart, wore a great deal of perfume and lace, and shared his deep faith in Christian Science.

They hadn't known each other long before their first argument— Delphine was emotional and temperamental, and it mystified Maurer, who was always so calm and cool. They had words, they fought—or Delphine fought, while Maurer avoided. She threatened, they made up, and the conscientious Maurer always seemed to be left with a deepening obligatory guilt. He constantly felt as if he let her down, and she seemed almost perpetually unhappy. When she threatened suicide, he was beside himself. If he didn't marry her, she would kill herself, and so, fearing conflict, he gave in.

When Maurer's summer lecture circuit ended, he joined Stefansson and the others for a few days on their Chautauqua leg, which was headed to Missoula, Montana. When Maurer told Stefansson he wanted to be married, Stefansson arranged for a minister there so that

Maurer could wed Delphine before he and the other men set sail for Wrangel Island.

Delphine took the train up from Niles, Ohio, and the couple was married on August 11, with Stefansson standing up as best man. They honeymooned for two days in Seattle before Maurer arrived at the dock where Knight, Crawford, and Galle were waiting for him. At nearly twenty-nine, Maurer was the old, somber man of the group, but that day he looked like a boy, with a shining face and huge, irrepressible grin. He and his new bride, it appeared, had worked things out.

Afterward, he wrote an apologetic note to his mother, telling her of his marriage and letting her know that he was sorry she could not be there for it. "But after meeting Stefansson and learning that I was going North for one or two years, and in view of the little trouble between Delphine and myself, I thought it would not be adviseable [*sic*] to go away without giving her the choice of marrying. It is unfortunate that we had a little trouble but that was all remedied and has been forgotten. She is a mighty fine girl . . . and is a brave girl to prove her loyalty as she did by coming out to Missoula to marry me."

*   *   *

J. T. Crawford was as philosophical about his son's new career as he was about most things. After the expedition was over, he was confident Allan would return to Toronto and resume his studies at the university. Until then, the professor would educate himself about the Arctic, and began by immersing himself in Stefansson's book *My Life With the Eskimo*, which Allan had recommended.

Before they left for Nome, Allan Crawford asked Stefansson to write his overwrought mother a line or two to reassure her of the safety of the journey. "Without an actual trip north it is scarcely possible to get out of people's heads the terrors of the North that have been planted there by countless books of fiction and of half-fact," Stefansson wrote to Helen Crawford. "I have always found the North a very commonplace and friendly country, just about like Manitoba or Montana and Dakota."

And, to Maurer's new wife, he wrote, "The polar regions are just as commonplace as Ohio. Lightning may strike you next summer but from that Fred is safe. Then there are all the multiplied dangers of civilization—railroad accidents, panics, fires and falling downstairs. If you can once divest yourself of these beliefs about the North that are untrue you will see that the few dangers of the North are paralleled by the same sort of dangers down here."

Maurer ordered his brother to sell all his suits and overcoats because they would be out of style by the time he was back to wear them again. They should save his trunks, though, even if they were in the way. Place them in storage if they must, but do not sell them. Delphine was to handle his monetary affairs while he was gone, which concerned him a bit. Finances flustered her, so Maurer wrote his brother John to ask him to help her as much as he could.

They should not worry about him this time out, Fred assured his family. He was not going for adventure, but to carry out specific plans, important plans. Also, they would be better prepared than the *Karluk* expedition, and this time there would be no chance for disaster. "Although we are going to Wrangel Island," he wrote his mother, "we are going to be living in comfort compared to the last experience up here."

Maurer's parents had come to America from Germany, like so many others, to make something of themselves. After putting himself through tailoring school, Maurer's father had eventually worked his way up to owning his own business. He bought the entire building where he had been working as an apprentice, and it became home to his family as well as to his own tailoring shop.

He didn't understand why Fred needed to go so far away. But David and Mary Maurer and all of Fred's siblings resigned themselves to the fact that Fred was returning to the place that had nearly claimed his life years before. They didn't approve or celebrate his choice, and they didn't necessarily understand it, but they figured it was his to make. He was a grown man, making his own decisions. He had made them before, and he would make them again, and there was little they could do to sway him.

Privately, though, Fred Maurer worried about his mother. His brother had reported her recent poor health and Fred was afraid that his returning to the North would weaken her. He would write her again, just as soon as he arrived in Nome, to let her know he was thinking of her.

Mr. Knight, for one, was proud of his elder son. He had seen Lorne through that first expedition and had endured being separated for four years with no means of communication. He had struggled with the worry, the fear, the anxious nights of wondering. He had noted the great change in Lorne when he had returned from his first expedition—more polished, experienced, deepened, wise.

"He has the utmost confidence and faith in you," Mr. Knight wrote to Stefansson, "and should you ask him to meet you on the Moon next week and if it were humanly possible for him to do so; he would be there knowing in his heart that you would not fail him. You can bet on him at every turn of the road and we are proud of the friendship and confidence that you seem to have for him. We are so proud of the belief that we have that he will never fail you."

He and Mrs. Knight set up a calendar on the dining table where she could record the happenings of each day so that they could share them with Lorne in letters. They also planned to save the local papers for him, so that he could read them upon his return.

The Galles were trying their best to be supportive, but Alma Galle was anxious and wished Milton would change his mind. Mr. Knight had been so fond of Milton Galle in the days Milton had spent living with them prior to the group's departure that he sat down and wrote Mrs. Galle a letter of reassurance. He told her what a fine boy Milton was, how much they had enjoyed having him in their home, how safe he would be with Mr. Stefansson, and with Lorne to look after him. "We are proud that Lorne has become a real explorer," he wrote, "and we would be ashamed to try to hinder him in pursuit of his favorite occupation. The only concern you need have in this matter is, will he make good? He is on a good job, is as safe physically as if in Texas, and in the hands of men of good morals."

Afterward, Alma sat down and wrote to Stefansson. She felt so far removed in Texas from her son and all that was happening to him, and he had not even waited for her consent, but instead had left on his journey directly from the Chautauqua circuit before his parents had a chance to contact him. Milton had given her little to go on except that he was headed somewhere in the unspecified North for an unspecified length of time. He had only told her that he was sailing to Nome, Alaska, and from there that they would board another ship, which would take them through the Bering Sea, past Point Barrow, past Herschel Island, and from there to their final destination, "not for me to tell."

"We may have told you that we hesitated in giving our consent at once," Alma wrote to Stefansson, "but now . . . he has all our blessings and good will. I assure you, a few lines from you would be greatly appreciated. We are convinced that your influence and association with you have been greatly beneficial to Milton."

She only wished she could have seen her Sohnie's face—just once more—before he left.

* * *

Crawford, Knight, Maurer, and Galle were too distracted and excited to think too long of home or of the loved ones they would miss. Overnight, they became celebrities as word leaked out about their departure, and reporters swarmed them on the Seattle docks, trying to sniff out information regarding their mysterious destination. Stefansson had given them orders not to talk—not to family and friends, and certainly not to newspapermen—and so they remained proudly and delightedly silent.

The day before they sailed for Nome, Crawford, Knight, Maurer, and Galle met with John Anderson, another colleague of Stefansson's in his Arctic Exploration and Development Company. Stefansson had promised his explorers a salary, but when he wasn't able to deliver up front, they were offered shares in his company instead. The limited liability company had been given an authorized capital of $100,000, divided into $100 shares.

Because he didn't have the money to invest, Knight agreed to pay a share of his wages—$50—every month into an account. It was a safe investment, he assured his family—every bit as safe and sound as Stefansson's reputation. The $1,000 Maurer had borrowed for Stefansson from his brother John was designated toward purchasing ten shares of stock, and Crawford arranged to purchase $500 worth of shares by also authorizing $50 to be drawn from his salary monthly. Then, at the last minute, Crawford decided he wanted to purchase ten additional shares of stock, which he must pay off in a year's time. Galle was to receive no wages and purchased no shares, but was to obtain, as promised, a percentage of the profits of any furs he managed to bring back from Wrangel Island.

On August 15, Stefansson wrote his twenty-year-old commander a letter containing formal instructions for the journey:

Always remember the following: Although I have confidence in you,
you are in command through the accident of being British while
Knight and Maurer are not. They have valuable experience which
you lack. The wiser you are the more you will follow the advice of
your experienced men. If you can not reach the island in question
you should spend the winter on the mainland . . . and cross over
by sled in March or early April to raise the flag. This should be
done no matter if men of our or any other nation are already on

the island. You might consider the advisability of crossing to the mainland in March and sending out a wireless by the same means used by Amundsen. Whatever happens send me a night letter the first day after landing in Nome. You may give out any news that does not reveal anything confidential.

Crawford took the instructions to heart and vowed to himself and to Stefansson to follow them. "We will do our best," he wrote on August 18, the day they set sail from Seattle.

The Knights, Doris Jones, and Delphine Maurer saw them off at the docks. Miss Jones was prostrate with grief, ever much the grieving widow, even though she had been unsuccessful in convincing Lorne to marry her in a last-minute ceremony. The two girls clung to each other, united in their mourning, and refused to be consoled as they were parted from their men. Next year, they vowed, they would join Fred and Lorne on the island.

Mr. Knight secretly hoped that Lorne would get himself involved with an Eskimo woman up there on Wrangel Island, something he knew would disgust the silly Miss Jones and scare her away. If not that, he was tempted to pray for something—anything—else which might diminish her overly keen interest in his son.

It would take four or five days to make the voyage to Nome, and the men promised to write when they arrived. These would be their last transmitted letters for a year, until the relief ship reached them in 1922. Till then, their loved ones must wait anxiously, trusting in God and Stefansson that the four would return home safely.

"I guess this will be the last . . . for some time as it is 12 noon and at 3 p.m. the *Victoria* sails. Expect to hear from me end of September. Will send two similar letters, one father, one you, in case one is lost. Love to all, Allan."

The female shaman departed to the sky.
The soul of her son was there, tied fast to
a pole with arms and legs spread asunder.
He asked his mother, "Why do you come here?"
"I come to fetch you home."

—STORY OF A FEMALE SHAMAN
Reindeer Chukchee Folktale

Four

SINCE THE BEGINNING of seafaring history, cats have been considered good luck on voyages, and have earned their passage by hunting the rats that live in the dark crevices of ships. In 1914, Maurer had taken special care of the *Karluk*'s kitten, protecting her from his comrades when they were starving and wanting to make a meal out of her. And now the chief steward of the *Victoria* presented them with a tiny gray-striped furball with pert ears and big eyes. She was the prettiest one in the litter, and the steward felt that Maurer and the others should take her with them to bring them luck on their trip north. They dubbed her Victoria, Vic for short, and they vowed to look after her and keep her safe.

The voyage from Seattle to Nome that August was rocky, the ship pitching and rolling along the way. It didn't bother Maurer and Knight so much, and though Crawford was shaken a bit, he didn't miss a meal. But Galle, who had never sailed before, was knocked off his feet for most of the journey. The older and more experienced members of the team chuckled over it and felt for him, although they knew it was only a matter of time—and sickness—before he grew his sea legs.

Some of the crewmen of the *Victoria* quickly began criticizing the expedition and Stefansson, which was unsettling for the four young men. One of the more condemning crew members was denounced as a fraud by a superior officer, which made them feel better, but all the same, Crawford and the others couldn't wait to get off the boat and be rid of the company.

Of course, everyone was curious about where they were going and why. From the time they pulled out of Seattle's harbor, there had been questions. Galle, when he was feeling better, had a great deal of fun with it, training his three comrades to evade the inquiries with skill. It was most fun when they were all together and could answer as a group.

Where are you off to?

Knight made up an answer. Crawford invented still another answer, and Maurer said a third destination altogether. Then Galle would reply, "Past Point Barrow."

When the usually raucous Knight was asked in particular about a place near Herschel Island, he would answer quietly and politely. If asked about another location, he would answer politely again. Crawford would plead ignorance, saying he was new and because of that had been told nothing. Galle would ask ridiculous questions of the inquisitors, who became completely confused, and then Maurer would launch into a somber remembrance of his time on the *Karluk* until everyone was nodding off to sleep.

Due to its lack of harbor, Nome was always a nightmarish spot to disembark. The fierce weather and waves that crashed wildly against the beach only made landing more difficult, and so the *Victoria* was forced to cast about and make her way back down the coast to St. Michael's, where the men aboard spent four miserably long days. Finally, on September 2, the ship made another attempt at Nome and was successful.

When they at last set foot on its beaches, Maurer, Crawford, Knight, and Galle eagerly began to explore. There were additional supplies to purchase, Eskimos to hire, sled dogs and a skin boat to buy, and a ship to procure for the last leg of the journey to Wrangel Island. But it was also a time to see the town, the new and novel landscape, and to write last-minute letters to families and friends.

People had been telling them there was only one Nome. And now they understood what was meant by it. With its narrow streets of dirt—twenty feet wide, if that—and its empty, tumbledown buildings, Nome felt like a ghost town. It was a place where wealth had once ruled and where thousands of gold-seekers once roamed the streets. But where there had been bustle and optimism, now there was silence and despair. The tiny, makeshift buildings were vacant—no more gambling halls and saloons. Everything had vanished except the high prices, and the place felt lonely, grim, and defeated, vastly different and far removed from Toronto, McMinnville, New Philadelphia, and even New Braunfels.

When Crawford and the others hit the shores of Nome, they were told that the *Orion*, the schooner they had chartered to take them to Wrangel, was tied up in litigation over the ship's proper ownership. With the *Orion* unable to bring them north, frantic telegrams and letters were exchanged between the four and Stefansson. Finally it was decided to hire the *Silver Wave* for $175 per day. The ship was expensive but sound, the best available for the job, and her captain, Jack Hammer, had a solid reputation.

Hammer let them know from the outset that he refused to take them anywhere until he knew their destination. When it was clear that he wouldn't back down, Crawford was forced to tell him they were headed for Wrangel Island. Hammer didn't believe them. He couldn't understand why anyone would want to travel to that barren, icy rock. No one with any sense wanted to go to Wrangel Island, least of all four young men who seemed more suited to a weekend jaunt up the coast than a year-long expedition to an untamed scrap of frozen earth. Hammer thought they were joking. From that point on, whenever anyone asked where his ship was headed, Captain Hammer answered that he didn't know, but one thing was certain, wherever they were going was certainly not Wrangel Island.

With the ship in place, Crawford, Knight, and Maurer purchased a sled and harness and a team of seven dogs. However, the umiak, or skin boat, Stefansson had urged them to buy proved more difficult to procure. They couldn't find one for what they thought was anything less than highway robbery, and so they decided to wait to buy one until they reached East Cape, Siberia, which was to be their last stop before Wrangel Island.

Galle, unburdened by the responsibilities of the others, found himself with plenty of time to see the sights and write letters. He bought some Arctic photographs, which he started sending, one by one, to the folks back home. He sent a picture of a reindeer to the Knights, scribbling on the back: "Our future lies somewhere amongst those animals. And Wrangel Island." To his brother, he sent a photo of a team of sled dogs. "Bud—How's this for you?" he wrote. "I am to have 7 of them all winter, to care for: get the feed and drive." And to his mother, he sent an Arctic scene, all sky and ice: "There has been none of this since we left Seattle. We expect none of it till we come home again."

"We are having a nice time at your expense," Knight wrote Stefansson, "but I would rather by far be out on the 'Bounding Sea' bound for the place that we are bound for." The season was growing late and they were worried. Reports of ice conditions up north were favorable, but making it all the way to Wrangel Island was already questionable. Navigating around the island had proven a difficult and often impossible task for many experienced sailors, and so they prepared themselves for the worst. If they failed to reach the island by boat, they promised each other that they would mush there by dog team and sleds from Siberia. It was an easy trip to make across the shifting pack ice, Stefansson had told them, even though he had never made the journey himself. "A very simple undertaking."

*   *   *

E. R. Jordan, Nome's chief of police, was standing outside the jail as Ada Blackjack walked past. She was heading home, weary and discouraged, after finishing a housecleaning job. The work was decent, but it was hard to find and the pay was not enough to sustain her. When Jordan waved to her and motioned for her to join him, she immediately became nervous.

Ada had known U.S. Marshal E. R. Jordan for most of her life. Now he began telling her that he thought it would be a good idea if she went away, leaving her home, her family, and her son. There were people in town planning an Arctic expedition. They were looking for a seamstress and someone who could speak English. It would mean money and he knew she needed money badly.

Ada tried to understand what Marshal Jordan was telling her as they strolled on the beach. Allan Crawford was advertising for Eskimos for his expedition, and Jordan had promised him he would help find able and skilled workers. He had suggested the walk so that he could explain the opportunity to Ada and recommend that it would be best if she went.

Her reputation as a seamstress was excellent, if her reputation as a citizen was not, and it would be a chance for him to tuck her away someplace where she couldn't get into trouble, and drink too much, or make eyes at the miners who still lingered on the beaches looking for gold.

He knew she needed money, but he also thought she needed a change of scenery—to get away from the pain of being separated from Bennett and the heartache she still felt over her marriage.

Jordan explained to her about the man named Stefansson who was in charge of the expedition. Ada's younger sister was married to a man who had served under Stefansson for a year on his 1913–1918 Canadian Arctic Expedition, so it was a name she recognized.

But there was her son, Bennett, to consider. He was in the children's home, and he depended on her even though she wasn't there to look after him every day. True, she hadn't yet been able to save much money, and her housekeeping and sewing work had been sporadic. True, she felt unhappy and alone. But Ada wasn't certain she wanted to leave Nome and Bennett, and she was skeptical about sailing away on a boat.

More than that, she did not want to be the only Eskimo who went— but Marshal Jordan assured her that the men at the docks were hiring entire native families to go with them, to hunt and trap and sew. This made Ada feel more confident. Perhaps she could go if there were others like her. After all, it was a great deal of money. Fifty dollars a month, according to Jordan, which was more than Ada had ever seen in her entire life.

She would think it over, she told him. But she knew she would not go. She was deathly afraid of polar bears, and they would be thick up there. One might kill her and eat her and then she would never be able to return home. And when it came down to it, money or not, she could not leave Bennett. She had never been so far away from him, or from her home and her people. If those men down at the dock wanted a seamstress, they would have to find someone else.

Ada went home and told her sisters about the offer. The brother-in-law who had served with Stefansson told Ada it was hard work in the North. "You'd better not go," he said. "You can always come to our house and get something to eat."

It was true that she could barely keep food on the table. She needed money badly, not only for herself but for Bennett. How else would she ever be able to bring him home again? But then she thought of the polar bears and the separation from her family and son. Marshal Jordan said she would be gone for one year, and that was a very long time.

Everyone in town was buzzing about the expedition, so that she couldn't get away from it. Marshal Jordan clearly wasn't ready to give up trying to convince her that she should accept the position. Soon Ada began to reconsider.

She couldn't get the money off her mind. Fifty dollars a month. In two years, if she was careful, she could save enough to take Bennett out of the orphanage and bring him to live with her. She might even save enough to take him to Seattle, where he could go to a hospital and get the best medical care. They would cure him of his tuberculosis, and then he would be a normal, healthy child.

To aid her in her decision, Ada set out on foot in the direction of a ramshackle hut on the outskirts of Nome where a shaman lived. In exchange for the tobacco which Ada brought her, the shaman studied Ada thoughtfully. Yes, Ada would in fact sail to the island, she said. But Ada must know that there was only death and danger ahead for the expedition. Furthermore, she must be watchful of knives and fire.

The reading left Ada shaken. She had been raised to respect, even revere shamans—they wielded great power in her tribe—and she had seen them correctly predict death and danger. She was nurtured on the ancient myths that warned that undertaking any forbidden action would be rewarded with an accident or punishment of some kind. The prediction terrified her just as leaving home and family terrified her, but she tried to push her fears to the back of her mind. In the end, her hopes overcame her doubts, and Ada Blackjack, the shaman's warnings lingering in her thoughts, reluctantly agreed to join the expedition.

Stefansson had told Crawford that the best thing to do would be to hire an entire family—or multiple families, if possible—to travel with them, the men to hunt, and the women to sew. Eskimo hunters were essential for the success of any northern mission, but Eskimo seamstresses were also vital because the clothing they made kept everyone safe and protected from the cold.

Carl Lomen, whose Lomen Brothers store was one of Nome's most prosperous businesses, was enlisted to help and oversee the preparations—not only the purchasing of equipment and supplies but also the hiring of Eskimos. When looking back in later years, his brother and business partner Ralph remembered an order given to him by Carl— hire a prostitute. It was unclear if Stefansson had actually issued this order to Carl Lomen, or if it came from Carl directly. It was Carl who had enlisted the help of U.S. Marshal Jordan.

Once Ada agreed to join the expedition, Crawford made arrangements with Jordan to hire her, along with some local Eskimo families. Ada Blackjack, in particular, was said to be highly skilled at sewing. She could also read and write English. Yet Crawford was aware that the people of Nome scoffed at his hiring her and said that she would not be of any help to the men of the expedition. She was a drunk, some said, a loose woman with no morals, and they would never get an honest day's work out of her. It was not just Ralph Lomen who believed her to be a prostitute. However, this slander was never proven; nor does any evidence exist that would verify it.

Crawford, Knight, and Maurer ignored the talk and hired Ada; her $50 per month was to be deposited for her in the bank at Nome.

When Marshal Jordan introduced Ada to Allan Crawford, she immediately liked the lanky young man with his shock of dark hair, pale skin, and green eyes. He was polite to her, soft-spoken and respectful, his voice clipped and cultured.

Crawford, in turn, saw a diminutive, childlike woman of twenty-three, with a broad, open face, wary black eyes, and a shy smile. He thought she was pretty, for an Eskimo, and seemed tidy and clean. Crawford had been told by Stefansson, Knight, Maurer, and others that Eskimos were prone to being sullen and melancholy, unkempt and dirty, but Ada seemed none of these things.

She was told to report for work September 9, which was to be the day of sailing. She was given some cash with which to purchase needles, thimbles, linen thread, and sinew. She was also issued clothing for the journey—as well as eleven towels, three handkerchiefs, and one belt for herself. And, perhaps her very favorite item of all, she was given one Eversharp pencil with which to keep notes or write letters.

The reporters had smelled a story when the four men hit town, and they hung around the docks and tried their best to finagle interviews, information, and a destination out of them. They assumed it was gold they were after—perhaps treasure discovered on the earlier *Karluk* expedition. The newsmen were, of course, interested in Maurer and just why he would want to return to the Arctic after the hell he had been through previously.

Galle relished feeding them his mischievous, nonsensical answers until they were utterly befuddled, but the reporters were clever, persisting until they managed to trip up Crawford, who admitted their plans to the *Nome Nugget*. They were going to travel along the Siberian coast, he said at first. But when the reporters pressed him, he let it slip about Wrangel Island. It would be an exploratory expedition, he said, quickly recovering, and there was absolutely no truth to the recent articles which had indicated that Stefansson was trying to establish a colony on the island. The reporters who had penned any articles suggesting as much must have been confused, he added.

By September 8, the *Silver Wave* was nearly loaded with supplies and equipment, and Crawford paid Captain Hammer his $600 deposit. "All in all it has been a great time," Galle wrote of their stay in Nome, "but it means work from tomorrow on and I aim to plow right in for better or for worse."

When it came time to depart, none of the Eskimo families they'd hired showed up for the sailing. Only one of the locals arrived at all— Ada Blackjack. This would never do, the men knew. The workload would be too demanding for one pair of hands, and they would need to be well prepared and well outfitted for winter. Even more than this, there was decorum to think of. What would their parents say—what would anyone say—if a single young woman—no matter her race— were to live alone on an island with four young men?

Crawford and the others made a last, futile attempt to persuade the families to change their minds, but none of them was willing to go. The Eskimos felt there was too great a risk, and that the trip would be too dangerous. Ada absolutely did not want to be the only Eskimo, but the men were desperate—they couldn't afford to leave Nome without any hired help and couldn't afford to count on finding Eskimos when they reached Siberia. They certainly didn't want to delay their departure any longer—and so they promised Ada that they would hire more Eskimos before reaching Wrangel Island.

Ada was suspicious. She did not think it proper for her to travel alone with four men, no matter how well mannered they seemed. She thought of running away, of staying at home. She talked to a woman she knew, an Eskimo named Mary, who had worked as a seamstress on one of Stefansson's previous expeditions. Mary knew Lorne Knight, and now she told Ada she must go with him because he was a decent man, and he would be good to Ada out there.

Ada had made a promise, and once she made promises she didn't like to break them. So she decided to keep her word and go.

It seemed wherever Crawford, Knight, Maurer, and Galle went— the docks, the saloons, the stores, the streets—someone was there to tell them they would never reach the island. There was too much ice and the seas were too rough, the naysayers said, but Knight shrugged it off and chalked it up to men who didn't know what they were talking about. "Some places get bad reputations for no cause whatsoever as do some people. Witness myself with the motoring public of Yamhill County," he quipped. Knight even came up with a nickname for those who doubted them—croakers, he called them.

There were those they met, too, who doubted Stefansson, and seemed only too happy to share their opinions. It seemed typical, some pointed out, for him to launch an expedition before he had the money to equip it properly. It also seemed typical, others said, for Stefansson to leave the dirty, dangerous work to someone else. To send young, untrained men out into the deadly Arctic to an island where Stefansson himself had never even ventured to go.

*   *   *

The *Silver Wave*, with Crawford, Knight, Maurer, Galle, and Ada Blackjack aboard, pulled out of Nome's harbor at 4:00 P.M. on September 9, 1921, nearly seven years to the day from when Maurer had been rescued from Wrangel Island. It was a gorgeous afternoon, sunny and with enough breeze to fill the sails.

Milton Galle wrote a last, uncharacteristically serious letter to Stefansson. He had shrugged off his family's concern and, in his frenzy and excitement, had been almost cavalier about their feelings. His mother had fretted and pleaded, and tried her best to be supportive, and he had cut her off and dismissed her, only thinking of his great adventure.

Now, as he faced the voyage ahead, and the fact that he was off to the unfamiliar Arctic without a last look at the faces of his loved ones, the enormity of the venture struck him.

"I wish to write you as a last thanks till I see you next year. I believe I can hardly thank you enough," he wrote. Stefansson would be speaking in San Marcos, just outside of New Braunfels, some time during the next few months as part of his lecture circuit. Galle hoped he would make the time to see Alma, to talk to her, to ease her mind. "If you can spare the time would you write to her and let her know when you will speak there and then if you can spare more time talk to her while there. I am sure she would feel a bit easier if you should do that than she feels now. Again, sir, I wish to thank you as much as I can."

*   *   *

On September 10, the *Silver Wave* sailed into East Cape, Siberia. The ship was boarded by the Russian governor, who seemed pleasant but agitated. Through an interpreter, he demanded that Crawford reveal where they were headed and their reasons for traveling. But instead of being scolded, Crawford and his comrades were laughed at when they stated their destination. It seemed they had run into croakers, once again. *You'll never reach that island.*

They were also warned. It became very clear to the four explorers that the Russians believed they, and not Britain, owned Wrangel. Crawford had been careful not to tell the governor of their true purpose in going to the island, but they were warned just the same that the Siberian Patrol might pay them an unexpected visit there at any time.

At East Cape, they bought some extra sinew and white sealskin, and then they did their best to haggle over an umiak with the local merchants, who were, as Knight observed, a bunch of robbers. The prices for the skin boats were just too high—$120, which was at least double the usual cost—and so instead they obtained a heavy wooden dory from Captain Hammer and a small skin boat for five silver dollars. They assumed the wooden boat and the tiny umiak would be fine, and that the dory would serve them the same way an umiak would.

While they loaded the additional supplies onto the ship, Ada watched and waited for them to bring more Eskimos on board. But none of the Eskimos in East Cape were willing to go with them to Wrangel Island. They feared the men and the mission.

Ada wanted desperately to turn back, to go home, to be returned to her sisters and her mother and Bennett. She agonized privately, without talking to her four companions. But it was too late. She had promised Crawford and the others. She had said that she would work for them and help them, and she had already traveled so far.

All too soon, the shaman's prophecy seemed to come true. Almost immediately, they were battered by high winds and swelling, heaving, rolling waves. They couldn't walk the decks for fear of losing their balance, and they clung to the walls, the railings, the door frames, to steady themselves. Forty-four hours were lost in the storm after leaving East Cape, and the small skin boat washed overboard and was gone. After the storm dissipated, the engines broke down—as if exhausted from the effort—and the *Silver Wave* sat in the middle of the sea while the crew worked on her. The wait, the delays were excruciating. A day and a half later, when the engines were finally running again, Crawford, Knight, Galle, Maurer, and even Ada were greatly relieved.

As they sailed at last toward Wrangel Island, the ship ran into a vicious gale from the west, which rocked the vessel violently. They were, much to their chagrin and the joy of the fish, noted Knight, "the sickest mortals that ever heaved." Crawford alone seemed to withstand illness, but Galle stayed below deck, clinging to his bunk, and Knight and Maurer weren't much better off. They groaned in their beds and cursed the sea.

When they headed closer and closer to Wrangel Island without asking him to alter course, Captain Hammer was shocked. Even after traveling to Siberia, he had been incredulous about the supposed destination and now, he finally realized, they weren't just pulling his leg. They actually wanted to go to Wrangel Island, although he still couldn't understand why. It was a place no one ever visited on purpose.

Crawford was the first to spot the peaks of Wrangel from the ship's deck at noon on September 14. The coast itself was expansive and flat, but the island seemed to rise farther inland, climbing into dramatic gray mountains. Snow dotted the crowns of the hills, but they had yet to see a single ice cake.

The sight of land, to seasick Galle, was the most beautiful vision he had seen for as long as he could remember. To Crawford, the outline and color of the place looked like the country around Lewiston, Idaho, which they had visited with Stefansson on his Chautauqua tour. Ada thought the island looked enormous, but they told her it was only a small piece of land. She felt the desperation building inside her as she thought of the ship leaving her on that island and heading back to Nome, but she held her tongue and willed herself to be strong.

On the fifteenth, the *Silver Wave* anchored half a mile off shore because there was a strong surf running from the southwest, and Captain Hammer thought it was too dangerous to sail into the harbor. At 7:00 P.M., the four men landed by dory on a high sandspit from which they could spy a promising abundance of driftwood. When they stepped onto the island—just miles from Rodger's Harbour, where Maurer and other members of the *Karluk* expedition had been rescued years before—they noticed that fox and bear tracks appeared plentiful.

They unloaded their equipment and supplies quietly and efficiently because they remembered the warning about the Siberian Patrol. Remarkably, the unloading went off without a hitch. Luck seemed to be with them. The weather was good, the offloading had been easy, and they had finally reached their destination.

All of their provisions were on the island by 11:00 P.M., and afterward they returned to the ship to eat a meal and to spend their last night for at least a year in warm beds with real sheets and pillows. Before turning in, the men sat down to write letters home.

Knight penned words of devotion to his mother and the promise of great adventure to his father and brother. Galle composed a telegram to his family, telling them they should find out from Stefansson how long the stay on Wrangel Island would be, and mentioning that he hoped he had enough film for his camera to last the duration.

"Keep note of all the interesting things that occur during the winter and let me know next spring," Crawford wrote to his mother. "I am not sure whether I will be out next year or not—possibly not. Don't write current events except Canadian Politics. Love to you all, good-bye, Allan."

For Maurer, the words did not come so easily. His first step onto Wrangel's soil after seven years was surreal and thrilling. To be there again, and so near to Rodger's Harbour, where he had lived for all those months and nearly died, was indescribable. He had prayed for salvation in the summer of 1914, when he was starving and when his body was wasting away before him. Yet he had known for some time that he must go back.

In some way, he felt that he had died years before, just like a character on the old whaling ship he first sailed on in 1912, an Eskimo man nicknamed Billy the Bum. Billy was a small, shrewd man with a homely, wizened face and a knack for wheedling tobacco out of you. The Eskimos aboard ship shunned him and Maurer once asked why.

Billy, they told him, had fallen ill fifteen years earlier, and was pronounced dead by the people nursing him. They had constructed a crude coffin made of boards from a ship, and, after dressing Billy in his fur clothing, they had placed him inside and closed him up. Then they carried the coffin up a nearby hillside to a place where his ancestors were buried and laid him there with great finality.

Later that night, after the proper rites had been performed over his still, cold body, Billy the Bum "in total disregard of the proprieties of well regulated Eskimeaux society," miraculously revived. He was able to push the lid off his coffin and crawl out. Then he wandered down the hill to the houses of his friends to let them know he was still alive. His sudden, unannounced reappearance inspired many members of the tribe to hysteria. They argued with Billy that he was dead and should, out of common decency, return to his coffin. But Billy had always been stubborn, and, as he was still very much alive, he refused—much to their dismay—to be dead.

From that moment on, Billy was viewed with great suspicion and people feared him. He had served them a mean trick, and they knew that he couldn't be trusted.

A man supposed dead who really lived. Maurer was fascinated by the idea, and by the fact that the same man's friends and family weren't happy to see the man alive after all he had gone through to rise from the dead.

"The old island looks familiar," Maurer wrote to his mother aboard ship, "and when I set foot ashore today for the first time in seven years, I was a little thrilled as the memories of our former experience came to me. But we are here for a new purpose and I hope to forget my past here. This will be my last letter to you for sometime, at least for the next year, so don't worry over my silence. I hope all of you will write next spring for I shall be mighty hungry for news. Best wishes for your health and happiness from your ever loving son, Fred."

PART II

WRANGEL ISLAND

A land more severely solitary could hardly
be found anywhere on the face
of the globe.

—JOHN MUIR, *1881*

ASSOCIATED PRESS
September 28, 1921

✳

Stefansson's Party Digs In

An advance party of Vilhjalmur Stefansson's fifth expedition into the Arctic has arrived at Wrangell Island, where it will "dig in" for the winter. Stefansson announced today on receipt of a relayed telegram from Allan Crawford, of Toronto, leader of the party. Stefansson said the party consisted of four white men and four Eskimos who sailed from Nome, Alaska. They will be the first white men to spend an entire winter on the island.

Five

IMMEDIATELY AFTER PUTTING ashore on September 16, 1921, the four men raised the British flag in the name of King George, Monarch of the British Empire, and claimed Wrangel Island for Great Britain.

From the deck of the *Silver Wave*, Captain Hammer watched with suspicion as the Union Jack was planted and the men appeared to read from a document. He couldn't hear their words from where he stood, but the message of the flag was clear. The *Silver Wave* was an American ship with a largely American crew, and Hammer had the sneaking feeling that he and the rest of his countrymen had just been duped into aiding a bold political maneuver on behalf of the British Empire.

But on Wrangel Island, standing atop a hillside in the shadow of the British flag, Allan Crawford, Lorne Knight, Fred Maurer, and Milton Galle signed their names to an official proclamation, and celebrated the first victory of their expedition. They had raised the flag, from what they could tell, at a point somewhere between Doubtful Harbour and Rodger's Harbour, where Maurer had fought for his life in 1914.

I, Allan Rudyard Crawford, a native of Canada and a British subject and those men whose names appear below . . . on the advice and council of Vilhjalmur Stefansson, a British subject have this day, in the consideration of lapses of foreign claims and the occupancy from March 12th 1914 to September 7 1914 of this island by the survivors of the brigantine *Karluk* . . . raised the British flag and declared this land known as Wrangel Island to be the just possession of His Majesty George, King of Great Britain . . . and a part of the British Empire.

While the four men sealed the proclamation with tallow, enclosed it in a bottle placed inside a slender box, and buried it in the earth, Ada Blackjack walked down the beach, her eyes on the ship. She watched as the *Silver Wave* pulled away from the island and pointed its nose toward Alaska. She knew she was going to cry and she didn't want the men to see her. She could hear their voices as they celebrated and she walked on so that she would be away from them. She wanted to call the ship back so that it could take her home. She was frightened to be so far away with strangers.

She walked and cried until she could barely see the flag the men had planted. And then she stopped, looking out to sea.

"If I turn back, who is going to sew for them?" she said to herself. She wiped away the tears as they fell and continued to watch the ship. "I promised them I would sew for them, and I must keep my word."

*   *   *

The *Silver Wave* returned to Nome, carrying letters from the men to the loved ones at home and correspondence to be sent by telegram from Crawford to Stefansson. Captain Hammer didn't want anyone—particularly his own government—to believe he had assisted another nation in taking possession of an island which could have just as well been claimed by the United States. And so he reported the flag raising to the authorities in Nome. The news spread rapidly and soon there were a number of infuriated Alaskans who felt something needed to be done to stop this suspicious venture.

*   *   *

Wrangel Island rises gloomily from the sea. The rocks, which cover much of the island, are a jumble of coarse and sharp slate, most as large as a grown man's hand. Even with this jagged shell, the earth supports mosses and lichens, and richly burnished fields of wildflowers of brilliant gold, periwinkle, magenta, violet, and blood-red. As the members of the expedition landed, summer lingered in blooms that held on stubbornly even as the temperature hovered just above freezing. The earth was bare of snow and ice, but the air had a bite that promised both, and with the stormy season beginning in September, they all knew that it was only a matter of time before winter was upon them.

Some eighty miles long with a width ranging between twenty and forty miles, Wrangel is bordered by the Chukotsk and East Siberian seas. It has rivers, streams, and lagoons. Two mountain ranges—one jagged and sheer, the other gently sloping—stretch from west to east, with the highest point, Berry Peak, rising 2,500 feet. A layer of low clouds shrouds the island from the view of approaching ships, so it is almost always tucked away, Brigadoon-like, from the world.

In the north, the mountains flatten into the expansive Tundra Akademii, which covers nearly half of the island, while the southern tip, where the men and Ada settled, is lined with low black gravel beaches and peninsulas that jut out into the water. There the bluffs drop to thirty feet or so before disappearing entirely, and the water off the shore is far more shallow than the water that hugs the northern side.

The weather was a surprise: a gentle breeze, sunshine burning through the perpetual cloud layer, and no ice at all. One of Maurer's most lasting impressions of that island had been the ice—ice everywhere, locking in the land from all sides and cutting it off from the world below. He had cursed that ice in 1914, when he was starving and in despair, waiting for a ship. And now, there was not even one ice cake to be seen.

After planting the flag and reading the proclamation, Wrangel Island's newest colonists set their watches for the twelfth International Time Zone and worked sixteen hours straight trying to set up camp. They pitched three tents on the sandspit—one for living quarters and two for supplies. There were no trees on the island, but there was a seemingly endless supply of driftwood, and with it they managed to construct the frame of a house against a steep hill, using the sheer side of the bank for one wall.

They would cover the remaining three sides with snow blocks in October or whenever the snow arrived, and build a storm shed off the front, where they could stock wood and other stores so that they wouldn't have to brave the treacherous winter weather whenever they needed supplies. The floor would be made of split logs, and the roof, inspired by dwellings Maurer and Knight had seen in their earlier travels, fashioned out of sod. For extra insulation they pitched two tents—one ten feet by twelve feet, the other eight feet by ten feet— end-to-end and sewn together inside the house. Crawford, Knight, Maurer, and Galle slept in the larger portion of the tent, while Ada's quarters were in the smaller tent, which doubled as the kitchen. They placed a woodburning stove in each space, with the stovepipes extending through the roof.

Upon opening boxes of their supplies, Knight noticed that some of the items he had ordered in Seattle hadn't made the trip. Even the supplies that had made it left something to be desired, like the rotten potatoes and the box of prunes that turned out to be full of maggots. The seven dogs they had purchased in Nome were also in wretched condition, but Crawford and the others would do their best to fix them up, feeding them excessively to fatten them.

In spite of it all, there was no denting their collective optimism and exhilaration. For Crawford and Galle, it was simply a great and glorious new adventure. To Knight—who, on his earlier expedition with Stefansson, had sometimes lived on half rations, with no driftwood for fuel—

this island, with its roaming polar bears, piles of driftwood, and flocks of birds, was paradise. For Maurer, all of the memories of his previous days on the island flooded back with staggering force and then swept away again like the tide that rushed against the gravel beach, as he realized that now, at last, he had the chance for absolution. He could endure here and beat the place that had once very nearly beaten him. And for Ada Blackjack, it meant money, which equaled survival.

Quickly and easily, they fell into a routine. They carried out scientific and exploratory work during the days, and when they weren't hiking across the island or studying its vegetation, wildlife, or minerals, they were writing entries in their journals, shooting craps for chewing gum, and eating candy. The friendly Arctic was just as Stefansson had promised.

Galle began work on a tool chest and helped Maurer and Knight cut and stack wood, while Maurer organized supplies and made a door for the front of the house. Crawford arranged his meteorological instruments, eager to put them to use, and built a table for the kitchen and some furniture for the house. Knight repaired the dog harness and sled, which had somehow been damaged in transit, and made another sled, for wood hauling, out of some lumber they had brought with them from Nome. They constructed gun cases and made sleeping bags out of blankets.

They had brought with them some parkas made of reindeer skin, and Ada fastened hoods to these. She worked diligently—sewing and cooking—and they were relieved. When the Eskimo families had broken their promise, the men worried they were making a mistake by bringing Ada Blackjack alone. But she seemed content and comfortable. She was shy and desperately afraid of bears, but a good, hard worker, and they all got along fine.

As the days passed, they became used to each other and quickly learned that Crawford liked to tell bad jokes, Knight liked to invent silly poems, Ada liked to sing hymns, and Galle could always be found writing. Everyone but Ada kept a diary, and Galle kept three journals. The first held just notes, which he jotted down throughout the day so that he could remember them later. The second, his notebook, was written in longhand, and then copied into his third, a loose-leaf binder, on his precious Corona typewriter, which he had forbidden anyone else to touch.

Fred Maurer was the only one of the men who claimed any sort of religion that—as Lorne Knight pointed out—didn't have to do with making money. Maurer was a Christian Scientist, but every night before bed he swallowed a couple of Dr. Pierce's Pleasant Purgative Pellets. The pills boasted a wild kaleidoscope of uses—"sick headache, bilious headache, dizziness, constipation, indigestion, bilious attacks, and all derangements of the stomach and bowels." His companions could only make guesses as to which particular malady Maurer was seeking to heal as, night after night, he never missed a dosage.

Exploring the island consumed much of their time. They took long walks inland or along the shore. Crawford and Galle strapped on backpacks and attempted to scale the largest mountain near their camp to leave a record and monument. It was an opportunity for Crawford to conduct some geological studies and for Galle to test his mettle at mountain climbing. In New Braunfels, he had climbed the bell tower of his mother's church. Now he was scaling mountains on a remote Arctic island and growing his very first beard. "I shall not shave or dress up until next year," he wrote, "when Mr. Stefansson and several other white men will come."

Polar bears, foxes, walrus, owls, seagulls, terns, and ravens were an everyday sight, while seals, so far, were few. Knight and Maurer reassured themselves that more would come with the ice. The surf was too strong for the wooden dory, which was too awkward and heavy to launch easily, and so they needed to be content with watching the animals from a distance.

No one knew the first thing about guns. They were expected to kill their own game, but only Maurer had any real experience with firearms, and it quickly became clear that he wasn't a great shot. On their first day they had each grabbed a rifle, determined to bring in a walrus. The walrus continued his nap, oblivious to the fuss he was causing, as one wishful hunter shot to the right, one to the left, one aimed too low, one too high. Only Ada refused to try her hand at hunting. Weapons of any kind terrified her—especially guns—and the sharp noise made her cover her ears.

They got their first polar bear one week after arriving. Galle saw it first, from the bluff just two miles west of camp. Maurer and Knight went in pursuit, and after a few failed attempts brought the creature to its knees—their first catch. The ground was so uneven and rocky that sledding was impossible and they realized they would never be able to drag him home. They saved the skin, cached most of the meat, and brought some back for the dogs. After that, bear sightings were frequent. The creatures were so prolific that—to Ada's horror—you could see them in every direction. They now understood why, during his brief stay in 1881, naturalist John Muir had dubbed the island the Land of the White Bear.

They saw the first flakes of snow on September 20. When the snow began to fall more heavily days later, they were confined to their tents to read and write. Seven days after that, they experienced their first brush with an Arctic storm. The temperature dipped to 17.5 degrees, and a bone-chilling wind from the east arrived, bringing a blizzard. Gradually, ice began to appear just off the beaches, drifting in from the limitless horizon until the floes ground to a halt against the shore. The island was a vast place for such a small party. Every day, its five human inhabitants watched as they became increasingly locked in for winter.

*　*　*

Two weeks after landing, they noticed a change in Ada. It started with a sniffle here and there, and somehow worked its way up into sobbing fits, until she was crying uncontrollably.

Crawford knew little about Ada before hiring her, only what Marshal Jordan had told him: that she was a good worker and a skilled seamstress. They knew she had a son and that her husband, Blackjack, had married another woman. The men had heard that he'd divorced Ada, but sometimes she claimed that he had drowned, and other times she said she had divorced him for abusing her, so they were never sure what to believe.

She longed for Bennett and her sister, she said. She was horribly homesick. The men treated Ada as well as they knew how. When she burst into tears or was too distraught to work, they were gentle and they tried to be understanding. She seemed, noted Knight, like a child of eight or ten, not a woman of twenty-three. "We will watch her and take good care of her," he wrote in his diary. Yet they became more and more unsettled and wary because as the days went by she began to behave strangely. Sometimes she worked diligently and efficiently, but other times she would set her work aside and sit, sullen and close-mouthed, refusing to speak. Both Crawford and Knight logged Ada's odd or difficult behavior in their journals, so that they would have a record of it for Stefansson when they saw him next summer.

Also disturbing to them was that she seemed to be increasingly infatuated with Allan Crawford. It started innocently enough—admiring looks, coupled with sighs, an eagerness to please him and be near him whenever she could. But it soon became clear to everyone that what Ada was expressing wasn't merely a simple, schoolgirl crush, but a deep, escalating passion.

Crawford was mortified by the attention, and Knight, Maurer, and Galle at first delighted in teasing him. They made themselves sick from laughing over Ada's swooning and Crawford's red-faced discomfort. *What beautiful green eyes you have, Crawford,* they would sigh at him before they erupted into laughter.

For Ada, the choice of Crawford was an easy one. Maurer was cool and standoffish and seemed much older than all the others, although he was kind to her and he spoke Eskimo. She found Knight bombastic and frightening. She was nearly as afraid of him as she was of the polar bears that roamed the island. From her diminutive standpoint, he seemed as large as a polar bear and just as fierce, with his raucous laugh and booming voice. Galle was a nice boy. He didn't treat her like an inferior, as she was used to being treated by white men, and he didn't call her "the native" or "the woman" as Maurer and Knight did. To him, she was just Ada. They played cards together and she told him stories, which made him throw his head back and laugh just like music, and he was genuinely warm and thoughtful. But he was so boyish that he could never be a father to her son.

Only Crawford, with his polite demeanor, his limitless patience, his impressive sophistication, and his dashing mustache, made Ada sigh and flutter. She decided that she loved him and she wasn't afraid to let the others know it. She had made up her mind. She planned to marry him and become Mrs. Ada Blackjack Crawford.

*　　*　　*

If they were to succeed on Wrangel Island, the men needed Ada to work. But, as the days passed, she would only pick up her sewing sulkily and concentrate for a while and then set it aside. She moved out of her tent and into a snowhouse to be alone, and she refused to eat or to talk about how she was feeling. At a loss, Galle, Maurer, and Knight decided to let Crawford handle her because he was the only one with any influence. They resigned themselves to the fact that they just might have to make their own clothing for the winter. They were already cleaning and stretching their own bearskins and Knight was forced to make all the seal pokes, or bags, because Ada didn't know how.

Every time they scraped their knives against the animal hides or polished their guns, she watched them with wide, frightened eyes. She seemed afraid and edgy, as if she were always ready to jump out of her skin. Somehow, she had decided that they were going to kill her.

Ada kept Crawford up one night, all night, begging him to protect her from the others.

"Oh, Crawford," she sighed. "Oh, your beautiful green eyes."

Then she turned to the men. "Well, I haven't much longer to live, so please get your gun and shoot me when I am asleep."

Then, in the following breath, she beseeched them to save her life. Afterward, she read aloud from letters written to her by friends and began to cry.

She worked irregularly, some days sewing industriously or washing dishes, and other days doing nothing. "When the mail goes out next summer I can tell you how she finishes up," wrote Knight in a letter he hoped to mail to his parents when the relief ship came. "This isn't so funny to you but we are in continual misery from laughing when we think about her goings on."

The men tried one thing after another to persuade Ada to settle into a predictable routine. Crawford sweet-talked her; they denied her supper; they made her sleep outside in the cold. "Have tried coaxing but find that sternness is better," Knight observed. When she asked Crawford for a religious book, Knight loaned her his grandfather's Bible. He and Crawford paged through the book with her, showing her the beautifully colored illustrations and the passages that said everyone should work faithfully and be kind to others. For days after, Ada worked hard to prove that she, too, was kind and faithful. But soon she was moping about camp again, not lifting a finger.

And then something happened to take their minds off Ada. Crawford had a seizure. He turned deathly pale, his pupils enlarged, his features contorted, and he suddenly lost consciousness. He was out for a full thirty seconds. The others panicked as they tried to help him. Then he awoke just as suddenly as he had collapsed, and he seemed fine but shaky. He had no idea what had caused it. He had no history of medical troubles—no epilepsy or any other diseases that might trigger such a thing. He was physically sound and he took good care of himself. The fit was gone just as soon as it had come on, but all of them, Crawford especially, were left shaken and hoping to God it wouldn't happen again.

The next day, October 14, the sea was completely covered with young ice. The view from the island was already flat and endless, and the whiteness now seemed to spread into infinity.

*　*　*

By October 22, they had moved into their winter house, which was cozy and comfortable, if not quite as warm as they would have liked. The thermometer dipped below zero, and there always seemed to be a strong, fresh wind blowing through. As winter set in, they began to lose track of the days, and their growing confusion about the time was reflected in their diaries.

None of them had any experience trapping, although they planned to trap plenty since they would be paid for the furs they brought back. Arctic foxes were profuse and so they set numerous traps near the camp and beyond, and Galle set out ten traps on the nearby tundra. But either the foxes were too slippery or he didn't know the first thing about what he was doing. Time after time, he brushed the snow off the traps and set them back, and time after time they were empty.

Sealing was still impossible, but they had, at last, begun hunting the bears which grazed through camp. Bears—their skins and their meat—were worth a hundred foxes, according to Stefansson, and the thought was comforting. If the seals and the foxes remained uncooperative, at least they could count on the bears. They cached the meat wherever the animal had fallen, and made trips to collect meat for the dogs whenever they needed it. There was still no reason to hurry, to try to bring it all home. There were bears aplenty—too many to shoot—and they hadn't even made a dent in their stores. Besides, whenever they were really hungry for fresh game, there were birds. After a couple of shots, one of the men—typically Knight or Maurer—

was usually able to kill one. Owl, they quickly discovered, tasted a lot like chicken.

One of their best dogs, Snowball, died in November, leaving them with only six to face a long winter of sled work. The dog feed had run out already and they were cooking up cornmeal for the animals. The dogs had been living without shelter, not unusual in the North as Eskimo pups usually slept outside, burrowing in the snow. But as the temperature dropped and the winds increased, the men built a house for the dogs with a separate alcove for each, connecting it by a covered tunnel to their own house.

November progressed, and they began to notice that the bear population had thinned somewhat; for the first time, the importance of saving any meat they could find became evident. Ada, for one, was relieved to see the bears go. She had moved into the winter house now, her igloo being too cold, but the bears still worried her day and night, and she was terrified of being eaten alive. She had heard that Nanook knew poor people and did not hunt them like others. But she was rich now, with $50 a month, so he might come for her. There was a story she remembered hearing, though, of a woman with a mean husband—mean like Blackjack—who met a bear and looked into its eyes all day from sunrise to sunset until the bear went away and never returned. Ada knew she would need to do this if she ever had the bad luck to meet a bear face-to-face.

*   *   *

They found Ada's footprints in the snow. She had been missing for a couple of hours, which was unlike her. The only thing they could figure was that she must have been frightened away by the bushy set of whiskers Knight had been growing so proudly, whiskers that would, as he boasted, make a Bolshevik envious.

Near the tent, they found a box that contained Ada's prized Eversharp pencil and a finger ring she loved. Then they found a note, which let Crawford know these treasures were for him so that he would remember her.

He set out with Knight to look for Ada, finding her footprints headed inland toward the mountains. They followed the tracks for an hour, wondering where she'd gone and if she'd actually trudged the ten miles it took to reach the mountain range. The men had become familiar with the island in the three months they had been living there, but Ada hadn't explored it to any great extent, preferring to remain near camp.

In the distance, a dark mound blotted the endless white landscape. From the shape, it could have been a rock or a patch of earth, which had somehow forced its way up through the snow. But as Crawford and Knight came closer, they could see it was Ada lying on the ground. Now she was probably dead of frostbite, which would weigh on their consciences forever.

As they drew nearer, Ada darted up out of the snow. She was going away from them, whichever way would get her there. She knew they didn't want her, only tolerated her, and she yearned to go home, although she was convinced she would never see Nome or Bennett again. She never should have come in the first place. As she ran, a bottle dropped out of her pocket, and when they picked it up they saw that it was liniment. What she was doing with liniment, they had no idea.

Crawford and Knight raced after her, their heels kicking up snow and ice and the dirt beneath. When they caught her she began to scream. When they demanded to know why she was running away, she told them she wanted to die and that she had drunk the liniment to poison herself.

She was mortally afraid of Knight. She had seen him sharpening his knife that morning and she thought he was going to kill her with it. She was homesick and unable to concentrate on her work, and now she was sure that Knight was planning to kill her so that she wouldn't be a burden anymore. Because she knew she was a burden. She felt it. The shaman had told her to be wary of knives and had promised there would be death.

Once they returned Ada safely to camp, the men decided that she should be separated from Crawford. Knight, Maurer, and Crawford had already agreed to establish two camps, ten or fifteen miles apart, in order to have a wider trapping ground. Maurer and Knight remembered all too well what could happen when men were confined in a small space, lying idle, waiting for winter to end, having nothing new or diverse to occupy their minds. There could be quarreling, boredom, discouragement, even violence, as there had been on the *Karluk* mission, when one man had shot another dead in his bunk.

Now, in mid-November, they would separate, taking turns with different partners, two men stationed at each camp, giving them a break from the tedium of their everyday lives, and giving them a break from each other. If they wanted to see the others, it would force them to walk and keep active, and they would set traps between the two camps so that they could visit these along the way. There had been some initial friction between Maurer and Galle, which had quickly dissipated, but Galle would stay with Knight and Ada at the primary camp, nearer to Doubtful Harbour, while Crawford and Maurer would move closer to Rodger's Harbour, ten to fifteen miles away along the southeastern shore. They were certain that Ada's unhappiness came from her unrequited passion for Crawford. Maybe she would forget about him if she no longer saw him every day, they figured, and maybe there would finally be some peace.

Crawford, Maurer, and Knight left camp at 6:15 A.M. on November 18, Galle staying behind to tend to his traps. As Ada watched Crawford go, she began to cry. Now, if she wanted to see him, she would need to walk fifteen miles, and the thought threw her into despair. Crawford alone—or the idea of him—kept her alive, and now she did not know how she would stand life without him.

She had confessed her feelings, had told him that she wanted to be with him, but Crawford wasn't having any of it. He was ashamed of the attention, had grown uncomfortably red and silent about it, and had tried to discourage her as gently—but firmly—as he could.

At the very thought of him, she would fall into a chant, which resembled more of a howl. *Oi, oi, oi, oi, oi, oi.*

She repeated it again and again, rocking herself back and forth, and somehow the repetition of the word made her feel better.

Oi, oi, oi, oi, oi, oi.

Every time one of the men felt gloomy, the others would only have to *oi, oi, oi* until the gloom disappeared and they were sick from laughing. Ada—Oofty, as they'd taken to calling her, or, even more commonly, the Nymph—may not have been doing any work, but at least, they felt, she was good for making them laugh.

She wanted to go back with Crawford and live at the other camp, to be near him in case he changed his mind about marrying her. If he wouldn't have her, she was willing to marry any of the rest of them, she announced, a fact which made them all wince. "This may all sound funny for the reader," Knight wrote after her revelation, "but I can assure him or her that it is NOT funny for the four of us to have a foolish female howling and refusing to work and eating all of our good grub. Heaven only knows what she is liable to do to herself or one of us and to be continually watching her gets rather monotonous."

On the evening of November 18, Knight and Galle set off for the other camp, but not before Knight warned Ada to stay home. She had a way of looking at him, stoically, stubbornly, which made him know she wasn't going to listen. He repeated the order again, more emphatically. She must stay home and not follow them.

The next day, as the men were hard at work at the new camp, Ada appeared, worn and peaked from the fifteen-mile hike. She had come, she said sweetly, matter-of-factly, to see Crawford and Maurer, and to tell them hello.

Knight was three times Ada's size, and now he bundled her up easily and strapped her to the sled, ignoring her screams. She must learn to obey them if she was to be anything but a hindrance to the expedition. They must find some way to make her listen. He and Galle bid good-bye to Crawford and Maurer and took her home. The next morning, of course, she was gone again.

They found her at the other camp, where she had awakened Crawford and Maurer early that morning, her eyes eager and happy, her lantern swinging from her fist. This time, Crawford threw her out of the tent and refused to let her back in. He made her sit outside until Knight came to fetch her. The men talked it over and decided that if they didn't teach her a lesson once and for all, she would never learn. Her work had gone undone, winter was approaching, they had little clothing to protect them from the cold, and her unruly behavior had distracted them from completing other necessary work.

Knight hitched up the dogs to go home and ignored Ada as she sidled over to him, a persuasive grin on her face. Suddenly, she was as agreeable as she had been difficult, and now she wanted a ride home. Knight told her that if she wanted to go home, she would need to walk back herself or sleep outside all night. Then he left her at the trapping camp, and as he rode away he could hear her howls. As she stood there, head thrown back in a wail, Crawford and Maurer returned to their tent and wouldn't let her in.

Five hours later, she stumbled into the original camp, exhausted and distraught. The next day, when she refused to patch a pair of boots, Knight tied her to the flagpole until she promised to do the work. Kindness had failed, he noted, so now he would try forcefulness. As far as he was concerned, she could stay there for hours.

She began to chant *oi, oi, oi* while she was tied to the flagpole, and paused only to ask Knight to fetch his Bible and read it to her. She hoped that this might give him a change of heart and inspire him to untie her. When he stubbornly refused, she offered him money to let her go, a dollar and fifteen cents, which was all she had. Again, he refused. She then asked both Knight and Galle to marry her, and they told her once again that they had wives outside. "But if at first you don't succeed try, try again, seems to be her axiom," observed Knight dryly, "and if she don't lay off of us for a while we will all be nuts by spring."

Eventually, after three hours bound to the flagpole, Ada at last ceased howling, and when Knight felt she had calmed down enough and when he tired of her grumbling, he set her free. She retired to her bunk, where he could hear her reciting from his grandfather's prayer book and singing hymns.

On Thanksgiving morning, Knight gave Ada her usual work orders before he left camp. She was to make some mittens and skin socks and begin scraping a deerskin while he went to the trapping camp. When he returned later in the day, he found the work untouched, and Ada just arrived from a walk out on the ice. She had followed a fox track, she said. The Eskimos believed that there were spirits who lived in hollow hills and disguised themselves as foxes. Ada knew that if she followed those tracks, she might walk into those hills and be treated kindly. She also knew that she might marry one of the people from the hills, as was often the case in the stories she had heard. It would be nice to live up there with people who were kind and who understood her, but instead she was sent to bed without any food.

She left again the next morning, leaving a trail of footprints heading for the trapping camp. No food appeared to be missing, but one of her nightgowns and a suit of underwear were gone. This time, Knight didn't go after her. It was the day after Thanksgiving, and he had spent his holiday haggling with her. Now he and Galle were celebrating, and they would just wait to see if she came back.

When she hadn't returned by the following morning, Knight hitched up the dogs and set out for the other camp. Crawford and Maurer hadn't seen her, but Galle reported finding her tracks heading along the beach and then zigzagging northwest. He had followed them for miles without sight of her. A cold wind was blowing from the east, blasting the snow about, and it was well below freezing.

On the morning of November 27, Knight and Crawford hitched the dogs to the sled and followed the tracks Galle had seen. After an hour plowing through the blistering wind, they spotted a dark form on the horizon. Peering through their field glasses, they could see it was Ada. She was walking slowly, wearily toward them, dressed in her night-gown and underwear, her usual camp suit, and a double Siberian native reindeer suit on top. She looked, Knight observed dryly, "like an inverted sack of spuds."

Once again, they bundled her onto the sled and brought her home. Crawford tried to talk to her, to find out why she had left and where she had been, but Ada wouldn't answer him. She had taken a few pieces of hard bread with her, she said, but that was all she would tell him.

The next day, Ada did nothing but wash a few dishes, and when Crawford asked her if she planned to run away again she answered maybe. Knight had warned her that if she didn't work she wouldn't eat, and for the next two weeks the only food she had was what she could steal, which was mostly bread. He didn't want to torture her, but as long as she refused to hold up her end of the bargain, she would have to be punished. He felt that discipline was essential. As it was, she was holding them back, causing double the work for all of them, and she hadn't done anything except get in the way. "She will not work and sits about and disobeys orders and eats up our food and is being paid fifty dollars a month for doing the opposite always," he wrote in his journal. "I'll bet I can get a job in the bughouse at Eslem when I get back."

No one wanted Ada on the expedition now. Hiring her was, ac-cording to Lorne Knight, a decision he soon felt he would regret for the rest of his life. "If there is anything serious happens to her," he wrote, "it will be a reflection on Mr. Stefansson and us when we get back to Nome."

Even the tolerant Crawford at last reached a point when he felt there was nothing left to do but threaten to dog whip her. None of them would actually take a switch to a woman, even Ada, but they were tempted. The first order of business when the ship arrived next summer was to make sure she was on it. She would never be of help to them, only a hindrance—she couldn't take care of herself, much less the work she needed to do for them—and it was worth staying on the island an additional year, just to have her off it and far, far away from all of them.

The truth was that Ada did not mean to make them miserable. She wasn't a joke, she wasn't a nymphomaniac, and she wasn't a "Foolish Female," as they called her. Instead, she was homesick and she was terrified. The men didn't want her there. She knew that. And Crawford, no matter how she tried to persuade him, didn't love her. She knew that, too. But her heart yearned for him because she had never met anyone like him, and she trusted him and believed that he alone would keep her safe. She did not know why she must be separated from him when she was so afraid of Knight and of the bears that wandered through camp.

There was a name for what she was feeling, although she didn't know it, and the men didn't know it. Arctic Hysteria sometimes develops in people who are trapped in a cold place with endless day, or, worse, endless night, as was the state of things by then. The polar night had officially begun November 21, when the sun dropped below the horizon, to remain there until January 20. Sixty-one days of darkness.

The victim of Arctic Hysteria is easily frightened or startled; he or she often runs away, in search of relief, and sometimes commits suicide; a fit can begin with a moan or a sigh and then grow into sobs and just as quickly stop, with the victim returning to normal as if nothing had happened; the victim becomes sluggish and sedentary; and there is an inclination toward "utterances of erotic expression."

One authority on the affliction dubbed the Arctic the "nest of hysteria," reasoning that the extreme cold, which keeps people cooped up indoors and which deprives them of necessary fresh food, is to blame. The most acute cases were found in Eskimos who were used to warmer climates and then moved to colder ones. Wrangel Island was a great deal more brutal than Nome, and as the days and nights passed and the cold only grew more severe, and as the sun disappeared from the sky, it was normal for desperation to creep in until the victim—in this case, Ada—craved sunshine and warmth "as only a dying person can."

It was this, most likely, which made Ada's eyes constantly red and watery and which left her voice raw. It was also the fact that she was used to the "white man's world" in Nome.

She had become accustomed to living in the city since she had left the mission school. No one had ever taught her to set a steel trap or shoot a gun. She knew little about fishing, nothing about hunting, and guns and knives terrified her. She had never built a house or a shelter to live in, and she had never needed to live entirely off the land. She did not know how to be resourceful, like so many of her people. She had never learned how to ration provisions or how to make a seal poke to store the blubber they would need in winter or how to kill a seal so that she wouldn't lose him to the water afterward. She could sew and she could cook, and that was all.

She did not know why she had thought she could live out here. No amount of money could be worth what she was facing—the self-doubt, the homesickness, the loneliness, and the fear that she would never live to see her son again.

The announcement made by the *New York Times* that Vilhjalmur Stefansson had hoisted the British flag on Wrangell Island came as a complete surprise to the authorities here. The British Government has had nothing to do with his explorations and has received no notification of his action. Inquiries in official quarters showed much indifference as to the fate of Wrangell Island, and it appears likely that Downing Street will leave the Government of the Dominion of Canada to deal with Stefansson's actions as it pleases.

Six

CAPTAIN HAMMER'S NEWS of the flag raising on Wrangel Island caused a great stir at the U.S. State Department. The story printed in the Nome *Nugget* drummed up enough negative public opinion to condemn Stefansson and his four young explorers as underhanded and dishonest. A protest was sent by Alaskans to Washington, D.C., and when the *New York Times* learned of it, they asked Stefansson for a statement. His secret mission at least partially revealed to the world, Stefansson spoke up. In his mind, it was free publicity, and he was skillful at spinning press accounts to suit his purposes. He hadn't been ready to go to the press so early in the venture, but he would head them off now, feeding them what he wanted to see printed. Besides, his men had been living on Wrangel Island for months, which, he felt, meant that the status of the island was secure.

The *Times* article was published in the fall of 1921, featuring Stefansson's own statements about the expedition and his young exploratory team. Stefansson was careful not to give too much away. The group he had sent to the island was only the vanguard for a grand and elaborate British expedition, which was to join them later the following summer. He expected they would remain there for two to three years, gathering scientific data and mapping the island.

"I shall not announce the plans for the expedition until Spring," he stated, "probably not before March." He mentioned nothing about colonization, nothing about political claims, although he casually and pointedly referenced the time his *Karluk* party had spent there, which, he asserted, "effected a renewal of the British right of occupation of the island."

He also hinted at the future of the island as a place to farm reindeer and as a viable spot for the fur industry. Allan Crawford and the others were merely there to make preparations for the larger expedition to follow. Some twenty-five applications a day poured in, Stefansson boasted, with offers of thousands of dollars to fund the undertaking, but he was more interested in recruiting men fueled with the spirit of adventure.

"Of what use would this ice-encompassed island be to any nation?" asked the *New York Times*. Other papers picked up the story and gave their own opinions on the matter. The American press damned Stefansson for claiming property that might very well belong to the United States. The Canadian papers implied that he was crazy for even attempting to take Wrangel Island for the dominion of Canada in the name of its sovereign Great Britain, while the British press expressed grave concern about what Stefansson's private venture would do to British-American relations. In Washington, D.C., the U.S. State Department launched an official inquiry into just which country held the rights to this remote no-man's-land.

On March 11, 1922, Stefansson wrote a letter to Canada's newly elected Prime Minister, Mackenzie King. King was unfamiliar with Stefansson's current activities, and so the explorer detailed the background and history of Wrangel Island. He also requested support for his claim to the island, and, if that couldn't be given, he asked King to allow him to move forward without opposition. The subject was put to discussion in the House of Commons on May 12, with Prime Minister King pronouncing, "The Government certainly maintains the position that Wrangel Island is part of the property of this country."

As far as Stefansson was concerned, this was good news. It would, in his opinion, only be a matter of time until the government backed him officially and fully, at last relieving him of the financial responsibility of the enterprise.

One week later, the U.S. State Department completed its investigation, concluding that "Wrangel Island, claimed by the explorer Stefansson for Canada, in reality is the property of Russia." Furthermore, it was the State Department's opinion that, due to its icebound condition, the island was of no real value to any country.

*   *   *

The hunting was frustrating. Either the weather was too vicious, or the seals too far out on the ice, or the foxes too elusive. Every now and then, one of the dogs—those that remained—managed to catch a fox, and the men—mostly Maurer—had been able to shoot a few. But the traps were worthless and the bears were scarce. Crawford, Knight, Maurer, and Galle thought back to their first weeks on the island, when polar bear tracks had overlapped each other on the ground and they hadn't attempted to hunt them. And now the bears were gone. Every now and then, a stray white form was glimpsed in the distance, hulking away from camp, but when the men gave chase they usually came back with nothing.

By December 1921, the weather was rotten and kept them confined to their house for weeks on end. Ada woke first to start the fire and make breakfast, while the men lay around "like plutocrats," according to Knight. They got up when they felt like it and went to bed when they were sleepy, and they spent their days chopping wood, hauling ice, and feeding the dogs. Galle wrote in his journals, invented humorous lyrics about the others, and plucked away happily at a pair of deerskin pants he was making; Maurer stretched out in a corner and read; Crawford, ever the diligent student, added to his scientific notes; and Knight, who liked to think himself in charge, tackled whatever task needed to be done, like making a sled-raft covering with the sewing machine. Afterward, they were so weary from all that exertion that they had no choice but to rest and read and lie about until bedtime.

Now, Ada, miraculously, worked harder than any of them. She sewed, cooked, washed dishes, scrubbed their clothing clean, and scraped skins. She rose at 6:00 A.M. to bake bread. She was pleasant, cheerful, and friendly. It was hard to believe there was ever a time when she hadn't been doing her share.

The change had literally happened overnight. On the first of December, Ada had stopped speaking to them. On the sixteenth, she packed both her suitcases and walked toward the mountains, returning later empty-handed. She said nothing about where she had taken her suitcases or why, and she said nothing about why she had gone. Knight and Galle refused to let her in the house unless she promised to start sewing. Ada wouldn't promise—wouldn't even utter a word— and so they banished her to the old snowhouse.

A light breeze was blowing from the east, but otherwise the weather was calm. She sat in her igloo and listened to the wind and was grateful for the break from gale and snow. The winter had been the harshest she had ever known. To Ada, it was an omen of bad things to come and it meant that the ship would not be able to break its way through the ice to them in the summer.

Knight and Galle awoke on December 17 to the beginnings of a blizzard, converging upon them from all directions. The snow came frenzied and thick, blotting out the sky until the rest of the world seemed to vanish, leaving only their small house and whirling, enveloping white. The numbing cold inched inside where they huddled, until it was an effort to move their hands and mouths.

They let Ada into the house, where it was at least warmer than in the igloo. When she assumed her usual sulky, silent posture and shook her head at her duties, Knight told her she would have to sleep outside while she refused to work. The wind howled like an animal, and the air was a nasty blast of white. It was a cold to beat anything in Nome, and it was so much nicer inside by the stove.

Ada looked at Knight and made a decision. "What should I make?" she asked.

"Mittens and socks," he told her, and watched skeptically as she brought out her sinew and began to sew. She labored until supper, her dark head bent over her needle, when Knight told her she could stop to eat. From that point on, she cooked and sewed and made herself useful.

She had not even sighed over Crawford—that Knight and Galle could hear—for weeks, and she hadn't mentioned the subject of marriage for some time. In her heart, she pined for him, but she knew now it was hopeless. With time and acclimation to her surroundings, Ada's case of Arctic Hysteria had lifted and with it gone, her tumultuous mood and ardent desperation for Crawford seemed to subside. When she was told that Crawford and Maurer would be coming home for Christmas, her spirits lifted noticeably, but there was no mention of Crawford's green eyes.

Christmas day brought Maurer and Crawford, and a fox from Galle's traps. The Wrangel Island community spent the entire day eating, even when they weren't hungry. There was a feast of bread and butter, potatoes, cake, and hot coffee, and after dinner they played poker for smokes. The weather cleared, and life was good.

*　　*　　*

Ada sat as still as a statue, slowly freezing to death. Knight had headed out early that morning for the other camp, Galle had gone to check his traps, and they had left Ada alone. She had been good lately, had tried not to cause a fuss or to be of any trouble to them. She had begun to work again because she knew they needed her to and she knew they would make her sleep outside if she didn't.

But now she sat in the house, surrounded by the cold darkness, and listened to the heavy footfall outside. There was a sniffing and a snorting, thunderous footsteps and labored breathing. *Nanook.*

There had been no warning because Knight had taken the dogs with him to the trapping camp. Ada had been doing her chores, as she had on all the rest of the days since December 17. But now there was nothing to do but sit very still and try not to make a noise. Otherwise, Nanook might find her there and kill her. The fire had died out long ago and the temperature inside the tent now matched the one outside. She needed to put more wood on the fire and get it going again, but she couldn't move. All she could do was sit and pray.

She held her breath for a long time until she heard Galle come home. He saw the bear, sniffing about the tent and storeroom, but there was no sign of Ada. With one clean shot, the bear fell dead to the ground, and Galle dove into the tent, looking for her. He found her in the dark, sitting rigid and fixed, a look of terror on her face.

On the first day of 1922, Maurer and Crawford sat inside their tent at the trapping camp eating breakfast. They were packing up to move back in with the others because the trapping camp had been a bust—just one fox to show for the entire time—and taking the trouble to walk back and forth between camps seemed pointless. Also, two camps burned twice as much wood as one and it taxed the dogs too much to drive them constantly back and forth between the two sites. They could conserve more dog feed if they let the dogs rest, so they decided it was best to live together at the main camp until the trapping improved and the foxes appeared—if they appeared at all.

Their tent was cozy enough, tucked inside a snowhouse, with a snow shed built off the front. As they ate, Maurer was sitting nearer the door and raised the tent flap to search for something in the shed when he found himself face-to-face with an enormous snout, two beady eyes, and a powerful, crushing jaw. The nose was twitching from the smells of their breakfast, and the great teeth were gnashing, the gastric juices dripping down the coarse white fur, in anticipation of a meal. The bear scarcely acknowledged Maurer, just kept sniffing at the supplies in the storeroom and at the tantalizing scent of the food, which wafted out from the main tent. There was blood in his eye, a look Maurer had come to recognize. He knew when an animal was hungry, and this bear was ravenous.

Maurer dropped the tent flap, grabbed Crawford and scrambled to the farthest corner of the tent. How could they have left their rifles outside? Captain Bob Bartlett, on the *Karluk* expedition, had always stressed the importance of carrying a weapon and of never going unarmed up there, where polar bears considered them prey. Now, here was Maurer, cowering in a corner with a hungry bear just feet away, because he had forgotten that simple rule.

The door to the shed was too tight a squeeze for the bear, and the walls of the snowhouse were strong, but the bear—a massive, brawny giant—was stronger. A shudder of the house informed them that the bear had decided to shoulder his way in. Maurer let out a blood-curdling war whoop, which didn't frighten the bear as intended, but only seemed to entice him closer and faster. Crawford and Maurer grabbed whatever they could find on the floor of the tent and started throwing it at the animal—firewood, pots, pans, and finally the dishes. Their aim was good, but the bear was determined. His great black nose twitched from side to side and the slobber seeped from his mouth. They plucked up bits of wood and thrust them into the fire and then took aim. As the sharp, licking flames pierced its skin, the bear gradually withdrew.

Crawford was better dressed for the cold and plunged out of the tent after the bear, grabbing his gun and taking chase. The bear was a hundred yards away by now and Crawford dropped to his knees and pulled the trigger. Nothing happened. He shook the gun and smacked his hand against it, but the cartridge was frozen. It would be the last time they would leave the guns outside, the last time they would be caught unprotected. Taking advantage of Crawford's handicap, the bear raced off. Maurer had dressed in a hurry and now took up the chase, but the bear was too fast.

*   *   *

Within days, Crawford and Maurer returned home to the main camp for good. Although Ada still directed longing glances at Crawford now and again, she was on her best behavior. There would be no more embarrassing displays or declarations of undying love. He did not want her and her attentions only seemed to upset him and the others, and so she would stop.

Concerned about the deepening winter cold, the men convinced her to wear army pants, which would be warmer and more practical than her skirts and dresses. But the smallest size they had was 35, which bagged off her waist and legs until they belted the pants about her. Crawford took Ada's picture, posed against the tent, looking almost jaunty in her new getup.

She was one of them now, and even though they still called her Oofty, she had earned her place by showing them she could work hard. Crawford and Knight repeatedly cracked jokes about the other's hometown, and they kidded their resident Christian Scientist about his Purgative Pellet habit. Ada received some teasing of her own for the grief she had put them through, while other fodder came from her pride about her mission school upbringing. She was fond of reminding the men of her education, and she liked to show it off by asking them for books. This amused her companions, and when she asked for a book about God, they couldn't resist giving her *Gargantua and Pantagruel*—the story of a giant and his son—published in 1534 by Rabelais, the Benedictine monk who resorted to a pseudonym when he wrote his racy, satirical novels.

"Now I will admit that God is mentioned in it," Knight confided to his diary, "but not in the way that it is mentioned in the church."

They watched as Ada turned the pages, nodding her head solemnly

over several passages. After a page or two, she would close the book
and lie back on the ground, eyes shut, to meditate and sing hymns.
The men tried to contain their laughter. "I wonder what the missionaries would think," wrote Knight, "not that I give a darn."

*   *   *

On January 25, the sun first peeked over the horizon at just 5 degrees.
Every day, little by little, it crept higher into the sky until, by the end
of the month, there was light enough for reading by 10:00 A.M. It
would grow dark again by 2:00 P.M., unless it was cloudy, in which
case they could barely read or shoot, and polar bears became invisible
to the eye. There was a constant red glow from the south, where the
great burning orb rested. But this hint of light failed to bring the
warmth they craved. January had brought blizzard after blizzard, and
the men and Ada were restless and itchy, confined to their makeshift
house.

In February, the weather continued to rage at them, shaking a violent, threatening fist over the island. Crawford celebrated his twenty-
first birthday on February 1, and he talked with Knight of establishing
a camp on the northern coast of the island for drying meat. They also
discussed the possibility of building a camp on the ice for sealing.

They talked over everything. Crawford was in charge, but everyone
knew that Knight had the actual say. Crawford conferred with him on
every decision, much more so than he did with Maurer. Galle and
Ada were the only ones never consulted, but it didn't bother either of
them. Ada was content to do her work and carry on with her duties,
and Galle, who had never liked being tied down to a job or family or
any obligation, enjoyed the freedom to tend his traps and wander off
into the mountains whenever he felt like it.

Galle also helped Ada prepare what game they caught. They had a
good time together and Ada enjoyed his company. He was so jolly
and thoughtful, always telling her funny stories about his sister and
brother and his home in Texas. She thought he was brilliant because

he knew all sorts of languages, and was always writing down his words on his shiny black typewriter, and reading book after book the others had recommended. He asked her to teach him her language and to tell him Eskimo tales, which she would do because she liked to hear him laugh and to see him watch her.

The temperature fell to minus 40 degrees in February, leaving the men and Ada huddled close to the stove through the night. On February 25, it dropped to minus 47.5 degrees. Storms sprang up for days at a time, swirling hurricanes of snow that left their skin raw and bones numb. For too many days, they were confined to the tent, keeping up with their general duties and trying not to think about the lack of game or the debilitating gales that blew through camp, leaving snow waist-deep and a fresh layer of ice over the sea.

On March 6, Milton Galle turned twenty. The weather was gentler, but there was still snow and a prolonged fog had crept in. Mid-month, the temperature climbed as high as twenty degrees during the day, and the men celebrated the relative warmth. They practiced making igloos and shooting their rifles.

Vic, the cat, had by now earned the nickname Snoops because of her investigative nature. She loved to prowl about the camp and stir up the dogs and eat anything she could find, edible or not. At night, the men or Ada would put out the fire, and she would crawl into one of their sleeping bags where she would remain, snug and warm, through the night.

The fiercest wind yet blew in April, and there seemed nothing to do but haul wood and ice and remain at camp. There was no game to be had, no tracks to be seen, but a raven taunted them daily, soaring over their heads, just out of reach. Day after day, the raven appeared, circling ominously over camp. The men went out hunting, even though they saw no other sign of life, and sank to their waists in the snow. On March 27, the snow, at last, had begun to melt, and the temperature rose to a balmy 40 degrees, the warmest day they had seen.

With the relief ship due in a few months, Crawford and Knight

turned their thoughts to Melville Island, which lay off the coast of
Nova Scotia. As far as they knew, no one had conducted any important
geological work on the island, and they felt the Canadian government
might be convinced to send them there without salary in the winter
of 1922, once they returned home and thawed out. Crawford was a
geologist, after all, and hoped to use his standing and connections in
the Canadian Geological Survey to get them there. The only variable
that might stop them was money.

In spite of the age disparity and their differences in temperament,
the two men thought highly of each other, and Knight admired Crawford's brains and his savvy. He was one of the smartest and most
modest men Knight had ever met. "I'll put C. up against anyone I
know except Stef," Knight wrote in his journal.

Crawford and Knight longed to make a trip around the island, but
knew they wouldn't be able to do so without dog feed. They had been
cooking all the dogs' meals for months, mostly rolled oats and rice,
and once the oats ran out, then rice mixed with flour. The men and
Ada weren't in any danger of starving yet—after all, they hadn't completely depleted their stores—but they began to feel a nagging worry
about the lack of game on the island. The supplies wouldn't last forever, and then what would they do? Since January, they had only
managed to get nine foxes, two bears, and one seal. Maurer was the
most skilled hunter, but Crawford was the luckiest, bringing home the
bears and the seal; most of the foxes turned up in Galle's traps. Another one of the dogs had died of violent convulsions, and they laid
his body out on the ice next to his dead companion. When they
noticed one day that the bodies had been gnawed at, they laid the
traps out around the dog carcasses. Suddenly, they had foxes.

But that wasn't enough, considering they were out hunting, rifles
slung over their shoulders, as much as the foul weather would allow.
Day after day, they set out, searching for fresh animal tracks with
increasing frustration. Now and then, they found an old pair of tracks

but rarely fresh ones. It made no sense. All the game seemed to have vanished.

By May, the snow began melting rapidly, dissolving into the cold, black tundra. It still snowed that month, but the weather was improving. They were grateful for it as they moved to a new camp for the summer. The walls of their house had begun to melt and now they were living in a puddle of water, so they moved the supplies to drier ground, one hundred feet away, and pitched tents.

The men and Ada began to look toward June and July with excitement and anticipation because the ship would be arriving then. Their time on the island hadn't been wretched or even terribly difficult, but they were weary and they were ready to see new faces and restock their dwindling larder with fresh supplies. The potatoes, onions, rolled oats, and beans had given out, and the only bacon that remained was three or four rancid slabs. They had plenty of hard bread, tea, and coffee, a handful of rice, and a bit of sugar. At the end of May, they watched helplessly as flocks of geese and ducks flew overhead, but none fell to their rifles. Crawford, Maurer, Knight, and Galle watched, too, as the seals began to creep out onto the ice, knowing they couldn't be reached because the ice around shore was too thin and the seals too far out.

Ada was homesick, just as they all were, and she told them so. She had turned 24 on May 10, and longed to return to home and mother, just as Maurer missed his wife and family and talked of the nice things he would do for them when he went back to New Philadelphia. Crawford spoke the names of his mother and sister with wistfulness, and Lorne Knight liked to talk of everyone—his brother, his parents, and, of course, his Miss Jones. It helped to know the men were homesick, too, and Ada seldom broke down into crying fits and rarely let her feelings interrupt her work now. They would all be brave together and the men were grateful for that. It would have been too much, on top of the shortage of fresh meat and the bleak weather conditions, to have Ada carrying on like she had before. Now they were growing fond of her, and Knight noted in his diary that they would miss her when she returned with the ship that summer.

*   *   *

The second day of June was their worst so far on the island. A blinding gale and snow whipped up without warning, and large drifts were building rapidly on the ice. The seas had opened up a bit in May, which raised their hopes for the ship. But now there was no open water to be seen anywhere, and the weather was nasty—cloudy, dark, drizzling, blowing.

They managed to kill a few birds for specimens, but they were too thin and small to eat. The seals continued to elude them, even with the Eskimo retriever, a device for hooking seals out of the water and reeling them in. The seals were just too slippery. Even if the men were somehow able to hit one, the animal would slide off the ice into the water before they could reach it. They tried the crawling method of hunting—also inherited from the Eskimo—sliding along the ground on their bellies toward a sleeping seal. Pausing whenever the seal glanced up to check for bears, as it did frequently, and then inching forward again as soon as the seal's head had dropped back to rest. The method took dark clothing and endless patience, and sometimes a bit of wriggling to convince the seals that you were one of them. But there still wasn't much to show for it.

"Our names should be 'hard luck' or 'incompetent,'" Knight wrote in his diary, and it was difficult for them not to be critical of themselves. If only the umiak hadn't been lost overboard. If only they were better with guns. If only they knew what they were doing.

It would be good to see Stefansson, to hear news of the outside world, and to read the letters he would bring them from their families and to give him the ones they had written. It would be good to feel connected again, to feel a part of the world below, and to find out what progress Stefansson had made with the British government.

*   *   *

Back in New York, there was no money to be had. It was the middle of June and Stefansson had no relief ship and no funding. No one wanted to help him; he had no borrowing power; and the Canadian government had sent no further word regarding the status of its support. The U.S. State Department sentence had been severe and had hurt his chances tremendously. This meant it was up to Stefansson to find the money and the boat.

The families of the men on Wrangel Island were writing to him constantly. Delphine Maurer was anxious to go north to join her husband, and hoped to win a spot on the relief ship. The Galles wrote letters and gathered the ones they had saved from Sohnie's friends and girlfriends, and were afraid they might forget to include something in the box they were sending to him. The Crawfords and the Knights, too, wanted to send packages to the boys. Mr. Knight asked for information about the expedition—could they expect Lorne home that summer? Lorne's grandfather was ninety-four years old and gradually failing, but he did not intend to die until he saw his grandson again.

Mr. Knight was concerned by the newspaper accounts he was reading. Stefansson had been quoted as saying that none of the party had been aware of the purpose of the expedition—to claim the island for Britain—which the Knights knew wasn't true. All those men well knew what they were getting into. Stefansson had made it clear to them. So why was he telling the papers something different?

Stefansson himself was broke, and while he assumed the men would be fine out there—it was the Friendly Arctic, after all—he thought it best to appeal to the Canadian government on a humanitarian level. Whether they approved of the expedition or not, those men might be sick or injured, needing medical attention. This was to be a relief expedition and not a rescue, but lives might very well be lost if a ship was not sent and soon. To the Minister and Deputy Minister of the Interior, Stefansson wrote, "Please urge upon Council that there are on Wrangel Island four men in Canadian service whose lives are in danger."

His friend Orville Wright, aviation pioneer, had donated $3,000 to the cause, but Stefansson needed more. He asked the Canadian government for $5,000, to cover the supplies and the chartering of the ship. In answer, the government—which still refused to wholly and officially support his claim to the island—offered him $3,000 for his relief trip, but no more.

Stefansson had been negotiating for a ship with his agents in Nome, and had located a schooner named the *Teddy Bear*. Stefansson had known her captain, Joe Bernard, since 1910 and thought well of him. Bernard was told nothing of the political implications of the expedition, only that it was a commercial venture. He was instructed to take along three white men and a group of Eskimos to Wrangel Island, who would serve to relieve Crawford's team of their duties.

Stefansson made a bargain with Bernard that the skipper would receive $1,000 of the government's donation if he failed to reach the island, and the remaining $2,000 if he was successful. That first $1,000 was exhausted quickly on supplies, crew's wages, insurance on the vessel, and all the other costs involved. If Bernard didn't make the island, he was going to lose money on this journey, but he felt sorry for those young men out there, and the woman they had taken along with them. There was another ship's captain anxious to go, but Bernard wanted to be the one. He knew the other captain, and knew he wouldn't break his back to reach that island. He knew the other skipper would just take one long, intimidated look at Bering Strait and all that ice and head back.

John Muir had described in excruciating detail the enduring fog which enshrouded the land in 1881, the forbidding, close-packed ice that stretched endlessly along the coast. Bernard knew that the ice could crush and shatter violently, and that a ship was almost as vulnerable as a person to the churning and grinding of the floes. The odds were slim that any ship could get through this late in the season, but Bernard vowed to be successful or die trying.

* * *

The old camp at Rodger's Harbour was just as Maurer remembered it. Relics from his stay there were littered across the ground. Scraps of the tent remained. Rusted tins of pemmican. A knife. A bit of animal skin or dog harness. Maurer and Galle had made the forty-mile hike to Rodger's Harbour to examine the trapping possibilities. Anything could have been better than the godforsaken place where they were camping now.

The graves of the men from the disastrous 1913 *Karluk* expedition were still there, of course. Fred Maurer had helped to dig those graves, had lowered their bodies into the cold, hard earth. He had erected the crude wooden cross which had stood watch over them, stiff and proud, like a soldier. The cross had now ceased its watch, and lay broken on the ground, blown down by the winds that continuously brutalized the island.

August 23, 1922

Dear Mr. Maurer:

The schooner Teddy Bear, *under command of one of the most experienced arctic navigators, Captain Joe Bernard, sailed from Nome Sunday afternoon, August 20th, for Wrangel Island. With good luck they should be back in two weeks.*

The Teddy Bear *carried three white men and some Eskimos who are to spend the next winter on Wrangel Island. I am hoping that one of the men who were there this year will remain another year in command of the newcomers, but I do not know which it will be.*

Vilhjalmur Stefansson

Seven

THE RIVER reached wider than the Yamhill in Oregon. Knight stood with his canine companion, loaded down with blankets, socks, an extra pair of boots, and some tea and sugar, and surveyed the long stretch of water. The Skeleton River. Such a chillingly appropriate name.

He'd left camp on July 7, intending to live off the country for a few days alone. Taking one dog, he'd headed east first for Rodger's Harbour, where he spent the night at the *Karluk*'s old camp. He left a note for Stefansson, in case he should land there with the relief ship, and he examined the grave of the *Karluk* men and the fallen cross that now lay impotent on the ground.

The next day he had set out for Waring Point, on the southeastern coast of the island. It was then that he first ran smack into the Skeleton River. Skeleton Island itself was a mere spit of sand on the eastern side of the river. Half of an empty pemmican tin lay on the ground near the remains of a campfire, which had burned long ago, further evidence of the *Karluk* party, now long since gone. The ice was thick along the beach here, and the hills inland were still capped with snow. Crossing the river was easy once Knight traveled on the ice that hugged the shoreline for two hundred yards or so.

At Waring Point, the sky opened and the rain began to pour. Why hadn't he thought to bring a tent? Miserably, Knight and the dog had huddled in to wait out the storm. Other members of the *Karluk* expedition had lived here as well, and the debris from two long-abandoned campsites lay nearby, but no tents remained in which to seek shelter. There were raggedy scraps of canvas here and there, pinned beneath rocks or frozen fast into the snow, and from these he made a windbreak and managed to sleep for four hours.

For three days, Knight and the dog had waited out the rain. The dog ate nothing, and Knight had only what he could kill—one duck and a couple of ratty crowbills with very little meat on them. They were a team, Knight and the dog, both hungry as could be and wishing for cover. The dog's feet were tender and he was weak from not eating, so Knight had a hell of a time getting him to move when the rain finally ceased.

It was snowing when Knight and the dog broke camp on July 10 and turned south toward home. Knight's boots were wearing raw and he was exhausted from the horrible weather and lack of food. He wanted to get back to the main camp as soon as possible, and thought he'd take a short cut to the river by following the wind. But when the wind shifted, he stumbled off course and ended up twice as far away as he should have been.

And now he faced the river, the Skeleton River, wider than ever and running swiftly. He looked left and right, and there was that river, just stretching out in either direction. The mouth was some 250 feet wide; the current swift and strong. To cross it would be suicide. There must be a way around. Knight gave up for the evening and sat through what felt like a hurricane, not sleeping, watching the dog rest, and drinking some tea. He built a fire, but it didn't do much good because he had no shelter and the wind and snow and beads of ice beat down upon his head and face.

The next morning, he shook off the snow and stretched his frozen limbs. Then, leaving his blankets and other baggage behind, Knight and the dog walked to the north bank of the river to find a place to cross. Eight hours later, he still hadn't found an opening, and his legs were aching from trudging through wet snow, standing water, and ankle-deep mud. He attempted to cross at points where the river looked more shallow, but the current was swift and he lost his footing. The dog was all in, and so was Knight, so finally he said to hell with it and plunged into the icy cold depths. The shock of the freezing water knocked the breath out of him, but he lifted his camera, extra rolls of film, and matches above his head in a pair of water boots, and together he and the dog swam the river at its narrowest point—two hundred feet or so. Knight struggled to keep his breath, and fought against being swept downriver.

Somehow, they made it, and crawled up onto the beach on the other side. Knight's watch had gone dead, but from what he could tell it was about five hours later when he and the dog found themselves at Rodger's Harbour, where they celebrated with a raging fire. One of the dog's legs had gone lame and the soles of Knight's boots had worn away completely, but they hobbled the rest of the way to Maurer and Crawford's old trapping camp, where Knight collapsed and slept a much-needed eight hours. When he awoke the next morning, he was stiff and hurting, but six miles later he was back at the base camp drinking black coffee and feasting on seal meat, and feeling just as "jake" as could be.

* * *

The *Teddy Bear* left Nome on August 20, 1922, carrying all the correspondence for the men and a fresh team of colonists to plant on Wrangel Island. A letter of instruction from Nome businessman and Stefansson acquaintance Ralph Lomen to Allan Crawford joined the sack of U.S. mail that had been saved up since last September. Mr. Stefansson, the letter stated, wanted Crawford, Knight, Maurer, and Galle to remain on the island for another season. He hoped that at least one of them would stay to command the new recruits. Supplies were being sent, though it was hard to know what the men were in need of, and they would also have a fresh team of dogs. "We will be glad to welcome you back in Nome," Lomen concluded, "and sincerely hope that the past winter has been kind in all respects to the entire party."

A strong northerly gale soon altered the ship's course, but those on board—Captain Bernard especially—were optimistic about their success. While they sat out an uncooperative northerly wind at Cape Prince of Wales, however, they received some disturbing news. The schooner *Sea Wolf* had just sailed in from Kotzebue, bringing word that all ships sailing into the Arctic that summer were locked in ice. The ice conditions, they warned, were unusually bad this year.

Undaunted, the *Teddy Bear* steamed ahead. On August 24, she entered the ice pack off East Cape, Siberia. Bernard had expected ice, and had known they would run into a good deal of it, but there were some breathless moments as they struggled with a southeasterly gale. On August 28, they reached Cape Wankarem, where they were delayed a day due to the pack. The ice here was thicker, more precarious, and they would have to wait it out before moving forward.

All the while, back in New Philadelphia, Toronto, McMinnville, and New Braunfels, the families waited anxiously. They had sent letters, telegrams, and packages to Captain Bernard, to be delivered to their boys. John Knight knew that the four men on the island would have the option of returning home or remaining at their Arctic posts, and personally he hoped that Lorne would stay. Lorne's grandfather was gone now, after suffering a hard fall. It was assumed that Crawford and Galle, neither of whom had been away from home for this long, would be homesick and anxious to return. Maurer, who seemed to have the call of the North in his blood, might just stay. And as for Lorne—as much as Mr. Knight missed his son, he was so proud of all he was doing, and he would be prouder still if Lorne remained on Wrangel.

"Of course, we . . . would love to see Lorne home again," he wrote to Harry Galle, "but, there is a greater thing for him now, to show his metal [*sic*] and go on than to come home much as he may wish to come home. I feel sure that they will report all well and in good spirits and hope they will all volunteer to carry on because that expedition means something big yet."

And to Stefansson, he wrote: "We would greatly love to see him and have him with us again but I don't believe that he would be justified in coming out now and leaving the work unfinished and I hope he will see it that way."

* * *

The snow on Wrangel Island had melted away in July, and Crawford, Knight, Maurer, Galle, and Ada turned eager and expectant eyes toward the horizon. Daily, they observed the movements of the ice— whether it traveled three quarters of a mile off shore, or began to close up, or drifted out away from land and then back in again. By July 28, the ice was completely out of sight, and their hearts rose. They were sure that it would only be a matter of days before the ship arrived.

Who would go back with it and who would stay? It was such a tremendous adventure for everyone. As eager as the men were to see home and family, they were also anxious to remain and carry out their mission. But Ada, they felt certain, would return. She was still painfully homesick and the thought of being so far removed from her son made her eyes darken and her smile fade. Crawford, Maurer, Galle, and even Knight all noted that they would actually be sorry to see her go.

They had read and reread all their books four or five times. Sometimes, after they finished their chores for the day, they went to bed by 2:00 P.M. Other times, while Ada worked at her sewing, the men remained in bed all day, rising in the evening. Because they were bored, they passed the time gambling and making idle wagers. The more opinionated Galle and Knight were especially fond of this pursuit. With his usual good-natured cockiness, Galle bet Knight $5.00 that the President of the United States earned a salary of $75,000 with $25,000 in travel expenses, and Knight vowed to show him up as soon as they got home and found out the real answer. Galle also amused himself by trying to catch birds so that he could attach messages to their legs.

The four men tried their hands at photography, Knight attempting to capture the moonlight on the ice; Crawford photographing a polar bear where it had fallen on the beach; Galle filming a whale vertebrae. They wanted to remember everything they had seen. Galle and Crawford were the most prolific photographers, washing and printing the films they had shot, and drying the pictures over a lamp or in the oven, until the chemicals finally ran out.

The stars were visible on some nights, breaking through the constant cloud barrier. The northern lights gave them regular shows, spectacular in their glowing and strobing greens, reds, blues, and golds. There was an undeniable beauty to this land.

The summer had brought grass three inches high and the delicate blooms of the island wildflowers. Ada and Galle would go walking sometimes, collecting flowers, which they took back to camp. Galle could identify most of them, although there were some that even he didn't know. He became excited over these and would tell Ada it was a new species, and she would help him collect his specimens so that he could study them and show the others.

Some days, Ada fished in the streams for hours, trying to hook tomcod, like they had in Alaska. But she never saw a tomcod, and she never caught anything. Sometimes she accompanied the men on hunting trips to help them bring back the game they killed. She and Galle collected roots from their daily walks and she boiled them up with the meat, and she found some greens which tasted like watercress, only sweeter.

She and Galle had been toying with different ways to serve seal blubber. The company had been boiling everything since they landed on the island nearly a year ago—which was in the Eskimo style, and the way Ada was accustomed to cooking things. But in August, Galle told them he was sick of boiled food, and thought it might taste better if they fried up some bear steaks in the fat they had stored. This tasted good to everyone, and for a while was the preparation of choice.

Since they had landed on the island, Galle had taken an increasing interest in the food preparation. He liked to help Ada with the cooking and began to view it as a kind of game, determined to find ways they could keep their diet interesting. With great care, he noted their menus in his diary, including verses he created on the subject, which helped to cheer him after a particularly dismal meal. "If you are at a dinner—a big one lets say,—Find your place as soon as you're able; If in the confusion you strike the wrong side, you shouldn't step over the table."

Knight was always picky about his food. He hated the taste of fox, and he liked his meat overdone. Ada, meanwhile, had never cared for bear meat. It tasted too strong, in her opinion. But the bear meat that Galle fried up tasted delicious to her, just like beefsteak.

They were eating fine, but there was a faint nagging of hunger now as, little by little, supplies ran out. Galle and Crawford dipped hard bread in grease all day long, but could never seem to feel satisfied.

Whether it was bear, duck, goose, or seal meat, they found it all tasted better served with candy. When they exhausted the ready-made sweets they had brought with them to the island, they attempted to make their own. Night after night, Galle experimented with different recipes because he was determined to satisfy his sweet tooth despite a throbbing abscess growing on his upper molar. It hurt like hell, but he wasn't about to stop eating or making candy.

Crawford, meanwhile, made the maps. The work was appealing to his disciplined, curious mind, and he embraced the responsibility with characteristic enthusiasm and dedication. He left often to explore the land, and when he came back he would spread out his papers and draw lines and numbers. Once he went away for an entire week, which was, Ada thought, a long time to be without him, and when he came back he said he had climbed a high mountain and looked in every direction. From what he could see, the island—if it were in a straight line—would stretch one hundred miles long and thirty miles wide. He also said that a ship making at least four fathoms could probably make it through to Doubtful Harbour. This was important because they were all thinking about the ship that should soon be coming for them.

They were collecting the skins of the animals they killed, and storing them in flour sacks. They had four full sacks so far, all fox, which they would take back with them for money. Ada wouldn't get any of it, but that was okay because she would have a great deal of money—$50 a month for every month she'd been there—waiting for her when she returned. She didn't mind it out here so very much anymore. The homesickness still crept up on her, rushing in waves, but for the most part it had subsided and she knew that if the ship came, she would be going home soon. She enjoyed the work she was doing. The men told her what to do and she did it and did it well. It was good to feel useful.

On August 9, Crawford, Galle, and Maurer left on an exploratory journey along the coast. They planned to mimic Knight's earlier trip, with Galle turning back at Skeleton River, and Crawford and Maurer continuing on to Cape Waring, or Waring Point, for a few days. It was the first time Ada had been left alone with Knight, this man she had come to fear. Ever since she'd begun working again he'd been friendlier to her and spoke more pleasantly. She would help him with whatever he needed while the others were away so that he would keep being nice.

He killed a polar bear while Crawford and the others were gone, a great, fat one. "Can you imagine the Smith Bld. falling?" Knight boasted in a letter he composed to his parents. "Well, that is the way he hit the ground." After breakfast, he and Ada skinned the bear but didn't bother to collect the meat because he told her they had enough ducks and geese to keep them fed. But he was lying. They needed the meat but he knew there was no way he would be able to haul it home right now with only Ada to help him. It was his hip that was giving him trouble. It had been bothering him since he'd returned from Skeleton Island and it just seemed to be getting worse.

Besides, he rationalized, they were doing fine with food. They had eaten well since the end of June. The hunting had been more successful, either because they were finding their rhythm with a rifle or because the game was more plentiful, and they had caught over forty seals alone. In the Eskimo way, they cut up a seal after it was killed, removing the blubber from the outside of the body. This they would slice into strips and store in the pokes, or sealskin bags. In this way, they accumulated some two thousand pounds of oil, while also saving the meat from the animal by drying it and storing it.

Everyone's spirits were brightened by a catch, but toward the middle of August, long after the three had returned from their exploratory trek, they grew frustrated once more. Luck seemed to have disappeared. The sky opened, offering a fall of snow which draped the earth in white. The men couldn't reach the seals. The bears all but vanished, and not even Ada, who had eyes like a telescope, could spot any. They could hear walrus in the distance, but couldn't see them thanks to the heavy fog and the rafters of ice, which were forming off shore. A ship was expected every day, and the ice was an unwelcome sight. To each other, the men and Ada remained optimistic and cheerful. A ship would come soon. It was, no doubt, delayed by the ice, and would be here before too long. But in private, each of them watched the horizon and worried.

As their unease increased, the five inhabitants of Wrangel Island kept themselves as busy as possible. On exploratory walks, the men discovered mammoth and mastodon tusks and bones scattered about, emerging from their ancient snowy graveyard as the sun melted the land. They found animal teeth and ivory, an eerie reminder of the lives that had preceded them on the island.

On August 28, Crawford gathered everyone—including Vic—for

their one and only group portrait. They sat together, huddled close, as the wind whipped at them from the west. Galle held Vic in his lap, while Ada edged close to Crawford. Their faces and hands were kissed by a thin layer of dirt, the men's chins so cloaked in whiskers that their families might not have recognized them.

Knight was the most drastically changed, although all the men were leaner now. His stout, oversized frame was narrow and slender. His face, previously round and apple-cheeked, was slim, and he looked, for the first time, almost handsome. Maurer's beard was bushy, his blond hair falling nearly to his shoulders. Crawford barely resembled the dapper, well-groomed boy of the previous year. His smooth, cherubic face was now sharply angled, his dark hair tangled and wild. Milton Galle had grown into his features, and his parents would hardly have known the tall, good-looking young man with the weathered brow and the tousled mane of hair. Ada, too, had changed. The cheekbones stood out in her pretty, elfin face, and womanly lines etched the corners of her eyes and mouth.

They were physically and mentally worn down and worn out, and trying to ignore the increasing evidence of wear and tear on their bodies. Crawford had a bad hand; Maurer constantly complained of lethargy; Ada suffered a wrenched back; an agonizing ulcer was growing on Galle's lower jaw; and a week after he returned from crossing the Skeleton River, Knight had noticed a soreness in his feet and a stiffness in his joints, especially his hip. He tried to ignore it, suspecting rheumatism, but by the following week, he was forced to stay close to camp. His right thigh hurt the worst and it made walking painful. He crawled into his bed and stayed there for several days, only getting out of it when absolutely necessary. He hated being idle, hated not doing his share, hated having free time to think about when and if the ship was actually coming, but the pain was quick and surprising and he knew he needed to heal. Much as he detested the thought, he would just have to rest up until the rheumatism passed.

*   *   *

Letters and telegrams from the Galles, the Crawfords, the Knights, and Delphine Maurer streamed in to Stefansson in New York, asking for any information he could spare. "Fear mishap has befallen *Teddy Bear*," read the wire from Professor Crawford. "Would it be advisable to send another boat equipped with wireless to its relief. Is relief by airship impossible?"

It was the iciest season anyone could remember in that far northern region—the worst ice conditions in twenty-five years. At Cape Wankarem, the skipper of the *Amy* had warned Captain Bernard about continuing north. Bernard persisted in spite of it, following the edge of the pack toward the west. But the ship was not strong enough to withstand the pressure. Ice sliced into the plank, above the iron sheeting, and her propeller was bowed and twisted by the crushing floes. Fifty-five miles west of Cape Serdze, on the northern shore of Anadyr Bay, Siberia, Bernard and his men took a break from their halting progress to survey the situation. From the highest elevation, the report was grim—nothing but a solid wall of ice across the horizon in the direction of Wrangel Island.

Bernard consulted with his crew. They didn't see any hope of moving forward and worried about the danger to the ship if they should press on. What's more, from the reports they had received from other ships, and from what they could see themselves from the ship's lookout, all the approaches to the island were blocked by ice. There was no chance of getting near the island and it would be difficult to make their way to Crawford and the others on foot. They would have to return to Nome.

The *Teddy Bear* arrived in Alaska on September 22, and Bernard sent the news of their failure to Stefansson on the 25th. "*Teddy Bear* unsuccessful. Encountered arctic pack, propeller damaged. All navigators here predicted failure due to unusual ice condition."

It was a bitter disappointment for Bernard. He knew the families would be wanting news, that they would be beside themselves when they found out the mission had failed. Although quoted in the newspapers as being "deeply concerned" for his party, Stefansson had confidence that the men were fine, that all would be well till next summer, when a ship would definitely be able to reach them. Upon sending the four young men and Ada to Wrangel Island, Stefansson had considered the fact that, due to the fickle nature of the ice, they might have to spend two winters there without relief. The worst malady to expect was homesickness, he conjectured. But Bernard wasn't so convinced. "If a native could live there," he was quoted as saying in the *Denver Post*, "I'd say those fellows could hang on. But no native has ever lived there."

Stefansson could have attempted a sled trip from Siberia to the island, he explained, but he didn't consider it necessary. "We had no reason to fear that assistance was needed and no reason to think that the skill of the men already there was inadequate to meet the situation." Therefore, he concentrated instead on his writing and his public speaking, which would, he hoped, help to sway the government to his side.

When the families received the news of the *Teddy Bear*'s failure, they reached out to Stefansson in alarm. "Is there nothing we can do?" Professor Crawford telegraphed. "Is it too late and dangerous now to send another boat?"

"There is," Stefansson wrote back, "no more need to worry about them than if they were in some European City or an ordinary place and were merely not in the habit of communicating with you. In other words, the only worries you need have for Allan are the same which he may reasonably have about you, and his chance of being safe and well next fall is the same as your own."

Delphine Maurer wrote him, too, asking for guidance. She trusted in the Lord, but she needed added reassurance. "As I see it," Stefansson wrote in return, "there is no cause for special anxiety about the men on Wrangel Island. They are as likely as you or I to be safe and well a year from now."

It was difficult in New Braunfels to get any news of the far North, so it was a friend of a friend of the Galles who first read the news in a New York paper that the *Teddy Bear* had failed to reach Wrangel Island. The article was passed on to Harry and Alma, who were left digesting the bitter failure of the relief expedition through third- or fourth-hand information, as well as the fact that Mr. Stefansson had not contacted them directly.

Trying to sound brave, Alma wrote to Stefansson. It wouldn't do to raise a fuss or to let him know how despondent she was. She felt desperate, fearful, but Stefansson was not to be bothered with that. He had his own worries, and she assumed he was just as hard struck by the failure of the ship as they were. "How welcome any news will be that you can forward to us about our boys can hardly be expressed. Had almost given up hopes of hearing anything further this year, but are anxious to know how near Captain Bernard came to the island. That we cannot hear from our boys is to be regretted, but that mail could not reach them even more so. I feel that news from the world would have made another winter indeed more pleasant . . . and we are all hoping that our boys will pass as pleasant a Christmas as possible."

"This means merely that the men on the island are cut off from communication for a year," Stefansson replied, as he had to the other parents. "They are just as safe on their island as Robinson Crusoe was on his—a little more so because there are no cannibals in that vicinity. They are just as likely as you or I in Texas or New York to be safe and well a year from now." Galle and Crawford might very well be so homesick, he said, that they would consider a journey to Siberia. While it would not be a dangerous journey, thanks to the American and Russian traders who were scattered along the coast, as well as the nomadic reindeer herders, he hoped they wouldn't attempt it because it would be expensive.

John Knight added his own words of comfort. "They are safe," he wrote again to Harry Galle, "and I hope well, and their failure is a word that is not yet written."

*   *   *

The men were very interested in the movement of the ice, and Ada understood that it was important if a ship was to get through. Sometimes the ocean cleared out and their faces brightened, and sometimes the ice came back in and they worried. Ada wondered how far the ice reached into the ocean. Did it spread as far as Nome? Did it reach to Russia? She decided to take a trip one day to see. She set out on her own until she came to the foot of a mountain. She thought she might climb it as far as she could and look for the end of the ice. But a thick fog rolled in and the sun began to fade, as it always did, so Ada turned back toward camp, still not knowing where the ice began.

Their luck had been good in June and July. The sealing had been strong, and they had shot more ducks and geese than they could count. But as July merged into August and then into September, their misfortune returned. "I shoot, no luck," Galle summed up. They launched the dory on September 2, and all four of the fellows went after the herd of walrus that had taunted them for weeks. Maurer and Galle each shot and killed one, but bringing them home wasn't as easy. The creatures were massive, and the four men could collect only a portion of the meat. They loaded the sled with a walrus skin four feet thick, ten feet long, and eight feet wide, dragging it across the ice. They dropped it at camp and went back for the meat. They were just nearing home when they capsized on the ice and lost all but one shoulder and a portion of the liver—just fifty pounds of their catch.

Ada cooked the walrus heart with some roots. They fried up the meat they'd managed to save, but it was extremely tough. Safe to eat, but that was it. They switched from walrus steaks to walrus stew as the meat ran thin, and then began boiling it again. They made bird stew, and Galle even experimented with frying hard breadcrumbs.

They scooped them up eagerly with spoons, and the concoction tasted nice for a change. When the walrus meat turned sour it was better tasting, and as the game began to dissipate, they were grateful to have anything at all to make a meal, even walrus flippers, which were practically inedible.

Ever since they arrived on Wrangel Island, they had eaten what they pleased without rationing. Hard bread alone was devoured several times a day, at meals and between meals. But with the thinning game, and no rescue ship yet on the horizon, they began to ration supplies. It was Galle's idea to break out one box of bread and issue two pieces a day to each person. In this way, one box would last them twenty days. Crawford approved the plan, but when he broke into a box one day early, Galle was furious with him.

"Coffee has taken place of tea," Galle noted in his diary on August 24. "I don't like it." They had been drinking tea every day from 4:00 till 6:00 P.M., but now they must ration it. The sugar ran out, but they had plenty of saccharine, which they used liberally.

They stored the meat of the seals in two large barrels. Once they filled these, they would begin drying the meat so they would have it for winter, should the ship fail to make the island. Skins hung about camp, drying, while other skins still waited to be cleaned. They had six seal pokes now, filled with some 1,200 pounds of blubber.

"At a dinner if anything happens amiss," Galle wrote in his notebook following one of Maurer's frequent attacks of biliousness, "to appear quite unconscious is best—It's bad form to notice the little Faux Pas, They should pass unobserved by the guests."

Galle had been taking aspirin for the ache in his jaw, but it didn't seem to help and the pain nagged at him all day long. As he was eating one night, the ulcer in his mouth broke and left him in agony. None of them had medical knowledge, so they would just have to do their best to stay well. Galle must try to ignore the excruciating pain of the ruptured ulcer because there was nothing else to be done for it except to take medicine for a headache and pray for the ship to come.

*   *   *

The rain returned at the end of August, and they threw tarpaulins over the tents to keep the water out. All too soon, it felt like winter again, as the fog, the snow, and the cold came creeping back. Unfortunately, so did the ice. The horizon turned white, as they watched the ice gradually float back into the harbor. The snow came thick and heavy, and the ice grew until it blanketed the sea. Every day, they awoke hopefully to a strong breeze, but were treated only to the sight of that thin, pale skin over the ocean. Soon, the ground was entirely covered in snow. But they still hoped for a ship.

On September 7, Crawford took a walk to the hills to have a look at the ice. From where he stood, he could see that it was broken up to the east, with leads of water trickling through. It was thick ice, must have been, because it seemed to be holding back the huge floes which crowded and strained beyond. On September 10, Knight trekked a mile and a half inland and climbed a high ridge. To the west, there was ice. To the east, there was ice with a wide lead breaking up the white. To the south, again all ice.

They prayed for a strong wind, and whenever a gale whipped up, they celebrated. "Let her blow," Knight wrote in his journal. "The harder the better." It may have made it unpleasant for them, but they knew the wind could help carry the ice off shore. Sometimes in the distance, they spotted what they thought looked like a water sky far out to sea, which meant there had to be open water somewhere. As the darkness increased steadily, they lit candles and hung a lantern outside the tent to attract the ship. But with each day that passed, pushing them deeper into September, the ice stubbornly showed no movement.

There would be no ship this year. By the middle of September, Crawford, Knight, Maurer, Galle, and Ada had to face that crushing disappointment. The window of time had ended, just like the window of time for summer had come and gone, leaving in its place sleet, drizzle, fog, snow, and gradually darkening skies. They would have to spend another fall, winter, and spring before they could hope to see relief. They had come to Wrangel Island to occupy it, claiming it for Great Britain, and they had come to study, to explore, and to assimilate knowledge of the area. They had done these things, had accomplished their mission, and now they must face another winter.

They would need to reorganize their daily lives. Supplies must be hoarded. Rationing must be adhered to. They must find a new camp because they had exhausted their wood supply for two miles on either side of their present position, and it would be easier to move the camp to wood than to move the wood to camp. If they had only known sooner that the ship wasn't coming, it would have been easier to reorganize, to save and to ration, and to move camp before the weather had grown so difficult and before they stood facing the swift approach of winter.

Crawford and Knight left camp on September 20 to search for a good location. That spring, Galle had found a site on the inside spit of the harbor mouth, just two and a half miles away near Doubtful Harbour. Now, Crawford and Knight surveyed the spot with a critical eye and found piles of driftwood and the first open water they had seen in a while.

As usual, they said nothing to Galle or Ada about it when they returned, but Galle sensed that they would be moving just as soon at the weather allowed. There was no mention of when or how or what the camp would be like when they got there. He suspected they were planning to make one big trip with the dory, hauling supplies and equipment, and that he would just get the word in the next few days. Probably, he assumed, he would simply awake one morning to " 'Get the hell up, we are going to move to-day.' " But when a frigid gale swept in, bringing wind and snow, they waited it out for several days before beginning the transfer.

Actually, when the time came to move, Galle awoke to, "Coffee for you." Then they began the long and tedious task of transporting everything to the new site. Once there, they chopped and piled wood, and erected two ridgepoles and six upright rails, nine feet tall, for the walls of the new house. It took thirty-odd rafters slanted upward with poles crossed on top to construct the ceiling.

Because they were surrounded by ice on all sides, they wouldn't be able to use the dory to move their equipment and supplies as they'd hoped, but would have to haul everything by sled. At the new campsite, they were treated to the sight of ducks—several hundred of them—and seagulls and ravens. They would make the most of the new place and of their situation. They would push aside their disappointment over the ship, and focus on the work at hand.

Crawford and Knight began pondering the idea of making the trip across the ice to Siberia next spring. It was a journey, they estimated, which would take anywhere from one hundred to two hundred miles, depending on their route. Once ashore, they would head some five hundred miles on foot down the rugged and wild Siberian coast to the nearest wireless station, which meant either Russia's Emma Harbor or Nome. They had five dogs in fair shape and a sled Knight planned to strengthen for the task. It was, in his opinion, just another opportunity to "demonstrate the 'Living off the country' which has never failed yet as far as the Stefansson expeditions are concerned."

Galle certainly didn't expect or feel the need to be consulted about their plans to cross to Siberia. He had known his place from the outset of this expedition and had accepted it happily. Crawford and Knight were in charge, with Maurer as consultant. But Galle overheard them talking to each other in hushed tones, dropping words or phrases, which made him suspect a "mysterious dash" to Siberia.

On the way back to the old camp from setting up the new one, Knight at last told Galle of the plans to cross the ice next spring. It would be Nome, not Siberia, if they could make it there, he said, but did not mention the reasons for the trip. They would need a good bit of money to take with them, he told Galle, and asked if he had any. Galle had only $2.50 and told Knight he was welcome to all of it. "K keeps conversation pretty nonsensical," he noted later. "Of course, I can figure their motives." And, Galle added, Knight had said that he was reluctant to make the trip, but he *had* to.

*   *   *

The stiffness in the back; the pain in his hip; the general lethargy and weakness. Knight tried to tell himself it was all due to rheumatism, brought on by the swim through cold water. But the feelings were disturbingly, alarmingly familiar.

In the spring of 1917 on his expedition with Stefansson, it had started with irritability, followed by a melancholy that he couldn't seem to shake. Afterward, he was plagued by sluggishness and joint pain. Then there was shortness of breath and dizziness. Knight had heard of scurvy, of course, had known it was caused by a deficiency of vitamin C, knew that limeys had taken their nicknames from the preventative lime juice issued to ships of the British Navy in 1795, and knew that polar explorers must be watchful of it. But beyond that, he'd never given it much thought.

Back then, he had liked to boast that a fat man was protected from the cold, but for some reason he always seemed to feel it more than the others. As they had traveled across the snow and ice, his feet were dangerously chilled, but he urged his teammates to keep moving. It was his heel, and when he stopped to nurse it, it really began to hurt. He wasn't able to bathe out there or change into dry clothing, and was eating mostly dried vegetables and fruits, and fried, boiled, or roasted meat. Then they switched to pemmican and hard bread. There was dry meat, too, but Knight's teeth were too tender to chew it. From April 7 to May 12, 1917, he ate no fresh meat at all, and he lived largely on rolled oats, rice, sugar, and cocoa.

On April 25 of that year, he thought he had caught a bad case of spring fever. He was gloomy and his energy was waning. One of his young comrades, Harold Noice, felt it, too, only he also suffered from a dull ache in his right knee. From the beginning of the expedition, Knight had found the homely, bookish Noice pushy and ingratiating, while Noice thought Knight simple and crude. But suddenly their ill health gave them something in common.

One week later, Knight felt the first shooting pain in his hips. Then his legs. He was fine during the day, but by nighttime he was in misery. He didn't want to move, didn't want to work, found it hard to concentrate on anything. He also discovered that he could easily pick chunks of loose flesh from his gums.

Alarmed, he told Stefansson at once. Scurvy, was the instant diagnosis. He would need fresh meat or fruits and vegetables immediately, nothing dried, fried, boiled, or roasted, which would only destroy the natural and curative Vitamin C. Knight, Stefansson, and their comrades spent hours looking for seals, but got nothing. The pain in Knight's hips increased until he couldn't leave his snow house. For three days, he lay inside, despondent and irritable. The smallest thing would aggravate him or make him lose his temper. He was unable to speak, to sleep. "I would have given anything in this world," he wrote in his journal in 1917, "for a magic button which would have landed me between the clean white sheets of my own bed in my own room back home. Mother would have been standing over me, worried pink. I could see her—. I had come North of my own free will. What a fool!"

On the fourth morning, Knight and Noice—who was so weak he had to be pulled on the sled—were willing, if not terribly able, to travel again. Knight's teeth were so loose he could have plucked them from his gums without a struggle, and the gums themselves were as soft as American cheese, so that chewing on a wooden toothpick was like chewing on a knife. Every bone ached, every movement pained him. His breath came quickly at the slightest motion.

The secret to his recovery was eight fat caribou tongues, presented to Knight and Noice by Stefansson in mid-May. The tongue was the choicest part of the animal, according to Stefansson—and the two gorged themselves. They cooked up the tongues in cocoa, and after the feeding enjoyed their first comfortable night in several weeks. The next morning, there was tongue again for breakfast, boiled and underdone, in order to preserve the precious nutrients they would need to heal. They nourished themselves on leftover broth the rest of the day, as well as the marrow of the deer, and any other meals thereafter were eaten raw. After four days of this diet, they were fit to travel again. Knight's legs still gave him trouble, but by June 17, the pains were gone and his gums had healed completely. He was good as new.

Five years later, the pain was still vivid in his memory and in his body. Too vivid for his comfort. But he said nothing about it to anyone because if he voiced his fears he believed they might really come true and he didn't want to believe that the scurvy had returned. Even as the nagging feeling grew, he tried to talk his mind and body out of it, and he kept his discomfort to himself. He would not be a burden and he would not have the others worry about him.

Galle noticed that Knight grumbled a lot lately about all the hard work he had to do, which seemed funny given that he was doing the least amount of work of anyone, Ada included. Ever since he'd come back from his trip to Skeleton River, Knight had seemed increasingly lazy. Galle was wrestling with the pain of the abscess on his molar, the ulcer on his jaw, and he was hungry and tired and cranky like everyone else. But they were here to work and to study and Galle would not allow his own pain to get in the way of that. Therefore, he was disgusted when Crawford dragged his feet while chopping wood— or when Maurer continually talked of being sleepy all the time—or when Knight lay in his bed all day.

Knight was full of facetious remarks lately, and he seemed irritable and out of sorts with his companions. They should be getting up at a regular hour, Knight complained. And on September 18, he reprimanded Crawford for calling him from his bunk and gave Crawford strict orders not to disturb him until morning. During the night, when the others were asleep, Knight would finally rise to make coffee and eat something; then he would sit back down to read until 10:00 A.M. Afterward, they were treated to one of his typically sarcastic comments about the noise level. Crawford and Maurer were turning in around 10:00 P.M., while Galle stayed up reading. Knight went to sleep last of all, and the next day, when Crawford prepared the breakfast at 1:30 P.M., Knight awoke grumbling and swearing about his short sleep. "Now what can you do?" Galle wrote. "You can't shoot him, you can't hang him, so what are you going to do?"

While Knight snapped at the others and stayed close to his bunk and struggled with the throbbing in his hip, Ada watched. He had been different ever since he returned from his exploring trip, but he wouldn't admit it. He seemed to have lost a lot of his strength and his energy. He complained about his back. It was sore, he told them, and sometimes he lay in bed for days, trying to nurse it to good health. He felt weak, he said, and weary.

The others didn't seem to notice—only seemed to get mad at him and lose their tempers—but Ada worried. There would be no ship this year, so they must keep him well. If he fell sick, there were no doctors until next summer and only the four of them to care for him.

Dear Sister,

I am somewhat composed now, and can talk about it, but I admit I was pretty well shot to pieces at first, because I lived all summer in the expectation of receiving letters from our dear boy. And then to hear that the ship couldn't reach them was a great disappointment. If I only could have heard the single word "safe" I would pacify myself for another year. But I have hope, and I won't give up, and when I do begin to doubt, I only have to look at his picture we have of him in his fur suit, and somehow it spells to me that all's well, and I bare up. I see no failure in his face. He deserves the credit and not we, although we waste away, worrying over his welfare.

Alma Galle

Eight

A WATER SKY HAUNTED them in October, making them dream of
the open ocean that lay far beyond their sight. The five citizens of
Wrangel Island went about their duties with a little less enthusiasm, a
little less vigor, and tried, all the while, to hide their disappointment
from each other. They had counted on a ship. They had each realized
there was a possibility that a ship might not make it, but they had
somehow never stopped believing that relief would come that summer.

Ada was taking it especially hard. She was very quiet, much more
so than usual. She thought of Bennett and her family and of Nome,
and she wondered again why she had ever agreed to come. She was
making a pair of moose-hide mittens for Crawford, but her heart wasn't
in her work. She had enjoyed feeling useful, enjoyed making socks or
mittens for the men. But now she worked mechanically, trying to turn
her mind away from her sadness over the absence of the ship.

They finished the move from the old camp to their new one, several
miles away, on November 16, just days before the sun once again
disappeared until spring. Because of the rough terrain and lack of
substantial snow on the ground, they were forced to pull the sled on
the sea ice that clung to the beach. The move was made tricky because
recent snowfalls had blanketed the thin ice, which broke easily with

too much weight. Before you knew it, you could be plunged into freezing water.

During the day, the temperature rose to minus 4 or minus 2 degrees, while at night it dropped to minus 13 or minus 20. It was too cold for snow, and that meant there was no snow suitable for building blocks to wall up their house, so they were forced to erect their old tent. They had a good Maplewood stove and plenty of wood, so each night they built up the fire and the five of them huddled around it trying to think of conversation. After spending so much time together, every day for over a year, it was sometimes an effort.

They left the dory at the old camp because they knew it would be useless to them now as there was nothing to hunt. Last year, the bears were everywhere, but this year, even though the men searched for them, hunted for them, kept a constant watch for them, "there hain't none," as Knight observed.

There were seals in the distance, but the would-be hunters could never seem to get close enough. Crawford woke one morning before anyone and walked for forty minutes following the ice offshore. The seals were within reach here, but the tricky part was capturing them after they were shot. He surprised one of the unsuspecting creatures, as well as a gull that had landed on it, but the seal disappeared as soon as he fired and he left the gull where it fell.

Crawford returned to camp, discouraged, shoulders slumped, and described to Knight where he had lost the seal. Knight took Galle with him and they hiked offshore to the spot. Through field glasses, Knight could see a seagull feasting on something in the distance. When they hiked out to it, they saw it was the remains of Crawford's gull. And there, just twenty feet away in the slush and snow, was a splash of red against white. The seal lay under the slush, a small male without much meat on its bones. But at least it was something.

Afterward, the lead—or trail of open water—closed over and they knew there would be no more sealing. Knight shot a duck but it got

away. Fox tracks were scattered along the beach, but the men and
Ada never actually saw the creatures now, even though they had set
out new traps and checked them every day. The seagulls had vanished.
Crawford made a crab net, which he set out in a hole in the ice, but
he managed to catch only a quart of small and tasteless shrimp.

They lived on walrus skin because there was nothing else except
some hard bread and tea. The weather turned nasty in the heart of
November, wet, slicing snow and icy gusts of wind. A pounding surf
split the ice offshore from underneath, leaving fragments that pushed,
clamored, dueled, and jostled for position. The water sky shone in
the far horizon, promising an open sea, and for a time Ada and the
men let themselves hope again for a ship.

After they settled into the new camp, Ada began to sew skins for
Knight and Crawford to take with them on their long journey across
the ice to Nome. It had become clear to them, as winter rolled on,
that they would need to do something to improve the food situation,
and that they would not be able to wait until spring to make the trek.
They would need a full outfit for the trip and there was much to do.
Ada repaired their old clothes and worked on sleeping bags, mittens,
socks, and blankets of skins. She scraped the seal and fox skins they
had collected and then sewed new clothes out of them. They hoped
to depart around January 15, 1923, depending, of course, on the
weather, the ice conditions, and the dog feed. Right now, the dogs
were subsisting on bear skin or dried sealskin and blubber, and if the
dogs were still weak and undernourished, it would be difficult to travel
very far with the sled full of supplies they would need to take with
them.

Knight had grown thin and haggard since September. Still he said
nothing about his health to anyone until one day Ada overheard him
mention to Crawford that he believed he had a touch of scurvy. He
didn't want to make a fuss and didn't want the others to know. The
pain in his hip and legs remained, but perhaps they were a bit duller
now, or maybe he was becoming used to them. His stomach troubled

him, and he thought he might have indigestion, so he rested until he felt better. Knight was convinced he would be fine and that he could make the trip. The sooner he and Crawford got started, the sooner they could reach open water and seals.

By December 21, there was enough snow to form blocks for the sides and roof of the house. And by Christmas Eve, the snow roof was completed. On Christmas Day, Ada and the men gathered in their newly completed house while the snow fell fast and heavy outside. They feasted on salt seal meat and a piece or two of extra hard bread each, and went over the plans for the trip to Nome. After working on bolstering the dog harness, Knight started repairs on the sled. Crawford, meanwhile, was occupied making ridgepoles and uprights for the tent they would use on the trip.

As another year on the island came to a close, Ada wondered where she would be if she lived till next Christmas. Would she be back in Nome with her sister? Would she be cleaning houses again and taking on sewing work? Would Bennett be well and healthy and living with her once more? Perhaps they would have a house where they would live after she took him to the hospital to cure him.

Ada and the men couldn't understand why the game had been so thick their first season on the island, when now there was very little. Ada was unfamiliar with hunting and the conditions in the wild Arctic, but she was surprised by the abundance and then the lack of game. She and the others had counted on the fact that the bears, seals, and foxes would remain thick. They didn't know that sometimes the animals simply chose to frequent another location from year to year, and that there was a domino effect in place—because the seals were gone, the polar bears must look elsewhere for food. As one outsider observed, "There are so many 'ifs' in Arctic exploration that it was folly to let the boys go up there with so few supplies."

There were two reasons for attempting the trek to Nome, the first and foremost their need for food because they felt certain that their existing provisions would not sustain them until summer. The second was that Crawford and Knight wanted to get news of their time on the island to Stefansson. The men figured they might be able to reach Nome in sixty or seventy days, if the ice and weather conditions allowed. Stefansson was most likely wintering on the mainland, and Crawford and Knight both had a hunch that he did not head north on the relief ship that past summer, so they were sure to run into him in Alaska. "If one can go by 'hunches', my 'hunch' tells me that V.S. did not come north this summer and that we are doing the right thing in making this trip," Knight recorded in his diary.

The darkness and the cold made January a dangerous month to travel. The sky was dim, the weather and ice conditions unpredictable. Crushing, vaulting floes, open water, and sudden blizzards were to be expected. Now, Crawford and Knight would need to find their way in the faint glow of the barely awakened sun. But as far as they could determine, they had no choice. There wasn't food enough for all of them and they must find help soon. They intended to set out just after Christmas, but the weather turned and the snow blew in until it was impossible to see more than a foot in front of their faces. For days, the wind howled and gusted and the snow drifted with surprising ferocity. The north wall of their house blew away and the men and Ada were so frozen they could barely build it back.

The sky cleared by January 4, and Knight and Crawford began gathering their belongings in earnest and loading the sled. Crawford packed his diary, but left his accounts of minerals and fossils in his trunk back at camp. They loaded the sled with 700 pounds of supplies, including thirty days' rations of seal blubber and Pilot bread, which was all the food they had for the journey, and a few pounds of dried meat for the dogs. When that gave out, they would feed the animals the four sealskins they were bringing as well. Seven hundred pounds was a heavy burden for five weakened and undernourished dogs and two weary men, particularly for traveling over uneven and unstable ice.

Just in case their hunch was wrong and Stefansson was not on the Alaskan mainland, Crawford and Knight left letters for him with Maurer and Galle so that he would understand why they had gone and what their plans were. They would head the one to two hundred miles due south to the Siberian coastline, and from there down the coast to Cape Serdze, Whalen, Diomedes, and finally across the water to Nome.

Knight knew firsthand the dangers of ice travel, and Crawford understood them intellectually. They knew that even though it was winter, the ice wasn't solid all the way across the sea, and they knew it could shift and break beneath them as they traveled, particularly with as heavy a load as they were pulling. They were all too aware that there was a chance they might not make it to Nome, and so they wrote last messages, just in case. Maurer would be left in charge on the island, and so they left the letters in his care.

"Game is *scarce*," Crawford wrote to Stefansson. "When I saw how sparse seal and bear were I decided it would be unwise to stay here with the dogs all winter. It is hard to say what we shall do if we arrive at Nome and find you are in the north. We will of course follow any advice you may have left. Otherwise we will use our own judgment."

Knight's letter was more typically to the point. "Of course I am not afraid of starving to death or freezing (thanks to the things I have been taught by you) but I am well aware that accidents are liable to happen to one in this country as well as on the 'outside.' So if I pass my 'checks' kindly send whatever remuneration I am entitled to, to my mother or father at McMinnville, and rest assured that I am ever grateful for the favors you have shown me, and the opportunities that you have made for me."

To their mothers and families, Knight and Crawford left a last good-bye, in case they should not return. "Crawford and I are about to leave for Nome," Knight wrote, "and as accidents are as likely to happen to one in this country as anywhere else, I am leaving this letter for you. I am also leaving a letter for the manager of the Stef. Ex. & Dev. Co. asking him to send whatever money is due me, to you.

However, if <u>something</u> does happen to me I will be thinking of you until the very end with all the love any one ever had for their Mother. This also applies to Dad & Joseph."

And Crawford wrote, "From my accrued pay, my shares in *The Goblin* and anything else of value I should like a fund to yield $25.00 annually set aside as a cash scholarship in U.T.S. for the student getting highest marks in Chemistry and Physics at the test exam. The rest to be held in trust for my brother John till the age of twenty-one. My regret on leaving is that I had not given you more information in my last letter to you about the fact that you might not hear from me in 1922. You may be sure my last thoughts were of my father and mother and of Marjorie and Johnnie. I hope I have been a dutiful son as sons go and that I have ended honourably."

At 1:00 A.M. on January 7, 1923, Crawford and Knight and the five dogs started out, heading due south. The going seemed smooth and they made good time. Maurer, Galle, and Ada watched until their dark figures quickly disappeared into the night. Now the three remaining at camp had only to wait for their return.

*   *   *

Their good start quickly turned bad. The sled was overloaded for the dogs, who were soft and weak from inactivity. The darkness was constant and perilous and caused them to misstep frequently and tip over the sled. Each time, they would pile the tumbled supplies back on and plod ahead. After the next tip-over, and the next, they did the same. They managed to lose two ice picks and a pot lid before it was all over with, and to make matters worse, a strong breeze was blowing in from the east. The first day's travel took them six miles east of camp and about a mile off the coast.

The following day was better, the wind letting up and the snow holding off for now. The sled glided easily over the ice, which was hard and tightly packed as concrete, and they traveled from 8:20 in the morning—as far as they could tell by their inaccurate watches—

until 2:30 in the afternoon, when it became too dark to see. They made camp under the shadow of the graves at Rodger's Harbour.

The next day was clear and calm, but Crawford and Knight discovered they were both too weary to travel. Their hands, feet, and legs were chafed from the exertion, and their muscles ached. They slept all day and broke camp early the following morning, once again heading due south. It wasn't long before they hit a patch of soft snow that left the dogs straining to get through. Knight slipped into the harness and helped pull, although it took all of his strength. Two miles later, they arrived at a field of rough, uneven ice. They knew they would never be able to make it across with the dogs and the sled.

They turned toward the east and traveled four miles along the shore until they reached a towering pressure ridge near Cape Hawaii. There was no use continuing because they would never be able to climb it with the supplies and the dogs, and so they made camp and talked about their options. A fierce wind built from the west and the snow was beginning to drift. Crawford and Knight tried to shake their growing discouragement.

The next day, they were again unable to travel because of the gale and snow. "The going ahead looks very bad," Knight noted in his journal, "and as we only have five dogs in poor condition and the weather is very cold, it is needless to say that going is very difficult. Unless we get started south soon, I am afraid that we will have to go back to the main camp and then go West looking for a way through the rough ice."

* * *

It was disturbingly peaceful with Crawford and Knight gone. Galle, Maurer, and Ada tried to keep busy so that they wouldn't think about the danger their comrades might be facing, the fact that they might never see them again, or the shortage of food around camp. Maurer and Galle attended to their traps, and Maurer managed to catch one fox, which was, after their dry spell, cause for great celebration.

When they weren't working, Ada told them stories, which Galle especially seemed to love. His favorite was Ada's favorite—"The Lady in the Moon."

"One time," Ada began, "there was Eskimo girl who did not want to marry. One day when she was out getting Salmon berries, she find skull of man. This skull she take home to her camp and hide in the reindeer skins of her bed.

"Well, one day when she is gone out berrying her father looks into reindeer skins on her bed and finds the skull of man. He takes the skull . . . and he throws it away as far as he can, over the cut bank into the water.

"When the girl comes home at night . . . she cannot find skull. She goes to father to ask him, 'Where is that thing I have in my skins?' And he is angry and says, 'Go to the cut bank and in the water you will find skull if you want him so much.'

"On cut bank she . . . rolls way down in water. Pretty soon she opens her eyes and looks round. Then she knows she is in the ocean only it seems just like on land.

"There she sees the man of the skull. She begs to stay with him for she loves him very much; but he say no, and drive her out of his camp. Then the man calls out to her and tells her if she wants to go home to her father she must do what he says, 'After a while you will come to a fork in the trail and one will go to the right and one to the left. You must keep to the left trail if you want to get home to your father and your mother.'

"After a while she comes to the forks of the trail and there is the road just as smooth on the right, and the rocky narrow road is on the left. Sure enough, the road is narrow, and full of stones. She look across and the road to the right is so nice and smooth, and so she just runs across to the right-hand road and begins walking fast along the smooth road.

"She heard the man calling—'Keep to the left, if you want to get home and see your father and mother.' But she kept running, and as she looked back the trail behind her fades away and she was way up in the air, with no man behind her and only the smooth trail leading the way to the sky.

"The girl kept on walking until she came to a land and it was the moon, and it had mounts and a ravine and a river. A spirit or medicine man . . . told the girl . . . that there was an old woman who lived up there. If she would go to her camp the old woman would look after her and not let the man in the moon get her.

"When she got there, a bear was stretched out in front of the cabin. She was afraid the bear would eat her, but if she turned back the man in the moon would get her, and she was afraid of him. So she stepped right on the belly of the bear. He growled but he didn't eat her.

"Then she stays with the old woman and helps her. But all the time she wonders about her father and mother and if they are dead. One night the old woman takes up one plank out of her floor and tells the girl to look down. She looked out through the hole in the floor to the earth. She could see it all spread out like it was in her hand but a long way off. She could see water and earth. Then she could see people.

"The girl kept thinking about her father and her mother and crying. So the old woman said, 'Well, if you want to go home, I will tell you how you can go! Get to work and make sinew thread, and mittens— some seal mittens; some reindeer skin.' So the girl made the sinew rope and braided it like she braids her hair, and a bag full of mittens. Then she starts out and throws out the rope from the moon to the earth.

"She puts on some mittens and she climbs down the braided sinew rope, and when mittens wear out she throws them away.

"She climbs down and down until at last there is only one pair of mittens left and only a little sinew rope. Now the old woman had told her to keep her legs straight when she got on the earth. For if she had straight legs she would be young just like she was when she went to the moon, but if she curved her legs, she would be bent like an old woman.

"So when she had on her last pair of mittens and only a little rope, there was nothing for her to do but drop, and she did, trying to keep her legs straight so she would be young as she was when she left the earth. But it was too far and her legs bent. There she was, bent almost double like an old woman, and she couldn't straighten up. She was an old woman.

"She hurried fast as she could to where her mother and father lived. All she found was a sunken place, where the house had fallen in a long time ago. And that is the story of the Lady in the Moon."

The girl in the story had returned home from her great adventure only to find that it no longer existed—her parents were gone, her house had vanished. And she was, once more, alone.

* * *

Crawford and Knight huddled behind a snow wall, which blocked them from the wind. They had thrown a tarpaulin over it and now sat shivering and cursing the stoves, both of which had inconveniently and infuriatingly decided to stop working. After several hours, Crawford, at last, was able to get one operating halfheartedly, but the damage was already done and they were freezing.

It had been a miserable trip so far, and they were making no progress. No matter which way they turned, no matter which direction they started off in, they always came to some sort of insurmountable obstacle—rough ice, broken ice, pressure ridges. The sled was weak and threatened to snap and the dogs were nearly broken themselves. The provisions were in danger of running out any day, and the ice hugging the island was so treacherous that there was no chance of reaching the level pack ice that lay beyond.

Knight and Crawford discussed every option, but could come up with nothing. The cold was eating into their brains, just as it pierced their skin and crept into their blood through toes, fingers, and noses. Crawford's fingertips were badly frozen, which kept him in constant, excruciating pain. He had, Knight observed, the "poorest hands for this country of anyone whom I have ever seen."

None of it would have been so bad if Crawford could have stood the cold better or if Knight had only felt well. But at last he had to admit to himself and to Crawford that what he had been most afraid of for all these months was true. He had scurvy. Not just a touch of scurvy, but an unshakable, growing case of it.

He was easily winded after hiking or helping to pull the sled, and he felt "weak as a kitten." The pain in his legs was worse at night, and he discovered on his legs and arms numerous hard, red spots, some as large as a pinhead, some smaller. They were thicker below his knees and elbows, and when he ran his fingers over them, there was no pain, but he could feel the bumps on his skin. He experimented by picking some of them off, and found they were fairly deep set.

"I am nearly all in (I hate to admit this but I am sure I can't help it), for my scurvy has been coming back for the last month or two although I have said nothing to anyone about it, Crawford excepted," he wrote with great discomfort in his journal. "When we started I was in hopes of fairly good going and a chance to get fresh meat but I find that my legs go back on me in this rough ice where I am forced to get in harness to help the dogs."

He and Crawford decided they must return to the main camp, where they would lighten the sled's load, and then Crawford with Galle would start out again to the south. Galle was the strongest of them all and the healthiest, and he and Crawford, with their youth and good sense, would have a better time than the rest, even if neither had experience traveling the ice. "It will be impossible for all of us to stay at the main camp," wrote Knight, "for there is just enough grub there for three people . . . to last until the seals and birds come. I would like to make this trip but I really do not feel able."

On the morning of January 15, they started back home. Along the way, a gale blew up from nowhere, blasting them in the face with snow. They shifted directions, but so did the wind, and three hours later they gave up and camped once more near the gravesite at Rodger's Harbour. The wind had frozen both of their faces badly, and Knight felt the cold more than usual because of his weakened condition. "We hoped to make home tomorrow," he recorded, ". . . but—This is the first blow we have had all year from the West, and naturally it had to come as we were going home in a hurry. Oh! Well-l-l-l-l!"

They were stranded the next day, nursing their frozen cheeks and chins, desperate to get back to camp but forced to wait because of the weather. The gale seemed vengeful, and they were exhausted. On January 17, the howler blew on and the snow formed over the small tent they had pitched over a makeshift structure, carved out of snow. The stove, still barely working, was dripping kerosene, and there was nothing to eat but cold blubber and hard bread.

On January 18, they were able to crawl out of their icy dungeon long enough to build a wall of snow around their shelter and cover it with the tent and a tarpaulin. They fed the dogs some sealskin and then crept back inside to shield Crawford's frozen fingers and cheeks and Knight's numbed face from the wind. With the gale shut out and the stove going stronger, they were able to make some tea, so that they soon were, according to Knight, "nice and warm and swilling tea like a couple of Englishmen."

The next day they made it nearly as far as the old trapping camp from the previous year. Between the fresh breeze, Crawford's newly frozen big toe (thanks to a pair of wet socks), and Knight's scurvy, they were unable to make the final push for home. Knight could barely walk, and the flashes of fire in his legs and hip were becoming sharper and more pronounced. Wearily, the two invalids erected a snow house with a canvas roof and climbed inside to rest.

Knight didn't think his chances very good to make it back to camp the next day without some help. He thought Crawford should go on ahead and bring Galle back to get him. They had seen not one single animal on their short and frustrating journey—only a few old tracks scattered here and there. Knight couldn't remember the last time he'd eaten something fresh or anything, for that matter, which would have helped him fight the scurvy. Sour seal oil was their only antiscorbutic food—the kind that would cure or prevent scurvy. He had been forcing himself to eat it for days, but there was no relief. The pains increased, as did his fatigue. To make it worse, there were several deep, raw cracks in his heels, which made walking next to impossible. That night, with great discouragement, he wrote, "Of all the trips I have ever participated in, long or short, this one is the worst for hard luck (or is it incompetence?)."

*   *   *

Knight and Crawford stumbled into camp the morning of January 20, both of them worn out and frozen. Crawford was in obvious discomfort from his frostbitten foot and fingers, and his face was black and blistered from the cold. Knight's cheeks bore the same marks, and he limped as he came into camp. He didn't complain, but his face and his eyes revealed the pain he was in, and Ada watched him and worried. Their arrival had been a shock to her and to Maurer and Galle, who had expected them to be nearing the Siberian shore by now.

While the two travelers rested, Maurer and Galle tended their traps and Ada continued to sew. Ada noticed that Knight was a good deal weaker now, although he was trying to pretend he wasn't. Knight did not confide in the others as to why he remained so pale and why he was still exhausted long after Crawford's energy had returned.

As usual, Crawford asked Knight for his opinion and guidance. Knight felt, and Crawford agreed, that it made more sense for three of them to make the trip now instead of two because three would have a better shot at it. When traveling that time of the year, on the unpredictable ice, it was vital to make a quick camp at night. If three of them were to go, one could build the igloo, while one tended to the dogs, and the other unloaded the sled. This way, they were inside in just twenty minutes or so, tucked safely away from the bitter cold of winter.

Also, food was dangerously short in camp, and because of this, Knight wrote in his diary, "it is essential for the party to split." There was simply not enough game on the island to feed more than two people. All would be fine because, before leaving them in Seattle, Stefansson himself had suggested they could make the trip if they felt they needed to. It would be stupid for Knight to attempt the journey again. He recognized that and made up his mind to accept it. He would stay on the island and keep the camp, and Ada would help him.

It meant that Ada would be alone with Knight. The idea frightened her because he still frightened her, but she held her tongue. It was not her place to object to Crawford's orders. Knight, for his part, was just as unhappy with the situation. He knew people in the outside world might frown on a single man and a single woman living alone. He and Crawford had discussed the matter at length, and although neither was crazy about the idea of Knight and Ada staying there together, they felt there was nothing else to be done. Exceptional circumstances sometimes required exceptional solutions, such as being left alone with a native woman—a native woman anxious for a white husband, in fact. And Crawford, Maurer, and Galle would do a lot to soften any criticisms that might arise when they reached Nome.

On January 21, the temperature dropped to minus 51 degrees, and the sun rose above the horizon for the first time in months. As was always the case after Crawford sought Knight's counsel, he now gathered the entire group and announced his plans. Maurer and Galle absorbed the news quietly and without any argument or fuss. But Maurer, for one, did not approve of the plan because he, more than anyone, knew the dangers of such a journey. He possessed minimal experience traveling over ice, but he certainly had more than anyone else in their party. Captain Robert Bartlett, who had taken command of Stefansson's *Karluk* crew after Stefansson abandoned ship, was the bravest man he had ever met, and even Bartlett, he knew, had been wary of the trek when he attempted it in March of 1914. To Maurer's mind, staying on the island was safer, but he was not in charge, and he believed that nothing he said would sway Knight or Crawford.

Galle, too, was unhappy about his orders. He wanted to stay, not go, and worried that it was a foolish and dangerous move. But his job was not to argue. He was to support Crawford and also Knight, as Stefansson had said, and so he would do so.

Ada was told to outfit the men for their journey. As she worked speedily and efficiently, Knight had to admit that the seamstress had improved dramatically from the previous year. There was no more mooning about, no more moping, no more throwing herself at Crawford's feet. Instead, she worked seriously and solemnly and did what she was told to do.

No doubt, none of the men would have been willing to leave Knight and Ada alone had they any real idea of the seriousness of Knight's illness. Knight had managed to convince Crawford that he could heal himself. Maurer was taken into confidence, to a lesser extent, and Knight made a case to his two comrades that he would be in no more danger if Crawford and the others left than if they stayed. Knight believed that the key to his cure would come from seal oil or a good catch of polar bear or foxes. Even so, Crawford was anxious about his friend's health and he did not want to leave Knight behind. But they had not been able to come up with a way around the decision.

In the days before departure, Ada and the men worked against minus 56 degrees to load the sled with supplies—three twenty-pound cases of hard bread and two five-gallon cans of seal blubber. They strapped on tents and various tools and equipment, and some of Crawford's prize geological specimens, and hitched up the five remaining dogs. The three men also packed up their diaries, Galle taking both his loose-leaf binder and his notebook, while leaving his notes behind. They would make it across the ice to Siberia and from there to Nome. If they didn't truly believe their journey would be successful, they would have left the diaries with Knight for safekeeping. They promised to come back with a ship in the summer, as soon as the ice opened, for Knight and Ada, and if the ice was still too formidable, they would journey to the island by dog team next winter.

Galle took Ada aside and assured her he would be back for her. She was not to be scared, she was to do as Knight said, and she was not, for any reason, to touch Galle's Corona typewriter, which he would have to leave behind. He left no last letter home to his mother, father, sister, and brother. Galle was determined to come back, and he knew that he would see his family again some day.

"Knight is troubled with scurvy," Crawford wrote to Stefansson before their departure. "As the five dogs are scarcely enough, he was dubious of making the trip as his strength is undermined. My plans are unchanged except that I am taking Maurer and Galle with me . . . although I would like to leave one of them with Knight. I think it is wisdom to do this, as it would be disastrous to return a second time."

"The chief reason for our leaving is the shortage of food," read Maurer's letter to Delphine. "There is not adequate food for all, there being only ten twenty-pound cases of hard bread and three pokes of seal oil to last until next summer. The prospects of getting game between now and next summer or sealing season are very poor, so we are leaving behind enough food for the two remaining here. Leaving here I'll be headed south in the direction whence I left you and all; whether I reach my goal or not remains to be seen. If the fates favour me, I'll have the pleasure of telling you all about it in person, if against me, then some one else, no doubt, will tell you all."

Maurer had returned from this very same island nine years before. He would do so again, by duplicating Bartlett's journey, and by bringing the help they needed, to Knight and to Ada.

"My dear Mother," he wrote, "I am leaving this letter behind in care of Knight . . . in case an accident should befall me, or all three of us. Should the worst come to pass, I want you to know Mother that I have only myself to blame for my ending and that I'll remember to the last moment, the kind loving tenderness you have shown me as my mother all through my life. I have not once forgotten it, nor shall I ever forget. Farewell! A long farewell to you and all."

On January 29, they set off for Nome, via Siberia. It was a beautiful, clear day, and warmer than usual. Everything seemed to be in their favor as they headed quickly to the south and soon disappeared from view. Afterward, Knight and Ada were struck by the silence. No neat, incessant tapping of Galle's typewriter. None of his boyish laughter or loud, challenging bets over one thing or the other. No more teasing Maurer as he swallowed his nightly Purgative Pellets. No more hearing him wax on about all the things he was going to buy Delphine when he returned home. No more of Crawford's patient mediation or feeble jokes about Seattle or excitement over his geological findings.

*   *   *

Knight worked hard at making the camp more convenient for two people, stacking wood and organizing things here and there to make it easier for the two of them to run everything themselves. There was still much to be done, but they would get to it with time. When the snow melted in the spring, they would need to dig away the walls and roof of the house and clean out the boxes they had stored outside.

His left leg was swollen just above the knee and was causing him a great deal of pain. Still, he was able to get about on it, even if it hurt. He assumed it was from the scurvy, but felt that with some rest and some fresh meat, he would be good as new in no time.

Ada began keeping a calendar in a little notebook, drawing boxes for each of the days of the months in pencil, and writing the month at the top. She started with January, crossing off the days as they passed. In the inside flap, she wrote simply, "Why Galle leave?"

"I wonder what people will say about my staying here alone with the female?" Knight wondered in his journal. It was Knight's opinion that Ada was actually happy about the situation, "for as I stated long ago, she is most anxious to 'get' a white man. No chance as far as I'm concerned." He tried to focus on the humor of the situation, on her past lustful behavior, on Oofty, on the Nymph, because it would take his mind off the fact that he was ill—more ill than he liked to admit.

Knight and Ada each could have six pieces of hard bread a day until the seals and birds returned. They had kept two pokes of seal blubber and six gallons of bear oil as well. Knight also had hopes of trapping foxes and maybe a bear. In just a couple of months, he figured, the female bears should be emerging from their hibernation with their young ones, and then they would have plenty of good, fresh meat. "Come on bear," he wrote in his journal.

His life would depend on the fresh meat he could secure. Ada would be of no help. He found her fearful and temperamental and, as good as she was at taking orders now, he didn't actually believe she could think or act for herself. She had never shown him she was particularly resourceful or clever. He worried about what might happen if he grew weaker, sicker, and if he had to rely on Ada to take care of him.

On January 30, a screaming gale blew in from the east. The door to the house was locked tight by the drifting snow and Knight and Ada were trapped inside. They didn't mind because they had plenty of wood piled up by the stove. While Vic the cat curled up for a nap, Knight read a book and Ada busied herself with her knitting, and they spent a cozy day in companionable silence.

The next morning, when the wind was just as vicious, Knight tried to push aside his nagging worry. The storm promised perilous, changeable ice. By now, Crawford, Maurer, and Galle should have crossed the island and entered the pack for their journey across to Siberia. They would be maneuvering the loaded sled and the skittish dogs over stirring, shifting floes of ice on the open sea. The pack could split and crack as suddenly and violently as an earthquake. Depending on the hazards they encountered and the path they were forced to follow—or, if need be, forge—through the ice, the trek might be anywhere from 140 miles to 200. The fresh snowfall would cover the sea, making it harder to determine a safe and solid path. They might crash through into the water with one false step, and be lost in a moment. Or they might be blessed with a clear, smooth course, which would lead them home.

Probably, Knight reasoned, they were far enough south by now to be out of the eye of the squall. The wind was most likely catching them from the side, which would slow their progress, but not deter them completely. They should be out of harm's way by now, he told himself.

On February 1—Crawford's twenty-second birthday—the gale seemed to have gathered force. It was, Knight noted grimly, "blowing and drifting as hard as I have ever seen it." He didn't want to think of how vulnerable his comrades were, in the midst of the volatile ice pack, and he didn't want to think of what might happen to them.

PART III

SURVIVAL

I must stay alive. I will live.

—ADA BLACKJACK

Sunday Times (London)
January 1923

❄

Stefansson Quits; Gives Up Exploring
Will Devote His Future to Telling of Possibilities in the "Friendly Arctic"

Vilhjalmur Stefansson yesterday announced his retirement as an explorer.

"I am through with exploring," he said. "I do not intend ever to set foot in the polar regions again. I want to make a new start in life while there is yet time."

Asked what he considered to have been his most important discovery, Stefansson said:

"The fact that the polar regions were a state of mind, that they were a friendly place to live in for the man who used common sense."

As for enlightening the world concerning the real nature of the Northern regions, which he already has done to a large extent in his book, "The Friendly Arctic," Stefansson explained that he would continue to write and to lecture on the conditions as he found them.

Among the popular fallacies is the belief that the Arctic is the coldest place in the world, whereas, according to Stefansson, it is colder in some places in Montana than it ever is at the North Pole.

For the intrepid young men who may find the lure of the Arctic irresistible, there is ample opportunity for exploration, according to Stefansson, who has concluded that the North Pole is by no means the most difficult point on the face of the globe to reach.

Nine

ADA PUSHED OPEN the tent flaps and searched for Knight. He had gone out some time ago to chop wood, and should have been back by now. Crawford, Maurer, and Galle had left them just one week before and Ada was still anxious about being left alone.

Suddenly she saw him, several feet away, lying on the ground, limp and still. Ada felt her heart rise into her throat as she took a step forward. Knight couldn't be dead. If he were dead she would be all alone, and then who would care for her? She took another step and another until she was standing over him, looking into his pale, gaunt face.

Thank God, he was breathing. She knelt over him and tried to wake him. It took a good five minutes—or so it seemed to Ada—but finally he stirred, the life coming back into him. He woke to see her anxious face, pinched and strained, peering down at him.

"I'm all right now, Ada." His speech was halting, his voice soft, but he wanted to reassure her because he could tell she was terrified. "I just felt a little faint."

Confused and frightened, Ada pulled him to his feet. He leaned heavily on her as she helped him into the tent and once there, utterly spent, he crumpled into a pile on his bed. He began to talk to her then, telling her for the first time how ill he was. It was scurvy, as far as he could tell, and it seemed to be getting worse. He had tried to keep it from the others, but Crawford knew, and Maurer a little, but now he could not hide it. His mood was gloomy, as he lay on his bunk, and he told Ada that for the first time he was scared. "I guess we shan't see Nome again," he said darkly.

She told him to stay in bed and rest, and promised that she would finish chopping the wood. She was used to it, she said, and had done that kind of work at home. The last thing Knight wanted to do was lie helpless in the tent while Ada took care of him. But when he found himself too weak to lift his head, he consented.

Ada went outside and took up the axe and began cutting the wood. Afterward, she collected snow for their drinking water, and then she took the map Maurer had left them of his trapline and followed it to his traps to check for foxes. As usual, there was nothing, and she turned back to camp, discouraged.

She had no idea Knight was this ill. No one had told her. Why had they not told her? She couldn't understand, but one thing was clear. Now *she* must take care of them until he was strong enough to get out of bed. She prayed he would recover enough in a few days to look after her again.

As long as he was flat on his back or sitting up in his sleeping bag, he felt fine, and so Knight stayed in bed. They had on their bookshelf a copy of Spoffard's *New Cabinet Encyclopedia*, which contained a good deal of information on scurvy. Knight told himself he wasn't frightened. He just felt like he'd had the wind knocked out of him. And he wasn't fully and completely convinced he had scurvy. After all, hadn't he been chopping and hauling wood and going off hunting just days before?

He sat up on his bunk, opened his diary so that he could make notes, and studied the encyclopedia entry. The disease had bred in prisons, armies, and poorhouses and on ships for years—anywhere men were gathered or confined and fed at public expense on cheap food that was to last a long time and feed a number of mouths. Sailors in the old days had largely eaten salted food and no vegetables, which was why so many of them became afflicted.

According to Spoffard's, scurvy began with fatigue, loss of strength, and a sudden dejection of spirits. Knight thought this was all accurate in his case, except for the dejection. As far as he was concerned, he had felt no gloominess, no excessive moodiness, no agitation.

Next came bloating of the face. There was none that he could see.

Followed by rapid respiration from the smallest movement. Yes, unfortunately he did have that, and he could tell he also had a touch of fever right now.

Then the teeth would start to loosen. Knight felt the two loose teeth in his upper jaw. All the others seemed fine.

The gums turned spongy. His lower jaw felt normal, but the gums surrounding his two loose teeth were decidedly soft and rotten.

The breath became offensive. No doubt from the bad teeth, but for now he thought his breath wasn't any worse than usual.

Bright and discolored spots on the body. They weren't necessarily bright, but there were some black and blue marks that looked more like bruises on the back of his left leg, and a black streak, half an inch wide, across the back of his knee, which was painful only to the touch. The red, pin-sized spots were fading, which was a good thing, but there was a band of purple on the back of his left leg, six or seven inches in length and about the same in width. In addition, his left leg was noticeably swollen and hard to the touch. His right leg was less inflated and lacked the dark spots.

Old wounds reopened. None that he had noticed.

Severe pain, growing worse at night. Not anymore, but it had certainly been true a month ago, and his joints—especially his shoulders and knees—ached.

Dry skin. No.

Smaller quantity of urine. The frequency was less, but the quantity was not.

Rapid but faint pulse. Yes. He checked it frequently and it usually rated seventy-two beats per minute.

Bad as all this was, the rest was too horrible to read. Hemorrhaging in the loose tissue under knees and eyes and also in the armpits. Overwhelming weakness and exhaustion, leading ultimately to death from malnutrition as the appetite gradually failed. But that was a long way off. He had only just become ill and he knew the cure he needed. On the bright side, after all—and he was determined to find one—he didn't have any signs of headache and his spirits were good and he would be fine once he was able to eat some fresh meat. He just needed to get his strength back so that he could go hunting.

The encyclopedia recommended a good diet of fresh vegetables and lime or lemon juice, which Knight would have been more than happy to administer to himself, had he access to them. Instead, he filled himself with the only antiscorbutic food they had, sour seal blubber, even though his appetite wasn't very big and the stuff tasted rotten. He had been eating as much of it as he could stomach since he and Crawford had returned from their aborted attempt to reach Nome, but he was feeling worse, not better, since then. Now there were only two pokes of seal blubber remaining, and he didn't know what this would mean for him and Ada if they couldn't find game to replenish it.

The dizzy spells began not long after Crawford, Maurer, and Galle had left for Siberia. Knight felt the earth spin every time he made a sudden movement, and he lost his breath easily. He became so winded just lifting a piece of firewood that he had to sit down afterward and catch his breath. He didn't remember the severe shortness of breath or the swelling in his legs from the first round of scurvy he'd suffered in 1917.

He dreamed of fresh meat. If only a bear would wander into camp. If only he felt strong enough to make it to Maurer's traps to check for foxes. No doubt there would be at least a fox or two found there, but he had been afraid to check until he felt better because what if something should happen to him? The traps weren't terribly far from camp, but if he should lose consciousness or have an accident, there would be no one there to help him. The thought of being helpless did frighten him, and he would not take that risk, no matter how much he needed the fresh meat.

He should get up out of his bed and go chop some wood to replenish their stock. He needed to gather ice to make drinking water, and he needed to go hunting, to try to find something for them to eat, and to do so many other things. "But on the least movement, especially rapid, I am puffing like a freight locomotive," he recorded. He wished Crawford and the others would come back because he could see now that it was going to be hard for Ada if he became completely bedridden.

For now, she seemed cheerful enough, but he wondered how much of it was for show, to make him feel better, and to make herself feel better. He thought she was probably more frightened and distressed about his illness than he was, although she wasn't showing it to him. He could hear her outside sharpening the wood saw. She had told him she would do everything that needed to be done around camp until he felt better and could get up again and take care of everything as he had before, and he had no choice but to let her.

Ada was terrified of running into a polar bear while she was out checking the traps. She carried a snow knife with her, but that was all, because she was still frightened of rifles, and she knew she wouldn't have the slightest idea how to defend herself if she was caught by Nanook. While she was out walking, she would pause now and then, every so often, and have a look around for bears, knowing she would faint if she so much as caught a glimpse of one.

She went out every day now, looking for food. There was nothing at camp, and Knight was too weak to hunt, too weak to do anything but rest in bed. Ada herself was feeling listless and tired, and very much alone. She missed Crawford and Galle and Maurer, but particularly Crawford and Galle. Everything had changed drastically and suddenly when they went away. Now Knight was sick and she must figure out how to help him and what to do to keep them fed, and she wished the men would come back and help her. She wanted to give up the trapping because there were never any foxes and it made her weary to walk all those miles every single day. Also, daylight hours were still minimal and she worried about being caught in the dark miles from camp.

But she made herself go out, following Maurer's map until she learned the way herself, and one afternoon, she spotted some fox tracks circling around the traps, and she knelt down and dug the trap out of the snow. It was empty, and Ada figured she must have hidden it under too much snow last time. So she baited the trap again, leaving it uncovered.

The next morning, when she checked the traps, she found a fox lying in one of them. Her first one. Ada was proud and exhilarated. No one had told her how to fix the trap or to uncover it and leave it in the open. She had figured that out on her own and now she would have food to take to Knight. The very best part of it was that she had done it all herself.

She remembered having read a book about northern people that said foxes were good eating. She cooked it over the fire until the meat nearly fell off the bone. Although she gave most of the meat to Knight, she tasted a little and thought it wonderful. Just like chicken.

Despite the meat Ada had proudly brought back to camp, Knight's decline was swift. Perhaps he had lived with the disease ever since his trip to Skeleton Island the previous July—all those long months of minor aches and pains that were easily explained away. Rheumatism seemed such a hopeful, foolish notion now. Why had he not looked closer and read the signs? He could have hunted while he was able and while he'd had the help of Crawford and Maurer and Galle. He should have been eating as much fresh meat as they could catch last September, when the pain in his hip grew sharp and his leg gave him trouble.

Two weeks ago he had been chopping wood and shooting his rifle, and now he was confined to bed without the strength or energy to sit up. The purple and black marks on the backs of his legs had grown lighter, then darker, and now they were lighter again. Ada examined them for him daily, and now she noticed that the marks had merged together to form one enormous patch. There was a spattering of spots on the back of his right leg as well, and slender, hairlike slivers appeared under his fingernails. When he applied a bit of pressure to them, he felt a shooting pain.

Every joint ached. His gums bled easily, and the two loose snags—as he called the wobbly teeth in his upper jaw—dropped out on their own. He was alternately ravenous and uninterested in food, not that there was anything to eat other than seal blubber. Despite her daily trips, Ada had not come back with another fox. "When I say that I don't feel like eating," Knight wrote, "what I mean is that I don't feel like eating the things we have here. I am continually 'hankering' for fresh meat."

He was plagued now by a mild headache that aspirin couldn't seem to cure, and when he tried to rise from his bunk, after a week spent lying in it, the earth began to spin and he fell back into bed. He felt fine—almost normal—when he was lying in bed, but he was anxious to be up and out and feeling useful. He tried reading, but was bored with everything they had, and he wrote regularly in his journal, even though his knuckles sometimes throbbed from the exertion of holding the pencil. It was important to him, though, that he record how he was feeling and what was happening to him, so that he would have documentation to show Stefansson once the ship came.

When there was any change in coloration of his black and purple marks, when his calf turned blue, when his gums began to swell, when his face grew colorless, his lips bloodless, and his eyes bloodshot, he wrote it down. But he was retaining his humor. "Thank fortune, I still feel like . . . sleeping, which I still do wonderfully well."

He had a gnawing, wolfish hunger for meat. He craved meat and thirsted for it, and most of his waking hours were spent imagining the taste, the smell, the texture against his tongue. He forced down the seal blubber, but it had become foul to him, and he wrote in his journal about his yearning for "<u>fresh raw meat</u> and lots of it."

Ada was trying, he knew, but she was hopeless with a rifle. Unless a bear happened to just wander into camp and lie down in front of them so that he could shoot it from his bed, there would be no chance of getting one, he noted in his diary. The rifle was too heavy for Ada and she became so rattled during the lesson Knight gave her that they put it aside and decided she should, instead, concentrate on the fox traps.

But day after day, nothing turned up. Each morning, Knight lay in his bed, reading or sleeping, trying to pass the time until Ada returned. He couldn't even sit up now to write in his journal, so did the best he could, writing while lying down. Would there be a fox today? Would he have meat? But each time Ada came home, her hands were empty.

On February 14, when Knight and Ada were sound asleep in their beds, a bear passed through camp. They slept peacefully, with no idea that the meat they had been praying for was just yards away. In the morning, Ada found the tracks, coming in from the east and heading out toward the west. They were the largest bear tracks Ada had ever seen in her life, and she and Knight could only imagine the succulent meat they would have enjoyed. Still, it gave them hope. If one bear had come, perhaps there would be others.

"Oh Yes! My desire for cold water is enormous," Knight wrote. "I am sure I drink at least 3 quarts a day." As soon as Ada brought in snow and melted it down, he drank all he could, yet his thirst never seemed to feel quenched. His pulse beat faint and slow until he shifted in his bed and it sped up like a "trip hammer." A wonderful turn of events. Now he was just fine—as long as he lay perfectly still and didn't sit up, breathe, or move in any way.

Ada examined his legs again and discovered that the left one was changing back to its natural color, while the right leg was also improving, though more slowly. His urine was scanty, but he still slept well—that was one thing—and his appetite had returned. No more loose teeth for now, and over all, he felt stronger and better than he had in some time. All things considered, things were beginning to look up.

No matter how hard she worked, though, Ada saw that Knight was increasingly annoyed with her. His illness was affecting his moods and he was alternately melancholy and placid, irritated and calm. As his symptoms developed and worsened, so did his ill humor. He told Ada she was not doing her best, she wasn't trying hard enough to get them the fresh meat he so desperately needed. She was lazy, thoughtless, stupid. He had a million criticisms.

Ada knew she annoyed him, but there was little she could do. She was not feeling well herself, and although she didn't know it, was suffering from the early symptoms of scurvy. She was tired, weak, and dispirited, and longed to give up. The work was hard, she was weary, and Knight complained all the time. It was too much for a person to bear, and so she snapped right back at him and they fell into a brooding silence, which was more unpleasant than the sharp exchange of words. On the days when she felt particularly wretched, she would stay inside the house and ignore the traps, much to Knight's annoyance. But as soon as she felt stronger, she put on her boots and mittens and went out into the cold to gather wood and tend the traps.

Finally, on February 20, Ada, Knight, and Vic enjoyed a good feed when Ada brought home a fat female fox. The skin was peeling off the ends of Knight's fingers, but he didn't give a damn. He had a "full stomach of underdone meat," and was feeling the best he'd felt in a long time.

Their luck seemed to be changing. Breathlessly, Ada awakened Knight on the morning of February 27 to tell him a bear was coming toward camp. She was nervous, excited, frightened. With bears, her first instinct, always, was to run and hide until they disappeared, but she knew Knight was counting on bear meat so that he could feel better. She had seen the great, lumbering bear along the beach, approaching from the east, and it seemed to be moving slowly toward them. Knight told her to holler when the bear was within 200 yards of the house. He had to conserve his energy, and simply sitting up would tax him too much, so he would wait until the creature was within shooting distance.

It was getting closer, she told Knight; she could see it coming. Closer, still. Closer. The bear seemed a long time arriving, but Knight willed himself to be patient. He lay there, trying not to move, trying to conserve his energy for the kill. Finally, Ada climbed onto the roof of the house and raised Knight's field glasses toward the direction of the bear. But there was nothing—only a dingy yellow cake of ice, floating in the water. Her polar bear.

On the days when the traps were empty—which was largely the case—Ada stored the oil she had saved and served up a portion of it for meals. On those days, that was all there was to eat, with a bit of hard bread for dipping. She continued to adjust her trapping methods to try to find the right combination, the right way of setting the traps, the right location, until, in March, she at last found success. First another female fox, a thin one, scant eating, but meat just the same. Then a male fox. Then another female, a nice, fat one this time.

Suddenly, Ada had struck gold, and not always in the traps. She had found another method for killing them which worked, too. Because the animals were so naturally curious, she found that she could often creep close to them before they ran away, and with a heavy stick, she would hit them over the head to stun them. Then she would bend their heads back until she heard their necks snap, and she would carry them home and skin them.

In spite of the increased intake of fresh meat, Knight showed no signs of improvement. Perhaps it was the fact that he could barely swallow the meat because his throat was so raw, or perhaps it would simply take time—and a consistent diet—for his health to be restored. On March 3, he wrote, "Troubled some last night by severe pains in my back. Reading and lying on my back day-dreaming about 'outside' to kill time, which goes rather slowly. It is bad enough to be laid up 'outside' where one has newspapers, good food, a comfortable <u>clean</u> bed and someone to talk to, but I just lay here in my dirty, hairy sleeping bag and read books again for the fourth or fifth time."

The pin-sized red spots returned and a dark line stretched across the skin of his left elbow. It looked suspiciously like the band on his leg, although it had been some time since Ada had examined him, since it meant moving from his sleeping bag. If he shifted at all, he knew, he would be left winded for a good half hour or so afterward, and he just couldn't risk it.

The fingers on both hands lost their sense of touch and his eyes watered, especially when he read or wrote. For some reason, the left side of his body was giving him more trouble than the right. The muscles of his left arm felt strained and weak, and there was a sprinkling of red spots covering the skin. His left shoulder ached, his left eyelid was swollen and red, and the gum of his upper jaw on that side was severely inflamed. The left side of his chest felt constricted, causing him a great deal of pain when he breathed.

To make matters worse—as if they could be—his body began rejecting the blubber he'd been living on. Because his throat was so tender, he couldn't always swallow the fox meat, but the blubber, or oil, slid down more easily. Now, however, he couldn't seem to stomach it. "Cannot eat the food we have here," he wrote. "I am surely hungry but I cannot positively swallow either hard bread or blubber."

Constantly checking for game to improve their food supply, Ada found numerous fox tracks at the mouth of the harbor nearby. She was always on the watch for newer, better places for her traps. She set twelve in the area and the next day, March 12, caught three fat foxes.

Because of his tender gums and missing teeth, eating was difficult for Knight, but he drank fox soup and forced himself to swallow the underdone meat. Fox meat never went down easily for him or sat right in his stomach, but it would do until they could get a bear, and he was grateful for the nourishment.

That night, he had his best night's sleep in weeks, and he awoke feeling refreshed and optimistic. His spirits brightened as, over the next several days, Ada brought home one fox after another. With the regular feedings, the swelling in Knight's gums decreased, the red spots on his arm began to fade, the pain in his legs subsided, his color came back, and his spirits soared. He was, in his opinion, "as thin as a side show freak," but he was beginning to feel more like himself. One morning, he even caught himself whistling—in his head. "Not that I don't want to whistle, God knows. However this is in spirits only for I am as weak as a cat."

He was getting better. Ada could see it and was relieved. She had done her best while he was bedridden to tend to the wood and the traps, but the responsibility unnerved her and she prayed to Jesus for Knight's return to good health. Now she could see him growing stronger and soon he would be up again and she would no longer have to worry.

While Knight slept or read, Ada stitched gloves or socks for Galle and Crawford. It was her way of keeping them present, even though they were very far away.

Knight and Ada did not talk much when they were alone together. He thought—frankly—that, "as a conversationalist, the woman is the bunk." But sometimes Knight felt talkative and would tell her stories and fairytales. She especially liked "Jack and the Beanstalk."

"Once upon a time," Knight would begin, "there lived a poor widow who had an only son named Jack. She was very poor, for times had been hard, and Jack was too young to work. Almost all of the furniture of the little cottage had been sold to buy bread, until at last there was nothing left worth selling."

Ada loved the magic beans—"the most wonderful beans that ever were known"—the singing harp, and the hen that laid the golden eggs. But she especially loved the aspect of mother and son, who struggled through hard times, only to live happily ever after in the end.

She and Knight never spoke about *if* Crawford, Galle, and Maurer would get back from Nome, but *when* they would return. They both had faith, even on the dark days, and they needed to believe that relief would come soon.

March 1923

Mr. Knight—

We have read and reread Mr. Stefansson's books, and we know that Mr. Lorne was fully capable of guiding the boys in the right way, and if our boys followed his advice they were perfectly safe. And we also know that Mr. Lorne has gone thru more serious and probably more dangerous trips than our boys even now had to do, for the fact that they were stationary.

We are more and more anxious every day to see how Milton stood it all, and cannot wait the time for his return. We compare him often with his boy friends here at home, who are more or less all at school, and still care-free, while Milton has desired to endure and sacrifice.

For us, time hangs heavy on our hands only because time requires such patience, but we think, "From day to day in every way the time comes nearer and nearer."

Alma Galle

Ten

—————

ADA OFTEN LOOKED out over the ice, praying for the sight of a dog team. And even though it was far too early in the season, she watched the sea for a ship. She told Knight that she knew Crawford and the others would return to them; Galle had promised her they would.

She still kept up with her sewing, the cooking, and the dishes, but now she added to this the work of three men who were no longer there and one man who was too sick to help. February had slipped into March and still Knight was confined to his bed. While Vic kept him company, Ada added new soles to her felt slippers, stitched herself a belt, tended the traps, hauled the wood she chopped, mended the stovepipe, scraped and cleaned the skins they had collected, and figured out a way to wash her hair. To protect her eyes, she learned to use snow goggles, which shielded them from the blinding white of the ice and the harmful glare of the sun, but which felt awkward on her face. She also constructed additional fox traps out of oil cans, hoping these would help to double her take.

And she began to keep a journal. Ever since they had sailed from Nome, Knight, Crawford, Maurer, and Galle had written their thoughts and the happenings of the day in notebooks. Ada had watched them sometimes, after they settled on Wrangel Island, and noted how diligently they added to them and how much they seemed to value them. Knight was growing so weak that it was becoming more and more difficult for him to write and record what happened, and so Ada decided that she would begin her own journal, making note of whatever Knight wasn't able to put down.

He wasn't much company anymore, not that they had ever truly enjoyed each other or had anything to talk about. But now the scurvy left him too weak to speak sometimes, and it was hard for him to tell her "Jack and the Beanstalk." Ada missed the others, especially Crawford and Galle, and she missed her son and her people. Perhaps if she kept a diary, she would be a little less lonely and sad, and it would give her the feeling, at least, of having someone to talk to.

She hadn't ever set her thoughts down on paper before, and so she wasn't exactly sure how to begin. At first she tried to write the kinds of things the men thought were important—all about the foxes she caught, or how she checked the traps every day, or what the weather was like, and if she had a headache or an upset stomach.

Knight was not getting better. She knew this now. And everything depended on her. If he was to get well, she must be the one to make that happen, so she must trap every day and she must find enough for two. She would give Knight the larger portion because he needed it more, but she would also keep some for herself so that she could stay strong enough to hunt and work.

It worried her that the foxes had stopped coming to her traps. On March 23, she found that three of the traps were missing. The next day, there was nothing, and the following day the wind was blowing so hard that she was forced to stay inside.

On March 26, she discovered that a fox had been in the oil cans, springing the trap, which was now empty. She spotted three foxes in the distance, one dragging a trap, which clung to its foot, and later that morning she glimpsed a polar bear. At the sight of it, Ada's heart seemed to freeze in her chest. Knight had been praying for a bear, and she knew they needed the meat, but she could only remember the words of the storytellers in her village, painting pictures of the malevolent Nanook who consumed humans or took human form to punish them. It was the first bear she had seen in many weeks, and Ada was only able to breathe deeply again when it gradually melted into the whiteness of the horizon without so much as a glance in her direction.

She managed to catch the fox with the trap on its foot on March 28. "It has caught trap by trap that funny," she wrote with amusement, proud once more of being able to bring game home to Knight. Later that day, she noticed a pain in the side of her face, and her eye seemed to swell a bit. The next morning, she was barely able to write in her diary because her eye was nearly swollen closed. Still, Knight was relying on her. So she pulled on her army pants, donned her snow goggles, and went out to chop wood. Afterward, she visited her trapline and found one fat male fox.

But the next day, her eye was so swollen that she couldn't see at all. It was even worse the next day, which meant she and Knight were both forced to lie in their sleeping bags, with no one to feed them or stoke the fire. Ada did what she could to heal herself, dipping into their first aid box for some ointment and a cotton bandage.

She was laid up for the next two days, and on April 2 began to notice a little improvement in her eye. The swelling seemed to have decreased a bit, but the eye still throbbed and gave her a headache, and now one side of her neck was aching and tender. Knight was desperate for food and help, and urged her to go to the traps. "But my eye is very ach," she wrote, "so I cannot go out when my eye is that way because in evening I could bearly stand the ach of my eye and one side of my head."

She might die here. She did not know what was wrong with her, but perhaps she also had scurvy and she might never be able to get up from her bed again. Who would take care of them? And what would Bennett do without his mother?

She took the pencil she used to write and opened her journal. "If anything happen to me and my death is known, there is black stirp for Bennett school book bag, for my only son. I wish if you please take everything to Bennett that is belong to me. I don't know how much I would be glad to get home to folks."

Ada lay there and prepared to die, but the next morning she noticed that the swelling had gone down. The day after that, it went down a little more, although her stomach began bothering her and her eyes seemed foggy. It had been three days now since she had ventured out of the tent.

On April 5, she was able to walk outside and carry in snow to melt down for drinking water, and the day after she was able to chop wood. She and Knight opened a can of biscuits and feasted. Her strength was returning, her stomach felt better, her eye was all but good again. And then the wind began to blow so hard that she couldn't leave the tent for another day. With her eyes healed, she worked at a pair of yarn gloves for Galle, and when the gale at last blew itself out, she set out once more to the traps and found one fox.

While Knight slept or simply lay there, gazing up at the ceiling, unable to move to read or write, Ada cleaned fox skins and cut some skin for boot soles and soaked them. She worked on them when she came home from trapping, chewing the sole to soften the skin and make it more pliable for sewing. As her dark head was bent over her work one night, Knight told her he was feeling rotten.

It was rare for him to admit how he felt, and so Ada knew the pain must be getting worse. Day after day, as April progressed, the traps yielded nothing until finally there seemed to be no use trapping any-more. Ada still checked daily, but she always came home empty-handed. March had seen plenty of foxes, and although they hadn't provided a good deal of meat, they had helped Knight improve to the point where his hopes began to rise again.

Now, as Ada examined his legs, she tried not to react in a way that might upset him. But in her diary she wrote, "We look at Knights legs my! They are skinny and they has no more blue spots like they use to be." The spots had disappeared, but he seemed to be growing weaker. Ada held up his head now to help him drink, but on April 17, he refused tea because he said he had a headache.

Four days later, with Ada still unable to catch anything, Knight was despondent and restless. His temper rose as he lay there, a helpless invalid with nothing to do but stare into space and think about the days when he could run and ride his motorcycle or just sit up in bed without feeling like the world was spinning off its axis. He was angry and he was fed up and he was sick of himself and Ada and this island.

It was so miserably, horribly unfair that he should be sick. That anyone should be sick at all. Was it any wonder he gave his grand-father's Bible to Ada? She had been so thrilled—like a child at Christmas—when he told her she could borrow it indefinitely. Perhaps he shouldn't have because it was an heirloom, and his mother trea-sured the fact that he kept it. But what use did he have for it now? Ada pored over the book, lingering over the vibrant illustrations of Jerusalem and other Biblical places, absorbing every word, an eager student.

The changes to his body were intriguing, in a horrific way, and at times he stood outside himself to observe the deterioration. How quickly this or that function failed him, how this part of him would rally for a while and then give in, as if defeated by a much stronger foe. He hardly knew what to expect next, and it was with a morbid fascination that he awaited and observed each new discoloration of the skin, each new swelling, each new bodily failure.

He had taken this big, sturdy body—a little soft in places, perhaps a bit too stout—for granted. Except for the earlier bout of scurvy, he'd enjoyed good health, but this round far surpassed the previous one and so far had been an entirely new experience. He had always been larger and stronger than his friends and peers. He liked being an imposing figure, in terms of height and width, but now he was just skin and bones, barely held together by tissue. His limbs were so fragile, his bones so brittle and angular, that Ada had to place make-shift pillows of cotton beneath his joints to cushion him in his bed. They eased the pain only a little. It was as if his very bones ached and throbbed, and they threatened to snap with every movement.

He couldn't remember when he had left his sleeping bag, even for the necessary trips outside to urinate. Now he did everything in his bed, and it was up to Ada to clean up after him. It was humiliating, and laughable in a better situation.

Ada was building the fire when Knight started "to cruel" with her. He told her Jack Blackjack must have been a good man, not a bad one like she'd said, and that he was right to treat Ada mean. Ada deserved it, Knight said, because she was callous to him and treated him badly. "He never stop and think how much its hard for women to take four mans place, to wood work and to hund for something to eat for him and do waiting to his bed and take the shiad out for him," she wrote in her diary.

If his words about her former husband were an unfair attack, his words about her dead children were unforgivable. He said it was no wonder they had died because she probably didn't take any better care of them than she did of him. The words cut Ada more than any words she had ever heard in her life. No one had ever said such hurtful things to her, and after all she tried to do for him, making herself sick so that she could barely see, and still going out to look for meat for him when she felt weak. But she wasn't trying to save him, he accused. She didn't want him to live. He would write to the people of Nome and tell them just how she had treated him and then she would be sorry.

She was starving, yet she had given him the bulk of the meat she had been able to catch. She needed meat, too, but Knight needed it more, and she always gave him the choicest parts of the animal, saving only the head and kidney for herself. She didn't understand why he said such nasty things to her after all she tried to do for him.

"This is the wosest life I ever live in this world," she wrote. "Though it is hard enough for me to wood work and trying my best in everything and when I come home to rest here a man talk against me saying all kinds of words against me then what could I do."

If Knight died, she didn't know what would become of her. And she suddenly was more afraid than she had ever been. If he died, she would be alone on that island. He had lain in his bed since the beginning of February, and now it was April 21 and she had no hope that he would be able to rise soon. He was so painfully brittle and thin, and she did not know when it would be that a ship would come, although she watched the water every day to look for it.

"If I be known dead," she wrote in her diary, "I want my sister Rita to take Bennett my son, for her own son and look after every things for Bennett she is the only one that I wish she take my son don't let his father Black Jack take him, if Rita my sister live. Then I be clear. Ada B. Jack."

The following day, Ada stayed in the tent because she could do nothing but cry. Her heart was sick and she was frightened and she couldn't forget the hateful words Knight had said to her.

On April 24, she washed her hair and read Knight's Bible all day to comfort herself. As she drank a cup of tea, she thought of the people who might be in church that morning or that night and what they might be doing or wearing or praying for. Still stinging from Knight's words, she was feeling weak, and two days later, with an armful of wood she was bringing home, she nearly fainted. She slipped into her bed early that night, and awoke the next day from a deep, drowsy sleep to a dark house. A glance at her watch told her it was 4:00 P.M. She knew she should get up to bring in more wood, to look after Knight's food, and to eat a bit herself. But she was so tired that she shut her eyes, telling herself she would get up later that evening to make some tea and look after a few things. When she awoke next, it was morning.

The wind howled outside the house and threatened to blow the walls in. Ada didn't feel at all well and stayed snug in her bag, Vic curled at her feet, doing nothing but reading the Bible and writing in her journal. She hoped to find strength in Jesus and in God, she wrote, because only God knew what would happen to her. Knight complained that he was sick and Ada didn't answer him because there was nothing to say. She was sick, too, and there was nothing she could do. He somehow got up the strength to throw a book at her—it wasn't the first time—and still she said nothing. But before she went to sleep, she filled his cup with water and fresh ice and a pick, so that it would stay filled through the night and so that he could chop at it if he wanted to, and then she turned her back on him and went to bed.

On the last day of April, the wind continued to rage at them from outside the tent. Inside, Ada was grateful that Knight was still living and that she was still living. Each day that they were alive was a day to be thankful for. "If I happen to get back home I don't know how much I would be glad God is the only one would brought me home again," she wrote. "There is no one pity me in this world but God even there is no hand would help me but God, with his lovingkindness and mighty hand."

The first of May brought the sun, peeping through a hole in the roof, and again they were still alive. Two days later, Ada saw a snowbird and the sight rejuvenated her and filled her with hope. The birds would come soon and perhaps the bears and seals and foxes, too, and then they would be fine and Knight would be well again. Encouraged, she took a walk to her traps but found nothing. Still, she was hopeful.

That night, she had a dream that she was in a foreign land and Knight was there, too, but they were the only ones. Then Knight left her to go to Siberia, taking one dog with him, and Ada was completely and utterly alone.

When she awoke, she knew she would not be defeated by aches

and pains or the raging weather or her own fear and discouragement. She would ignore Knight's harsh and cutting words and not let them pierce her where she was most vulnerable. She made up her mind to live instead. "I will not let Bennett have stepmother," she said to herself, and that was that. From that point forward, she would concentrate on keeping herself alive and taking care of Lorne Knight. He needed her—even if he did say such cruel words to her when he felt poorly—and she would not let him down.

*   *   *

Gradually, the birds came back. Ada noticed ducks appearing in the sky and she borrowed Knight's gun and tried to shoot one as they flew overhead. She stood there first for several minutes, trying to get up her nerve to pull the trigger. It was the noise that frightened her as much as anything. She had always covered her ears when the men fired their rifles because the sound was so violent and terrible. Now, as the birds soared past, she knew she must make a decision. Summoning all her courage, she pulled the trigger.

As the gun turned and twisted spasmodically in her hands, the power and noise terrified Ada. Knight was right. She was lousy with a gun. She would never be able to shoot anything unless she studied and practiced. "I thought to myself, I must not waste ammunition—I must learn to shoot."

She set up a target of empty tea tins near camp. The rifle was almost too heavy for her to lift, much less to hold, and the recoil bruised her shoulder. If she could only prop the gun against something or on top of something so that she could aim it properly and pull the trigger without having to worry about the weight of it. She examined the gun, holding it differently, trying to figure out the best way to handle it. But when nothing worked, she gathered some of the tools they had in camp and, out of driftwood, built a kind of gun rest which she could prop on her shoulder so that she was shielded from the kick of the rifle.

She practiced daily until she was frustrated and her shoulder was sore, but gradually she began to see an improvement. She only hit her target twice on the first day of practice, but she thought that wasn't bad for her very first time handling a rifle. She didn't want to waste ammunition, but she knew it was important to practice, and so she was back at it the next day. At first, she shot sitting down, missing the target three times in a row. For the last shot, she lay on her stomach and hit the target with a smack. Then she stood up and took aim, and hit the target again.

She suited up in a new pair of army pants, and set about breaking them in. They quickly became caked in dust and dirt as she worked at building a knife case and a gun case for the rifle, in order to protect it from the cold and the weather.

When Ada felt sick with a headache now, she took aspirin all day, hoping it would go away so that she could concentrate on her work. When she had stomach trouble now, she still went out to the fox traps.

On the morning of May 10—her twenty-fifth birthday—Ada awoke to the sound of a steady dripping. Her first thought was rain or perhaps droplets of water trickling off the tent. But when she shook the clouds of sleep from her eyes, she saw the red flowing from Knight's nose. He was holding a one-pound tea tin beneath it to catch the stream, and it was already half full. His face was a frightening shade of blue, and when Ada tried to help him he turned his face away from her and from the tin.

"Knight," she called over and over again. But he refused to answer. Finally, he managed to tell her he was better. The nosebleed had been going on for some time, but now he seemed to be over it.

He needed her, but he hated relying on her, and because of this he often resisted her efforts on his behalf. Now she asked if he might eat some hard bread, fried in oil, if she were to make it for him. It was the only food they had and they were both sick and tired of it, but he needed strength.

After she fed him, she fetched his shotgun and headed out to hunt. Lately, she had begun carrying the rifle with her on her walks, and this time she went out toward the islands that rose out of the harbor. She was still uncertain of her skill with the gun, still wary of the weapon. But at least she could shoot now without feeling faint, and she could shoulder it thanks to the portable platform she had built.

She watched as a seagull flew over her head, and without pausing to be afraid, she raised the gun skyward and shot. The bird dropped from the sky and landed with a smack against the earth. It was the first bird she had ever shot with a rifle. For months, Knight had mocked her inability to shoot. He thought she would never learn, that she was hopeless, and that her intense fear of guns would mean she would never be of any use with one. But she had proved him wrong again.

Because of his tender gums and missing teeth, eating was ever more painful for Knight, but Ada made some seagull broth and fed it to him. Afterward, he said he felt much better. Not too long after, she was able to shoot an eider duck through the head, but was disappointed because she had actually been aiming for its breast. Her earlier triumph at being able to hit something at all had disappeared, and as she grew more sure of herself, she expected better results.

Polar bears still haunted her, even though she hadn't seen any in weeks. But one morning, Ada awoke to find a mother and cub hovering outside the door of her tent. While Knight lay helpless in his bed, Ada crouched behind her own bed in fear. She was terrified the bears would find her and eat her and she would end up trapped inside one of their bellies. Knight couldn't protect her now and he wouldn't be able to shoot the gun, no matter how close the bears stood to him, because he simply didn't have the strength. They needed the meat desperately, but Ada didn't trust herself to kill them. When she shot at ducks, her gun stayed steady, but "when I shoot at polar bear, my gun shakes in big circles."

"I said to myself, what shall I do—what shall I do? If I shoot the mother bear and only wound her, she will get me—If I shoot her cub, she will be angry and eat me up—What shall I do?"

Knight told her she must save their precious few soft-nosed bullets for shooting polar bears because they were more powerful and more deadly than regular bullets. Instead of lodging in the animal's flesh or passing through it, the soft-nosed bullets would explode upon impact, shattering vital organs, so that death was more assured. Now Ada grabbed Knight's rifle and dragged it toward the tent opening. Then, she tore open the door and fired her gun in the air to frighten the bears away. She watched as they sprinted across the snow, leaving camp, leaving her.

Afterward, she built a platform above the house so that she could climb up and watch for bears along the horizon. She dragged the solid, weighty planks of wood from the beach and, using all her strength, hefted them onto the four ridgepoles. It was cold, numbing work without mittens, but her own were torn and unusable and she had not had time to make new ones. But she managed to nail the planks together so that her platform was sturdy. Next time, she would be prepared, she promised herself. Next time, she would see the polar bear coming. And next time, she would have the nerve to shoot it.

1. Ada Blackjack's parents with three of their children. (Ada is believed to be the oldest child, standing here behind her siblings.)

2. Ada Blackjack's mother, Maggie Delutuk.

3. Ada Blackjack and son Bennett, Nome, Alaska.

4. Ada in the latest fashions. (Date unknown, taken before the expedition to Wrangel Island.)

6. Vilhjalmur Stefansson, organizer of the expedition.

5. Ada with Bennett and sister Rita on the porch of her home in Nome before joining the Wrangel Island Expedition.

7. Ada in Eskimo costume.

8. Allan Crawford, official leader of the Wrangel Island Expedition.

9. Fred Maurer, survivor of Stefansson's 1913–1914 Canadian Arctic Expedition, and member of the 1921 Wrangel Island venture.

10. E. Lorne Knight, second-in-command.

11. Promotional poster for Fred Maurer's lecture stint on the Chautauqua circuit.

12. Nineteen-year-old Milton Galle of New Braunfels, Texas.

13. The *Silver Wave*, before sailing for Wrangel Island.

14. View of Wrangel Island on the approach.

15. The camp on Wrangel Island.

16. Allan Crawford with expedition cat, Vic.

17. Milton Galle walking into the wind on the gravel beach.

18. Lorne Knight displays his catch.

19. Fred Maurer in winter gear.

20. Ada Blackjack scraping skins.   21. Milton Galle making a seal poke.

22. Allan Crawford carving snow blocks for the winter house.

23. Building walls of snow to surround the tents for winter.

24. Ada in riding pants.

25. Summer camp in June 1922.

26. Crawford and Maurer skinning a walrus.

27. Displaying the walrus skull in camp.

28. Ada with a polar bear.

29. One of the many bears shot around camp.

THE *NATION*
Wrangel Island

✳

In connection with reports in British newspapers to the effect that an expedition led by Mr. Vilhjalmur Stefansson had raised the British flag on Russian territory, to wit, on the Isle of Wrangel in the Arctic Ocean, the Government of the Russian Federal Soviet Republic addressed itself to the British Government in a note of May 24, 1923, asking to be informed as to whether this act had taken place with the knowledge and sanction of the British Government.

To this inquiry no reply has been forthcoming.

The Government of the Union of the Socialist Soviet Republics, being wholly unable to understand the absence of the requested explanations, and having in the meantime learned that new expeditions are being planned by British subjects to the Isle of Wrangel, finds it necessary again to state that it regards the Isle of Wrangel as an integral part of the Union of the Socialist Soviet Republics.

Russian sovereign rights to the island have never been questioned by any other government, and it has been generally looked upon as Russian territory. Therefore the Federal Government is compelled to notify the British Government that it regards the raising of the British flag on the Isle of Wrangel as a violation of Russian sovereign rights.

Eleven

ADA DREAMED she was surrounded by people. There were people everywhere, swarming around her, and Bennett was there, too. She was looking at pictures of the people swimming and Bennett pointed to them and said, "Swimming pool."

"Who told you these are swimming pool pictures?" she asked him, and then she awoke.

She wished she was home where she could see her son and have someone to talk to. She longed to go to church and hear the people singing hymns. She read Knight's Bible whenever she had a spare moment, and she had just finished the Old Testament. Now she would begin reading the New Testament. The words were comfort and solace and she grew to crave them. She prayed the Lord would carry her home so that she could join in the singing one day.

There was a distant moaning and a rumbling that told her the walrus had returned. When Ada turned her gaze toward the ocean, she could see them basking on the ice offshore. The birds had come again as well, and the sky was thick with them as they soared back to their island nests, but now she could not seem to get a single one with her rifle. The fox traps remained empty, and she added some seal oil to them, hoping it would help attract the evasive little creatures. A walrus would last both Ada and Knight for days and would help

Knight feel better. But there would be no reaching the walrus on foot. The ice was too unstable, the animals too skittish, too massive, and too ferocious when angered.

The dory remained at the old camp, and she knew it would be useless to her, even if she could somehow drag it from there to the water. A dory would be too cumbersome, too awkward. Better to have a skin boat, which was much lighter and which she could maneuver more easily. So she decided to build one. She had never built a skin boat before, but she had seen them, had watched as men in her village had made them, and so she worked the skins and formed the base and gradually, little by little, its shape began to emerge, like a sculpture from clay, and Ada knew that it would work.

As Ada grew stronger and taught herself how to shoot and how to shape a boat out of skins, she could see Knight growing weaker. His nose bled constantly now. He could barely manipulate his bed pan, which Ada had placed beneath his sleeping bag. She had cut a hole in the bag, which would fit around the pan, and every day, when the pot became too full or too offensive, she carried it outside and emptied it. She tried not to be sickened by the stench, the mess, but Knight's bodily functions were failing him fast and he had little control now of his evacuations. Sometimes he wasn't even able to adjust himself over the pan in time, and then Ada had to clean up the filth in his sleeping bag while he lay there, helpless to do anything but watch her.

Lately she couldn't sleep because there was too much to think about and to worry about. Knight looked as if he might die any minute, some days more than others. He still had moments—brief ones—when he felt better, but these had become rare. She could tell by his voice then, which would sound stronger, clearer, more like his old self. But other days, most days, she could barely hear him or understand his words because his voice was so faint and halting, just a whisper, and she had to lean in close to hear him.

His stomach turned on him and he began refusing food. He didn't eat anything for nine days straight until finally she was able to persuade him to eat a fried biscuit. His spirit was there—she could see him in his eyes—but his body was giving out. He drifted in and out of consciousness—so that sometimes he was there with her and sometimes he wasn't. He was trapped in a deteriorating shell of bones and flesh, unable to free himself except in sleep, and Ada was afraid it wouldn't be long now before he was gone forever. She prayed that they would survive until a ship came.

It wasn't that Knight could be of any help to her now, but the very fact that he was there, breathing, meant that she was not alone, and that someone else shared this remote, forgotten place. His presence was a comfort to Ada, and she needed him almost as much as he needed her. He relied on her to care for him physically, to talk to him, to be there if he should need something, and she counted on him to keep her company and remind her that, no matter how lonely she felt, there was someone else to share this hell.

While Knight lay in his bed, Ada sat nearby and made herself some sealskin boots, a blanket coat, a parka, and a sun hat to go hunting in, along with a pack for carrying things. The little house was cozy, but the weather was blustery and cold, and fog hovered over the mountains. It snowed on May 19, unfolding a vast, smooth blanket of white across the earth, and burying all of Ada's traps. But the sun began shining in the evening, which meant there was more time for Ada to work outside at chopping wood, washing clothes, scraping skins, and, of course, hunting, which occupied most of her time.

Every day, when the weather allowed, she cleaned her gun and then set out with it and her shoulder platform to find some game. She had seen ducks, geese, gulls, ravens, and owls across the sky. But her aim was still unreliable, and she knew she must be careful not to waste her ammunition. Rather than come home empty-handed each time, she collected sweet roots to boil up into a stew.

If she made a mistake once, she didn't make it again. When she fell into the mouth of the harbor up to her ankles, she learned. When she shot too far to the left or to the right and frightened off the birds without hitting one, she took note. When she pulled the trigger, for-getting that she had already set the hammer, it nearly knocked her over, but she wasn't hurt. And she never forgot again. She also learned to keep the fox skins out of reach of the cat, who kept trying to eat them. All this she documented in her journal.

A storm roared in on May 27, blowing snow into the storm shed and threatening to invade the house. Ada had meant to go over to the old camp to see how the hunting conditions were there, but was forced to delay until the weather was calmer. When she did go, she was not prepared for how desolate the camp seemed. It was strange being back there, where the five of them had once lived together. There was evidence of all of them littered across the ground, but there was no sign of life. No animal tracks, no birds flying above, no indication that a bear or fox had ever been there. It was only six months ago that Ada, Knight, Crawford, Galle, and Maurer had lived here together and celebrated Christmas and talked of all their future plans. Only five months since Crawford, Maurer, and Galle had headed off with the dogs, so full of ambition and determination and hope.

*   *   *

The first week in June, Ada took a walk west of camp. As she crossed the harbor, a flash of white caught her eye, and she paused to study the seagulls, which seemed busy along the beach. They scattered as Ada approached, and she saw that they had been building a nest. She shot at the birds, but they flew away, and she had to content herself with stealing their egg.

On her way home, a flock of white geese suddenly took flight above her, and she raised her gun and took aim. She lowered the gun again, watching, but the geese continued their journey. A hundred feet or so later, however, one fell to the ground, and Ada scooped it up and carried it home.

"Look what I got," she called out to Knight as she entered the house.

He opened his eyes with difficulty and tried to focus them. "What is that, a seagull?"

"No, it is a white goose and one seagull egg."

His head suddenly cleared. Was the egg fresh, he wanted to know. Yes, Ada said. It had been warm when she first touched it. She broke it open into a cup and showed it to him so that he could see for himself. He wanted it fried, he said. He should have eaten it uncooked, of course, because the frying only killed the nutrients he so desperately needed, so that he might as well have eaten a hard biscuit as an egg. But food had always tasted better to him fried or overcooked, especially now that his stomach was so queasy. The egg was easier for Knight to eat than solid meat because he was now having to gum everything. Besides, his throat was raw and sore and the meat hurt going down. Ada cooked the goose tenderly, though, until the meat fell away from the bone, just in case Knight felt like attempting it.

She held his head, to give him a drink of water. And every morning and every night she heated a canvas bag filled with sand and placed it on his feet to keep him warm. He was so terribly cold because he was only skin and bones. The chill penetrated easily and deeply, and he lay shivering in his bed until Ada warmed the bags for him and built the fire even higher. She kept the fire burning continuously so that Knight would not be uncomfortable, although it sometimes died while she was sleeping.

Ada was growing weaker herself. She could feel her energy slipping away, but she still made herself walk the three or four miles it took to get to the traps every day, and then she hurried back to camp to chop, split, and stack wood for the fire, and to collect snow for drinking water. When she finally felt that she could no longer make the three-mile walk to the trapline, she set numerous traps in a circle about the house so that she could reach them more easily and so that she would be closer to Knight should he need her. There were just as many fox tracks in camp as there were on the trapline, so she felt sure they would be fine.

Day after grueling day, Knight would lie in his bunk and watch Ada work and sometimes he would offer his advice or criticism. When she placed her fox skins on stretchers, he whispered, "White ladies want wide skins and you must stretch them as wide as you can—you are stretching them too long."

Ada kept doing it exactly the way she had been told. "Some native men who got skins have been telling me to make them long in the stretchers," she replied.

"That's not right," Knight insisted. "White people who live outside like them wide."

Ada fell quiet because she had never been outside where the white people lived, except to Nome, and so she did not know how they liked their furs. But the Eskimos had told her to stretch them this way, and that is the way she would continue to do it, no matter how frustrated it seemed to make Knight. She knew he also disapproved of the way she left the claws of the animals on the skins because he and Crawford and the others had always cut the claws off theirs. But this was the way she knew to do it. She was in charge now, not Knight, and she would have to do exactly as she believed best.

*　　*　　*

Knight was so thin that he was frightened to shift in his bag at all, for fear his bones would snap in two, so he lay prone and still as could be. Ada placed the cotton pillows she had made him beneath his shoulders and hips to cushion his bones, and she filled the canvas bags with hot sand and placed these around his entire body to warm him.

She cared for him now with a mother's instinct. She had a son who was ill and would probably always be ill from tuberculosis, unless she could take him to the doctors to cure him. And she had had two sick babies who had died. She said to herself, "Ada, Mr. Knight is sick now just like a little baby and I will take care of him just like my own little babies that are sick and die."

When Knight's stomach refused to hold anything—not biscuit or blubber or fox soup—she remembered that soda and salt added to water were good for an upset stomach. She had drunk this many times herself and had felt better afterward. She told Knight she would make him some, but he refused it. He couldn't stand the thought of it. Ada felt she couldn't insist—even if it was something that might help him—because she could not tell a white man what to do.

Sometimes she read to him from his grandfather's Bible, which she carried around with her and treasured above all else. The words were so soothing to her.

"Ada," Knight said one day, as she was reading, "when we get back to Nome, I am going to give you this Bible." And that thought filled her with joy.

On June 5, Knight fainted in his bed. He was gone for a while this time—much longer than before—until Ada wondered whether he would ever come back. When he once again opened his eyes and searched for her, they both sat shaken and afraid. The next day—Knight's thirtieth birthday—Ada shouldered her rifle and set out with grim determination. Knight must not die.

Frustrated and angry, she shot her gun over and over that day, but only got one bird to show for it. And then she saw the polar bear. It was far out on the ice and was heading toward camp. Ada stood rooted, her legs unsteady, watching as the bear veered closer. First to the beach near camp, then a bit south again, and then west to the beach, and then south once more. She couldn't tell what path it was taking, but she knew it would only be a matter of yards before it was upon her. Hands shaking, she raised her gun and took aim. And then the sky opened and snow began to fall and soon she could see nothing but white. She waited there, watching, with the snow falling around her, until her legs finally moved again and carried her back home.

The next afternoon, she dropped a seagull with one shot, and pride replaced fear as she brought it home for Knight. They had not eaten meat in a very long time, and now they had enjoyed birds for two days in a row. Ada could feel her body responding happily to the feed, and she was excited to set out the next day to try again. With the field glasses to her eyes, she scanned the beach and could see two sets of polar bear tracks. One was fresh, probably from the bear of the day before, but the other appeared to be old. There was no sign of seal yet, but she knew it would not be long before the seals reappeared on the ice. She would make a rifle resting board for seal hunting, she decided. It was a type of hunting, she knew, that required great patience and the strength to hold a gun in place for hours, if need be, while waiting for just the right moment to shoot the seal. She would need the resting board to do this.

On June 9, she brought home one fresh seagull egg and one fat goose. The goose was carrying three eggs inside her, one already with a shell, so there would be added cause for celebration at tonight's dinner.

* * *

The lack of Vitamin C makes the capillaries fragile, which means they can and do rupture easily. The walls of the small blood vessels become so worn down, so vulnerable and delicate, that the slightest pressure causes them to shatter.

It seemed Knight was always bleeding now. His nose. His skin. Literally, every time he turned around. He thus lay like a statue in his bed.

Death would eventually take place from cardiac failure, internal bleeding of the lungs or digestive tract, or a fractured blood vessel of the brain. After a lengthy period of degeneration, during which one's body seemed to collapse inward, death could come suddenly and without warning.

There were several times in May and June when Knight thought his time had come. Once, when he fainted in bed. Another when he turned white as an ice sheet. And another and still another that weren't quite as clear to him now. When he had the strength he noted everything in his journal.

Nowadays, his body just did what it wanted and there was nothing he could do to control it. It didn't take formal medical knowledge for him to know he was in the advanced stages of the disease. The reality was that, even as deep as he was into the throes of scurvy, if he'd had a week's worth—or even just a few days—of fresh raw bear or seal meat, he could have been saved. A measly fox or goose or a gull egg here or there did little, particularly when he insisted on eating the meat overcooked or fried. But with plentiful fresh meat the chronic nosebleeds would have stopped in one day. The stabbing pain in his bones would have disappeared quickly, and his tender gums, a purplish red, would have healed in just three days' time. The hemorrhaging of his skin—that stormy mass of black and blue which now spread across all planes of his body—would have cleared up in twelve days. Such a short healing period for such a debilitating, drawn-out disease, which had rendered him bedridden and helpless now for almost five months.

His voice didn't seem to work anymore, but when he could find the strength to whisper, Knight talked to Ada about what would happen if he died. He asked her to put his diary and any of his other personal papers into his trunk. He kept the key in his trouser pocket, he told her, where she could find it if he should stop breathing. He also wanted her to look after his rifle and his camera, and to be sure to keep them dry so that they wouldn't be ruined. They must be returned to his parents and Joseph, and he wanted his family to be able to use them.

On his earlier expedition with Stefansson, during one of their many travels over the ice and snow, they had stumbled across the grave of a small boy. It was obvious that vandals had visited the site at some point, rifling the nails from the coffin and the clothing of the deceased. A single arrow stuck in the ground near the grave, and Knight figured it must have been a sort of exchange for what they had stolen from the boy. A feeble, if well-meaning gesture, perhaps, following a grievously disrespectful one.

Would they ransack his grave on Wrangel Island? Would strangers come one day to rob him of his boots or his belt? Or would he be buried at home near his ancestors? There was no question now in his mind that he was going to die before the ship came. The only thing that remained to be seen was where he would rest for eternity.

June 17, 1923
Mr. & Mrs. H. Galle
Newbraunfels, Texas.

Dear People;

I have been guessing that Mr. Stefansson would ask of the British Government, in return for the transfer of the Island to them, an expedition fitted out under his control and directions and that, from London, he would cable for a ship which he would already have located as suitable for his purposes . . . and would proceed to Wrangle Island which he would make his permanent base and they would penetrate the unknown regions north from there.

If this is done, it will be a modern, fully equipped and well manned expedition going for perhaps three years and our boys would be given their option of staying another three years or returning home.

I am getting anxious and so are we all and we wish we could hasten the time of hearing from Lorne and Milton. . . .

Hoping that I have been some comfort and assurance to you and trusting that we have some word soon that they are all well and have not been hungry, which I believe we will, I beg to remain,

YOURS VERY RESPECTFULLY,
J.I. Knight

Twelve

KNIGHT'S YOUNGER BROTHER, Joseph, was going to the Arctic. Stefansson himself had requested that he join him on the relief expedition that summer. Joseph wasn't quite sure what his role was to be, but he knew he would be taking part in the next stage of colonization on the island. He had no experience in the far North—or anywhere outside the Pacific Northwest—but he loved the outdoors and had spent a great deal of time in the mountains and the woods in his job as McMinnville's special deputy game warden. He was also eager to follow in Lorne's footsteps. Lorne was widely regarded as the bravest and most adventurous young man to come from their town, and everyone admired him for the work he was doing. He was famous now, and Joseph, at age twenty, wanted to be just like him.

He couldn't believe his good luck—that Mr. Stefansson wanted him. Joseph wrote to Stefansson to let him know that he would be a willing part of any venture in which the explorer wanted to include him. He planned to start training right away, so that he would be fit and ready by the time he was called to go. He may have lacked the physical strength and power of his brother, but he was taller at six feet two inches, and quickly growing into his lanky knees-and-elbows frame.

On June 13, 1923, Stefansson would return to New York from London, where he was trying to muster support for the relief venture, and would let the Knights know the results of his conference with the British government, and the particulars of the relief expedition to Wrangel Island. Till that time, Joseph and his parents must wait. But they were used to waiting. There had been years of it, beginning in 1916, when Lorne first went north.

Both Mr. and Mrs. Knight were proud of Joseph—the fact that Stefansson had asked for him specifically—just as they were indescribably proud of his older brother. They loved to imagine the look on Lorne's face when he saw his younger brother stepping off the relief ship. While they hated the thought of being so very far away from both their boys, they were consoled by the knowledge that their sons would be doing important work for the world and that they would play such critical roles in something so grand as claiming an island for Britain.

Stefansson, meanwhile, awaited word from the British cabinet regarding support of his proposed relief expedition. He had made the trip to London himself to appeal for help because the Canadian government had made it clear that they would do nothing—not even recognize Stefansson's occupation of the island—without the consent of their sovereign Britain. After all, the Union Jack and not the Canadian flag was planted in the cold earth of Wrangel Island.

Former Prime Minister Meighen had believed staunchly that Canada "should confine its territorial ambitions to that portion of the map lying between and about the 52nd and 142nd meridians west of Greenwich, and that to reach out towards Wrangel Island, which is nearer to Russia than any other country, might only give ground for similar incursions into those portions which we claim." Although there was a new government now, its leaders remained just as unconvinced.

Stefansson's own funds were largely exhausted and he had no hope of launching a relief journey without assistance. The money he had earned from his numerous lectures and articles was, according to him, being fed into the running of the expedition, and he had resorted to borrowing on his assets and accepting the offer of charity from friends.

It was already June of 1923, and Stefansson knew he must send a relief ship to the island earlier than last year's belated attempt. They would need to leave in July, early August at the very latest, in order to have a good shot at making the island. Although he had officially given up an active career as explorer, he still wanted to finish his work with the Wrangel Island Expedition.

He emphasized the difference between relief and rescue. In writing to Mr. O. S. Finnie, of the Northwest Territories Branch in Ottawa, he said, "the men on Wrangel Island are not 'stranded' there. From my point of view they are a colony, no more stranded than were the early settlers of Nova Scotia or Plymouth Rock." Of course, he was being bombarded with correspondence from the families of the men he had sent there. Mrs. Fred Maurer wrote him frequently, wanting to know all the particulars of the relief expedition, as did the Galles, who were always politely asking if there might be any information, and the Crawfords and the Knights, who were more direct with their questions. At this point, there was little to tell them except that he was doing his best to secure the funds he needed, and so he wrote them with the usual lines about how the men were as safe on Wrangel Island as they were at home. "Illness is, of course, possible but the danger of that is no greater than it always has been on our expeditions," he wrote to Mr. Knight. "It is a very healthful climate, the danger of illness is less than it would be in a city, and about the only drawback on Wrangel Island from that point of view is the absence of surgical care."

The men had taken a good amount of ammunition to the island with them, he was sure of that. Both Knight and Maurer knew the importance of conservation, and so he felt confident they weren't wanting for anything. If they ran low, they would know to save their bullets for the big animals, which could feed five people for quite some time. True, it had been disappointing when the ship had failed to reach them last summer, but Stefansson felt certain that the only trouble they were experiencing now was homesickness. It was possible, of course, that they had grown so lonesome that they had crossed the ice to Siberia in January or February, in which case there would have already been word of them from Russia. But since there had been no such word, Stefansson was content in the knowledge that all of his men, and Ada Blackjack, were doing just fine.

The British government was understandably distracted by the aftermath of World War I. The Nazi Party, under the leadership of Adolf Hitler, had held its first Congress in Munich that January of 1923, while the Allies of the Great War met in Paris to sign an agreement procuring one billion dollars from Germany to repay the United States for the cost of its occupation. The peasants of Russia, aided by Herbert Hoover's American Relief Association, had barely recovered from their country's great famine. And the British Government was faced with widespread unemployment, the failure of hard hit commercial industries, and political unrest.

Four young men and one woman—only one an actual British subject—posted on a remote Arctic island were hardly a priority for a country still reeling from the ravages of war. Since Britain had never officially offered its support for Stefansson's Wrangel Island venture, the whole expedition, from start to finish, had been nothing but a mortifying, internationally embarrassing affair. The less they had to do with it, the better.

Stefansson estimated that he would need $10,000—the equivalent of $105,000 today—to thoroughly outfit and launch the relief expedition. While the families of the four young men and Ada Blackjack waited for news of a plan, he scrambled to come up with one.

* * *

Harold Noice, after finishing a stint as an explorer under Stefansson in 1918, had struggled to make a name for himself on his own. What he wanted more than anything was to be as well-known an adventurer as Stefansson himself, someone who would be in constant demand, who would write and lecture and lead his own expeditions into the great, frozen wild. But there had been nothing. It wasn't for want of trying, of course, because Noice was as ambitious a man as ever fell into Arctic work. He had always imagined great things for himself and dreamed far beyond the limits of his immediate experience.

In 1923, he was a tall young man of twenty-seven, with a shock of dark hair, swept back and parted severely in the middle, and a round, puckish face. He had the pinched look of a mole who had just stumbled into sunlight—close-set eyes, appled cheeks, and no chin to speak of. He came from a family of farmers and there wasn't one adventurous soul among his ancestors. But he was raised, as were most boys his age, on adventure stories, and Noice left his hometown of Seattle just after high school to seek the real thing. The Arctic was the last place he had considered going. Instead, he pictured himself prospecting for gold in Bolivia, winding his way down the Amazon, or lion hunting in Africa.

He had enrolled in a technical school to study mineralogy and hoped for a life as a gold prospector, but before he finished his courses he met a man who was planning a photographic expedition into Alaska to take motion pictures of the scenery. It was a thrilling opportunity, and Noice jumped at it even though his parents—especially his mother—were unhappy about it. They had been reading the then-recent news accounts of Stefansson's 1913 Canadian Arctic Expedition and its tragic outcome—eleven men dead in the Arctic—and it was the last kind of life they wanted for their son.

Noice's mind was made up, however, and in 1914 he had set out with several other young men to travel up the coast to Nome to meet their expedition. But the man never showed, and Noice stayed aboard the ship that had carried him to Alaska. The captain was continuing on up to Banks Land and then to Cape Kellett, where they unexpectedly found Stefansson, who had been out of touch with the rest of the world for two years.

Noice ended up serving nearly that amount of time on Stefansson's 1916–1918 Canadian Arctic Expedition with Lorne Knight, whom he disliked intensely. Knight was just a bumpkin, in Noice's opinion, a great, bumbling fool, who seemed to think of nothing but having a good time. Noice was far more serious than that and he quickly grew impatient with people whom he believed were less intelligent. Knight had beaten him once in a fight, too, which had been as humiliating an experience as it was painful.

Noice had absolutely nothing in common with Knight except that they both worshiped Stefansson, or rather Knight worshiped while Noice coveted Stefansson's position. Noice had found Stefansson, the man, to be a great disappointment, and he harbored numerous criticisms of the explorer, which he made clear in a book he was writing, *With Stefansson in the Arctic.* Although he had no publisher as of yet, he was certain the book would eventually be printed, largely thanks to the inclusion of Stefansson's name in the title.

It was difficult for him to find work after the run with Stefansson, even though Noice tried to create opportunities for himself whenever and wherever possible. In 1918, after finishing with Stefansson, Noice purchased a five-eighths interest in an old trading schooner with the idea that he was now experienced enough to become an explorer. During that time, he enjoyed stomping up and down the deck of the ship as captain, while he and his crew surveyed and charted remote shores of the Northwest Passage and the Victoria coastline. In the summer of 1920, he had penetrated the interior of Victoria Island, and began compiling a dictionary of the Eskimo languages, the first of its kind ever completed.

In 1922, he went to New York, trying with no luck to sell a collection of ethnological objects to the American Museum of Natural History. He hoped to earn enough money from the sale to support himself and his writing, but he found no buyers. By spring of 1923, he finished his manuscript and found himself with nothing to do and no money. He stayed in touch with Stefansson, who was in New York at the time, and the explorer promised to help in any way he could.

It was natural that he would want to do so. Noice was a man who, in Stefansson's eyes, shared his beliefs and convictions about living off the land. And for all his criticism of Stefansson personally, Noice subscribed wholeheartedly to his theory, boasting that surviving in the Arctic was "easy if only one makes hay while the sun shines."

Stefansson knew that Noice was looking for any opportunity to go north, and so at the end of May, before he had sailed for London, the explorer mentioned the possibility of going to Wrangel Island in charge of the relief ship. The attention Noice would garner from leading such a journey might earn him enough prominence to make a good and solid living giving lectures, so it was quite an appealing proposition.

Stefansson had returned from London without a promise or a farthing from the British government, but Noice knew the explorer was still working on a way to send a ship north. Noice vowed to stand by until he was needed, and Stefansson, in turn, promised to keep Noice informed. They would put everything into place so that, once the money was found, the expedition could sail immediately. With this in mind, Stefansson's business partner, A. J. T. Taylor, began inquiring in Nome about possible ships available to charter.

Noice didn't have a cent to his name, and there were obligations back home that he needed to settle. Stefansson, once he had funding, was willing to take financial responsibility for these and for sending him money for his expenses. For Noice, this was the opportunity for which he had been waiting. He would go north again, and to Wrangel Island this time, the very setting of Stefansson's tragic Canadian Arctic Expedition. He didn't care if Lorne Knight *was* one of the men to be rescued—even though Stefansson was quick to emphasize it was a relief expedition and not a rescue mission.

With the British government refusing to offer the support Stefansson so desperately needed, he turned his sights to other prospects. He had an acquaintance by the name of Griffith Brewer, an English gentleman and the managing director of the British Wright Aeroplane Company, who had taken an interest in Lorne Knight after meeting him at the Ohio home of Stefansson's friend and Brewer's fellow businessman, aviator Orville Wright. Brewer had seen promise in Knight then and was won over by the young man's enthusiasm, and now he showed interest in Stefansson's relief venture. Brewer was not a wealthy man, but he was an industrious one, and he vowed to help in any way he could.

A. J. T. Taylor also offered his support, vouching personally to pay Noice's expenses from New York to Nome so that he could be on hand, just in case they could scrape up enough resources for the relief trip. Noice, who had recently dislocated his shoulder, which was now bound in a cast, left at the first opportunity. He spent most of the journey in the company of an intriguing woman named Frances Allison, who was several years his senior, a traveler and musician and divorcée. She made the trip a pleasant one, but when Noice arrived in Nome, he was startled by the unfriendly treatment he received from the other Americans there, who had followed the news of Stefansson's claim on Wrangel Island and were angry because they resented the fact that he was trying to steal this piece of land for Britain. When Noice arrived, word spread quickly as to his purpose there, and he was not welcomed.

Noice tried to explain Stefansson's point of view, but the people of Nome weren't interested in his explanations, and so, whenever he shopped for supplies or goods for himself, he found, time and again, the prices increased by levels that made purchases unaffordable. Only Carl and Ralph Lomen, prominent local businessmen, were good to him, thanks to an arrangement Stefansson had made with them to help supply Noice for the trip. But no matter the headache, the fact that he was going north again was worth all the hostility.

The Arctic had hooked him. To Noice, it was "challenging, calling, tempting, taunting, and I knew I could never break away from it." He dreamed now at age twenty-seven, as he had at nineteen when he was just starting out, of seeing his name in the papers. The headlines that would read *Seattle Boy Becomes Arctic Explorer.*

Stefansson had told him there was nothing heroic in the work of an Arctic voyager, but Noice disagreed. "Adventure!" Stefansson had scoffed. "There is absolutely nothing heroic in Arctic exploration, for exploration, like any other work, is easily resolved into certain simple rules, which, if properly followed, render it as safe and about as exciting as taxicab-driving or a hundred other things which are done in civilization and done without a suggestion of heroism either."

Noice was sufficiently chastened by the words, but it became increasingly clear to him that Stefansson's was a cold and scientific mind. As far as Noice could see, Stefansson talked but rarely acted, and spent most of his time in the Arctic reading novels or tapping away on his typewriter with his lily-white hands. Noice had wondered then, as he wondered now, "if this man had ever really battled with ice-floes, or even fired a gun at a target, let alone a bear, in his whole life."

As much as he may have coveted Stefansson's public position and fame, the more Noice came to know the man behind the legend, the less enchanted he was. In his eyes, Stefansson had "few 'human' traits and no human weaknesses." Noice vowed early on that he was never going to be like him. He would be his own man instead, and some day people would read about him in history books for the great things he had done, all on his own. By now, he had seen some of the very worst of the North, but he had not been swayed. He had seen some of the best, too, and, in his opinion, "the best was very good."

* * *

Ada had filled all the pages in her diary, using her prized Eversharp pencil to record her thoughts. It was hard to believe, flipping through the little book, that she had written all those words. Now, Knight told her to use a blank book of photo supply order forms to continue her journal because it was the only notebook they had left. She took great care with her first entry:

June 10. This very important noted in case I happen to died or some body fine out that I was dead I want Mrs. Rita McCafferty take care of my son Bennett. I don't want his father Black Jack to take him on a count of stepmother not for my boy. My sister Rita is just as good his on mother I know she love Bennett just as much as I do I dare not my son to have stepmother. If you please let this know to the Judge. If I got any money coming from boss of this company if $1,200.00 give my mother Mrs. Ototook $200.00 if its only $600.00 give her $100.00 rest of it for my son. And let Rita have enough money to support Bennett.

Death was constantly on her mind. She thought about it every time she looked at Knight's pale and haggard face—his sunken cheeks, his thin lips, his hollow eyes.

Knight was going to die. Ada knew it when she looked at him. He was "white like paper," and just bones now, with a thin layer of skin over them. His voice was growing weaker so that he could barely talk, and when he did it cost him whatever strength he still had. With a shaky hand, he inscribed his grandfather's Bible and gave it to her. "Presented to Ada Blackjack by E. Lorne Knight on Wrangel Island 1923." It was hers to keep now.

Ada was terrified that she was going to die as well. She was hunting every day and was certain that a polar bear would catch her and eat her, or that she would fall through the ice and drown. Her aim was improving, though, and there was at least some small comfort in her ability to shoot gulls and geese with regularity now. There were eggs, too, and Knight ate what he could of these. His throat was still too raw for meat and no matter how he tried, he wasn't able to swallow it.

Ada had been wearing her snow goggles, but one day her eyes, which had never adjusted to them, felt so gritty and strained and the light hurt them so much that she knew she was now snow blind. For three days, she was laid up in bed with her eyes closed against the pain, praying her sight would return. Knight breathed softly, raggedly, in his bed, so she could at least hear that he was still there, still with her.

On June 13, Ada was able to walk as far as the end of the harbor, where she found nine seagull eggs. Her eyes were strong enough now so she could shoot a gull from the sky, and her arms were quite full of birds and eggs by the time she returned to camp. Two days later, she caught a seagull in one of her traps, but once again Knight wasn't able to swallow the meat. He could only swallow a little bit of raw egg as Ada held his head.

Determined to improve her shooting further, Ada made another target and shot it twice with her rifle. It was all she dared to do, since the ammunition was beginning to run low. But afterward she picked up the target and brought it into the tent to show Knight what she had done. "Pretty good shooting," he told her, and Ada felt proud, as she always did, whenever he acknowledged her work. Even though they had had sharp words, even though she had never felt as close to him as to the others, she supposed they were friends now, and she craved his approval and respect.

By mid-June, the seals seemed to come from nowhere, returning to the ice floes offshore to sun themselves for hours. Their slick, dark skins glistened against the white of the ice, barely specks of black because they were quite far out on the pack. On June 18, Ada, with her rifle and her new rifle stand, went seal hunting for six hours. She crawled along the ice on her belly for three hundred yards after one seal, but when she fired at it, the seal dove into the water and was gone. For the first time in a while, she came home empty-handed. When she told Knight what had happened, he said that she was too far off from the seal to do any good. Next time, she must get closer before firing, at least one hundred fifty yards or less. And she mustn't forget and use the soft-nosed bullets when he had told her not to. Those were to be saved for the polar bears.

Eggs had become their safety net, but when Ada set out to go egg hunting on June 20, she discovered that her passage to the nests had disappeared. As the snow melted, the water level of the harbor rose; now there was no way across to the sand island where the birds nested. She would have to tell Knight that there was nothing again for dinner, but perhaps the next day would bring better luck.

{ PART IV }

RELIEF

"I'll just see where it leads to," thought Jack,
and with that he stepped out of the window
on to the beanstalk, and began to climb upwards.

—*"Jack and the Beanstalk"*

Untitled Poem by Lorne Knight, Summer 1923

❋

Here lies a Polar Explorer so valiant and bold
Who devoted his life to snowstorms and cold
All for prominence, so I've been told
And a few pieces of yellow filth called gold.
For nourishment he had snow and scenery
Which reminded him of the grim beanery
The grim beanery so greasy and grim
Would look like Paradise now to him.
Oh! Bring on your roast pork, apple sauce and pie
And some whipped cream before I die
Some of that wonderful potato salad, too
And sliced tomatoes with lots of goo-goo
And beans. Oh! Beans, that wonderful fruit
And then to end it all, just to make things suit
About a gallon of mother's canned fruit
And then a wonderful bewitching smoke
For as tobacco is concerned I'm dead broke.
But I'm going now where it's always hot
Where blizzards ain't and cold is not
Where everyone's happy and anthems ringing
But having no voice I'll be out of the singing
Don't weep for me now, don't weep for me ever
I'm going to do nothing for ever and ever.

Thirteen

————

ON JUNE 21, Ada stood over Knight and began to cry. He had once again slipped into unconsciousness, and she prayed that he would wake up and come back to her. *Don't leave me here alone*, she thought.

When at last he opened his eyes and saw her standing there, the tears streaming down her face, he was startled. "What is the matter, Ada?" he asked gently. She told him that she was afraid he was going to leave her. She needed consolation, but what could Knight say? She was right, wasn't she? He was going to leave her soon. He was fading quickly, even though he couldn't predict what the immediate cause of death would be.

Ada's tears were flowing and her sad face tilted down at him. She had done her best, after all, and he knew it wasn't her fault he was losing his last battle. She had taught herself to shoot and had hunted for him nearly every day and had seen that he was as comfortable as possible under the circumstances. She had not been able to save him, as he had not been able to save himself. But she had tried. And so he thanked her for all she had done for him, and he told her that she must be strong, that she must do her best to fight for her life and hang on until the ship arrived.

Afterward, Ada sat down at Galle's typewriter and slipped a piece of paper into it, just as she had seen Galle do numerous times. She had never used a typewriter before, and Galle had told her firmly that she must not touch it, but she felt there should be a record kept of the fact that Knight was very ill, in case anything should happen to him or to her.

Dear Galle,

I didn't know I will have very important writing to do. You well forgive me wouldn't you. Just before you left I've told you I wouldn't write with your typewriter. So I made up my mine I'll write a few words, in case some happen to me, because Mr. Knight he hardly know what he's talking about I guess he is going die he looks pretty bad. I hope I'll see you when you read letter. Well, if nothing happen to me I'll see you. The reason why I write this important notice I have to go out seal hunding with the rifle. Of course Knight wouldn't eat any meat he always say he's got sore throad. That's about all I well say in this notice I write. I may write some more some times if nothing happen to me in few days.
    With lots of best regards to your self from me

> *Yours truly*
> *Mrs. Ada B. Jack.*

Knight's words had comforted her, and that night, she slept. The next morning, she checked on him, as she always did, and discovered that he wasn't breathing. Then she knew that Lorne Knight was really and truly gone. He had died some time during the night.

It had been a long, excruciating illness, but now, at last, she felt he would have peace and be with God.

She knew that she should record the date of Knight's death because Mr. Stefansson and others back home would want to know, and if she were to die, too, of starvation or illness or from being killed by a wild animal, she would need to leave something behind that would tell what had happened to Knight. Once again, she sat down in front of Galle's Corona and placed her fingers on the keys.

Wrangel, Island.
June 23d. 1923.

The daid of Mr Knights death He died on June 23d I don't know what time he die though Anyway I write the daid, Just to let Mr Stefansson know what month he died and what daid of the month

written by Mrs Ada B. Jack.

Galle should be in Nome by now and would probably be coming back to the island by boat. She left the letters in the typewriter, just in case anything should happen to her, so that he would find them easily and could learn about their deaths, and she vowed to write something every day, so that he would know where she was at all times, just in case the ship should come while she was out hunting.

She did not have the heart—nor the strength—to stir Knight from his sleeping bag. To remove him from her sight would have been too much, and she couldn't bear the thought of not having another human to look at. If she left him in his bed, it would almost be as if he were still with her. To protect him from wild animals, she built a barricade of boxes around his body.

She moved into the storage tent to escape the smell of decay. She and Vic would just have to make the small space their new home, and she drove driftwood into the ground to bolster the tattered walls and ceiling of the tent. She built a cupboard out of boxes, which she placed at the entrance, and in this she stored her field glasses and ammunition. The stove she made herself. It was a rusty, rickety thing comprised of empty kerosene tins, but it worked well. She piled driftwood beside it so that she wouldn't have to go outside to fetch it. On top

of the stove sat her battered teakettle, and she stocked her food—
pieces of dried meat and bits of hard bread—in a small box.

She built a sleeping platform against the rear wall of the tent out of
empty crates and driftwood, and then covered it with reindeer skins
to make it softer. She made a rack for her thirty-forty rifle and her
shotgun, which she hung above her bed so that she would have easy
access to them should she be surprised by bears during the night.

Ada collected Knight's diary and reached into his trouser pocket
for the key to his trunk. But when she tried to turn the key in the
lock, it wouldn't budge. She had promised to put his journal in the
trunk, but she would protect it as best she could from the elements.
She left it in its box and set it out under the tarp which she had
propped up outside her tent for storing Knight's camera and other
items she wanted to keep dry.

Despite all of his cross words and criticisms, she missed Knight.
They had developed their own unique and prickly friendship, coming
to rely upon one another. Ada did not understand why he had to die
so young and leave her by herself, but she supposed that it must have
been the evil spirits that had caused his illness. She knew of such
happenings from her people, who had spoken of them often, and
besides, the shaman had warned her. Perhaps Knight had done something to anger the spirits. Perhaps they all had, coming there to the
island. If the spirits had claimed Knight, they might very well come
for Ada as well. She must be watchful and take good care of herself,
she wrote in her diary, and continue to read Knight's grandfather's
Bible—her Bible now—so that the spirits would not take her away, too.

* * *

Stefansson made it clear to Noice that if Crawford, Knight, Maurer,
and Galle wished to return home with the ship, Noice was to stay on
the island and take their place or hire men to do so. Noice had no
intention of remaining on Wrangel Island to continue British occupation, and he figured it was a safe bet that the men who were living

there now would be anxious to come back, with the exception of Knight, who just might possibly want to stay. In case he didn't, Noice thought it best to hire Eskimo families, with their dogs and sleds, who would be willing to stay behind.

The ship was called the *Donaldson*. Noice and the ship's owner, Alexander Allen, signed an official agreement stating that Allen promised to furnish Noice with a crew and provisions sufficient to cover their needs. In addition, he would supply the engine oil and coal necessary to run the boat. The *Donaldson* was to be completely outfitted and shipshape by the first of August 1923, and in return Noice, representing Stefansson, would hand over $1,000 in cash for payment for the first twelve days. Weekly installments of $83 per day would follow, to the end of a thirty-one-day period.

It had been hell, at first, finding a suitable vessel. There was only one boat available when Noice arrived in Nome, a rusty, abandoned ship, inappropriately christened the *Gladiator*, which hadn't been at sea for years. Because it was the only option, he was determined to figure out a way to make it work. He tore off the iron bark sheeting to investigate for leaks and was treated to a smattering of them, all the way across the stern. He would have to send the old tub out to be repaired, overhauled, completely rebuilt, at a huge cost of time and money.

It was at that point that Alexander Allen stepped in, offering his ship, the *Donaldson*, which was solid and sound but which possessed a musty, unreliable engine of only 40 horsepower. Allen volunteered to remove it and replace it with a new engine of 65 horsepower, which sounded just fine to Noice, and a lot better than the rusty, leaky *Gladiator*. Stefansson had been vaguely associated with Allen in years past, and Noice thought him a decent man. The ship was seventy-two feet long, had a seventy-four ton burden, and should—with the new engine—get them to their destination.

To staff the ship, Noice would take along Allen as navigator, a man named Hansen as captain, as well as two engineers and second mate Charles Wells, an Alaskan prospector and trapper. Noice wanted three

Eskimos to accompany him on the sled trip across the frozen sea to the island—should the ship be forced out by ice. He spoke the language so wasn't worried about dealing with the Eskimos, but as yet, he had only found one Eskimo willing to go. Too many of them feared the danger of the mission, of being crushed in the ice, of being swept away by the pack and the current. Before Noice could convince them otherwise, word spread of an accident in which one Eskimo sprained a wrist and another smashed a foot. It had happened while loading the ship with cargo, and now the remaining Eskimo refused to sail.

All reports of the ice conditions that season were favorable, and Noice hoped the route would be clear, smooth going, and that the *Donaldson* could reach Wrangel within two weeks. They would head toward—but not to—North Cape, Siberia, and if the ice was too thick and they weren't able to break it, Noice planned to land a depot of supplies there, in case the ship was crushed. If he didn't find Crawford or Knight or any of the others along the Siberian Coast, he would wait until the sea froze over completely so that he could cross to the island by sled. With his plaster cast now removed and his shoulder healed, he felt fit and ready for that particular challenge, although he hoped it wouldn't be necessary.

Noice jotted off a note to Knight's father to let him know the status of the relief expedition. If he couldn't reach the island by ship, he promised to find a way to reach the men and Ada. Mr. Knight was skeptical—he harbored a bit of prejudice toward Noice based on the stories he'd heard from his son—but he passed the news on to the Galles just the same because he knew that they, at least, would be comforted. "In case he could not reach the island by boat he would take Nome's best dog team and sled and an Eskimo skin boat and, in case the boat became impossible, he would take to the ice hauling the boat on the sled and in case he encountered open water which he would, he can ferry over and thus be sure to reach the island and the boys."

Although he feigned confidence, Mr. Knight wished it was someone else going after Lorne and his comrades. Noice was unnervingly unproven to be leading such an important expedition, no matter what Stefansson seemed to think. But perhaps Noice would make good on this one, and perhaps he really would get through. After all, years had passed since that earlier expedition with Lorne, and they were men now, not boys.

The only problem with Noice's plans was Stefansson. Both Noice and A. J. T. Taylor wired him repeatedly, urging him to send the money they needed if they were to move forward with hiring the ship and purchasing supplies. For weeks, they tried to reach Stefansson, each correspondence growing more beseeching, more frantic, more demanding. If they were to have a better shot at making the island than the *Teddy Bear*, they must leave soon. Noice did all he could to secure the equipment and stores they would need, and the Lomen brothers held the goods he had chosen while Noice tried without success to get word from Stefansson about the money.

But there was nothing, and the Lomens were unable to advance any credit to Noice. Alexander Allen, too, would have to relinquish the ship to someone else who could pay him upfront and soon. The *Donaldson* was the only suitable ship available that summer, and if they lost her, they lost their chance at Wrangel. Noice was all too aware that he was working with a two- to three-week window during which the sea promised—as much as it was able—to be open and clear of ice.

"It is unthinkable that Mr. Stefansson does not realize the seriousness of the present situation," Mr. Taylor wrote to the explorer's secretary, "and the far reaching and unfavourable effect that any public appeal for money will have upon him personally. There are only two sources that the money for this expedition should come from, the government or privately from us."

"Must load . . . while weather favourable otherwise surf may cause two weeks delay and jeopardize success stop unless receive credit august first will broadcast worldwide appeal for help," telegraphed Noice.

"Do not make me wait," he wired the next day when he still had not received a response.

To make matters all the more urgent, the Russian government began issuing threats in international newspapers. "The Siberian Government is outfitting a vessel at Vladivostok for a voyage to Wrangel Island," read an Associated Press dispatch, "with the avowed intention of capturing the little band of British explorers . . . and taking possession of the island in the name of Russia." "Soviet officials are antagonistic to the Wrangel party of occupation," read another.

The British government retaliated in the press, warning that the capture of Allan Crawford and his companions would be looked upon as the "equivalent to an act of war."

There were rumors that any ship sent to Wrangel from a country other than Russia must first ask permission from the Soviet government. If and when permission was granted, members of the Russian Red Guard would sail with the ship, confiscating any commercial property or furs collected by the expedition members. There were whispers of a Russian gunboat, which was supposedly sailing from Siberia for Wrangel with the sole purpose of protecting the territory from outsiders. And Noice received a direct missive from Siberia, announcing that a ship was being sent to the island to capture it and everyone ashore.

Without any word from Stefansson, who was still unexplainably silent, A. J. T. Taylor took matters into his own hands and wrote directly to William Cory, the Deputy Minister of the Department of the Interior in Ottawa. "A critical time is approaching," he said, "when if the credit is not established and the expedition consequently delayed, four men and among them, Allan Crawford of Toronto, may perish, if not from exposure, then possibly at the hands of the Siberians mentioned in Mr. Noice's telegram of the 28th."

Cory's response was short and to the point. The Dominion government had informed Stefansson that he must first obtain the support of the Imperial Authorities in England before he would gain the support of the government of Canada. "Until we are aware of the decision of the Imperial Authorities," wrote Deputy Minister Cory, "it is impossible to consider any application for a grant to aid any expedition to Wrangel Island."

Neither Taylor nor Noice felt it wise to go to the public for support of the venture. As Taylor pointed out in one of his many letters to Stefansson, such a maneuver could be harmful to the explorer's reputation, implying extreme governmental disrespect, going over the heads of the government and the authorities.

By the last week in July, the ship was ready to sail, but they would wait to load it until they received the amount needed for security— $12,600, or $133,000 by today's standards. Captain Cochran of the U.S. revenue cutter *Bear* hand-delivered a wire from the Siberian authorities in Anadyr, warning Noice again to telegraph Petropavlosk for permission to travel to Wrangel Island, and to stop at Whalen, where he must show his credentials and pick up two Russian guards.

Naturally, Noice and Taylor were alarmed by the Soviet threats, and again wired a message to Stefansson. "Siberian sending ship from Vladivostock to capture Wrangell stop must prevent capture by leaving immediately." It was Noice's instinct to disregard the threats. After all, the lives of four men and their Eskimo companion might be at stake, and until he had word from Stefansson to do otherwise, he would ignore the Russians entirely.

* * *

Each day that lonely summer, before setting out to hunt, Ada sat down at Galle's typewriter and wrote him a note about where she was going. She left a sheet of paper in the machine so that she could add to it daily because she did not want to risk the ship coming and not finding her in camp. She wanted to make certain her rescuers did not leave her there after they had come all that way to fetch her.

It was also a way for her to have a conversation with someone, now that she was alone. It was a way of talking to Galle, just as she had talked to him before he left for Siberia. She began lengthening the entries, confiding and sharing more about herself and her work, and reporting in again at the end of the day, telling him what happened and what she did, how the hunt went and how she felt about it. It was a comfort to be able to write those words, even if he wasn't able to listen and respond.

June 24th. I'm going to the other side of the harbar mouth do some duck hunding.

She brought four eiders home that day and then took pictures of her tent and herself, even though she hadn't quite figured out how to work the camera. She had seen Crawford set the contraption on a box or log and pull the string that snapped the shutter. When she tried to imitate his methods, her photographs only turned out blurred and dark. But she would learn to use that camera, she promised herself, so that she could leave a photographic record of her time as well.

June 25. Going same as yest rday. I got seven eiders.

When she got back to the tent, she plucked the birds and then hung the legs and the breasts to dry.

June 26th. I'm going to take a walk to the smale Island. I saw two Polar bears going in shore from the ice way over west of the camp. It's four oclock now. I write down when I saw them. I don't know what I'm going to do if they come to the camp. Well, God knows.

She collected three seagull eggs that morning and cooked them for her lunch. She drank them down with tea and saccharine and "had a nice picknick all by myself."

The very next day, Ada was able to kill her first seal. There were two of them, basking in the sun, and she fired one shot. The other seal slipped into the water, but Ada's seal lay still. She was filled with pride as she bent over the animal to examine it.

One week later, she shot another seal with Knight's rifle. She had fashioned a stretcher out of skins to haul the animals home, and she was sitting in her tent, cleaning the second seal, when she heard a noise outside her door. It sounded like a dog to her, and for one brief moment she believed it was Crawford, Galle, and Maurer come back to find her. But when she raised the tent flap, her heart stopped. Two bears, a large one and a younger one, stood fifteen feet from the tent, gazing down at her. In seconds, Ada was clutching her rifle. She knew that if she hit them in the shoulder or the foot and only injured them slightly, they would be angry and come after her, so she must not even try to kill them because she might miss. She raised the gun, as she had before, and fired over their heads until they turned and began to run away. When the gunfire stopped, the bears paused and looked back toward camp, considering. Ada raised her gun once more and fired five consecutive shots until they disappeared over the horizon.

June 28th. I clean the seal skin today and lat this afternoon Polar bear and one Cub was very close to the Camp and I didn't take any chances. I was afraid if I didn't hit it right I'd be in danger. I just shot over them and they wend away. I was glad thank the living God.

The bears they had waited so long for, that Knight had prayed for, had returned, but it suited her much better when they stayed away. Now, they haunted her. She found fresh polar bear tracks one morning outside the door of the tent. She investigated, but there was no bear in sight. One of her tins of oil, though, was licked clean, and she knew she would have to be more careful with her stores.

July 1st. I stay home today and I fix the shovel handle that I brack this spring and I saw Polar bear out on the ice and this evening I went to the end of the sand spit shot a eidar duck I shot him right in the head thank God keep me a live till now.

On July 4, Ada crawled on her stomach across the beach after a seal. She remembered what Knight had said about waiting until she was at least 150 yards from the animal before shooting, and so she tried to creep as close as possible. She cocked her gun and was just about to pull the trigger when an enormous cake of ice rose up between Ada and the seal, blocking her view. She moved quickly before the seal could disappear and took aim again, but the gun exploded with a deafening bang before she meant to shoot, and the seal slipped away, unharmed, into the water. Ada jumped to her feet and yelled, "Fourth of July," shattering the vast, impenetrable silence of the landscape. She may have come home empty-handed, but she had enjoyed a celebration, fireworks and all, she would note that evening.

She killed her third seal the following day, just a few yards from the back of her tent. The beach ran behind her little house, and she could see a seal some two hundred yards out on the ice. Once again, she fell to her stomach and wriggled, pretending she was another seal. When she was within range, she shot it once through the head, killing it instantly. She was ecstatic and thanked the Lord Jesus for giving her such a gift. The seal did not slip off the ice and into the water this time. It was hers and it was everything—skins for clothing, oil for lamps, and meat for food. She cut up the seal, hung the meat, and pulled the skin taut over the stretcher. If only Knight were there to share it with her, the victory would have seemed sweeter.

On July 6, she shot a seal at the harbor mouth. Because the seal lay a fair distance from camp and because the animals typically weighed well over six hundred pounds, Ada would need something to help her bring this one back to the tent. She had just fetched a poling line and started back toward her seal when she glimpsed something against the white of the sky that looked like a gigantic yellow ball coming toward her. A polar bear. Ada was four hundred yards from her tent, and now she ran back as fast as she could until she was safe inside.

She was afraid she might faint, but instead she climbed onto the platform she had built at the back of the tent and peered through her field glasses. She could see the outline of the bear and its cub as they bent over her seal—the seal she had labored for—and tore it to pieces. She was helpless to do anything as they devoured it before her eyes, but at least, she thought, "I am glad it is not me polar bear eats." She fired her gun toward them in anger, and watched as they scattered west and then east and then as they seemed to cross the harbor mouth, their noses pointed toward camp. She fired one more shot and waited.

Ada stood up on her platform until the sky grew dark and the fog billowed in like the soft, cold breath of the landscape. She decided it was better just to leave the seal to the bears. The next morning, she walked out to where her seal had fallen and found only smears of blood on the ice.

She purposely did not mention much about the polar bears in her diary. She knew that if the spirits were to take their revenge on her and she should die, that her diary would fall into the hands of others. And if her mother read mention of Nanook, she would always believe that Ada had been eaten by a polar bear and was living in his stomach, no matter how she had really died.

The mother bear and cub returned on July 7, circling the spot where the seal had fallen. Ada fired her gun at them, but missed, and they eventually wandered back the way they had come. She hunted for ducks then, but was unable to retrieve the one she shot because the ice on the harbor mouth was thin and would have given way beneath her. She returned to camp, discouraged.

She sewed a new flap onto the tent door, where the wind blew in through the holes in the canvas, and she added canvas to the tent frame to bolster her house. Ada did not know if a ship would come for her. Mr. Stefansson had not been able to make the island last summer, and there was a good chance Ada might face another winter without relief. Last September, she and the men had been unprepared for the ship's failure to reach them, and now she would ready her equipment and her house before the snow and the storms arrived—so that she would be ready for the worst.

She chewed up the sealskins to make them more pliable to mold into soles for her boots. She added new soles to her short boots. She practiced shooting at her target, and opened a new box of shotgun cartridges. She knitted fingers into her gloves to replace the ones that had worn away from all the work she was doing. And she began making a parka out of fancy reindeer skin and wolf trimming. It would be a beautiful parka and she felt she deserved it. It made her happy

to work on it, and she indulged herself for days, picking it up whenever she had time to add a new hook or to work on the hood. When
she finished it, she looked upon it with pride, with its fancy trim down
the front and around the hood. "It look like a parky alright," she
boasted in her diary.

On July 10, Ada rested in bed because she was frazzled and worn
from the exertion of her work, the constant, unending work without
a break. Vic lay against her, warm and breathing, and Ada opened a
new can of tea and thanked her heavenly father for letting her live
another day.

She was able to bring home two birds on July 16, gray ones she
didn't recognize. And on July 18 she shot two squaws and a duck.
She was storing her meat now, in case the ship didn't come or in case
Galle and Crawford and Maurer were unable to reach her by sled.
She would save the meat for winter because she would need it if the
game disappeared again. She filled up her food box with the seal meat
she had dried in the sun, and then she gently removed the seal skins
from the stretcher.

Ada often stood on the beach and looked out to sea, in the direction
of Nome—or where she thought Nome might be. She watched for
Crawford and Galle and Maurer or for a ship. It was time for a ship
to come. The water offshore was clear and calm and open. Ice still
hugged the shore in spots, but the space beyond was free of it. There
would be nothing to hold a ship back, to keep it from reaching her.
But on the morning of July 20, when she turned her gaze to the sea,
she saw the pack of ice to the west side of the harbor mouth and felt
a chill in her blood.

July 23. I thank God for living.

On July 24, there was a muffled roaring in the distance that let Ada
know the walrus had returned. She could not see them, but she heard
their foghorn cries for several days. She loaded her gun with brass
shells and went out after them, but got two old ducks instead and was
content. The game had improved. And when she went to sleep that

night, she dreamed she was singing cheers for the red, white, and blue.

She began another pair of boots, these out of reindeer skins and a set of old slippers, and she stitched herself some deer leggings. She threw out the molded hard biscuits and transferred the ones that were still edible to her food box. And she cleaned some seal flippers and stored them away in case the ship was able to find her, so that she could take them home and share them with her sisters "if the lord let me have it."

One night while Ada slept, the wind swept in and blew her skin boat out to sea. She had only used it twice, but she cried all day when she discovered it was gone. Then she cried all the next day and the next. It was too much. Ada was tired and she was weak and there was no one to help her. If she did not get up out of bed to forage for food, she would go hungry. If she did not light the fire, it would remain unlit. If she did not bring in the snow, there would be no water to drink. Eventually she grew tired of crying and pitying herself. She must get up and make another boat, and so she did.

This one was constructed out of canvas, although skins were preferable, but Ada did not have enough skins for a boat. She gathered driftwood for the frame and placed the wood, piece by piece, into position because the bottom must be built first. The boat should be more canvas than wood because the umiak must sit light in the water and she must be able to drag it easily across the ice and land. With the canvas stretched across the skeletal frame, Ada used her needle to sew the canvas into place until gradually it took the shape of a boat. The little vessel was nothing to look at, but it was sturdy and seaworthy, and she carved a set of driftwood oars to go with it. Every time she finished using it, she tied it up so that the wind could not take it away.

Her world was lonely and silent. Now that there was open water, there was no longer the crash of the ice pack, the long, low grind of the floes churning against one another, the deep and sudden splash of water as masses of the pack broke off and plunged into the sea, or the staccato burst like rifle shots that echoed across the island as the ice expanded. There was only the sound of her own voice as she spoke to Vic. She fussed over the cat like a mother and picked her up and held her in her arms and talked to her like she had talked to Crawford and the others. Vic was a warm, breathing creature, who responded with purrs and rubs and an occasional meow. Ada thought she would go insane without her.

McMinnville, Oreg. Aug. 8, 1923
Mr. H. Galle
Newbraunfels, Texas.;

Dear Sir;

You will note that the boys are supposed to be alive and I feel that this is an accepted fact although I am, of necessity, prepared to receive almost any kind of news when we do hear from them for they have been in a very inhuman situation for two long years and that is a long time for men to hold themselves in solitude and be normal.

Of course, all we have to worry about is that some of the boys may have developed sickness of some sort. This, however, does not impress me as cause for worry because they were all young and healthy and should have no difficulty in keeping themselves well.

Lorne made a statement to Life Insurance Companies before leaving on this trip to the effect that, he did not consider the hazard of life as great in the Arctic by 40 per cent as here in the modern city with all the swift moving vehicles.

As to the Soviet interference, I do not believe there is any danger because of the inaccessibility of the island.

We shall see and in the meantime, all we can do is to hope and sit tight. It will be a happy bit of news when we do see news of the expedition in the morning paper or when the telegraph messenger knocks at the door and delivers the first message from them.

Yours very respectfully;
J. I. Knight

Fourteen

BY AUGUST 1, Stefansson forwarded the money to Noice. He had finally succeeded in raising funds for the expedition. Now that he was back in communication with Noice and Taylor, he brushed off the Russian threats with irritation and confidence. In his mind, the Soviet Union had no more claim to Wrangel Island than anyone else, and certainly less than Britain now that he had officially claimed the island in its name. At the same time, he did recognize that the Soviets could pose a threat to his relief expedition. Reports had leaked into American papers, stating that an armed Russian expedition was being supplied and readied for capturing Wrangel Island. An article appeared in the *London Times*, stating that the Soviet authorities were prepared to confiscate the *Donaldson* if Noice did not ask their permission to sail.

The sailing of the relief expedition should clearly be kept as quiet as possible, and Stefansson told Noice to say nothing in response to the Russians, and to sail directly to Wrangel Island without calling first on any Russian ports. "Everybody London considers fear Soviet interference ridiculous," Stefansson said in his wire. "If Russia has claims they will be settled. All nonperishable property should be left Wrangell for resuming company business summer. News of Noice having money enough for certainty sailing should be kept from press if possible till moment sailing."

This suited Noice fine, but he secretly wished Stefansson hadn't made such a media production of the island's appeal as an air base. Otherwise, Russia might not be so interested and he wouldn't have to be so careful. As it was, if the outside route to Wrangel was blocked by ice, he would be forced to follow the Siberian coast, no matter what Stefansson said about it.

The funding for the trip came, at last, from Englishman Griffith Brewer. He was not a rich man, but he believed fervently that Allan Crawford and his team must be rescued. He had written an impassioned letter for publication in the London *Times* to bring attention to the plight of the "adventurous patriots" who had now been stranded in the Arctic for two years. "The British Wright Company two weeks ago voted the sum of $2,500 to pay for an auxiliary schooner to visit Wrangel Island from Nome, Alaska," his published letter read. "An additional sum of $10,000 must be deposited in the bank at Nome to safeguard the crew of the only other vessel now available. This sum, to be of use, must be found immediately."

While they waited for the money to come in, Brewer pledged his personal property at a bank and sent the money Stefansson needed immediately—$11,000—to Nome. It would be an advance on the subscriptions, which, he felt confident, would soon be forthcoming. In all, they managed to collect nearly $3,000 from subscriptions, with donations from several notable and enthusiastic Brits, including a former Secretary for the Colonies, and Miss M. F. Gell, granddaughter of the late Arctic explorer Sir John Franklin.

Stefansson had estimated spending no more than $5,000 on equipment for the relief expedition, but costs grew and multiplied, until the price rose to $17,000. All told, the entire Wrangel Island Expedition, from its outset in 1921 to the present, had cost $46,600, although much of the sum was yet to be paid.

Before setting sail, an agreement was drawn up between the North American Newspaper Alliance and A. J. T. Taylor, acting as Noice's attorney, and in his official capacity as vice-president of the Stefansson

Arctic Exploration and Development Company. The Alliance contracted to purchase for $3,000 the exclusive world newspaper rights to the story of the Wrangel Island relief expedition as well as the narrative of Noice. He must not speak to anyone else or grant other interviews until after he delivered his story to the Alliance, and to their associate, the *Toronto Star*. Likewise, no members of Crawford's party must speak to the press. Furthermore, the Alliance requested first option to Crawford's story and to the stories of Knight, Maurer, Galle, and Ada Blackjack. Noice would keep the money for himself.

The *Donaldson* set sail at three o'clock on August 2. In addition to his captain and crew who sailed with him, Noice planned to hire Eskimos at another port and also acquire their sleds, umiaks, and hunting gear. Second mate Charles Wells and the Eskimos would remain on Wrangel Island to continue the occupation for Britain. Noice was taking enough food, rifles, ammunition, clothing, sleds, scientific equipment, and a skin boat to last such a party for at least one year.

They arrived at Cape Blossom on the morning of August 6, 1923, where Noice and engineer Joseph Earl were forced, due to shallow water, to row eight miles to shore. In town, they purchased all the equipment they would need to repair the engine, as well as additional guns and supplies, and they hired an Eskimo family and two unmarried Eskimo hunters. They also took on eleven strong dogs and a fresh supply of reindeer meat.

The equipment and the dogs were rowed out to the ship, and only the Eskimos remained to follow in their skin boats. When they didn't come, Noice discovered he had another problem on his hands. A local missionary had descended upon the Eskimos, spouting that they would be going with people who were not Christians and who would leave them stranded on Wrangel Island so that they could never again see home or family.

Noice decided he needed to gather the Eskimos and urge them to follow him to the missionary's house. He rapped on the door and was greeted by the disgruntled missionary, dressed in a nightgown.

Noice proceeded to give the man an earful. As a "Christian fostering the spiritual welfare of the natives," he told him, the missionary should "permit them to go to the rescue of those in dire straits or worse and who if alive must be famished to see their families and friends."

His words were ignored, and Noice had no choice but to throw his hands up and turn away. "I am leaving at once," he told the Eskimos, "and if you fail me I will select my crew from points farther north." Exasperated, he returned to the shore, and before long heard the sounds of running feet behind him. Turning, he saw the entire party of Eskimos following him.

It was a sweet but brief victory. Afterward, the day just got worse. When Noice arrived on the ship with the Eskimos, Captain Hansen—a contrary, difficult man to begin with—refused to accept the additional supplies, dogs, or hunters. He gave no reason, but stood firm, and, when it was clear that no argument would change his mind, Noice was forced to ask for the skipper's resignation. Hansen left the ship and Noice was relieved that the rest of his crew was willing to remain. They raised ship's anchor and aimed her nose toward Point Hope, where they hired a second Eskimo family.

Even though he liked to fancy himself a skilled explorer, Noice knew little about navigation. Ship's owner Alexander Allen had pulled out of the venture at the last minute, fearing the Russians. With Hansen also gone, that left the extremely inexperienced Noice as captain and navigator. He quickly promoted first mate Hans Olson to sailing master, but the burden of responsibility still rested heavily on Noice's shoulders.

Wrangel Island, in a perfectly clear season with perfectly clear sailing conditions, was only four days from Nome by ship. Such conditions only occurred by chance a few days or weeks out of the year. The rest of the time it was difficult or impossible to reach the island by boat. Since they were already as far as Cape Blossom, Noice naively hoped to make the trip in two days, even though he would have set a record in doing so. The ship's new engines were running strong and fast, the vessel itself was snug and sleek and shipshape, and the crew and passengers now meshed harmoniously. "So far we have gone according to our schedule," he wrote to A. J. T. Taylor, "and I do not anticipate future trouble of any kind which will cause me to modify my plans."

From the crow's nest, they could see nothing but rippling blue-green in every direction and not one speck of white. They expected to meet ice at any time, but there was nothing. Then, on August 11 in the middle of the night, the temperature fell to 37 degrees, and at 4:30 A.M. the sea began to bob with white. They sailed through cautiously and before long the ice stretched across the horizon, infinite and unyielding. They edged backward until they found a lead of open water, and slithered through toward the southwest. They would follow the pack toward the island for as long as they could.

Then the fog was upon them, creeping in from all sides until they were surrounded. The ship maneuvered its way through blindly, plowing through the ice. The engines labored and pushed, but finally collapsed and fell stubbornly silent.

"What's the matter with the damn thing now?" Noice demanded as his engineers furiously took the equipment apart. A needle valve had broken, but they thought they could fix it. Noice climbed to the deck to wait it out, pacing restlessly. The engines could not have failed at a more ominous time. There was an iceberg dead ahead of them, and the current was carrying the ship toward it. It was a hulking, nasty mountain, water dripping off its sides, looming nearly as tall as the ship's mast.

Everyone on board seemed to stand frozen in place until they heard the miraculous chug of the engines. With one of the engineers at the carburetor and one at the clutch, they were able to back themselves clear. Noice clung to the rigging, barking directions, while the first mate steered her free of danger.

They spent ten breathless days bucking the ice floes, and the ship barely escaped plunging to the bottom of the sea. The *Donaldson*'s bulkhead was water tight, but Noice didn't know how long she could withstand the pressure. Steering through ice floes was exceptionally tedious and slow work. There was no such thing as sailing the open sea because the ice dictated your path. With every floe they dodged, every twisted, zigzagging lead they followed, they only added more miles to the trip. The bow was smashed and painstakingly repaired by covering it with an enormous walrus hide; the engines broke down again; and Noice was rooted to the deck the entire time they traveled through the pack. He and his first mate roamed the decks in the same clothes they had worn when the ship set sail from Nome. There was no time to change shirts or pants or underwear, barely time to eat. Noice climbed to the masthead barrel to strain his eyes over the horizon, searching for Wrangel Island, but there was no land in sight, only a low layer of fog, dark, thick, and stubborn.

At least he would have plenty to write about. Per his contract with the North American Newspaper Alliance, Noice had had to dispatch two to three hundred words each day before sailing, describing his plans and preparations, and any newsworthy developments and incidents. After sailing, he was to take pictures and keep track of all the excitement of the journey, so that he could later supply the newspapers with photographs and stories of the crew, the ship, and the rescued members of the Wrangel Island party. If all went well, he would have a terrific tale to tell when he returned. If all failed, he would make headlines of a different kind.

*   *   *

But whosoever drinketh of the water that I shall give him shall never thirst; but the water that I shall give him shall be in him a well of water springing up into everlasting life.

On the days when it was too windy or rainy to go outside or when she was too tired to move, Ada stayed in her tent and read about the Samaritan woman in the Bible who was talking to Jesus. The woman was drawing water from a well when Jesus asked her for a drink. "How is it that thou, being a Jew, askest drink of me," the woman replied, "which am a woman of Sa-ma-ri-a? for the Jews have no dealings with the Sa-mari-ans."

When Jesus spoke of living water, the woman did not understand, nor when he mentioned the gift of God. The woman asked why he thought himself better than others, better than the well, to offer such a thing as living water.

"Whosoever drinketh of this water shall thirst again," he replied. *But whosoever drinketh of the water that I shall give him shall never thirst; but the water that I shall give him shall be in him a well of water springing up into everlasting life.*

The woman had five husbands and she did not understand.

"But the hour cometh," Jesus told her, "and now is, when the true worshippers shall worship the Father in spirit and in truth: for the Father seeketh such to worship him. God *is* a Spirit: and they that worship *him* must worship him in spirit and in truth."

It was then the woman seemed to comprehend what he was saying. She knew the Messiah was coming and that he would be called Christ, and when he came he would tell them all things.

Jesus saith unto her, "I that speak unto thee am he."

The woman was not a smart woman, nor a good woman, nor a brave woman, yet she met Christ and he showed her what it was to believe. Because she believed, there would be salvation for her and everlasting life.

With great care, Ada marked the passages in the Bible that spoke to her the most directly. There were those that comforted and those that instilled fear in her heart, making her vow to be good.

But if ye will not hearken unto me, and will not do all these commandments; I will even appoint over you terror, consumption, and the burning ague, that shall consume the eyes, and cause sorrow of heart: and ye shall sow your seed in vain. . . .

And if ye walk contrary unto me, and will not hearken unto me; I will bring seven times more plagues upon you according to your sins. I will also send wild beasts among you, which shall rob you of your children.

Trust in the Lord with all thine heart; In all thy ways acknowledge him, and he shall direct thy paths. Fear the Lord, and depart from evil.

Ada embraced God fully and her daily Bible readings became increasingly important as the food became scarce and the holes in her tent grew beyond repair. It was August now, and the ship should have been there in July, as far as she could figure. The men had looked for one last year in July and had shown the first stirrings of restlessness by August. Perhaps no ship would come for her. The bay was rapidly filling with ice and Mr. Stefansson might not be able to reach her. She might very well have to face a winter alone, without the sound of another human voice, with only the shelter of her fragile tent, and with no food to sustain her other than the game she could hunt.

But God was near and she prayed to him to take care of her and to give her the strength to survive. Every day, she thanked God and Jesus in her diary, and asked God to forgive her sins.

She vowed to be grateful for each day she lived from now on, and she made sure to note her gratitude to God in her journal entries. "Thank living God . . . that help me every day and night if God be with me till I should get home again I thank God very much that he had mercy on me and forgive my sins," she wrote on August 1.

She prayed he would forgive her sins, just as Jesus had forgiven the Samaritan woman.

She was making Bennett a pair of slippers, sewing beads on them to make them handsome so that he would like wearing them when— if—she got home again.

On August 2, she shot five birds, and she thanked the good Lord for her bounty. On August 3, she collected some greens to boil up with the meat and saw a polar bear some distance away inland. But the bear didn't come closer, and the ice had opened up around the shore, and so she thanked God.

She finished Bennett's slippers on August 4 and set them aside so that they would be safe and ready for when she took them to him if a ship came. When she took a walk to stretch her legs she spotted a bear track on the east side of her tent, but no bear in sight. Not that Ada could see very far; the fog had crept in, thick and low, so that she couldn't see much past the beach. But the shore looked clear of ice cakes.

After she had finished reading her Bible, Ada picked up some of the books the men had brought to the island. She began to read about Frederick A. Cook, the explorer, who had spent two decades in the Arctic and Antarctic. The men had loved to read and sometimes they had lent Ada their books. Now they were her books and she would read as many as she could.

On August 5, she tried out her new canvas boat, launching it into the shallow water offshore and climbing inside with her gun. She was going duck hunting, and with the umiak she had a better chance of reaching the birds in their distant pool of water. There was frustration as she paddled out to them but couldn't seem to get close enough. But there was happiness and relief because the ice was moving west and beyond it the sea was open. If the sea was open, a ship might still come. The next day, she was able to shoot a gray bird with two eggs, and then she washed her hair and thanked "the Lord Jesus Christ the saviour."

She spent a foggy morning on August 7 at home, reading Frederick A. Cook, and opened a tube of dental cream and thanked God again that the ice had now disappeared in the sea. "So it looks like . . . I was going to see boat coming," Ada wrote in her diary. She could only see a mile or two into the horizon, but there were no patches of white to mar the blue-black surface of the sea.

She was desperately lonely and she missed Lorne Knight. Sometimes she slipped into his tent to visit him and to sit beside his body in silence. There was a comfort in having him near, even if he was no longer able to hear her or speak to her. She longed for him to return as she longed for the other three young men to come back with a ship to take her home. But she thanked her "saviour Jesus" for keeping her from loneliness because she was trying so hard to be good and to be grateful for all she had been given.

On August 9, she inserted a new fur lining inside her moose mittens and sheltered and bolstered her tent with logs. The temperature was dropping steadily, although the sun still sat high and bright in the sky, and Ada knew she must continue to prepare for winter, in case the ship could not get through. She would need to have a head start on the foul weather and cold which was to come. She must repair her tent as best she could to keep out the chill. She must stock wood and mend her clothing so that she would not risk frostbite when she was outside hunting.

There were walrus and bearded seals to the east of camp and close to shore, but the walrus were too far, the bearded seals too slippery. She hauled wood and took an entire roll of pictures of herself and a young bird she found. She set the bird on top of a box and took pictures of it, and then she knitted a seal net for hunting and thanked the Lord Jesus for another day.

She dreamed that night that the boss—Stefansson—asked her what she would have from the store, and she answered that it would be a case or nothing because she would be staying on this island for two years.

The next morning, when she awoke, she found the lard can empty of the seal blubber she had stored there and knew that once again a polar bear had come during the night to feast. She would have to be more careful if her blubber was to last the winter.

She finished her seal net on August 13 and began to knit a pair of winter gloves for her callused and toughened hands. She had worked them hard and they would probably never be soft or ladylike again.

She took more pictures of herself the next day and of a bird that she shot, and then took photographs of the mountains, which rose so majestically from the fog covering the earth.

There were more walrus off the beach on the evening of August 15, and again she wrote a diary entry thanking Jesus.

She saw the walrus on August 16, too, and that day made an eider duck cap for her mother, because she knew her mother would like it very much. The next day, she took one shot at a walrus whose giant form was stretched across the ice—the ice that had begun to return. She hit him once, but didn't kill him, but still she thanked her savior Jesus, "and I thank Jesus loves my little boy Bennett."

On August 18, she finished her right glove and began the left one. Her hands would be warm for winter, and that was something to be glad about.

On August 19, the wind blew in angrily from the west and the ice once again began sliding out to sea. Ada watched it and hoped it would go, go, go forever, until the sea was open for a ship. But the ice paused in the harbor and refused to move any farther.

On August 20, Ada finished her new pair of gloves and opened the last of the biscuits. After this tin of bread, the only food would come from the animals that roamed the island, if she was lucky enough to have good aim and strong enough to bring the meat back to camp.

In the distance, there was the sound of thunder. Walrus perhaps. The ice had drifted again and now lingered just below the belt of the far horizon. The path looked clear. The fog lifted. Yet again, Ada thanked the Lord Jesus and his Father that she was still alive.

* * *

Noice and his crew could not shake their sense of gloom. They had miraculously made it through the ice but had begun to despair of finding anyone alive on Wrangel Island. The low, black cliffs of the island pierced the belly of the fog. They were formidable. Beyond, the mountains rose, at once graceful and stark. "It seemed to us that no human being could find a foothold, let alone a living in such a desolate place," Noice observed.

When day broke and the forbidding shoreline was revealed as not just gravel but also moss-covered prairie, Noice felt his hope returning. A herd of walrus roared at the ship from the edge of the pack, and at the sight of them, the Eskimos aboard immediately brightened as well. They had spent most of the trip from Nome sulking and brooding, but the walrus restored their good spirits and told them, more clearly than Noice's words, that this was good country.

A skin boat was lowered and several Eskimos sailed off to hunt. They killed two of the massive walrus and towed them to a nearby ice cake and waited for the *Donaldson* to pick them up. When they were hoisted aboard, the rest of the Eskimos began to chant a traditional walrus song in celebration until the mood of the ship became festive and joyful.

As they approached the section of the coast where Noice expected to find Crawford, Knight, and the others waiting, everyone kept a lookout, some up in the rigging, some in the crow's nest, others on deck. "Prepare a special dinner for the marooned," Noice told the steward. His optimism was growing.

By Noice's guess, the *Donaldson* was near the old *Karluk* camp at Rodger's Harbour, where he expected to find the stranded party. But as he stood on deck, studying the land through his field glasses, Noice could see no sign of life on the shore. There were no tents, no evidence that anyone had lived there. The fog rolled back in suddenly, sweeping down upon them in great, gray clouds, and his vision was obscured. Noice ordered the ship's speed cut down to a quarter, and they crept at a snail's pace, hugging the shore as closely as they dared.

Ten miles farther, he and his men discovered an abandoned camp. Perhaps Crawford had moved his group to another spot on the island to summer or to winter. Noice and his men went ashore and picked through the debris, searching for clues, and found a slender, oblong box buried in the mud. Inside was a bottle, which contained a piece of paper sealed with tallow. Noice opened it and read the claim to Wrangel Island, in the name of King George, dated September 16, 1921. The names of all four men—Crawford, Knight, Maurer, and Galle—were signed at the bottom.

But although Noice and his men searched thoroughly for a monument or perhaps a cave where they might have left other records, there was no other trace of Crawford's party. Now with a nagging sense of worry and a bit of the old gloom returning, Noice steamed the *Donaldson* along the coast, through the fog that covered the sea, the ice, and the island. It was hard to see anything. They nudged the ship along, creeping along the shore, and stopping to investigate every large stone or mound they saw, in case it should offer some clue. They blew the ship's whistle continuously, hoping someone might hear it and come out to greet them.

Finally, on the morning of August 20, the Eskimos on deck let out a great, exuberant shout. They were pointing through the fog toward the shore, and when his eyes focused, Noice saw a figure standing on the beach. At first, he could not tell if it was real or ghostly, but as the ship drew closer he could see it was human.

Full speed astern, he ordered, and then brought the ship to a complete stop. They were near Doubtful Harbour, as far as he could tell. "Were we in time after all?" he wondered. "Certainly some one still lived upon the island, and soon we should know whether all survived or not." He gave orders to launch one of the skin boats and, with several of the Eskimos, Noice climbed into the umiak and pointed her toward shore and the figure, who stood facing them, hands outstretched in a silent plea.

*   *   *

All through the night, Ada had dreamed of a ship, but when she awoke she could see nothing but fog. The fire had died while she was sleeping, and Ada huddled inside early on the morning of August 20, building it back again. The warmth was always a comfort to her. Hearing a strange, rumbling sound in the distance, she assumed it was the walrus. She began preparing her breakfast of tea, seal oil, and a bit of dried duck. But the sound persisted, muffled by the fog, and growing steadily stronger. Ada stopped what she was doing and listened.

Then she picked up her field glasses and ran from her tent, up the ladder to her platform. The fog enveloped the land and Ada could see nothing. The rumble continued. She peered through her glasses, directing them out to sea, and strained her eyes until the fog shifted and there, like a phantom, was the mast of a ship.

Ada jumped from the lookout post to the ground beneath and rushed to the beach, the binoculars bobbing against her waist from the string she had slung over her shoulder. She walked right into the water and began splashing toward the ship.

And then she saw the skin boat with a white man and some Eskimos, coming toward the island. The white man had a shock of dark hair and a homely face and he was no one Ada knew. She had expected Crawford or Galle or Maurer. Perhaps they waited for her on the ship and she would see them again shortly, just as soon as the white man and his Eskimos came for her.

Noice watched her as they paddled closer, and as soon as he reached her, he leapt from the little boat to take her hand. She had the look of a hunter, he thought. She was dressed in furs, from head to foot, with a snow shirt worn over a reindeer parka trimmed with wolf skin. Her face was lined and dirty, toughened by brutal winds and cold and hardship.

They regarded each other silently for a moment, and then Ada tilted her face upward and pushed back her hood. "Where is Crawford and Galle and Maurer?" she asked. "Why is not Mr. Galle with you?"

The questions took Noice by surprise. He had expected to find all of the men on the island, just as Ada clearly expected to find them on the ship. He told her as gently as possible that he had just arrived from Nome and that there had been no word of them there. "I expected to find them all on Wrangel Island," he told her.

Ada's eyes widened and swiftly brimmed with tears. "There is nobody here but me," she choked. "I am all alone."

Again, Noice was stunned. What of Lorne Knight?

"Knight, he died on June 22," Ada told him. Her voice was broken; her expression dazed. "I want to go back to my mother. Will you take me back to Nome?"

Yes, of course, he told her, and then Ada collapsed. Noice had no idea how long she had been alone, but by the look of her toughened face, her scarred and callused hands, he knew she had been fending for herself for quite some time. Noice held her as she sobbed and assured her that she was safe now. Her ordeal was over. They would take her home.

She heard the man calling, "Keep to the left,
if you want to get home and see your father
and mother." But she kept running along the
smooth road, and just then she looks back, and she
is out of the sea and into the air; and as she looks
back the trail behind her fades away . . .

—ADA BLACKJACK
"The Lady in the Moon"

Fifteen

NOICE PICKED UP ADA and carried her to the umiak. They rowed her back to the ship and Noice ushered her below to his cabin and warmed her with a cup of hot coffee. She managed to eat some break-fast, and then, when he felt she was ready, he asked her to tell him what had happened to her and to the others. Every now and then, she interrupted herself to say, "I wonder if this is only a dream?" or "I can hardly believe that you have come."

Ada told him how Crawford, Galle, and Maurer had left for Siberia in January, taking all the dogs with them, and how a storm blew in the next day. She never doubted that they would make it to the main-land and then on to Nome, as they had planned. It never occurred to her that they might be lost in the ice and the winds and snow. Ada was distraught at the thought that her friends might be missing or dead, and Noice had no words to comfort her. There had been no sightings, no reports of three white men landing on the Siberian or Alaskan coasts.

Ada was convinced they would turn up somewhere, but Noice was not so confident. He knew how difficult it was to traverse the ice, and how fickle and volatile the pack could be. If a gale had blown up with force, as Ada had described it, the men might easily have fallen through the ice or been crushed by shifting floes.

Even with Maurer's knowledge of the Arctic, it would be hard to find a safe path over the water in such winds and blinding snow. Then there was their inexperience in ice travel—only Maurer, to Noice's knowledge, had ever made a journey of such peril, but that was over a different route and under the guidance of the seasoned and savvy ice master Robert Bartlett. Added to that, the men and the dogs must have been in a weakened condition when they set out on their journey. Ada had described the lack of food, the alarming shortage of game.

Noice had the crew fix up a small cabin for Ada on the *Donaldson*, and there she sat and wrote out the story of her time on the island. "I had hard time when he was dying," she wrote of Knight. "I never will forget that all my life. I was crying while he was living. I try my best to save his life but I can't quite save him."

Noice and Ada returned to the island by themselves after she was warmed and fed. The day had turned dismal, Noice noted, as he paddled the skin boat to the beach. Ada sat quietly, watching the shoreline. Surveying the camp, it was hard for Noice to believe anyone could have lived that way, in those conditions, for long. That Ada had done so, on her own for all those months, was a miracle.

Two thin and tattered tents were perched near each other. There was a scattering of broken boxes across the gravel of the beach. Ada pointed to the larger of the tents. "Knight—he dead man now—he stay inside over there. Better we go first to my tent."

She led Noice to the smaller tent, where there was a tiny cupboard of boxes in which she kept her ammunition and field glasses, and a crudely built canvas boat, tied near the entrance. Ada's gaze fell on it with pride. "After Knight die and birds and seal come I work hard to make a little boat so can get anything I shoot in the water," she said.

She led Noice into her tent, which hung like loose flesh from the driftwood spokes she had erected. Inside there was a decrepit, fire-eaten stove made of kerosene tins and a pile of driftwood. There was an old teakettle sitting atop a small box, which contained the remainder of Ada's food—bits of hard bread and a few scraps of dried meat. Noice's eyes skimmed the sleeping platform against the rear wall, the threadbare reindeer skins which covered it, and the guns which hung on the rack overhead. The tent was chilly and the cool air and mist drifted in through the holes in the canvas. "Such was the habitation in which this girl had slept, eaten, hoped and waited—praying that help would come," he observed.

It had always struck Noice profoundly how elements of the outside world lost all significance in the Arctic. "The white man's customs go the way of the mist. The world of newspapers, business, telephones, ballot-boxes, and jazz seems in memory no more real than his dream does to the sleeper awakened. Is it possible that somewhere there are people even now being ostracized by their kind for eating olives with a fork or peas with a knife? People who judge a man by his grooming, his bank account, or his ancestry? Our new world has stripped us to the fundamentals; and it is salutary, if not a little humbling, to reflect that these fundamentals—intelligence, character, and health—are not peculiarly human, that they are the same with men, with horses, with dogs, and with the ants."

Noice sat down on a box while Ada lit a fire. "I'm sorry I can't give you any good thing to eat," she told him, "but I make a little tea." The gesture was poignant. Soon she had the fire burning and the chill air of the tent began to warm. Noice watched Ada make the tea and began to relax to the hum of the kettle, the glow of the fire, when a gray-striped cat wound its way out from behind a box and walked over to Ada. She bent to lift the creature to her chest, stroking its fur, calling it by name—Vic, the expedition cat, looking fit and fat and content in Ada's arms.

They buried Lorne Knight on August 21. A simple wooden cross, bearing his name and the date of his death, was erected over his grave. Ada gave Knight's diary to Noice and he also collected some notes Galle had kept, along with Galle's typewriter. There was a large box of ivory that the men had gathered, as well as some walrus and mastodon tusks they had found. Noice confiscated these, along with the four sacks of furs they had managed to save. Ada herself had collected sixteen furs, which she kept tucked in a flour sack, and she sold fifteen of these to Noice at $28.00 each, which made her feel quite rich afterward. She didn't know—and no one bothered to tell her—that she could have sold them for $100 apiece in Nome or Seattle.

She did keep a few items from Noice—specifically Knight's field glasses and the Bible he had given her, the one that had belonged to his grandfather, which she wanted to return to his parents herself. She was desperate to keep the book, more than anything she had ever wanted to possess in her life, but she knew the right thing was to return it to Knight's family.

Ada and Noice remained on the island for several days while the crew and Eskimos unloaded supplies from the ship and Charles Wells organized his camp. Then they collected Ada's few belongings and Vic and returned to the ship. Ada took a last, lingering look at the island that had been her home for two years, and then turned away. She would never go back there because Wrangel Island meant only death and disaster, just as the shaman had predicted. She intended to live the rest of her days at home with Bennett and her family, away from bears and guns and death.

Once on the boat, Ada recognized some of the Eskimos from Nome and asked them about her son. How was he, she wanted to know. Was he happy and well? Did he miss her? Did he think of her? Did he know she was coming back for him? They told her he was doing fine. There was only one letter waiting for her, from a friend, and Ada felt her heart sink. She had hoped for and expected letters from her sister, telling her about her family and about Bennett.

The Eskimos aboard ship told Ada that if Mr. Noice were captain instead of first mate Hans Olson, they would have mutinied before reaching Wrangel Island. It was an odd comment and one Ada shrugged away. Noice had, after all, saved her life, and she would be forever indebted to him for rescuing her and bringing her home. She would always remember him for what he had done for her, and she believed that she would not be alive, if not for him.

Noice, meanwhile, sat in his cabin and pored over the diary of Lorne Knight. He was startled by what he saw to be the incompetence of Knight, Crawford, Maurer, and Galle—the stores they took to the island, the methods of hunting, decisions made. Noice felt he could have done much better. But the most shocking part of it all was Ada. Throwing herself at Crawford, tied to a flagpole, sent to bed without supper, made to sleep in the cold. Noice had heard rumors in Nome about the woman—that she was a prostitute—and the fact that she had been taken along as the only female with four young men seemed to him disturbingly suspicious. If the wrong people should get hold of Knight's diary, it would be humiliating for the expedition and everyone involved, himself included. A foolish woman; primitive punishments. It was indecent and the information contained therein could discredit the men and mar their reputations, he believed, as well as the reputation of Stefansson, should word of it ever leak out.

* * *

They sailed for Nome on August 23 and reached its harbor on August 31. As soon as he landed, Noice wrote out a telegram and wired it to Stefansson:

Nome, Alaska, Aug. 31–Sept. 4, 1923. Arrival last night Wednesday, Blackjack only survivor stop buried Knight August twentieth stop Crawford, Galle, Maurer left Wrangel January twenty eighth nineteen twenty three stop believe entire party perished you notify relatives of boys as you think best stop have left colony of two Eskimo families two unmarried Eskimo men, in charge of Wells stop equipped party for two years sojourn stop game conditions Wrangel apparently excellent stop failure of last expedition due to combination poor equipment and inexperience.

1. Crawford with rifle, preparing for the hunt.

2. Lorne Knight after his walk to Skeleton Island.

3. Milton Galle with Vic.

4. Crawford on the beach in summer as the ice closes in.

5. Fred Maurer watching for a ship.

6. Ada in hunting costume (self-portrait).

7. Ada and Knight's camp in May of 1923.

8. The rescue ship *Donaldson*.

9. *Donaldson* commander Harold Noice on the approach to Wrangel Island.

10. Ada, wearing the reindeer parka she made for herself, meets her rescuers (note the platform she constructed in the background).

11. Ada standing over Lorne Knight's grave.

12. Ada on the rescue ship *Donaldson*.

13. Ada and Vic aboard the rescue ship on the way home to Alaska.

14. Alma Galle, awaiting word from her son.

15. Professor Crawford, Helen Crawford, and Allan's younger brother, Johnnie.

16. Mary Maurer and Nigeraurak, or Nicki, the cat Fred saved from the *Karluk* expedition.

17. Ada with Georgia and John Knight outside their home in McMinnville, Oregon.

18. The diary of Lorne Knight, defaced by Harold Noice.

19. Ada as heroine (circa 1924).

20. Bennett in California, February 25, 1924.

21. Ada on porch, shortly after her return from California.

22. Ada, discovered by a reporter, gathering driftwood on the beach in Unalaska in 1935.

23. Ada trying to disappear in a crowd.

24. Ada with son Billy in 1973, posing once again for newspaper photographers.

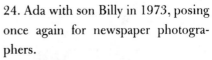

25. Ada in the home of the Maurers in the mid-1970s, working on her favorite puzzle.

26. Ada Blackjack, former Arctic heroine, at Palmer Nursing Home during her last years.

27. Ada's final resting place in Anchorage, Alaska.

Ada was anxious to leave the ship so that she could be reunited with her family and her son. But she was told by Noice and the other men aboard that she must wait. Ada did not understand this at first, but it soon became clear that the men held her under suspicion in the death of Lorne Knight. Ada knew she had done the best she could to look after Knight and to heal him, but now these men were asking her questions and telling her she must convince them that she did not murder him. Ada grew increasingly frantic and frightened. She had come so far and she was ill and tired. She wanted only to see Bennett and to know that he was safe. But now these men were asking her about poor Mr. Knight again and again, forcing her to relive the nightmare. At last, her sister Fina was allowed to come aboard with her family and stand by Ada.

Finally, after Noice and his comrades were satisfied, Ada was allowed to gather her few belongings—including Vic—and leave the ship. She enjoyed a tearful reunion with her sister Rita, who told her that the party of Wrangel Island had long ago been reported dead, and that they had given up hope of ever seeing her again.

For Ada, setting foot on the dirty streets of Nome felt like a wonderful dream. But she barely had time to enjoy the feeling of home and the familiar faces of family before she must face the reality that it was a changed world she had returned to. The first female U.S. senator had been elected in 1922; the first birth control clinic had opened in New York; Lenin had formed the Union of Soviet Socialist Republics (USSR); the first transcontinental airplane flight was made from New York to San Diego in twenty-six hours and fifty minutes; and President Harding had died while in office. But Ada's personal world had changed just as drastically. Jack Blackjack had died while she was away, drowned in a river. Her stepfather had also passed away, and her sister had had a baby. She had named the child Ada, in honor of her brave sister, who was lost in the Arctic.

Ada blamed no one for the disaster of the trip. She felt no animosity or resentment toward Mr. Stefansson or Marshal Jordan, the Nome chief of police who had encouraged her to go, or anyone else. "It was no one's fault but my own that I went up there," Ada said, "for no one would have forced me to go, but I wanted to go and thought I would never have another chance to go so I took it."

Noice, meanwhile, was detained by the Nome marshal, E. R. Jordan, and escorted to the U.S. revenue cutter *Bear*. The charge: He was warned before sailing for Wrangel Island by the captain of the *Bear* not to take any Eskimos to the island and leave them. After an intense two-hour session, Noice was released and free to go on his way.

One of the first things he did was to look up Frances Allison—the intriguing lady he had met on his trip to Alaska—who was still in Nome. Ada had given Noice her own diary as well, and he asked Frances to help him decipher it. Then he tracked down Carl Lomen of Lomen Brothers, the local businessman who had helped to outfit both the original and the relief expeditions, to show him the diary kept by Lorne Knight. He wanted Lomen to see for himself what Noice was up against and to ask his opinion about what he thought Noice should do.

*   *   *

Stefansson was in England when he received the telegram on September 1. Publicly, he reacted with shock. "Crawford's death is terribly tragic news," he told the *Twin Falls News*. "I knew the situation of the party was critical, but I did not expect this sudden end."

There should have been enough game to sustain the men, he told the papers. "One good hunter can provide food for ten dependents so long as his ammunition holds out," and his party had had plenty of ammunition.

In private, he felt it enormously important to "prevent, as far as possible, the ordinary distortions which the press is accustomed to give to any events that happen in remote regions under conditions not familiar to the average reader." In other words, Stefansson wanted to keep the whole matter as quiet as possible in the papers, which would surely paint his Friendly Arctic as a most unfriendly place. "I knew even before the details came out that freezing or starvation was not likely to have played an important part," he conjectured, "but I knew equally that the press always assigns any polar tragedy to the routine reasons of hunger and frost. Their doing so now would go a long way towards making fruitless the work for which our young men had died."

Their doing so would also go a long way toward surrounding Stefansson with the sort of controversy to which he had grown all too accustomed—his responsibility for the loss of young, inexperienced men who embarked upon Arctic expeditions under his command, or at his prompting, without proper training, equipment, or supplies. The last thing Stefansson wanted was to be embroiled in another scandal, and if the papers started printing the words *starvation, hunger, frostbite*, he would be in for disgrace and humiliation.

He telegraphed his business associates in the United States immediately to make sure they negotiated with the North American Newspaper Alliance for Allan Crawford's story and to inquire about the sale of possible movie rights. He also wanted letters sent to each family requesting the rights to the Wrangel Island diaries for publication. He sent word to Noice to secure Ada Blackjack's personal story and keep her from talking to interviewers. And he told his people to tell Noice to "minimize the starvation theory. Emphasize possibility breaking through ice both because less painful to relatives and favorable my success raising money to pay Noice's bills. Noice story yesterday has hurt our cause badly."

Then Stefansson wrote Noice directly to try to straighten him out about the reports he was giving before he did too much damage, and to discuss the issue of rights to the island documents. "We must keep our eyes on whatever silver lining there is to the Wrangel Island cloud," he said. "For one thing the tragedy has removed some of the previous apathy. The public interest has created a market value for the story. The things the boys believed in, worked for and eventually died for, can certainly gain nothing by being now abandoned. Both the publications and the lecturing will help."

*   *   *

Helen Crawford had a premonition that she would never see her son again. She fell into a deep melancholy in the winter of 1922, after the first relief attempt had failed, and had been inconsolable ever since. When the telephone rang at the Crawford house on Walmer Road some time after midnight on September 1, Mrs. Crawford knew that something was wrong.

The *Toronto Star* newspaper office had received word by cablegram from Harold Noice in Nome. Allan Crawford and his three male companions were dead. The conversation between one of the reporters from the newspaper and Professor Crawford was brief and to the point, and when the professor hung up the phone, he did not need to tell his wife what had happened. She knew by the ring of the phone, by the look on his face. Her eldest child was never again coming home.

One hour later, there was a knock at the front door, and a member of the newspaper staff stood on the step, bearing an eighty-word summation of the tragedy. Professor Crawford snatched it away, but before he could read it, Helen called out to him. She wanted to see the words for herself, to read them before anyone else, so that she could really know it was true.

Afterward, she gave herself up to grief. Unlike his wife, Professor Crawford had been confident Allan would survive. He had never been plagued by doubts or dark premonitions, and had been sure he would see Allan back at school in the fall, finishing his studies, resuming his vibrant, busy life at home. Allan was an athlete, scholar, friend, son, brother, model citizen. "Life looked so bright for him," his father lamented.

It would be hardest on Allan's mother. "He was her first born and her chum," the Professor told the *Toronto Star* that night. "Much as he meant to me, he meant more to her." He was reluctant to send the reporter away, afraid to be shut inside the house with his grief. It was easier to stand there, talking to a stranger.

The telegram from Stefansson came the next day, reading simply, "Deepest sympathy over terrible news." There was nothing more. No mention of the details, no information on Allan's death. All they were told was that he had died going for help.

The answers, they hoped, would be revealed in the days to come. They would have to comfort themselves with their remaining two children, Marjorie and Johnnie, and honor the memory of their fallen son with love and respect and pride. "He was a public figure, and his death is not merely our private grief but also a public matter," Professor Crawford told the press. "He was more than just our son and we must share him even in death."

And, thought Professor Crawford, they would get to the bottom of things, to find out just what had happened to Allan Crawford and why he had not come home.

*   *   *

All of the Maurers, including Delphine, anxiously awaited a telegram from Fred. The rescue ship, they knew, should be sailing into Nome's harbor any day now, and that meant there would be word from him. There had been no news of the ship turning back this year, as it had been forced to do last summer, and no reports of bad ice conditions on the sea.

Delphine had moved in with her parents in Niles, Ohio, ninety-one miles away from New Philadelphia. The last word she had heard from her husband came shortly after he landed on the island in the fall of 1921. He had sent a letter to her with the ship that had left him there. She had known Fred such a short time, and only enjoyed a handful of days with him as his wife before being separated from him for two long years. But she had remained faithful and true, and she wrote him regularly, even though she knew there was no way of sending the letters.

The waiting was the hardest part. Fred's parents, David and Mary, seemed to have aged considerably, and certainly their son's time in the Arctic took its toll on the health of each parent. But they were excited now, eager to see him, eager to welcome him home again.

Word came from Nome on September 1, but it wasn't the word they had expected or hoped for. Fred and the other men, dead on Wrangel Island. Only Ada Blackjack had survived.

Stefansson's telegram arrived shortly afterward: "Deepest sympathy to you all and Fred's wife."

All of Tuscarawas County was consumed with the devastating news. Fred had been a local hero, ever since returning from the Arctic in 1914 with the *Karluk*'s cat tucked under his arm, and the Maurers were well-loved in the community.

More information came later on the afternoon of September 1 from a United Press report. Something about Fred heading for Siberia with Crawford and Galle because of a shortage of food. Knight left behind, dead of scurvy. The other boys, missing.

Fred's brother John, who was now running the tailor shop for his father, told reporters that he, for one, did not believe Fred was dead. In his opinion, Fred and the others were merely lost somewhere up there. Perhaps they had taken the wrong direction. It was even possible they had been picked up by the Russians or that they were stranded somewhere on the Siberian coast, too ill or injured or lost to move. The papers were always full of news of Arctic explorers who disappeared into the frozen North, given up for dead, only to return a year or two later, unharmed. There were other possibilities, of course, he theorized. They might have eaten spoiled food and perished, or one of them might have become insane and killed the others and then himself. The last thing he was going to accept was that they had just vanished.

Meanwhile, Delphine prepared to come to New Philadelphia to be with Fred's family, and Mr. and Mrs. Maurer tried to comfort each other and their remaining children. "The Arctic has claimed a kind man," wrote the newspapers, while Nicki, the *Karluk* cat and Fred's prize souvenir from his time in the Arctic, was petted and pampered by her family.

* * *

In the early hours of September 1, Joe Abrahams opened the front door to his home on Academy Street in New Braunfels, Texas, and walked down the steps to fetch the morning paper. He picked it up, shook it open, and there, on the front page, was the headline. *Local Boy Missing in Arctic.*

There had been no word from Milton's parents, even though Joe was family, and so he rushed down the street, paper in hand, and knocked on the door of the Galle house.

Both of Milton's siblings, Alfred and Elsie, were away at college in Austin. With Milton expected back in the fall, the family had figured it was a good time for Elsie to leave home and follow her brother and her friends to school. So it was that Joe Abrahams found Harry and Alma at home alone that morning, and broke the news to them that Milton was dead.

There was no telegram from Stefansson, no word at all from the explorer. Instead, a wire arrived from A. J. T. Taylor and John Anderson on September 3. "We deeply regret to learn of the loss of the Wrangel Island party and your son Milton," it read. "Please accept our sincere sympathy stop cabled Stefansson to see if anything can be done through Siberian government to find trace of your son and party."

A telegram from Professor Crawford followed. "Deepest sympathy cabled Stefansson to request Siberian government to make inquiries for missing parties."

* * *

The telephone rang at four o'clock in the morning. Joseph Knight was the first to hear it, and when he picked it up, he heard the voice of the night officer for McMinnville on the other end. The man wanted to know if Joseph had heard the news, but when Joseph replied that he hadn't, the officer announced that he was coming to the house.

By the time he arrived, the Knights—Joseph and his parents—were awake, dressed, and fully assembled. The night officer clutched an early morning paper in his hand, which contained the first report of the relief expedition. The report was vague and brief, but it was enough to break the hearts of Lorne Knight's family.

Lorne was dead. While they had been eating and sleeping and enjoying every comfort of modern life, he had been dying just like a dog on a faraway island.

A later issue of the paper gave more details: Lorne, ill for months with scurvy, with only Ada Blackjack to care for him. The other boys gone to Siberia to find food and help.

Although they had understood—perhaps better than any of the other families—the dangers, the Knights had never really expected anything to happen to their boy. Mrs. Knight took it the hardest. She alone had fostered reservations about Lorne returning to the Arctic, and now she berated herself for not having stopped him.

John Knight thought of young Milton Galle, so full of promise and enthusiasm as he embarked on his first true adventure, and he felt tremendous guilt because he had assured the Galles all along that their son would be safe. He hoped they would not be angry with him or resent him, especially now when the families needed to pull together.

At least he knew what had happened to his son, as wretched as it was to know so much. But the Galles knew nothing and they might never know how their son died. He supposed there was a possibility— a slight one—that the three young men could have survived and were living somewhere, and he hoped the Galles would live on that and let it keep them optimistic through the upcoming days. He would hope and pray for them that Milton would turn up somewhere, and Allan Crawford and Fred Maurer, too.

The only comfort John Knight could find in it all—and it was much too soon to look for any deeper comfort—was that "they died in the discharge of their duty, they died with their faces to the front, that they did not show any white feathers, that they were no quitters, that they (if we could know) never complained . . . but carried on like real men."

Now he felt compelled to write to the Galles and try somehow to summon some words of comfort. And then he would wire Noice to find out if he had brought the body home so that they could look upon Lorne's face one last time and give him a proper burial. There was so much Mr. Knight wanted and needed to know, for himself and for his family—what Noice had seen out there and what the conditions of the camp and the island had been, whether Lorne left a letter or a diary or papers of any kind, and where his belongings were. Most important, he needed to know about Lorne's body. He was surprised Noice had not contacted him about it yet so that he could start making arrangements.

He would, he knew, always resent Captain Bernard for not being able to reach the island the year before. He wanted someone to blame right now, and Bernard seemed the best candidate. He should have tried harder, put forth more effort. But "this does me no good now," Mr. Knight wrote, "and does not restore our beloved boys nor can we ever right the wrong he has done them and us by his miserable failure."

He didn't know how he would ever again be able to think of his business. As words of sympathy flooded in from all over the country, he tried to take care of all that needed to be done for Mrs. Knight and Joseph and himself. First to write to the Galles, then to Mrs. Maurer. Lorne's fiancée, Doris Jones, must be told. And he must write to the Crawfords in Canada. The four families were now, after all, partners in grief and perhaps they could help each other.

His friends shook his hand or opened their arms and looked into his eyes with tears in their own, but they were speechless and there were no words to comfort such a loss. Stefansson's telegram, brief but sympathetic, did nothing to soothe their wounds. Mr. Knight couldn't even bear the thought that Joseph had nearly followed Lorne's path into the Arctic. He did not know what he would do without his other child.

On September 3, the Knights read in the paper that the ship *Victoria* was unloading cargo in Nome, which meant that she would soon be making her way down the coast to Seattle. They would be there to meet her at the dock so that they could talk to Noice and get the facts and collect their son's belongings and his remains. Mrs. Knight had been prostrate with grief, ever since the news broke, but still she insisted on collecting Lorne's body. "The ordeal is going to be awful for Mrs. Knight," her husband noted, "but . . . to refuse her would be worse than to take her."

Two days later, Mr. Knight still had heard nothing from Noice about Lorne's remains. Noice simply refused to answer his inquiries, and John Knight knew the *Victoria* was due in any day. He still had no idea if Lorne's body was on the boat or buried at sea or at rest on Wrangel Island. All of the old prejudices and resentments toward Noice arose once more. His grief over Lorne's death was painful enough. He should, at the very least, be treated with consideration over his son's remains.

"It seems to me," he wrote Stefansson, "that, all the glory this man Noice has gained in his expedition which he is making as spectacular and sensational as he possibly can, has gone glimmering in his failure to be the man equal to the occasion at a time when common decency should prompt him to lay aside his damnable greed for a few paltry dollars for column inches and been humanitarian about the matter."

Lorne's fiancée, Doris, was distraught over Lorne's death, and asked to make the trip to Seattle to meet the ship. Mr. Knight had to admit that, even given his reservations about her as a match for Lorne, she had been as true to his son "as steel," and so they would take her along, and keep her close to them.

There was just one thought that cheered John Knight in the midst of his personal heartbreak. The brave Eskimo woman who had taken care of his son. "How I wish I could make some suitable reward for Ada Blackjack," he wrote Stefansson. "She is the Heroine of the whole expedition. If it is ever in my power to suitably reward her, I hope I may not overlook the opportunity."

*   *   *

In Toronto, Noice consulted with A. J. T. Taylor about the diaries—Knight's and Ada's. He asked Taylor for permission to copy them and use them in his writings. As for Lorne Knight's diary, Noice wouldn't allow Taylor to look at the document, but he did hint at the objectionable material it contained. He made it seem more sensational, more shocking than it actually was because he wanted Taylor to think he had uncovered a scandal. Noice told Taylor that he planned to remove any offensive and questionable parts before he shared the diary with anyone. The newspapers would eventually find a way to get hold of it, and then there were the memories of the young men and the families to think of, Noice said, not to mention Ada herself.

Noice took it upon himself to fix the contents of the diary. There were two reasons, both urgent to him. The first was that Stefansson should not be allowed the chance to shift blame from himself to the four young men, and some of the information in the diary just might let him do that. There were certain passages that might enable Stefansson to twist the wording and reinterpret actions so as to deflect any fingers pointed in his direction toward the four well-meaning but incompetent men he had entrusted with his mission. It was just the sort of thing, thought Noice, that Stefansson would do. And, if Noice had his way, he would keep Stefansson from doing anything of the kind.

Secondly—and most pressing—he knew with a reporter's instinct that an edited journal would cause a sensation. No one should look upon this journal and see these things written, especially because they were not nearly as shocking as he was leading everyone to believe.

The more people wondered about the sections he removed, the more Noice would receive for telling the "true story." He was, first and foremost, an opportunist, and right now he smelled a huge opportunity, not only to make money but to gain the notoriety he craved.

Using a good eraser, he rubbed away numerous passages. Then he picked up a soft lead pencil and carefully drew hard black lines through the slanted impressions that remained on the paper, at times blacking out entire, lengthy sections. Whoever read the diary next would wonder what had been so shameful, so shocking that it had had to be destroyed. There would be a great scandal and plenty of press and only Noice and Noice alone would be able to answer questions about what the journal had actually contained.

Then, he ripped out pages 9–14, 19–22, 27–40, and 45–46 of Knight's diary, sealing them into an envelope. And he tore out the last ten pages and threw them away. He kept no record of them, made no notes of their content. Only Harold Noice would ever know what they had said. He would publicly vow never to speak of their contents to anyone.

*   *   *

Ada Blackjack could not go anywhere without drawing attention. She hated the crowds, the whispers, the stares as she walked down the street, the insistent way strangers called her name and reporters tried to trick her into talking to them. They tried to snap her picture, but she turned away and refused to speak. They were everywhere and they wouldn't let her alone, and all she wanted was to be with Bennett, to be left in peace, so that she could rest and recover.

She was a hero. The newspapers said so. She was the hero of the Arctic. The hero of Wrangel Island. They compared her to Joan of Arc and to Madame Butterfly, women she had never heard of. During her time on the island, she had dreamed of coming home, of the peace it would afford her, of returning to her simple, quiet life, which would be a comfort after all she had seen and endured.

She was constantly cold and tired and her feet still ached. There was a hunger in her gut which would not subside and she could not chase out of her head the image of Lorne Knight's lifeless body. She missed Crawford, and she missed her friend Galle, who had promised he would come back for her. She missed Maurer, too, with his kind manner and gentle voice, and she missed Knight.

Now she must make another life for herself and for Bennett. She would take the money set aside for her in the bank at Nome and she and Bennett would go to Seattle, where he could be cured in a hospital. Then she would make a nice life for them somewhere while she worked at her sewing or housework. She had done it before and she could do it again, and it would be easy now because she had lived to come home again, just as she had promised Bennett she would.

It was time to remake herself, to start afresh, and to give Bennett all the opportunities for a better life that she could afford with the money she had earned. Had it been worth it? A great deal of money had accumulated in her bank account while she was away as deposits were made each month from Stefansson's company. She was a rich woman now, or so she felt. But, like the girl in her favorite Eskimo story, she had come back home only to find her legs bent and broken, her body old and feeble, and nothing the way it used to be.

{ PART V }

FALLOUT

There was nothing for her to do but drop, and she did,
trying to keep her legs straight so she would be
young as she was when she left the earth.

—ADA BLACKJACK
"The Lady in the Moon"

MONTREAL STANDARD

September 9, 1923

❄

Mr. Stefansson Shows Results

As we pointed out in these columns some time ago, Mr. Stefansson's ambition to keep in the limelight was hardly worth risking the lives of three young men on a desolate Arctic island.

Since then, the three young men have died of hunger and disease, and Mr. Stefansson . . . is busy with the crocodile tears. The misadventure has obliged Mr. Stefansson to explain that he alone was responsible for the unfortunate expedition, and that Canadian Government had nothing to do with it. That it had not was no fault of Mr. Stefansson's, who begged hard enough that they relieved him of the expense.

The plain truth is, that the blood of these three young men is on the head of Mr. Stefansson. While they were starving to death on a frozen island to prove the Stefansson theory that an explorer could live off the country, Mr. Stefansson himself was prancing about from one luxurious spot of civilization to another, lecturing and telling what a hero he was. Meanwhile the three young men went on short rations, then on no rations at all, the food supply Mr. Stefansson had left behind being about one year short of the demand upon it.

For some time past Mr. Stefansson has been trying to wish himself and his plans on the Canadian Government. Not being successful in that he went north and discovered an island that had been discovered several times before—Wrangel Island, to wit—and tried to wish that on the Government. Failing again, he betook himself to England, and tried to wish this island, with which he had no business whatever, on the British Government. He failed in that also, but meanwhile, as we said before, the three young men on the island died.

After this it would be advisable for Mr. Stefansson to hold down his own islands.

Sixteen

THREE MEN WERE SPOTTED on the Siberian coast in September 1923. The report was telegraphed in from various Siberian coastal ships. Word of the sightings was sent to Nome, and from there wired to the Maurers in Ohio, the Crawfords in Toronto, and the Galles in Texas.

Until now, the question posed by all the newspapers was: What had happened to Crawford, Maurer, and Galle? In interviews, Stefansson stated that one of two scenarios must have occurred. The first was that they broke through the rough and tumultuous ice and drowned. Because the ice north of Alaska and Siberia was in constant motion, young, fragile ice grew between the heavier, more solid floes, making it dangerous for travelers. The fresh ice, when covered by snow, was hard to detect, especially in a storm such as the one the men encountered their second day out.

The second possibility was that they died during the long, cold Arctic night, taken by surprise by the unpredictable ice pack, which could split apart with no warning. There was the storm Knight had noted in his journal and that Ada had described—a blistering gale that sprang up just a day after they left camp, and which could have swept them away unexpectedly. This, Stefansson suggested, was the most logical conclusion.

But before there was ever a sighting of three men walking on the Siberian coast, rumors of a different nature began circulating. Fred Maurer's brothers John and Thomas believed them, as did Delphine, the Galles, and Professor Crawford. Maurer, Galle, and Crawford could still be alive. The threats from the Russian government must be taken into consideration. They had vowed to capture anyone who landed on the island. They had ordered outsiders to stay away from the island. Was it a stretch of the imagination to suppose that the Russians might have captured the boys, either on the ice or on the Siberian coast, and taken them prisoner?

No, Stefansson conceded to the press, it wasn't. Crawford, Maurer, and Galle might very well have made it across to Siberia and their loved ones might hear from them yet. The newspapers buzzed with the suggestion. "In view of the Soviet attitude, it is even possible that Crawford and his companions are prisoners."

"Is Allan Crawford still alive?" asked the *Toronto Star* on September 4. "Stefansson thinks so. If they succeeded, it would be nothing out of the ordinary in that region of slow travel for the news of their arrival in Siberia to be delayed up to the present. Trading vessels which visit that remote region, from American and Russian ports, will soon be returning. It is from these that Stefansson hopes to get any news that Siberia may have of the Crawford party. Until that time the whole world clings to the hope that the heroic explorer is still alive."

Sir Edmund Walker, president of the Canadian Bank of Commerce, told the *Toronto Star*, "The first thing for us to do is to cable Stefansson and Noice to ask their advice and their help and then send a party immediately to find Allan Crawford and his companions."

Stefansson, for his part, said he would defer to Noice on the matter. Noice alone knew how thoroughly he had searched the surrounding area for the missing men. With Wells's party now situated on Wrangel, Crawford and the others would be in fine shape should they return to the island from Siberia, where, perhaps, they had voluntarily spent the winter.

The disturbing thing, of course, was the friction between Russia and America. There were some unfortunate incidents in the past that had blackened the American image for the Siberian natives, such as when a Cossack officer was shot by an American captain, and when Russian police were taken prisoner and sent to Alaska. The latest tension, of course, now came from the claim on Russia's own Wrangel Island. Therefore, it was not without reason that the men from the Wrangel Island Expedition could have been captured and held against their will. Perhaps they were rotting in a Siberian prison even now.

Numerous trading ships had sailed from the Bering Strait toward the north coast of eastern Siberia and were expected to return by October 1923. If Crawford and the others were alive and safe, they would most likely return on one of those ships. Until then, Stefansson and the families would have to wait and not give up hope.

And then the reports came in of the sightings. Three white men walking along the northern Siberian shore. As soon as the cable from Nome was received, Thomas Maurer fired off a telegram to Stefansson: "Maurer's family believe Fred is alive in Russia. Request you investigate. Three men reported seen off Siberian coast."

Immediately, the three families rallied together. John Maurer had been gathering all the information he could on the fate of his brother, Crawford, and Galle, and he and Thomas shared the opinion that the men could very well have made it across the ice to Russia. Hadn't Captain Bob Bartlett made that same trip safely in 1914, after the ship *Karluk* had sunk? Why, then, was it so impossible to believe that these three young men could have done the same? It was some seven hundred miles from Wrangel Island to the nearest wireless station. The men could be wandering somewhere in northeastern Siberia, lost in a wilderness populated by only the most remote Eskimo villages. It could be months before they would reach anything resembling civilization.

The Maurer brothers appealed to their congressman and to the president of the Red Cross, who promised to send word to the Red

Cross outposts in Russia. They also sent a request to Secretary of State Charles Evans Hughes, asking him to appropriate sufficient money to send a party in search of the men. In Toronto, Professor Crawford contacted British government officials, who promised to do everything in their power to find the men. And in Texas, Alma Galle's brother Benjamin Nebergall also sent a letter to Secretary of State Hughes to ask, on "behalf of Milton Galle's grief-stricken parents," if the State Department was in the position to launch an inquiry into young Milton's fate.

Afterward, Mr. Nebergall wrote letters to the Honorable Morris Sheppard, U.S. Senator, as well as to the Honorable Harry M. Wurzbach, U.S. Representative from Texas. "If you can do anything to help this investigation along," he said, "it will certainly be greatly appreciated." An appeal was also made to Congressman C. B. Hudspeth.

The responses were quick. "I wish to assure you that I will do everything in my power to aid you and Mr. and Mrs. Galle in securing some information about their son," wrote Harry M. Wurzbach.

"I am at once transmitting your letter and the copy to my secretary at Washington," replied C. B. Hudspeth, "with instructions to her to at once call on the Secretary of State and render every assistance."

"I shall be glad to take up with the Secretary the matter of the investigation you refer to," penned Morris Sheppard, "and will advise you further."

*   *   *

The Knights and Miss Jones met Noice at the dock in Seattle on September 17. There were questions to ask about Lorne's illness, the Eskimo woman, Crawford's trip to the mainland, Lorne's diary, and any last letters home.

They followed Noice to his room at the Hotel Frye, where Mr. and Mrs. Knight and Joseph collected Lorne's possessions. Noice gave Mrs. Knight her letter from Lorne—the last one he had written, in case of his death. She was reduced to tears when she reached the line "all the love any boy could have for his Mother." When they inquired about Lorne's diary, Noice said that it would need to be photographed first by the expedition corporation, and once that was done the original would be sent to them.

But there was no body. Lorne, Noice told them, had been buried on Wrangel Island, just as the dead men of the *Karluk* had been gallantly laid to rest there, and Robert Scott had been buried a hero in the Antarctic. Noice had felt it a fitting tribute to Knight, to bury him where he fell, like a soldier in battle.

This news left Mr. and Mrs. Knight with an unspeakable emptiness, reaching even beyond all they had felt before. They knew Lorne was dead, and bringing his body home would not have done anything to change that. But it should have been their decision to make. They had yearned to rest their eyes on him once more, to have the sense that he had come home, at last, from his long expedition. And now they must face the fact that they would never see their son again.

* * *

On September 19, Senator Morris Sheppard received a letter from the Department of State about the Milton Galle case. The Department, it said, did not have any additional information regarding the members of the Wrangel Island Expedition beyond what was currently appearing in the press. However, the Department assured him that it would be certain to pass along any new information that might come to its attention.

There was no mention of the sightings off the Siberian coast, but William Phillips, the acting Secretary of State, did say that, "No information which would indicate that members of the expedition succeeded in reaching the Siberian mainland has been received by the Department from these sources." Furthermore, it was, according to the U.S. Coast Guard, impractical if not impossible for any ship to conduct an investigation for the men so late in the season.

There was also a discouraging reply from the office of Congressman Hudspeth. After an interview with the assistant to the Secretary of State, Hudspeth's secretary, Kate George, was told that American trading ships and a government vessel—the U.S. revenue cutter *Bear*— had called at every port on the Siberian coast in the vicinity of Wrangel Island, without finding any trace of the missing men. "He further stated that it would not be possible under any circumstances to send a relief expedition until about the first of June, next, as every port in that region is ice-bound from the first of October until that time. He did not state that it would be the intention of the Department to send any expedition even then, as they feel the cause to be about hopeless."

One week later, Sir Robert Falconer formally opened the University of Toronto 1923–1924 school session and paid tribute to former student Allan Crawford. Earlier, he had told reporters, "Certainly we cannot let an event like this pass by without some sort of tribute being made to his memory. Some sort of permanent memorial should be erected, something fitting to keep his deeds before the students of future years. Allan Crawford was a young hero, that is what he was, a young hero."

To the crowd gathered in the University of Toronto's Convocation Hall he said, "It is hard to abandon hope, but Canadians will always remember that this young man went forward with faith and that he deserves a place alongside the youth that fell in the Great War."

*　*　*

Stefansson arrived in the United States five weeks after the news of the tragedy broke. A. J. T. Taylor had written him with great concern to alert him to the bad feeling among the people of the press and the people of Canada. There was a great deal of ill will building toward Stefansson, and Taylor suggested they find someone to write something on his behalf before all hell broke loose.

Stefansson was sick of reading what he considered to be Noice's twisted words in the newspapers—words of hunger and starvation, words of Crawford and the others being desperately in need of food or help. Stefansson had not yet read any of the documents Noice had collected from the island—not Knight's diary nor Galle's notes nor Ada's journal—but he resented the implication that these men died of anything that could have been prevented. He believed that the truth would only come out after the diaries had been sorted through and read.

He reached New York on October 15 and was met by his associates, A. J. T. Taylor and John Anderson, who had traveled from Toronto to brief him on the latest goings-on. Noice had Knight's diary in his possession, they told him, and it contained controversial material, which could darken the news reports and make an already bad situation worse for everyone. Something about Ada Blackjack's conduct and the treatment of her by Knight and the others. Noice had destroyed the objectionable material, they said, without showing it to them first.

Stefansson met with Noice in New York the day after he arrived from England. Noice mentioned that he had taken time to sit down with Ada Blackjack and go over the lesser-known details of her story, since there were holes in the diary accounts. He then made it clear to Stefansson that, after having reviewed all the documents, he believed the men would be alive today if it weren't for their own incompetence. The outfitting of the party had been insufficient and inadequate, and he felt Stefansson should have traveled to the island himself to remain in command of the party. Noice also believed it was his right—given the contract he had signed with the Newspaper Alliance—to state this in his articles.

Stefansson was livid. He was already being condemned from Britain to Canada to the States over this fiasco, and he blamed it all on Noice for suggesting incompetence and inexperience to the public through the press. "Grotesque fallacy," one periodical had called Stefansson's leadership. "Neglect." "Lack of means and precautions." "Novices led away by a false lure and with little real knowledge of the problems with which they had to deal." "Needlessly perish." "Difficult to forgive."

"Could a land, from which comes so sad a tale, possibly be 'The Friendly Arctic' described by Stefansson?" wrote one newspaper.

"Wrangel Island is not worth the brave lives it has cost," stated another. "Mr. Stefansson, with his legend of 'The Friendly Arctic,' placed an estimate on Wrangel Island much above that of the Canadian people. He was not officially authorized to dispatch an expedition to the island to proclaim it British or Canadian territory. The value of the island, present or potential, is not to be weighed against the precious lives of Allan Crawford and his companions."

"No one can read the tale unfolded by Harold Noice who headed the relief expedition, so long delayed that it failed of its object by many months, without experiencing the deepest pain and anger at the tragic folly of the whole Stefansson enterprise," read an article entitled "The Un-Friendly Arctic," in *Saturday Night* on September 15, 1923. "Noice without openly censuring anybody makes it clear that the lives of all these victims would probably have been saved had there been any clear plan or adequate preparations in connection with Stefansson's Wrangel expedition. Thus they perished while the author of the wild enterprise was far away talking nonsense about the supposed strategical importance of Wrangel."

J. B. Tyrrell, Toronto mining engineer and geologist and a former member of the Dominion Geological Survey, also publicly condemned Stefansson. "We have no business at all on Wrangel Island," he told reporters. "The parents of Allan Crawford have my deepest sympathy in the loss of their son. It was a crime for Stefansson to send a young man like that to Wrangel Island. It would have been different if he had sent some old Norwegian or someone who had spent all his life in the Arctic. But instead he sent a youth who knew nothing about Arctic regions."

And one newspaper headline read simply, *Canada Humiliated.*

"There have been two victims of this ill-starred adventure," the article declared, "Allan Crawford, a patriotic Canadian, who found death among the ice floes of the Arctic, and a humiliated Canada."

Obviously, Stefansson believed, it had been a mistake to entrust Noice with the delicate and vital matter of reporting the news to the papers. Stefansson thought it was slanderous to say the men had been starving, so desperate for food that they had been forced to hike across the ice to Siberia. He was determined to keep Noice from continuing to say these things. Otherwise, everything Stefansson had worked for—his reputation and, in particular, his championing of the cause of the Friendly Arctic—was at risk of being obliterated.

Starvation as a motive for their fatal crossing to Siberia was highly unlikely, Stefansson told the press. "Crawford crossed to the mainland of Siberia because of the monotony of staying on the island," was his reasoning. He would say it again and again, for as long as the papers continued printing Noice's descriptions of a starving expedition, desperate for help.

* * *

By the beginning of October, there had been no more word about the sighting of three white men along the Siberian coast. Harold Noice told the *Toronto Star* that he, for one, felt there was no hope of ever seeing Crawford, Maurer, and Galle alive again. The *Belinda*, the *Blue Sea*, and the *Silver Wave* had all made inquiries while trading up north and had individually scoured the Russian shore, but no one had seen or heard of the men. "As to the utility of sending a searching party to Siberia," Noice concluded, "I do not think that anything could be gained by it, otherwise I would have gone myself."

Stefansson wrote to Maurer's insurance company to convince them to release to the Maurer family the money from their son's claim, and both John and Thomas Maurer felt ready to give up hope of seeing their brother alive again. They were unable to find out any more information about the sighting—were unable to locate the persons who had actually spotted the men—and all of the avenues they had explored had led only to dead ends. John received word from their congressman, telling them that the Siberian coast was now officially closed for the season. All boats had returned without reporting any further sightings of the three men. "So we must be patient until ice freezes over," John wrote to Harry Galle, "and we may hear something good later." For now, they must be satisfied—if one could be satisfied in such a grim situation—that Fred had never made it to the Siberian coast, but had, most likely, drowned on his way across.

Fred had worshipped Stefansson, and because of this the Maurers felt kindly toward the man. Fred had known the dangers of what he was getting into. "Don't you know that freezing is the easiest death there is," he had once remarked to a friend, "why do you worry about us?" The Maurer family could not blame Stefansson for a choice Fred made willingly. Instead, they reached out to the explorer, inviting him to their home in Ohio. Delphine wrote him frequently because it made her feel better and more connected to her husband in some small way. She had read all of Noice's damning accounts in the newspapers, but she refused to feel any ill will toward the man who had sent her husband on his last mission. "I am sincerely sorry for you," she wrote Stefansson, "and no matter what the outcome of all this may be, regardless of any other opinion concerning you please remember that Delphine is your friend among many others who are standing with you now."

Delphine was living with the Maurers, at least temporarily, and her zealous faith and belief that all would work out well in the end was a consolation to the family. Her enthusiasm and refusal to give up hope were a striking contrast to the denial that Mr. Maurer was experiencing. Both he and his wife were old and feeble, and he refused to accept the fact that Fred was never coming home. He expected to see him at the door some time in the near future, whenever he found his way back, but it was a stubborn, almost angry conviction that fueled his belief. Mary Maurer, meanwhile, tried to keep herself as busy as possible, so that she wouldn't worry and think about her child, lying dead on some ice floe.

Stefansson was due in Cleveland, Ohio, on a lecture tour sometime in early November. For the family, his upcoming visit gave them just what they needed—something to look forward to. Stefansson was their last link to Fred and each of them was eager to shake his hand and sit down with him for a few minutes and talk to him of the tragedy and of the beloved young man they had lost.

But when Stefansson arrived in Cleveland, he wired them to say he had become tied up and would not be able to visit them in New Philadelphia after all. Delphine was so desperate to see him that she prepared to travel to Cleveland on her own to try to gain an interview. But before she arrived, he sent her a telegram to say he must return to New York on urgent business and would not be able to see her.

Stefansson's urgent business was Noice. He refused to return Lorne Knight's diary to the Knight family, and was now claiming he owned the rights to it. What was even more infuriating, he also claimed ownership of Ada Blackjack's diary. She was the only survivor and the only eyewitness to all that had happened, which made her extremely valuable. Stefansson would fight Noice for her story because Stefansson believed strongly that it belonged to him. Noice planned to sell it for his own private profit, but Stefansson asked his people to investigate at once and to secure Ada's release first.

Letters flew back and forth between Stefansson and his business partners. There was some confusion over who owned the rights to the two diaries. Noice had found them and he was the one writing the newspaper accounts of the story. But, Stefansson argued, Noice had signed the contract with the North American Newspaper Alliance as a writer under Stefansson's own employment.

One thing was clear—Noice was not planning to give up the diaries—not to the families, and certainly not to Stefansson. The Knights were frantic for Lorne's journal, and the Galles insisted on knowing if

Milton had left anything intended for them—a last letter or note. The Crawfords, too, were anxious to read Lorne's journal for any news of their son, and Stefansson began thinking he might need to resort to legal action to restrain Noice from publishing the diaries.

On October 22, 1923, Stefansson telegraphed the Knights: "Unfortunately you were right about Noice trying to make money for himself from Wrangell tragedy our company probably owns diaries anyway but will you assign any rights you may have to me so I can legally restrain Noice from his attempt sell your son's diary to newspapers for his private gain."

From what they could tell, Noice was in hiding. Calls came in and telegrams were sent to him daily but were never answered. He was living at the Waldorf Hotel in New York, and had left explicit instructions with the desk to tell all callers that he wasn't in. He had apparently married wealthy musician and traveler Frances Allison, the woman he had met on his trip from New York to Nome, but had cut himself off from all of the friends he had in common with Stefansson, and he refused to answer the pleas from the families of the men who had died.

When Noice sold the Wrangel Island story to the *London Daily News* in mid-October, he violated his contract with the Alliance. In answer, Stefansson sold a similar story to Whitelaw Amalgamated Press. He would simply fight fire with fire, answering Noice's claims that the men died from their own incompetence and inexperience, not to mention Stefansson's poor planning and greed, with his own statements that the men had not been starving, that there had been no shortage of food, and that Crawford and the other two had simply gone to Siberia to send news to him. Furthermore, Stefansson stated, the idea for the expedition had not been his alone. "The expedition did not grow out of my mind only," he wrote, "but was really a composite product of the ideas of Lorne, Fred Maurer and myself—their eagerness, altruism and desire for adventure."

As Noice and Stefansson warred in the press, the families of the dead men sat at home in Canada, Texas, Ohio, and Oregon, not knowing what or whom to believe, and only wanting peace. While in Alaska, Ada Blackjack avoided reporters and prayed that all the fuss would be over soon.

* * *

Mrs. Knight had always been strong and logical, but ever since the news had come in about Lorne's death, she had been distracted, weepy, and walked around as if in a daze. Mr. Knight was similarly affected, and often found himself weeping in his office. "I do not try to conceal my tears," he wrote to the Galles, "for they are the safety valve to a pressure of grief which would cause my too full heart to explode unless they are allowed to flow." But he worried about his wife. She was unable to sleep, even when he and Joseph and Miss Jones bundled her up and took her away in the car to eastern Oregon and Washington to visit the country and to see some friends. He was afraid it would be a long time until she was her old self, and he missed her almost as much as he missed his son.

The Lodge of Elks had asked him to speak to them of the expedition, to tell the people of McMinnville all he knew of what happened out there. Friends and neighbors were naturally curious about the details, and although Mr. Knight dreaded having to relive his grief before a large group of curiosity seekers, he felt it was important and necessary to do so. There had been an overwhelming outpouring of sympathy from people around the country and he was trying to answer every letter or telegram or postcard. Now, at least, he would have the opportunity to address a group of well-wishers at one time.

They met in Portland at the Grand Lodge of the Knights of Pythias, where he was a delegate. Over two hundred men showed up to listen to him and to gaze at the large scale map of the Arctic he brought along. When he broke down in tears—as he did frequently now—he saw tears in the eyes of his audience. There had been grumblings—growing louder every day—from people who held Stefansson responsible for Lorne Knight's death. "They seemed to think that you had, in a measure sent this band of boys there with insufficient supplies," Mr. Knight wrote to the explorer, "and that, you had, in a measure abandoned them. This, we honestly tried to dispel and I believe that we did, in a very large measure, overcome the feeling but, it is due you to know that it exists."

There was no grave for Crawford, for Maurer, for Galle, but there was one for Lorne, high up in the North on Wrangel Island. Mr. Knight felt the right thing to do was to put a marker there, a sort of monument to the four lost boys who had given their lives for England. He thought it should be the Canadian government's responsibility, and with that in mind he wrote to the Crawfords to ask them to use whatever influence they might have to secure it. He wrote, too, to the Galles and the Maurers, to tell them what he was thinking and to ask that they all work together, because they would have a better chance if they all demanded it.

He also wrote to Stefansson, who said the British government might consider erecting a memorial in a public park somewhere. This, in Mr. Knight's opinion, would never do. The memorial should be close to the final resting place of the four as a tribute to where they last lived and died.

It wouldn't have to be anything terribly grand or imposing—although, in his opinion, it should—but a bronze slab covering Lorne's grave that would list the names of all four boys, their dates of birth and hometowns, and a brief history of the expedition. It would be a small way of memorializing these brave men, and of perpetuating their memory so that others would know in years to come who they were and what they had done.

* * *

While the families worried about Siberian sightings and Stefansson argued with Noice, Ada Blackjack somehow managed to disappear. She was still living in Nome, as far as anyone knew, but by October there had been no word from her or of her for some time. The Knights, the Galles, the Crawfords, and the Maurers were anxious to find her, to ask her questions about their sons, the conditions, and the island, but no one seemed to know where she was or what had happened to her. Mr. Knight wrote a long letter to Ada, asking her to write to him, and thanking her for taking care of his son. He enclosed several stamped envelopes—addressed to himself, to the Maurers, the Galles, and the Crawfords—and asked her to write to them. He wanted to meet her, and thank her for all she had done to try to save Lorne's life.

Continuing the search for the elusive Ada, Mr. Galle wrote to a Nome newspaper reporter named Scarborough, a fellow Texan, to ask if he knew anything about Ada's whereabouts. The papers said she was living in Nome, and Harry hoped that this man might be able to find Ada for him so that he could talk to her about why, once and for all, the boys had left the island and what their frames of mind were. Did they truly believe they could reach Siberia? "There are hundreds of questions I would ask her, were I to meet her," he wrote, "and we feel that you are the one person to turn to."

Mr. Scarborough had been on the dock in Nome before the men left for Wrangel Island. Did the boys seem fully equipped? Were enough provisions taken? If so, why then were they forced to journey to Siberia for food? In Noice's latest articles, he openly criticized Knight's intellect and skill as a leader, while also pointing out the flaws in the planning of the expedition. It was painful to hear Noice speak of Lorne Knight in this way, and excruciating to hear him call the boys incompetent. Alma Galle could not think highly of anyone who spoke so ill of the dead, particularly of men who had traded their lives in a valiant effort. Still, why did the boys run out of food? Why did they not take a skin boat if it was something they must have? Alma knew her son. He was smart and practical, and if he knew they must have a skin boat to survive, he would have made sure they had one.

The Galles had so many urgent questions that no one bothered to answer. Stefansson had yet to be in direct contact with them, and they felt brushed aside by everyone except Mr. Knight and John Maurer, who wrote faithfully. "I blame Steffanson [*sic*] greatly," a friend said to them; "he had no right to send or get up such an expedition without enough funds to <u>back</u> it <u>up all</u> the time."

The Crawfords, the Knights, and the Maurers had all received words of condolence from Stefansson. They wrote to the Galles, assuming they had heard from him as well. They also wrote to them of the precious farewell letters their sons had left them, of the bittersweet assurance of having those last lines of love. The Galles waited for Milton's final letter to be sent to them. It would be something, at least, to have a few words from him. There was a suitcase of Milton's in Toronto, they were told, that contained some papers of his, but they had yet to see it. The only thing they had received was an empty handbag, a parcel of old letters he had taken with him to the island, and some unopened letters from home. There was no sign of the Corona or of any last lines to Mrs. Galle, although she prayed that some would yet turn up. There was only a skin case for his snow glasses, with initials carved in the side—M.G.

On October 11, they heard again from Stefansson's secretary, Olive Wilcox. In Stefansson's eyes, young Galle had been an afterthought to the expedition, and now Stefansson continued to overlook his family. Instead of taking the time to communicate with them directly, he asked Mrs. Wilcox to inform them that there was no last letter. Milton had left nothing for them after all. "Evidently," Miss Wilcox wrote, "he was full of hope and thought it unnecessary."

* * *

Allan Crawford had collected numerous specimens on Wrangel Island, keeping careful records and notes, and categorizing his finds when he was able to identify them. Because Noice had no use for these mementos, he returned them to Professor Crawford. There were birds of different types with faded plumage and withered bodies; delicate blue and yellow flowers tucked inside a tattered cardboard box labeled Societé Algonquin Chocolates; two bottles, both a dark olive, that contained a variety of shellfish and caterpillars; and rocks, fossils, and grass.

Professor Crawford donated his son's collection to the Royal Ontario Museum, where the items were placed in a glass case at the top of the stairs of the mineralogical department. This way, he hoped, Allan's work would have a chance to be appreciated by the public.

For months, Professor and Mrs. Crawford, the Maurer brothers, Mr. Knight, and the Galles read every newspaper or magazine article relating to the expedition, which was how Alma Galle came across one dated August 28, 1923. The *Christian Science Monitor* had published the article, datelined from Russia, reporting that the three men had been lost after the British expedition disturbed the Russian government. August 28 was three days before Noice landed in Nome, bringing news of the tragedy to the world. With Noice still at sea on August 28, how then did the *Monitor* know that the men were missing? To the Galles there was only one possibility—the boys had been found or spotted in Russia, which meant they were still alive. They made copies of the article at once and sent them to each of the other families as well as to Stefansson, and they sent off a letter to the editor of the magazine to inquire about the report.

The Crawfords, for their part, did not believe it. There must be a logical explanation for the mention of the boys, though no one could figure out what it might be. They saw Harold Noice in Toronto and he described to them the fierce gale that had blown up a day after the three men set out on their journey, as well as their weakened physical condition. Noice did not believe the men could have reached Siberia, and the Crawfords had to agree, no matter how much they wanted their son back.

Stefansson wrote an article for the *London Times* on October 9, 1923, in which he made his usual comments about the abundance of game on Wrangel Island. In it, he compared Fred Maurer to Robert

Scott and Lorne Knight to Ernest Shackleton, a comment that alternately amused and enraged readers. Neither Maurer nor Knight, of
course, had experiences that touched those of the two legendary explorers, but it was a way for Stefansson to defend his choice of them
to the public.

"Other miscarriages in hunting, combined with the approach of
mid-winter darkness, compelled them to feed the dogs on groceries,"
he said. "It seems also that the party felt so certain that a supply ship
was coming that they spent a large part of the summer just waiting
for it. Optimism was again one of their stumbling-blocks." He also
wrote about "The unaccountable omission of a skin boat."

Defensively, perhaps deviously, Stefansson was quick to point out
the things his men could have done differently. They did not take
advantage of precious hunting opportunities. They were sloppy in
guarding their meat from marauding polar bears. Ada Blackjack did
not understand that some parts of animals were more effective than
others in preventing scurvy. Knight, who should have understood this
from his previous bout, apparently was ignorant of this fact as well.
The outfitting of the expedition was the responsibility of Crawford
and the others, not Stefansson, who had merely advised them to take
along an umiak, which, of course, they did not. Furthermore, this talk
about the men leaving the island because the food had run short was
utter nonsense. Noice himself had said that the game conditions appeared to be abundant during the few days he was on the island.
Clearly, the men were homesick or craving news from the outside
world, which was why they attempted the trek to Siberia.

To the Crawfords, Stefansson's thinly disguised criticisms of the
four young men were as insulting as Harold Noice implying Lorne
Knight was stupid. It was worse, in fact, because Stefansson was cast-
ing blame on their son, as commander of the expedition. When Stefansson heard of their disapproval, he wrote immediately to try to
pacify them. A mere misunderstanding, he told them. They must remember that reporters rarely were completely accurate. Furthermore,

he was only trying to protect the men and their families by taking blame away from anyone.

Professor and Mrs. Crawford had never criticized Stefansson. When they first received news of their son's supposed death, they were in sympathy with Allan's commander. But their friends despised Stefansson and what they saw as his cold, heartless tactics, and shifting of blame to anyone but himself. The man took no responsibility for what he did, for the harm he caused. But the Crawfords did not approach Stefansson directly. Instead, he heard of their unhappiness through his business partner, A. J. T. Taylor. Writing to them again, he asked them to contact him to clear up this grave misunderstanding, and to enlighten him on the offensive points.

The response he received was brief and succinct. Yes, there were one or two statements in the *Times* article that made them bristle. But Professor Crawford was unwilling to discuss the matter. "The blow is too recent and overwhelming," he wrote. "The loss of our son has been the most devastating sorrow of our lives, but nothing which we can say or do can bring him back or heal the wound. We are trying to forget our sorrow and to carry on for the sake of the living, and the less discussion there is, the easier it will be for us to do so."

But in private, they remained insulted by the man's depiction of what had happened on Wrangel Island. Allan was dead, and more and more, they believed they knew who was responsible.

* * *

Early in the fall of 1923, Ada and Bennett Blackjack packed up their belongings and left Nome for Seattle. Ada was intent on getting Bennett to the hospital there where they could cure his tuberculosis. And she wanted to go somewhere where no one would bother her or ask her questions or force her to relive the tragedies of the past two years. If she wanted to cure Bennett and heal herself, she would have to put everything familiar behind her and make a new life.

Although she kept to herself and didn't speak to the strangers who badgered her for information, her going and coming caused a stir in the press, as the Alaskans buzzed about her departure, and the Seattle reporters who had somehow managed to catch wind of it eagerly awaited her arrival. The lone woman to survive a two-year Arctic expedition was a prime news story, and people recognized her face now, even though she had never agreed to pose for pictures. The reporters managed to dig up old ones or coerce them out of people who knew her or buy them from Noice for a price.

Before Ada had left Nome for Wrangel Island in 1921, she was told not to sign a newspaper contract or agreement of any sort, and so she made a promise that she would not sign her name to anything. Taking it literally, Ada refused to autograph photos of herself now because she felt she would be breaking her word. She had also promised never to give interviews or speak about herself, and she adhered to this also. It suited her fine. She was a painfully private person, and to be suddenly thrust into the spotlight almost made her long for the solitude of Wrangel Island.

The Isle of Wrangell was officially incorporated as Russian territory, and the Russian flag raised thereon, by an expedition organized by the Russian government and led by Lieutenant Wrangell, in 1821–1824. Russian sovereign rights to the island have never been questioned by any other government, and it has been generally looked upon as Russian territory. This position is taken by British official sources, as well; for instance, the British official publication "The Arctic Pilot," admits that the Isle of Wrangell was discovered by a Russian expedition. It may also be noted that all geographic maps, including the British "Philips' New General Atlas," puts down the Isle of Wrangel as Russian territory.

In the year 1910, the Russian Hydrographic Arctic Expedition . . . made measurements around the island, and built thereon an iron navigation pyramid for the guidance of ships seeking entrance to the southwest part of the island, this pyramid being the first and only erection on the island. Thus the Russian government took concrete steps to assert its rights and its duties as the possessor of the territory.

Finally, in September, 1916, the Russian government formally notified all of the allied and neutral governments that the Isle of Wrangel, together with other islands and territory adjoining the coast of Siberia, constituted an integral part of Russian territory. This notification elicited no objection on the part of any of the governments so addressed, including the British government.

Seventeen

ADA AND BENNETT ARRIVED in Seattle on November 2. The local newspapers immediately published their speculations as to why Ada Blackjack had come. To rest and recuperate from her ordeal, some wrote. To begin a new life and turn her back on the North, others reported. To save her young son from tuberculosis. To join forces with Seattle native Harold Noice, who was in the city with his new wife, Frances. To head east with Noice, traveling the country to talk of her experiences.

Noice, like everyone else, was interested in her story, and it was no secret that he wanted the rights to it, as well as to the photographs she had taken on the island.

"I wonder what the plan is," the wife of one of Stefansson's former colleagues wrote to Mrs. Crawford. "Lecture platform for Ada and Noice, vaudeville stage, book by Noice and Stefansson, just what? Exploitation of Ada's experiences for all the money there is in it for Stefansson and Noice, of that I am pretty sure."

To Ada, Seattle seemed colder than Wrangel Island because there was a dampness in the air that she had not felt before. One of Ada's sisters lived in the city with her husband, but Ada and Bennett moved into a hotel. The hotel elevators frightened her so much that for the first few days Ada stayed in her room, afraid to come out. When she finally summoned up her courage to explore the street below, she was overwhelmed by the sounds, the smells, the people, the skyscrapers. She was terrified she would lose her way and never find the hotel again, and so she walked around and around the block for exercise, without losing sight of the building.

Before long, she ventured away from her block, taking Bennett with her to the movies. She would take him to the hospital soon, but first they would go to see films, which they both enjoyed. Their favorite movie star was William S. Hart, known for his realistic motion pictures about the Wild West, and Bennett loved the stories about Strongheart, the dog hero who triumphed over criminals.

There were stores in Seattle the likes of which Ada had never seen. She had a weakness for pretty clothes and hats and she often wandered into the children's department of various shops to find herself something smart to wear. She was careful with her money—she had paid a heavy price for it, after all—but she liked to look nice.

With its sheltered harbor, Seattle was the closest major port to the Far East. It was a prosperous, bustling city, and in many ways far prettier, safer, and more sophisticated than Nome. Once she became used to it, Ada felt comfortable there. She had met a man on the ship to Seattle, a waiter named W. Harvey who seemed to like her very much. For the first time since her return from Wrangel Island, she felt her spirits lift.

Even though technological leaps were bringing the far corners of the world closer together, with the Southern Transcontinental Long Distance Telephone Line connecting Los Angeles to Chicago, and President Calvin Coolidge delivering the first official presidential address on the radio, Seattle maintained a sense of separation from Alaska and the Arctic that suited Ada fine. She had no desire to see anyone from her past life or to talk of the terrible things that had happened.

* * *

It didn't take long for Noice to use Lorne Knight's own words against him in a smart and cutting article for one of the papers. Knight had written in his diary about feeling unlucky and frustrated, and, at times, overwhelmed by life on Wrangel Island. He wrote with his usual good humor of their frequent inability to shoot well or to find the game they needed, and he wrote honestly about their shortcomings. Noice took this as evidence that the men were ill equipped for the job they were given to do. It was this opinion he voiced to the newspaper, using Knight's own words to back up his theory. Stefansson's men were inexperienced and inept and never should have been made to assume such an undertaking.

The tenor of the piece, the flagrant exploitation of his son's words and life, made Mr. Knight regret that he hadn't thrown Noice to the floor of his hotel room and sat on top of him while Joseph confiscated all evidence of Lorne Knight.

Not for one minute had Mr. Knight imagined that Noice—even Noice—could stoop so low as to use the words of a dead man against himself. Lorne's journal was a sacred document to the Knights, and this man, if he could be called that, had taken it and twisted it and "prostituted it as a pirate would violate the chastity of a captive."

Imagine a person who would call another man a friend and then publicly ridicule him and call him stupid to all the world, using the man's own words to back up his argument. Mr. Knight was glad Lorne had thrashed Noice all those years ago in the Arctic. He just wished his son were alive to thrash him again.

"You are playing for notoriety as an explorer," Mr. Knight concluded in a letter to him, "for fame as an author but, in view of your unmanly, dishonest, and altogether despicable conduct in this matter, I hope that the filthy lucre you acquire from this matter will choke you."

Mrs. Knight and Joseph both discouraged him from sending the letter, and reluctantly he sent a much tamer one in its place and presented a copy of the first to Stefansson for his opinion.

Mrs. Knight, for her part, wanted nothing to do with the explorer.

She had been hearing whispers from friends and neighbors and people about town. There were criticisms of Stefansson and many fingers pointed in his direction. She decided she did not want to see him, as she had planned to do, when he passed through Portland on a speaking engagement.

But when Stefansson sent a copy of Lorne's last letter to him, Mrs. Knight relented. There, in her boy's hand, were words of loyalty and admiration for the man who had sent him north. In the face of death, Lorne had still believed in Stefansson and stood firmly by him. The Crawfords were making a bitter case against the explorer. The Knights' mailbox was cluttered with letters from Helen Crawford, accompanied by offensive newspaper clippings underlined and marked. But Mr. Knight kept these from his wife and, remembering the words of her son, loyal and steadfast till the end, Georgia Knight decided that when Stefansson came to town she would like to see him after all.

*   *   *

Professor Crawford did not want to hear of Charles Wells and the second colony of settlers sent up to take his dead son's place. He did not ever want to hear the name Wrangel Island again. And he hoped Stefansson would stay away from Toronto. He had too many enemies there and there were too many people—the professor and his family included—who never wanted to see him again. If Stefansson insisted on coming to Canada and speaking to the Canadian Club, as he was threatening to do, Professor Crawford vowed to go to the newspapers beforehand and charge Stefansson with criminal negligence in the outfitting of the expedition. If Stefansson stayed put where he was and stopped talking of plentiful game and the necessity of a skin boat to newspapers and lecture audiences, Professor Crawford would drop the matter entirely. But if Stefansson insisted on repeating these lies, Mr. Crawford would have no choice but to come forward with charges of his own. All of this he communicated to a lawyer friend named Mr. Spence, who relayed everything to Stefansson.

When word of the Wrangel Island tragedy first reached Britain, the government felt great relief that it had not been officially involved with Stefansson's enterprise. The Canadian government, however, soon found itself drawn into the controversy because Crawford's parents made it clear that they held both Canada and Stefansson jointly responsible for the loss of their son.

The Crawfords read the published excerpts of Lorne Knight's diary, poring over every word, every sentence mentioning Allan. When they finished, they read them again, focusing this time on the conditions of life on the island. In his interview with the *Times*, Stefansson had said there was plenty of game. But Knight's diary and Allan's last letter home clearly said game was scarce.

Stefansson did nothing to endear himself to the Crawfords by granting an interview, just weeks after news of the Wrangel Island tragedy was released to the world, in which he once again sang the praises of the far North. It seemed he was carrying on with his mission to prove to the world that the Arctic was a Friendly Place, to dispel what he still saw as the myth of that particular polar region—that it was dangerous, that it was inhospitable—and to convince the world that Wrangel Island was a desirable commodity.

*   *   *

Mrs. Crawford was becoming increasingly distraught, and Allan was all she could think about. Her daughter Marjorie and son Johnnie desperately needed her attention, and her husband worried about her, but the only distraction she found from her grief was a correspondence with the wife of one of Stefansson's former colleagues, Dr. Rudolph Martin Anderson.

Anderson and Stefansson had served together on two prior expeditions, most notably the Canadian Arctic Expedition of 1913-1918. While Stefansson had commanded the northern party of the venture, Dr. Anderson had directed the southern division. With the tragedy of the ship *Karluk* and the loss of so many expedition members, not to mention Stefansson's poor and questionable handling of the entire situation, there was a general loss of respect for Stefansson, and Dr. Anderson distanced himself professionally. When Stefansson published his book *The Friendly Arctic* (1921), in which he publicly accused Anderson and some of the other scientists of mutiny, Anderson angrily severed all ties with him.

Now his wife, Mae Belle Anderson, found herself in the role of counselor and confidante to Helen Crawford. The more Stefansson told the newspapers, and the more that was revealed about the Wrangel Island Expedition, the more the Crawfords grew increasingly disillusioned, hurt, angry, and resentful. Mrs. Anderson and her husband both had been ill treated by Stefansson over the years, and now Mrs. Crawford reached out to people who knew him far better than she to ask more about this man who had led her son to his death.

Mrs. Crawford wrote weekly to the Andersons' home in Ottawa, pouring out her heart to the kind and sympathetic woman on the other end. Mrs. Anderson was feisty, smart, and direct. Her words did much both to soothe and ignite Mrs. Crawford. "For some years," Belle wrote Helen about Stefansson, "I think he has been a neurastenic monomaniac, but that he would become such a dangerous liar I never dreamed."

"He will almost shed tears over the loss of your boy especially if you are around to see the tears," she wrote on another occasion, "but he will lie about him and his comrades the next minute if it suits the great ends that he has in view and feel himself a second Napolean [*sic*] in doing it."

And, she wrote, "He could have at least gone to Nome, to be sure that the best efforts were being made to rescue the boys, but he did not worry about that—all he could think of was his political schemes re. Wrangell. He never worried about any responsibility on any expedition. That is quite characteristic of him."

Ever since the *London Times* article had been released on October 9, Professor and Mrs. Crawford had been pondering a response to Stefansson's comments with an interview or article of their own. Belle encouraged Helen to do so. "I am glad that you are a woman of spirit and intelligence as well, and can see the advisability of defending your son's reputation. It should be done for the sake of historical accuracy if there were not another reason—to keep V. Stefansson from luring away other boys to his friendly Arctic."

In the Andersons' opinion, Stefansson, as usual, was trying to brush off any responsibility or blame and "make out that Wrangell is a fine place and it was not his fault that the men perished." He had sent them to a place where he himself would never have set foot, to live off the land, something, according to them, that he himself had never done. In their opinion, he would have starved to death in the time he spent in the Arctic, if not for the Eskimos who sustained him.

Professor and Mrs. Crawford, meanwhile, could not understand how the Maurers and the Knights could remain so passive, so blindly and openly supportive of the man who had killed their sons. Mr. Knight answered Mrs. Crawford's impassioned, embittered letters— the ones she wrote, as she herself admitted, in the heat of anger and against the wishes of her husband—with words beseeching her to lay aside her rage and resentment, which he believed only served to make her loss more difficult to bear. The families should bind together now, not divide. "Let us devote our strength, not to hatred and resentment," he wrote, "but to loving memory of our true and brave boys and we will be better off in the end."

Mr. Knight felt he had forged a bond of friendship with the families of the other men. He looked forward to their letters and to writing his letters in return to them. "They all bring to us a sound assurance," he wrote, "that, although we have never met, we are friends."

He also believed the four families should set aside one day out of each year to pay tribute to the ones they had lost. "To commemorate their lives together," he suggested to the other parents, "and on this day, each one of us write to all the others and renew our love and devotion to our heroes. We have a day that we should celebrate with a pause in our work and a tender thought for those who loved us so much and whose love we can not express except in tears."

They would decide together the day for the commemoration, but Mrs. Galle asked that it not be January 28, which was the day before Milton and the others had left for Siberia, and the birthday of her husband and daughter. Whichever day they chose, they would, promised Mr. Knight, "gather flowers and revel in their fragrance, imagining, if we can, that we are presenting them to our boys, never marring the occasion with resentment or hatred toward any one, and see if we can not all become better men and better women for the lives that have been given for duty."

The Galles continued to feel like outsiders. To them, the Arctic was and always would be a strange, remote unknown. No one had responded to Mrs. Galle's letters regarding the mysterious article, dated August 28, which appeared in the *Christian Science Monitor*. She had sent copies of the article to all the families involved, and had written to the *Monitor* herself.

Stefansson alone dismissed the article as inconsequential, concluding that the reporter, when talking of the vanished expedition, was clearly referring to the fact that the men had not been heard from by the outside world in two years. He had absolutely no interest in pursuing the matter further.

Eventually, an editor from the *Monitor* responded to the Galles with the opinion that the published date must have been a misprint. The magazine had hired a freelance reporter for the article and, the editor suggested, if Mrs. Galle had any further questions, she should address them to him.

It was another bitter disappointment, and Alma attempted to distract herself by directing the church choir, teaching her piano students, and keeping up with her various club activities. She tried to turn her sorrow into sympathy for the other families who had lost so much, thereby lessening her pain a little. But she knew that she would never fully recover. "We regret that he went as young as he was, and therefore reproach ourselves," she wrote Stefansson. "I do realize I could have prevented him from going, but it is such a tedious matter to write and say what we wished to express on him, as a boy of his age is often very apt to misunderstand what is really meant for his welfare. But he went and he worked and he realized and therefore I have longed more than I ever admitted to have a letter from him."

* * *

As he contemplated the aftermath of the Wrangel Island Expedition, Stefansson was most interested in securing Ada's story. He was anxious to prevent Noice from feeding a sensationalized version of her account to the papers, and he sent out word to various contacts, asking them to snoop about, without mentioning his name, to determine if Ada had been approached by anyone to sell or give away the rights to her story. He even consulted the Alaska division of the U.S. Bureau of Education, which acted as the official guardian of all Eskimos, who were considered wards of the U.S. government.

Stefansson first wrote to the Bureau at its Seattle office, asking if Ada had arrived in the city and the status of her situation. Yes, they replied, she was in Seattle. She sent a message through the Bureau thanking Stefansson for his interest in her, but saying that she had no need of any assistance at present. Stefansson fired off another telegram to the Bureau, alerting them that Ada's personal story had potential monetary value, and that they must protect her from being exploited by Noice or anyone else. Her story should be sold for her own benefit—not Noice's—through a good New York literary agent since New York was the literary hub of the world. Otherwise he feared that someone might influence her to sign away her rights for nothing. He believed her tale was worth several thousand dollars at least.

Gertrude Andrus, his contact in Seattle, wired Stefansson to let him know she had tried three times to see Ada Blackjack, and had waited four hours without a glimpse of her. A man named Harvey had told her that Ada had turned her diaries over to Noice without any sort of agreement, but that she still hoped to be paid for them.

The Alaska Division of Education wrote Stefansson shortly afterward to let him know that a series of articles by Noice in the *Seattle Times* included excerpts from the Ada Blackjack diary. Ada had refused the help of the Division, remaining enigmatic and elusive, but they were still planning to put forth every effort to protect her rights. In the eyes of the chief of the Division, Ada was heavily under the influence of a man named Harvey, who had worked as a waiter on the steamship *Victoria,* on which she had traveled to Seattle. They knew little about the man and so could not predict, at this point, whether he was working for or against Ada.

*   *   *

On November 28, John Knight left McMinnville and headed to Seattle to search for Ada Blackjack. He had heard the rumors that she was in hiding, that she had retreated from the world, and that she was under bad influences there and might not be cooperative.

The first person he met was Carl Lomen of Lomen Brothers in Nome. Carl and his brother Ralph Lomen were well respected in both Nome and Seattle, their father being the federal judge at Nome, and the brothers prominent businessmen and reindeer farmers. For Mr. Knight, it was a great pleasure to meet this man who had known his son. They sat down together and spent several hours talking of Wrangel Island and the tragedy. John Knight was invited to Lomen's home to meet his mother and sister and to spend the evening hearing their stories about the days they had spent with Lorne, Allan, Milton, and Fred. Mother Lomen said there had never been four finer men to travel into the Arctic, and she began to cry when she spoke of them.

They talked till well past midnight, and it felt good to Mr. Knight to speak of his son with people who had known him in the context of Arctic explorer. It was one thing to receive condolences and good wishes from neighbors and friends who had known Lorne as motor-cycle policeman, chief of police, or the son of John and Georgia Knight. It was another to speak with those who recognized him as an experienced and savvy Arctic explorer and who had appreciated the qualities in him that Stefansson had acknowledged—vigor, unflappable calm, and levelheadedness.

Carl Lomen warned Mr. Knight that Ada was refusing to see any-one, even her most trusted friends. She had placed Bennett in a local hospital, where he was undergoing treatment for tuberculosis. She did not want advice or assistance and seemed to want to be left alone, except for the company of the mysterious W. Harvey. Lomen wished Mr. Knight luck getting an interview with her, but thought it unlikely. Others had tried to talk to her, but she "closed up like a clam and refused to answer questions and became like a wooden Indian."

He would look for this Harvey person first, Mr. Knight decided, since he seemed to have Ada under a sort of hold. He went to the address he had been given, posing as a representative from a publish-ing company, but Harvey wasn't there. Nor was he in the neighbor-hood. No one he asked had even heard of Harvey.

Next he went to the Bureau of Education, where he was given the same address for Ada that Lomen had given him, and told by a man named Sinclair that he would be happy to have Harvey picked up by the police if they could come up with a reason. The man was bad news, Sinclair said, and a friend of Ada's brother-in-law. They were bootlegging and everyone knew about it, Sinclair claimed, adding that he had found Ada drunk on more than one occasion.

Mr. Knight began his search for her at a run-down shack on Eighth Avenue, where he'd heard she was living. For two days, he hovered around the filthy place, waiting for someone to come home. On the second day, he ran into a Swedish man who said he had lived in the shack for the past five years and had never heard of Ada Blackjack.

Mr. Knight returned to his room and called the hospital where

Bennett was staying. The people on the other end passed him from one person to another until, at last, someone cooperated and gave him a telephone number and an address. When he called, the landlady who answered announced that Ada was not there and hung up on him. Not trusting her tone, he headed down to the place in person and banged on the landlady's door. When she didn't answer, he barged in and said he needed Ada's correct address or he would have the woman arrested, and so she relented.

He raced to the rooming house where Ada was living and knocked loudly on her door. No answer. The landlord stood watching and promised to talk to Ada when she came in and to give her the message that Mr. Knight had been to see her. He would call at the Savoy Hotel, where Mr. Knight was staying, to let him know when Ada would be available to see him.

When the landlord hadn't called by Sunday, Mr. Knight again went to Ada's rooming house and rapped on her door. When there was again no answer, he roused the landlord and made him call to Ada through the door, to tell her he needed to talk to her. From inside the room, there was a muffled sound and then a faint voice. She would not get up, she said. Through the wood of the door, Mr. Knight shouted to her that he was Lorne's father, come all the way from McMinnville, Oregon, to see her and to thank her for doing all she could for his boy.

On the other side of the door, Ada rose from her bed and pulled on her bathrobe. It was 9:30 on a Sunday morning and she had not yet eaten. The room was cold and unheated. She wanted to be left alone. She had taken Bennett to the hospital to be cured, and now she must wait until he was well. The world had been unfriendly to her ever since she had left Nome for Wrangel Island. It had become even more unfriendly since she returned from the island, and she did not know whom to trust. Everyone seemed to want something from her, and she was tired. But this was Lorne Knight's father, all the way from Oregon, and she felt that she must see him, if only for a brief time, because Lorne had been kind to her and had been her friend.

Despite all that time Mr. Knight had spent and the distance he had traveled, Ada only sat with him for ten minutes. He was impressed by her quiet manner, her diminutive stature, and her dignity. She was withdrawn, shy, and didn't seem to want to say too much. Her speech was direct but halting. She seemed to regard him warily. But she was clearly intelligent, he thought, and a perfect lady.

Ada told Mr. Knight she had never heard the men quarreling or fighting. They were all good friends, they all worked hard, they all did the best they could, and were very nice to her. She told him of the polar bears who came to camp, but always at the wrong times, when they didn't want them or need the meat, and she told him how the supplies had run out, leaving them hungry and desperate.

She told him that Noice took her diary from her without her consent and without paying her, and that he also collected the pictures she had taken on the island. She had made one especially for Mr. Knight, a photograph of Lorne's grave so that he could see where his boy was laid to rest, but this Noice had taken, too. She had written to Noice herself, asking him to give these things back to her, but he did not answer and she did not understand why. As far as she was concerned, her diary belonged to the Knights because she only began writing it when Lorne was unable to continue his own. She had kept it for both of them, and now it was her wish that his family have her journal. "Why did Noice not give you Mr. Lorne's diary?" she wanted to know. "It was yours, you are his father and it belonged to you."

After the ten minutes, Ada appeared discouraged and weary, as if she did not want to relive old memories any longer than she had to. She spoke briefly of W. Harvey, who had registered at the rooming house as Jack Tanana, and whom she had met on the ship to Seattle. He was trying to get her on the vaudeville circuit, even though Ada wanted no part of it because she knew she could never stand up in

front of a crowd of people. He was also trying to sell her story to the
public and had gotten $35.00 out of the *Seattle Times* for an interview.
The very thought of this man made Mr. Knight uncomfortable because
Harvey was clearly after Ada's money, and he had so influenced her
that she was refusing to see friends and others who only wanted to
help her and protect her from such exploitation.

When he returned to McMinnville, Mr. Knight sent Ada an invitation to visit his family and stay in their home, along with the money
it would take for her to make the trip. It would be easier for Ada to
remain in Seattle near Bennett. Long trips held little appeal to her
now, and she didn't like the thought of being away from home, such
as it was. Still, Mr. Knight had seemed like a nice man and he had
sent her money to come. She needed to return Mr. Lorne's belongings
to his parents because she had forgotten to do so when Mr. Knight
had visited her. She thought maybe she would accept the invitation
so that she could give them Lorne's items. And besides, Mr. Knight
had come an awfully long way just to see her.

*   *   *

Ada didn't like most women, and Helen Lomen was no exception.
Miss Lomen had a picture of Ada that Ada hadn't given her and now
she was asking to have it autographed. Ada refused to do it because
she felt this woman had no right to have such a thing. Still, Miss
Lomen, as a favor to her brother Carl, who had been anxious to help
John Knight, was the one who sent the telegram to the Knights saying
that Ada was coming. She had also purchased Ada's ticket for her
because Ada did not know how, and she had taken Ada to the train
to make sure she knew where to get on and which one to take.

Ada arrived in Portland on Monday, December 10. The Knights
met her at the train station and packed her into the car. She stared,
wide-eyed, through the window as they drove the forty miles to Mc-
Minnville. She had never ridden in an automobile before, and except

for her trip to Wrangel Island, had never been so far from home. She told the Knights she would stay until Christmas if Bennett remained well at the hospital.

The Knights' house was old and modest, but to Ada it was a palace. She had never been a guest in a white man's home before and she marveled at the modern conveniences. "This is a beautiful house," she breathed, as she walked in the door. As she stood there, taking it all in, Joseph asked her if she knew about the radio. Ada had never heard of radio, and so he tuned it in for her and soon a man's voice was booming out of the box, filling up the room. Joseph told her it was a man talking live from another place, but Ada refused to believe it. To her, it must be a special phonograph.

Then there was music, which filtered in sweetly, and the Knights told her it was from Los Angeles, but that seemed very far away to Ada. And later there was music from Vancouver, and Ada knew where that was because it had been explained to her. She wanted to walk outside then and see the tower which brought the music to them.

That night, she ate good, hearty food, and afterward fell into the comfortable bed they gave her and slept restfully. The next morning, she awoke somewhat refreshed, and unearthed from her suitcase Lorne's Kodak camera, with his name inscribed on it, and the leather Bible, which had belonged to his grandfather. She was afraid the Knights would want to keep the Bible, but she knew that she must return it to them because even though Lorne had let her read it and had said she could have it, they deserved to have the option of taking it back. When they saw how much it meant to her, the Knights told her she must keep it always and Mr. Knight even inscribed it to her. She belonged to the Methodist Church, she told them, and promised to treasure that Bible for the rest of her life.

The Knights were moved to see what she had brought them. These few objects were, in a way, pieces of Lorne, which they could touch and hold. Ada had forgotten Lorne's field glasses in Seattle, but she promised to send them when she went back. She had withheld all these items from Noice because she worried he would not give them to the family, just as he had not returned Galle's typewriter to his parents, and because Knight had made her promise to see that his things reached his mother and father.

The Knights were struck by her intelligence and her good manners, even though she did not speak readily. Her answers to their questions were mostly yes and no, and she would suddenly stop herself in the middle of a sentence and just fall silent. But when she began to speak of the four men and Wrangel Island, she became more talkative and she would often weep. Her fondness for the young men was obvious in the great emotion she expressed. At all other times, about all other things, she remained reserved.

Galle had been especially jolly and very considerate of her, and they had become great friends. Maurer was always very polite, and Crawford—whose very name elicited a deep sigh—was a gentleman. Knight was a good boy, too, although he had had such a hard time of things. This made her very sad, but the Knights sat there looking at her and she felt she had to find the words to tell them about their son.

She had first noticed a difference in Lorne when he returned from his exploring trip in the summer of 1922. By the time he and Crawford left for Siberia in January 1923, he was quite ill but trying to hide it from the others. Forced to turn back, he watched Crawford, Maurer, and Galle retrace his steps while he stayed behind with Ada. Later, she said, he had regretted not keeping one of the men to help Ada with him. She had to care for him all alone, and he had worried.

On the island, she sometimes had nothing to eat but hard bread and tea. There were days when she would try to eat it but could not swallow it. She would chew and chew, but the bread still would not go down. At those times, she told the Knights, she would think, "Well, I must live for my mother and for Bennett, my little boy at Nome," and then she would take a drink of tea and force the food down.

Noice had twisted some of her words for the newspaper stories and it upset her. She didn't understand why he had said some things, such as that she was well and fat when he found her on the island, when actually she had lost thirty pounds by the end and weighed little more than ninety pounds at the time the ship came. Nor did she understand why he made up other things and said they came out of her mouth.

She did not like the comments Noice made about Crawford and Knight and the others—the cruel and insulting remarks about their capabilities. She had been reading the papers and his words hurt her. She also felt her own rights were not being respected as they should. He said things about her that cut deeply—implying that she had done something harmful to Mr. Lorne's diary and that she had something to hide from the world.

Ada's sisters thought Noice dishonest and sneaky, particularly since he had taken Ada's diary and photographs from her and refused to give them back. Ada wanted them because she thought the Knights should have what she had written and she also hoped she could earn some money from their sale. Mr. Knight tried to convince her to wrestle the diary away from Noice and give it to Stefansson, so that he would have the complete record of the expedition. But even though she had confidence in Mr. Stefansson and believed him to be honest and true with the Eskimo people, Noice, not Stefansson, had saved her life. According to her, "Noice saved my life and he brought me from the Island to my Mother and Bennett and I can't go against him."

Everyone in McMinnville wanted to meet Ada or catch a glimpse of the heroine of the Arctic. Many were just curious, calling to feign interest in visiting with Mrs. Knight as if they hadn't read in the local paper that Ada was in town. But others genuinely wanted to meet Ada because they had known and loved Lorne. A steady stream of visitors flowed in and out of the house, and Ada enjoyed meeting most of them. There were some who thought she was a cannibal and asked her rude and insulting questions, and then she simply clammed up and sat staring at the floor. But most were respectful of her and hung upon her every word.

Mrs. Knight took her visiting to the homes of some of her lady friends, and Ada admired them greatly—such elegant people with such lovely manners. She particularly liked a woman with brilliant red hair who seemed to be everything that Ada wished she herself could be—polished, sophisticated, beautiful. In Mr. Knight's opinion, however, Ada had nothing to envy and "could teach some curious self conceited women a good deal about how to be a lady and yet, these same people would ask her questions as if they deemed her a wild woman."

People brought her presents for herself and for Bennett so that it was like Christmas every day she was there. Joseph gave her his very own Kodak camera, which was small and compact, and Ada was delighted. Mrs. Knight gave her the silk American flag presented to Lorne when he had been initiated into the Elks, and again she was pleased. The Knights gave her a handsome wristwatch with wide leather straps and a large face, and when Mrs. Knight slipped it onto Ada's wrist, she let her sleeve fall over it so that it was hidden. When she did not wear it the next day, Mr. Knight told her he would like to take it to be engraved, and she admitted that it was too large and heavy for her wrist. When Mr. Knight exchanged it for a smaller one with fifteen jewels and a solid gold bracelet, Ada was thrilled. She had never received such a beautiful, extravagant present. They had it engraved to say, TO ADA FROM MRS. KNIGHT, 12-15-23, and Ada wore it every day for the rest of her visit.

Mrs. Knight had been weeping daily since the tragedy, but not while Ada was with them, and it was good for her to have this time with the one person who could offer her firsthand information about her son. Because they now thought of her as family, the Knights and Ada dressed in their finest and visited the local portrait studio to have some formal pictures made. She was, to them, "nearer to us than almost any one else outside of our own relatives," and they came to love her for her sweet reserve, her earnest good manners, and her tender heart, as well as for all she had done for Lorne. To them, she was and would always be a hero, and they knew without a doubt that she had done all she could for their son. Perhaps if she had been more experienced or more savvy she could have done more, they would later write, but she was human and it was impossible for anyone to stand in another's shoes and say how this and that should have been or how he or she would have done it instead. The Knights loved Ada just the way she was, and could find no fault in that.

Ada was as proud of those portraits as were the Knights. The Knights were not fancy people, but they were fancy to her, and here were two white people who had taken her into their home and made her feel accepted and appreciated and loved. After all she had been through, all she had suffered, it felt like a miracle to sit with them at breakfast or to listen to the radio with Joseph or to see the gold sparkle at the end of her arm.

When a letter came from the hospital in Seattle saying that Bennett had contracted measles, Ada began to worry and longed to go home. She was still enjoying her visit, particularly the afternoons when everything was so bustling and energetic. But at bedtime, she wished for Bennett and every morning she said wistfully that she wanted to go back.

She stayed a week in all, and on her last night there, she and Mrs. Knight headed uptown to see the sights and do some shopping. Ada said she did not think she would wear a hat this time, as she always did when they went out, but that she would let everyone see that she was an Eskimo girl. As Mr. Knight noted, "What a lot of rubber there is in the McMinnville necks."

On December 16 the Knights drove Ada to Portland, where she would catch her train to Seattle. Before her departure, a reporter from the *Portland Oregonian* telephoned the Knight house to ask if he could have an interview with Ada because "she was the most famous Eskimo in the world." When the Knights and Ada arrived at the train station, the reporter and a photographer were waiting. As she always did with strangers—particularly reporters—Ada shut her mouth and refused to say a word. They offered her $5.00 to pose for a photograph, but still she declined.

As Mr. Knight escorted Ada through the gate at the station, the photographer snapped a picture of her. As the flash exploded, Ada muttered, "Damn. That makes me mad."

Just a few days after she settled back into her hotel in Seattle, Ada received a letter from the Knights, asking her to come live with them and to bring Bennett. "You are all we have left of the Wrangle [*sic*] Island expedition," they wrote, "and we feel that you are now almost a part of our family. We would be glad if you would like it, to have you live with us so that we could repay you for what you did for Lorne."

It was a touching offer but one Ada felt she had to refuse. She knew that she needed to close the door on Wrangel Island once and for all so that she could begin to live again.

* * *

Noice had heard that Ada Blackjack was a prostitute. That, according to Carl Lomen, was Noice's justification for mangling Lorne Knight's diary and holding on to Ada's. Not that Lomen had actually been allowed to look at the mutilated pages, but Noice had described the material when they met, just after he returned from the island. It was because Ada was a prostitute, said Noice, that she had refused to work when she first went to the island—she thought she had been hired for sex only and not as a cook and seamstress. When the men told her she was expected to cook instead, she refused to lift a finger. It was Noice's belief that the four had lured Ada to go on the expedition under the pretense that they knew what she was because they felt it was the only way to get her there. But they had no interest in her sexually, and so Ada, who was used to friendly relations with men, was deprived of any such contact for two years.

Noice's remarks about Ada were the first Lomen, Taylor, or Stefansson had heard of Ada being anything other than a seamstress. There had been rumors, of course, of a bad reputation in Nome, of too much drinking and too many men. Marshal Jordan certainly was familiar with her history and had encouraged her to go along on the journey and get away from town, but there was no evidence that Ada was a prostitute.

To his friends in New York, Noice told a different story. He said to them that he had removed certain pages of Knight's diary because they revealed the fact that Ada eventually adapted to her job as seamstress, but the young men tried to persuade her to work as a prostitute as well. To anyone the least acquainted with Crawford, Maurer, Knight, and Galle, it was a ridiculous charge. All had been attracted to and attractive to women, but Maurer was happily married, Knight happily engaged, Crawford happily studious, and Galle happily free. What's more, the earnestness and sobriety with which they treated their mission was apparent to everyone. To imply that they had gone up to Wrangel Island to cavort with a prostitute was ridiculous. It was, as usual, impossible to know what to believe or if anything could be believed, given Noice's reputation for dishonesty.

Stefansson could not come to any conclusions about the entire mess until he had the chance to view Knight's diary himself. He had not yet been able to recover Ada's journal and the expedition photographs, but he was prepared to prosecute Noice if he didn't receive them, something his lawyers made very clear to Noice. Not long after the warning, Noice's attorney alerted Stefansson's lawyers that his client was ready to agree to a settlement which stated that he would turn over all diaries and papers—and Galle's typewriter—to Stefansson's company. This was good news not only for the families but for Stefansson, who planned to write a book on the venture, using the diaries and other papers as material.

Explorers counted on selling books and stories about their travels and adventures. They earned their money—sometimes thousands of dollars—from publishing diaries, giving lectures and slide shows, and traveling about, talking to anyone who would pay them to hear about their exploits. Stefansson was no different in relying upon this option, but Noice had taken it away from him. Noice may have cornered and won the newspaper market, but Stefansson would win the race in the book world.

Stefansson wrote to Mr. Knight to let him know he would soon be sending him a copy of his son's journal, which was written in two volumes and which Noice indeed did finally send him. And then Stefansson began to read through it—only to find much of it obliterated. Thirty-eight pages in all from Volume I were missing, and an additional ten pages were missing from Volume II. Dark, angry pencil scratches slashed through the text, blackening whole passages here and there, and the last entry, dated March 23, 1923, was torn off in mid-sentence. Stefansson immediately wrote another letter to Mr. Knight, warning him of the diary's condition.

The Knights received a typed copy in early January of 1924 and immediately sat down to read it. It was at once heartbreaking and comforting to read Lorne's words. But the erasures, the torn pages, the obliterations were shocking, even though Stefansson had given them notice. It was such a betrayal and desecration of their elder son. Why would anyone have done this?

On February 4, Mr. Knight received an envelope in the mail from Noice. Inside were pages 9-14, 19-22, 27-40, and 45-46 of Volume I, most of which dealt with Ada's refusal to work and attempts made by the men to punish her. No mention was made of why Noice had originally removed the pages or why, after taking such time and care to destroy them, he had decided to reunite them with the diary. And no mention at all was made of the last ten pages of Volume II, which were still missing.

* * *

The parents of Crawford, Knight, Maurer, and Galle set aside September 1 as the day to commemorate the memory of the four young men. Since it was the anniversary of the day they had learned about the loss of their sons, it seemed the most appropriate date for a memorial. On January 1, 1924, Mr. Knight typed up the document and then he and Georgia and Joseph signed their names to it. He sent it on to the Crawfords next, and then to the Maurers, and finally to the Galles.

"We hereby designate the First day of September of each year," the agreement stated, "and we dedicate it as a day on which we shall commemorate the lives and deeds of our heroes, Allan Crawford, E. Lorne Knight, Frederick Maurer, and Milton Galle by each writing, on that day, letters to the others and, when possible, bestowing flowers upon some invalid in their names, thus keeping alive, in a fitting manner, the loving memory of those who perished doing their duty in the interest of the advancement of civilization."

J. T., Helen, and Marjorie Crawford, David and Mary Maurer, their children John, Joseph, and Kate, as well as Delphine Maurer, and Harry, Alma, Alfred, and Elsie Galle each added their names to the list.

* * *

Ada Blackjack met Vilhjalmur Stefansson for the first time in January 1924, when he passed through Seattle. August Masik and Aarnout Castel, former members of his 1913–1918 expedition, escorted her, along with Bennett, to Stefansson's hotel. The first thing she asked him was whether he believed that Crawford, Galle, and Maurer were safe somewhere in Siberia. When he told her it was unlikely, Ada fell silent. She still could not accept the fact that they were dead.

Ada and Stefansson met again over the next several days, and each time she was more adamant. Crawford and the others were prisoners in Siberia. She was sure of it. Or else they had been murdered upon setting foot on land.

Mr. Knight had warned Stefansson about Ada's reticence. Stefansson now told her of a book he was writing about Wrangel Island and the expedition, but she was wary about being interviewed. He offered her a share of his royalties, should the book do as well as he expected, but this still didn't sway her. It was only after she had spent some time with him and felt more secure and safe with him that she began to talk more freely. She did better on a one-on-one basis, he noticed. She resisted anything that seemed like a direct interrogation, so Stefansson soon learned to sit very silent so that she would open up.

The point Stefansson was most interested in was whether or not Ada knew anything about the missing and mutilated pages in Lorne Knight's diary. Noice had claimed, at first, that Ada was responsible, even though he had told both Carl Lomen and A. J. T. Taylor in September that he planned to censor the journal. When Noice was reminded of this, he retracted his story and said, instead, that while he was responsible for a portion of the diary's mutilation, it was Ada who had removed the ten missing pages. He had blacked out select passages, but she had destroyed the rest to hide her guilt from the world.

When Stefansson asked Ada about the journal, she looked up at him quizzically through solemn brown eyes. There were no missing pages when she gave the book to Mr. Noice, she was sure of it.

Was it possible that Knight could have torn the pages out himself?

"I will tell you I'm sure that Mr. Knight did not torn the leafs off his diary," she answered. "I don't know what the people are doing against me anyway. I'm just telling all I know and all I seed and I cannot do more than that."

January 1924

Dear Ada:

I have had a great desire to meet and speak to you. Mr. Knight has written us about . . . what you told him about the boys and some of the things that happened while on Wrangell Island, and he was so good as to mention to us that you thought Milton was such a jolly and considerate fellow. I could ask you a lot of questions could I speak to you, for I am longing to know a great many more things of him. Do you know if he wrote home often? Was he always happy or did you sometimes notice that he was quiet and thoughtful? What do you remember about the day they left for the ice trip? Do you suppose they really believed it was safe for them to make the trip? Were they strong and healthy when they left or were they weakened from lack of proper food? Did Milton say nothing to you as a message to us, should he not return? And do you know if Milton really did not have a letter for us?

I know I am asking a lot of you, to answer all these questions, but I am as homesick as ever for him.

Mr. Galle, our daughter Elsie, and son Alfred and I wish to extend to you our thanks for all you did for the boys and for Milton and for what you may write and say to us about him. I am sending you under separate cover a little remembrance for yourself and son. We hope you will always remember Milton and his mother who sent it.

Mrs. Galle

Seattle
Jan 30 1924
606 Columbia St

Dear Mrs. Galle

I received your nice presents to me yesterday and Bennetts presents
Oh my Bennett was very glad about his cup that you sent to him
And he ask me who sent me this cup Ma and I told him that Mrs
Galle and he said I thank her very much And as soon as I got my
presents I went over to my sister and saw it to her and she was
very thank for many nice presents from people

I thank you very much for the presents I didn't have much to
say Close with best wishes

Very truly
Mrs. Ada Blackjack.

————————————

Eighteen

FRANCES ALLISON NOICE, "Fanny" to family and friends, was at least ten years older than her husband and had already been married four times. Her own brother, John Allison, thought her mentally and emotionally unstable, but Noice couldn't see past his love for her. She was sophisticated and smart and beautiful, a talented writer and musician. She had taken an enormous interest in the Wrangel Island Expedition and had helped him sort through the diaries of Lorne Knight and Ada Blackjack.

Yet as soon as she became involved in her husband's work, Frances began to resent his initial heroic depiction of Ada Blackjack. Ada was no hero, in Frances's opinion, especially considering her shady reputation in Nome before joining up with the expedition, and her efforts to throw herself at Crawford and the others. The more Noice glowed about Ada in print, the more jealous Frances became. She decided that Ada was an evil person and that she had been taken to Wrangel Island for depraved, immoral purposes by those four young men. Frances even suspected her husband and Ada had been involved romantically and sexually on the voyage home.

At first, Frances asked her brother to contact Thomas Dibble, the city editor of the *New York Evening Journal*, to write a derogatory piece on Ada Blackjack and her own husband. When Dibble refused,

Frances turned to her father, millionaire banker William O. Allison, asking him to do a bit of detective work for her. She wanted a background check and character report on Noice.

The strain took its toll on their young marriage, and Noice and Frances separated briefly. It was not the first time Noice had dealt with Fanny's unreasonable jealousy or paranoid imaginings about other people, but he loved her and simply decided she was not well. He told himself she would get over it.

When Noice proposed an exploratory trip down to South America, Frances agreed to reconcile and they planned excitedly for the expedition. She would write while Noice took moving pictures. Noice asked John Allison to accompany him to the Fort Lee Processing Labs in New Jersey, where he tried out a camera and purchased it. While they viewed their projected test images, Noice told John that Fanny's ideas about Ada Blackjack were all in her head and "her statements concerning the matter sheer poppycock."

There was apparently an awful scene as Noice and Frances boarded the ship for South America, and not long after, John Allison received a hastily scrawled statement in the mail. It was from Noice—or so it said—and in it he withdrew everything he had said at the processing lab about Ada Blackjack and Wrangel Island and changed his story to suit Fanny's. "Knowing my sister well," John Allison wrote, "this note bore the signs of having been dictated by her. A case of 'you do what I say and write this, or else.' " Allison gave no heed to the note, but he did pity Noice. All who knew Fanny realized she needed to dominate everyone and do her best to control their every thought, feeling, or action.

She was determined that Noice should not celebrate a woman who, in her estimation, had so shamelessly chased those four tragic young men and who had done nothing to save Lorne Knight as he lay dying. He should not persist in writing words of praise about such a barbarian. Frances made it clear to her husband that either he must tell the world what she considered the *real* story of Ada Blackjack, or she would go public with it herself—from the protestations of passion for Crawford to the shameful punishments inflicted upon her by the men.

Noice knew his wife had worked up an irrational jealousy of Ada. He knew it was silly for her to be jealous, but there was no way of explaining that to Frances and making her understand. He also knew that she was serious in her threats.

Noice was showing promise as an explorer and writer, but Frances was determined that he should have no chance at either. Even during their temporary separations, she did everything she could to ruin him and his career. And so she wrote to Stefansson, who, it was widely known, was having problems of his own with Noice.

Frances arranged a meeting with Stefansson and invited her brother John to join them. Sitting at the luncheon, it was hard for John to believe that anyone could take his sister's wild, unfounded accusations and ideas seriously, but Stefansson seemed to accept them readily and willingly. "I sensed," John wrote afterward, "a kind of conspiracy between Frances and Stefansson to ruin Noice's career."

*   *   *

There were still painful tubercular lesions on Bennett's chest and neck, and he was drawn, pale, and weak. The doctors had released him from the hospital, unable to do anything more for him. Ada had hoped for a miracle, but instead the progress was slow, the prognosis uncertain.

There was a friend of Stefansson's who was living in Seattle but who planned to travel to California and had invited Ada and Bennett to join her. Her name was Inglis Fletcher, but everyone called her Peggy, and she was a novelist and a great, exuberant, laughing woman. Peggy had met Stefansson in Washington during World War I while she was working for the Red Cross. He had encouraged her to write and she had never forgotten his friendship. She even became his lecture agent at his request.

Ada usually did not care much for women, but she liked this one.

Mrs. Fletcher was forty-four years old and had a son who was nearly Bennett's age and who had also been seriously ill. When Mrs. Fletcher showed a true and deep interest in Bennett's health, Ada couldn't help but like her. Bennett was the most important part of Ada's life, and being a good mother was, to her, the most important work.

At first, however, Ada turned down the invitation. She did not want to make another long trip to yet another strange and unfamiliar place, and she was anxious to return to Alaska. In Seattle, at least, she knew her sister and her brother-in-law, and the Lomens, and Harvey, but in California she would only have Peggy Fletcher. So Ada said no. But when Bennett's doctors assured her that it would be good for the boy to have sunshine in February and a fresh change of scenery, and that it would help him to heal, she reconsidered.

Mrs. Fletcher was planning to visit some friends in Los Angeles who were the owners of Bennett's favorite canine movie hero, Strongheart. They lived on a farm outside Hollywood, where Bennett could run and walk and play in the sunshine. Stefansson was anxious for Peggy to befriend Ada, to interview her, to get her story down on paper. He had already commissioned Ada's old friend Marshal Jordan, Nome's chief of police, to talk to her and to type up the account, and this he did when he came down to Seattle. Afterward, Jordan managed to convince Ada, on Stefansson's behalf, to sell the rights to her diary and papers to Stefansson for $500. Ada wasn't sure what it was she was selling, but there was such pressure to do it and there was money being offered—quite a lot all at once—and so it was hard to refuse. She was told simply that she must sign here and here and then money would be hers, and so she did. Peggy Fletcher asked an attorney friend of hers in Spokane to draw up a document to make it official.

Mrs. Fletcher had arranged with Stefansson to pay for Ada's trip, but Ada changed her mind about traveling a dozen or so times before she and Mrs. Fletcher actually left, deciding alternately that she would go and that it was "too much trouble to go on trip." When she had once again determined to accept the invitation, she went with Bennett to the New Washington Hotel in Seattle to see Mrs. Fletcher and talk about what she should pack. There was much Ada needed for herself and for Bennett. She wanted a new dress and some shoes, and she thought Bennett should have a suit. She and Peggy Fletcher talked about the kind of clothes Ada would need in the warm California climate, but when Peggy pulled on her coat so that they could go shopping, Ada said again that it was too much trouble to go on the trip. She would need too many clothes and was afraid of looking shabby and destitute.

When Peggy assured her that the dress she was wearing would be just perfect for the boat, Ada was disappointed. She was painfully self-conscious about the fact that her clothes were tatty and that she believed she was too dark-skinned and uncultured for the white man's world. Sensing this, Peggy took her arm and led her to the street below so that they could browse the Seattle stores. If Ada wanted a new dress before sailing, she would get one.

Down on the street, Ada once again worried about the trip. It was too much trouble and too much anxiety, and she didn't understand all that would need to be done. She seemed helpless and frightened and close to tears, and before Peggy could stop her, she hurried off in the rain with Bennett. Peggy strode after them until she caught up and tried to persuade Ada to let her take them home in a cab so that Bennett could get out of the wet and the cold, but Ada kept walking.

Something more was clearly troubling Ada, but Peggy Fletcher could not figure out what it was. She could talk to Ada, but she was afraid that she wouldn't get very far. She could tell Ada was not ready to open up, and Peggy did not want to risk scaring her away completely. But the older woman was determined to win the younger woman's trust, not because she had promised Stefansson, but because there was something about Ada that made Peggy want to help her.

Peggy walked over to Fredrick and Nelsons, where she bought a suit, a pair of coveralls, a pair of rompers, stockings, and a hat for

Bennett. She phoned Ada at her rooming house afterward, but when Ada did not answer Peggy arranged to have the clothes delivered to her room.

If Ada decided to join Peggy on the boat the next day, it would be wonderful. If not, Peggy did not want to press her any more than she already had. She would buy Ada and Bennett one-way tickets, which would total $80, and then help them arrange to come back on another boat for less money. Later that evening, Peggy dined with friends, and when she was finished there was a message awaiting her from Ada. She had received the lovely clothes for Bennett and thought, if she had something new and suitable to wear herself, she would like to go to California after all.

The next day, Peggy Fletcher gave Ada $20, and with this Ada purchased a handsome suitcase, two pairs of tan stockings, a pair of shoes with straps, two cotton blouses, and a navy serge suit. She was short ten cents when she made her final purchase, the suitcase, but the clerk waved her away and told her not to mind. Now Ada would be equipped for her journey.

The landlord and landlady at the rooming house were happy to see Ada go. She had kept her room like a pig, the landlady said, with furs draped around the floor. And a man, whose name they didn't want to mention, had brought her booze some nights until Ada could be heard screaming drunkenly "like an animal," and waking the neighbors.

On February 7, Ada and Bennett joined Peggy Fletcher on the *Emma Alexander*, run by the Admiral Line of the Pacific Steamship Company. Peggy was relieved when the ship pulled away from the dock with Ada safely on it, and unable to change her mind once more. But Ada was glad to be going. She had not said a word to her sisters about the trip because she didn't see them much anymore. They made her feel as much like a sideshow curiosity as the reporters and the gawkers. They stared at her as if expecting her to look different and they asked her for money too often now. While she didn't mind giving them a dollar or two, she did not like to keep handing out forty or fifty. She had only wanted to be alone in Seattle, while Bennett healed, but there was never any peace. Now she would go to Los Angeles, where she and her son could try again to start anew.

On the second day at sea, Ada spent only an hour or two on deck before becoming seasick. She retreated to her cabin and her bed, and Peggy Fletcher sat with her for an hour or so and chatted. Ada was not yet sure she could trust Peggy, and so she spoke briefly of Wrangel, testing the waters, telling Mrs. Fletcher of Maurer's hunting prowess and the seals she had shot. "You must shoot their heads," she told Peggy firmly, and then fell silent.

Later, she spoke of money matters, which were always on her mind. She worried about money constantly, especially now that she had some. She was easily led and influenced, although extremely frugal. She seemed at once helpless and fiercely independent. It was hard for Peggy to imagine, looking at Ada as she lay on her bunk, her cheeks apple red, her hair black against the pillow, that this pretty, fragile woman had endured for so long and so well on Wrangel Island.

From her bed, Ada said she thought she might travel back to Seattle by train instead of ship, as long as the ticket would not cost too much. She was miserable from the gentle, rocking rhythm of the water beneath the boat. She told Peggy that she planned to head back up to Nome by June and that she couldn't wait to be home again. Seattle had been terribly damp and chilly, and she had caught the first cold of her life there.

Then—Knight had been so sick, she said suddenly, as if she couldn't hold the feelings at bay anymore. So weak that she must hold his head up to give him a drink. Her voice broke when she spoke of him, and the tears came quickly, but then she fell quiet once more.

Peggy quickly learned that when Ada did not want to talk about a subject, she would simply say, "Well, I don't want to say anything about that." Peggy was struck by Ada's direct way of speaking. Ada's own mother, she confided to Peggy, was unable to express herself.

She would, according to Ada, "just sit still and say nothing." Ada preferred to sit still, like her mother, and absorb everything. She simply sat in silence until she thought of the next thing she wanted to say. And then, Peggy learned, it would come: "I have been thinking," Ada would begin.

"Do you think in English?" Peggy asked her.

"No, in Eskimo."

Peggy longed to take notes as Ada was talking, but she was afraid doing so would only distract Ada and make her clam up again. So as soon as Peggy returned to her cabin each night, she would sit down and write a long letter to Stefansson containing everything she could remember about her time with Ada.

The other passengers on the steamship clamored to meet Ada, who, as usual, only wanted to be left alone. People were naturally curious and asked all sorts of questions about her experiences on Wrangel Island. They wanted to do things for her and help her because there was something about Ada that inspired that impulse. But she did not want their help or ask for it. She used as few words as possible in answering their questions, and she never spoke of Wrangel to anyone except Peggy Fletcher.

Ada was reluctant to tell her story, but she was afraid "they" would murder her if she didn't. She wasn't clear about who "they" were, but she seemed adamant that it would happen. She had been brought up on ancient superstition and, as a result, was often quick to suspect and fear the unknown. Mrs. Fletcher soothed her and explained that Ada was already a part of history and therefore her story was a part of history. She reminded Ada of the Eskimo storytellers who kept the records and stories of the tribes alive by passing the tales onto one another. "It is like that with white people," she explained, "only they write theirs down."

"Oh," Ada exclaimed. "Is that it." And she was satisfied.

The reporters found her, as they inevitably did. As always, she refused to talk to them or have her picture taken, and she seemed to have an uncanny ability to pick them out of a crowd. As soon as she spotted one, she would whisk Bennett away to their cabin, where they would hide until the newshounds gave up and went away. Some took their revenge by publishing stories of the snubbing she gave them. They made fun of her native dialect and her "halfbreed" son.

One day, when a newspaperman managed to corner Ada, he wanted to know, "Were there many wild animals on Wrangel Island?"

He stood there for fifteen full minutes, waiting for the answer. Finally, Ada spoke, "A few." But that was all she said.

It was better to hide in her cabin where no one could find her. She did not believe this talk about being a hero. In the Arctic, she had done what she had to do to survive and what she needed to do to get home again to Bennett, without any thought of glory or praise. And now strangers were staring at her on the street and rushing to embrace her and applauding her. More than anything, she wanted to forget, but they would not let her. The cold, the fear, the polar bears, the hunger, the sickness, the death. When she thought of it, she confided to Mrs. Fletcher, "it always makes me have a choke in my throat and tears come to my eyes."

Every now and again, she would offer Peggy, unprompted, a piece of the puzzle. It usually had to do with Lorne Knight's illness. It seemed to be the aspect of the venture that most disturbed her because she circled it, kept coming back to it, revisiting it and the emotion she had felt at the time.

Bennett, unlike his mother, chattered constantly and asked questions about everything. "Too many questions," said Ada. "Not like me. Always my people say I never ask questions about anything." Whenever Ada felt Bennett was talking too much, she spoke his name softly and he fell silent. He tried to teach Mrs. Fletcher the Eskimo language. Horse, he would say, and then give her the Eskimo word for it. She would forget it and he would repeat it, and on they would go. Ada watched the whole time, smiling with pride. Bennett was a smart boy, clever and quick.

Sometimes when Ada was feeling particularly weak or ill, or when she preferred to remain out of the public eye in her cabin, Peggy would take Bennett up to the deck, where they would walk and look out over the water together. He loved to watch the gulls and to imitate the cry of the ducks. He chattered happily, without his mother to make him hush, and he boasted to Peggy about the reindeer they had in Nome, which he would ride fast across the shore.

Peggy noticed that Ada took pride in dressing Bennett nicely and keeping him clean and tidy, just as she enjoyed dressing herself in one of her many dark blue serge suits. Ada took great effort with her appearance, and the people they met aboard ship seemed impressed by her poise and good manners. Most of them had never seen an Eskimo in person before, which was reason enough to stare, but Ada further surprised them by not fitting their preconceived image of the unkempt, uneducated heathen.

There was a man in her life, Ada confided to Peggy one day, a man named Harvey. He was her friend and right now he was on a ship called the *Alameda*, which was cruising in the waters of southeast Alaska. Ada did not say much about Harvey, but Peggy had certainly heard the rumors back in Seattle, and was of the impression that he was not a very good "friend" for Ada to have.

Ada spent most of her time in her cabin, having her meals delivered there. When the service was too slow for her liking, she would call Peggy on the telephone in her room and ask her to bring ice water so that she wouldn't have to go out in the midst of people to get it. Ada seemed thirsty all the time, and as soon as she was finished with a glass of cold water, she craved another. Bennett drank glass after glass himself and devoured the ice in chunks.

Ada told Peggy that she wanted to go back to Oregon sometime to see the Knights. She liked them very much. She thought she might like to buy a little boat and go into the fishing business in southeastern Alaska with her cousin. Or perhaps find a restaurant or hotel in Nome, where she could wait on tables and her sister Rita could cook. If her mother would agree to move to southeast Alaska, though, that is where Ada thought she would most like to go because she had heard there was good work there for sewing.

Peggy suggested the movie business in California—perhaps a film studio might hire her to make fur clothes for their northern pictures. Ada was skeptical about that, but knew she must find something because she was afraid of running out of money. The way she figured it, she could only spend about $20 a month or she would not be able to get back to Nome. There was money in her bank at home, but she didn't want to touch this because she was saving it for Bennett and her mother.

On the evening of February 9, 1924, Ada felt well enough to venture up to the deck. There was a festive masquerade dance, and Ada stood very still and watched. As the maskers marched down the deck, she drew closer to Mrs. Fletcher, not understanding what it meant. As Peggy explained the custom to her, Ada watched a dancing girl dressed in a thin, beaded costume. After a long while, she tilted her face up at Mrs. Fletcher and smiled, "If I have a dress like that on Wrangel Island, I think I freeze to death very quick."

*   *   *

At Mr. Knight's request, the Crawfords, Maurers, and Galles each received a copy of Lorne's diary from Stefansson. They had been warned about the missing pages, but seeing the blacked-out passages was much more disturbing to the families than hearing of them. It was distressing to read about the lack of food, day by day, and the inability to find enough game. They suffered as they read, in a way they had not suffered before, because now they could picture all too vividly what their boys had been up against.

For the Galles, who had had no last letter to comfort them, and who still had not been allowed to see their own son's notes, Lorne Knight's journal brought some consolation. For Mrs. Galle, it was a chance to see her son again, as described by Lorne. She was proud to read of Milton's ambitious and fearless three-day excursion to the mountains by himself, and she was comforted to find no mention of sadness or depression. She had suffered guilt at letting him leave, even though he had taken himself off without a look back, but now she felt a little better about him, and about his decision.

"When thinking of . . . Milton the young, growing, and slender boy . . . and Milton developing into the hardened, strong man, I can hardly realize it was our boy," she wrote to Stefansson. "He was out all the time keeping busy and seeking diversion and occupation and I am glad. He showed himself what I had wished for, that, once he had gone, he would be man enough to do his best and overcome difficulties as well as was possible."

Reading Knight's diary made the Galles long even more to read Milton's journal. To know that such a thing existed but that they weren't allowed to see it was maddening. They had heard no word from Noice about it, but Mrs. Galle could not keep silent. She had done that long enough. So she wrote to Noice, to ask him to please send their son's notes, and then she wrote to Stefansson to tell him, knowing he would be displeased.

She would not blame anyone for the tragedy, as the Crawfords did. It was true that there was still a great deal about their son's last journey that they did not know. But "I am more at peace to believe that everybody did all with the best of intentions and that Mr. Stef only thought of doing the best for the boys. He will see, better than me, where the fault or mistakes lie."

Others continued to blame Stefansson, however. H. H. Langton, of *The Canadian Historical Review*, observed at the time, "The truth is that Wrangel Island was a most unsuitable place for trying the experiment of 'living off the country.' Mr. Stefansson had never been there; he knew its resources only by the report of survivors of the *Karluk* disaster. But from their report he knew that there were neither caribou nor musk-oxen, as there are in the islands of the Canadian Arctic, and he knew that the *Karluk* survivors had all but starved."

Beyond newspapers and magazines, former associates began to speak out as well. Captain Bernard, leader of the 1922 relief expedition attempt to Wrangel Island, noted that the man was " 'done for' from Seattle to Ottawa," and that no one had anything good to say for him. In Nome, Stefansson was known as a champion liar, as well as in New York, Boston, and Washington, D.C.

William McKinlay was the only scientific member of Stefansson's *Karluk* expedition to survive the disastrous 1913 trip to the Arctic. His memories of the expedition embittered him toward Stefansson for the rest of his life. "If I would venture any criticism, then it would fall entirely and exclusively on Stefansson," he wrote of the Crawford tragedy, "because of his unscrupulous efforts to present to the young men a picture of Wrangel Island that never was."

Stefansson ignored the press, and concentrated his efforts on writing his own definitive account of the expedition for publication. He had written most of the story, the history and background of the venture, the events of Wrangel Island during 1921–1923, and the aftermath of the discovery. But now he needed the input and cooperation of the parents of the four young men. Specifically, he was most interested in biographical sketches of each of the men, which he asked the parents to write for him, and also any photographs they might have in their possession relating to the expedition.

Do not give him anything, Mae Belle Anderson warned Helen Crawford. "Mr. Knight thinks in his innocence that V.S. is going to make a book out of his son's diary. The diary will be only a small part of a book on Wrangell Island, which will be full of the old lies. Moreover when the book is published he will find that V. S. is not to blame for a solitary thing. The boys will be to blame—perhaps his son—for *all* the tragedy. Stefansson is very strong at quoting dead men."

She was referring to the diary of John Hadley, a passenger on the *Karluk*, who had survived the tragedy but died in 1918 in the influenza epidemic in San Francisco. After Hadley died, a mysterious document appeared, which Stefansson quoted at length in his book *The Friendly Arctic*. Hadley had also kept a diary during his time on Wrangel Island in 1914, but that document and the one that surfaced after his death were suspiciously opposite in viewpoints, opinions, and grammatical structuring. Stefansson had invented the second diary to suit his own purposes, critics said, but Hadley, of course, was dead, so there was only Stefansson's word that the document was authentic.

There was also the matter of unpaid salaries, which did nothing to endear Stefansson to the families. As supportive as she was of Stefansson, Delphine Maurer was forced to write inquiring about the money due Fred, which had still not been paid. Stefansson had written to her of the money he stood to earn on an Australian lecture tour, and the fact that they offered him double for the following year, so surely there must be money to pay Fred's salary. Emotionally, she was sustained by her deep, unshakable religious faith, while her parents were able to care for her financially. Delphine had managed to return to work herself, yet she wanted what was due Fred, and she had to press Stefansson for an answer.

Eventually he responded, saying that the Stefansson Arctic Exploration and Development Company had no money in its treasury. He blamed the deficit on Noice, who, he said, had spent their money and run up their credit recklessly before sailing on the relief trip. He would try to cover the amount due Maurer with a personal check, but Stefansson estimated his debts relating to the expedition as being between $20,000 and $30,000. As Mae Belle Anderson remarked to Mrs. Crawford, "Stefansson could not manage a peanut stand, my husband always said."

Letters from Mr. Knight and the Galles followed, and then one from the Crawfords' attorney. Mrs. Galle wrote that, "Now that a year has passed since the tragic news and little hope that I held out for the boys is vanishing, I am about to ask you for more about Milton's affairs and agreement with you and the Company, upon leaving for the north." Milton had never told her exactly what he was to be paid or what his agreement with Stefansson was, but it was now time to find out and receive his due.

According to his records, Stefansson owed $1,450 to Allan Crawford, $10 to Lorne Knight, $100 to Fred Maurer, and nothing to Milton Galle, who was only to be paid in furs. Stefansson hoped to be able to pay all that was legally due to the relatives by the middle of March of 1924, but first, he told them, he must pay back Griffith Brewer and settle other debts, including the $17,000 he claimed Noice had accrued in bills in Nome. Now that Noice was married to a wealthy woman, though, Stefansson told the families, perhaps they could get some of the money back from him.

In the meantime, Stefansson offered to sell Wrangel Island, first to Canada for $30,000, then, when the government ignored the offer, for $27,000 to the United States. When the United States also failed to respond, he offered the island to the Lomen brothers. Of course, it was preposterous. Stefansson no more owned Wrangel Island than he owned France.

* * *

Ada grew into her sea legs by February 10, the fourth day of her six-day voyage. Now that she was able, she took a stroll on the deck of the ship and stood at the railing to stare at the mountains that hugged the shore. They made her wish she was back in Nome, with the ice and the snow. But when the ship docked in San Francisco and Peggy took Ada and Bennett for a ride through Golden Gate Park with some friends who met them at the dock, she sat straight and still with her hands clasped on her lap, exclaiming over and over again to herself, "Oh, Oh!"

There was such beauty here, and a kind of grandeur of color and form that she had never seen before. Flowers bloomed in February, and the sound and smell of the nearby sea awakened her senses. She found the celebrated redwoods glorious. At one point, she turned to

Peggy and said, "If my mother could see this, I don't know what she would say. Maybe she would say nothing, just like I do."

And later, as she gazed in wonder at the vibrant colors of the flowers, Ada said, "I do not know why white people want to come to Nome where there is ice and snow when they have everything so beautiful like this."

Before they returned to the ship, Peggy stopped at the ferry building to send a wire to Stefansson. They passed a florist shop on the way, and Ada paused in front of the window. Her face lit up as she stared at the flowers. They were just like the ones she had seen in the park—bright and bold and beautiful. On impulse, Peggy purchased a bouquet of violets and gave it to her. Ada's eyes, when they found Peggy's, were filled with emotion and surprise. "Are they for me?" When Peggy said yes, Ada could hardly believe it. No one had ever given her flowers before. The gesture was simple but enormous to Ada.

When they returned to the ship, Ada told Mrs. Fletcher that she had never in her life seen such wonderful cars, met so many nice people, or been on such a beautiful ride.

Peggy left Ada in her cabin, tired and happy, but before she went away she told Ada she was going to write a letter to Mr. Stefansson and asked if she wanted to give him a message.

Ada nodded, her eyes shining. "Please tell him I thank him for trip."

THE *NEW YORK WORLD*
February 11, 1924

❋

Spurned Eskimo Woman Is Blamed for Arctic Death

Out of the Arctic last summer came a romantic story of three white men presumably lost on a dash across 100 miles of ice from Wrangel Island to Siberia, of a fourth man who died on the island and of a heroic Eskimo woman, Ada Blackjack.

Yesterday, in a cozy room at the Villa Richard, Fort Lee, N. J., Mr. Noice told a group of friends a far different story. Ada Blackjack, he said, was not the heroine he at first believed her to be. Instead, he explained, she played a mean role in a grim tragedy she could have averted.

Earlier stories, in which Mr. Noice himself paid tribute to the woman's courage and faithfulness, were based largely on statements made by her and on parts of a crude diary she kept.

Some entries in this record, at first thought to be unreadable, have recently been deciphered by Mr. Noice and his wife. These, the explorer said, revealed that Ada refused to aid E. Lorne Knight, actual leader of the party, as he lay dying on the island and that she probably saved her own life on food that would have saved Knight from starvation . . .

Since the chief need was warm clothing, they took with them Ada Blackjack, who was to be seamstress and cook. She quickly proposed marriage to Crawford, Mr. Noice said, and, when repulsed by him, remarked that she had left Nome determined to marry one of the four white men.

None could see Mrs. Blackjack as a mate, however, and from that time her cooperation lessened. She often refused to work, Mr. Noice said, and gave the little group no end of trouble . . .

Knight lay in his tent, almost wholly dependent on the Eskimo woman for his food. He appeared for a while to improve . . . but other entries told of the woman refusing to visit the traps, which were set near the tent . . . when Knight asked her to search for game.

Later information also reveals that the woman knew how to handle a rifle and was a good hunter, Mr. Noice said, although she had claimed she could not shoot.

When the Noice expedition reached Wrangel Island late last summer, Knight's emaciated body, weighing only ninety pounds, was found in his tent. Mrs. Blackjack was well and fat. The party's original food supply had not run out.

Mr. Noice said he intended to bring his disclosures to the attention of the Explorers Club and to start some kind of inquiry which would establish the facts officially.

Nineteen

THE ARTICLE WAS printed in the *New York World* on February 11, 1924. *Spurned Eskimo Woman Is Blamed for Arctic Death*, raged the headline, while above the text it said in summary: *Wrangel Island Explorers Refused Proposal of Marriage, Rescuer Noice Discloses Here. When Three Left Camp, Knight Died of Hunger. Though Man's Body Was Wasted by Starvation, Ada Blackjack Was Healthy.*

In Noice's mind, there were numerous reasons for coming forward with this information now. The public was being made aware of the mutilated diary, and accusational looks were being cast in his direction about the missing ten pages. He might have told Carl Lomen and A. J. T. Taylor that he planned to censor the diary, but no one could really prove that it was he, and not Ada Blackjack, who had removed those pages. He would own up to the erasures and pencil blackenings, but try to make people suspect that Ada was responsible for the missing pages. Then there was Frances. She had been urging him, threatening him, for some time to come forward and discredit Ada before she did so herself. He must have considered it better for him to discredit Ada, knowing how ruthless and vicious Frances could be.

Just to make sure that Lorne's father saw it, Noice sent a copy of the *World* article to Mr. Knight with a note that read, "I thought you might be interested in the enclosed clipping which shows that I have a different viewpoint of the Wrangel Island story, as that first published I obtained from the Eskimo woman. It is thru Mrs. Noice's efforts that the second story is brought to light, and it is thru her desire to give the boys a square deal, which she felt I had not done, that these discoveries were made. It caused her much suffering until these facts were made known."

*   *   *

On February 12, the sea grew noticeably calmer and the air was balmy and warm. They would dock in Los Angeles at 5:30 that evening, an hour and a half later than they were scheduled to arrive. As the ship passed the coast just below Santa Barbara, Ada studied the mountains and said to Peggy, "The hills look like Wrangel. Only the hills were higher on Wrangel, all covered with snow in winter and black in summer."

Although Ada had managed to avoid photographers at each stop, one of them had somehow snapped a shot of Bennett sitting in a sand pile. Peggy Fletcher had purchased a paper in San Francisco, not knowing the picture was in there, accompanied by a two-column article about Ada's trip to Los Angeles.

Ada studied the photograph and the story with a frown. "Here is my name. If I had known there would be all time papers to get story I would stay in Seattle." She paused. "If they tell things not true I'll give them hell."

Peggy had kept quiet while Ada sat staring at the article in fury. Finally, Peggy told her that if she wanted to go home now, or if she only wanted to stay a week in California, that was all right. No one wanted her to do anything she wouldn't enjoy.

Peggy had left her then to meet some friends for lunch. She wasn't certain what she would find when she returned to the boat—if Ada and Bennett would be gone or not. As soon as she was back on board, she raced down to Ada's cabin, only to find Ada there with her good mood restored. Together they made for the deck, but a swarm of reporters and photographers descended upon Ada, and she flew to her room, where she had remained until they were well past Alcatraz.

Afterward, Ada showed Peggy that she had bought three copies of the paper with Bennett's picture. She would not read the article again, but Ada could not help but be proud of Bennett's photograph. It was a handsome photo of him, and she said she was even planning to send one to Harvey.

In the safety of her cabin, with the reporters diverted, she had seemed happy again, and she began to tell Peggy stories. Ada had grown up hearing folktales from her grandmother, who was a tribal storyteller herself, and who told them to Ada when she was just a little girl. Now she told Peggy about an Eskimo man who married a polar bear, and about a woman who met a polar bear and looked into its eyes from sunup to sundown until the bear went away, and about the Lady in the Moon. This was Galle's favorite Eskimo story, she said, and was told to her by her mother when she was very young.

Peggy listened as Ada told the story about the girl who left her home and her loved ones to chase the man she wanted into another world. And how the man rejected the girl, leaving her frightened and alone, and so far away from everything familiar. Ada's soft, low voice described the dangers the girl faced, in a strange and unfriendly land, and how she found the Lady in the Moon to live with, so that the girl would be tucked away from everything that might harm her.

She told Peggy of the girl's yearning to be home, to see her family again, and of the Lady in the Moon's warning to her. The girl must save herself and find her own way, but she must be careful how she traveled. "Now the old woman had told her to keep her legs straight when she got on the earth," Ada said, her voice hushed. "For if she had straight legs she would be young just like she was when she went to the moon, but if she curved her legs, she would be bent like an old woman."

Ada had a unique and poignant way of expressing herself, and seemed to have inherited her grandmother's gift for telling stories.

Peggy was mesmerized, and willed herself to remember every point of the story so that she could write it down in her cabin later.

The weaving of the tales seemed to make Ada homesick for Nome all over again. She suddenly yearned for salmonberries, seal oil, and sour leaves. It had been too long since she had tasted any of those, except for seal oil, which she did have on Wrangel Island.

That night, Peggy stayed up until two in the morning, writing down "The Lady in the Moon." Since the ship had departed, Peggy had been trying to understand Ada, to get to know her. Ada's natural reserve made it difficult, as did her inherent distrust of strangers. But perhaps Ada had just told her much of what she needed to know. Perhaps, wrote Peggy, Ada saw herself as the girl from "The Lady in the Moon."

* * *

John Knight was horrified by what he read in the newspaper. The insinuations were terribly upsetting—that Ada had purposely ignored and mistreated his son. He felt he knew Ada better than this, and that the young woman he and his family had come to know and love would never be capable of anything so horrible. At once, he sat down and wrote a statement, which he wanted to send to the Associated Press. He sent it to Stefansson for approval, and they agreed that Stefansson would publish the statement in his book.

During the six months when Ada Blackjack was the sole companion of our son Lorne until his death, there is nothing in his diary to indicate that she did not do what she humanly could for him and for herself.

I have seen and talked with Ada, have discussed this matter with her, and I am fully convinced that she was grossly maligned when, "In a cozy room at the Villa Richard, Fort Lee, N. J., Mr. Noice told a group of friends a far different story." He says that Ada refused to aid Lorne and that she could have saved his life if she had tried, and that is why I am writing this article. We have had Ada as a house guest in our own home, and she has been admired and lauded by our friends and the friends of Lorne. I cannot allow the stigma to be placed upon myself and my family of having entertained a person so gross and monstrous as Noice would have her appear now.

Noice has crossed himself when he says now that he found Lorne's emaciated body and that "Mrs. Blackjack was well and fat." In his earlier articles he described Ada when he found her, as a frail little creature weighing less than 100 pounds and in a condition bordering on collapse. She tells us herself that she weighed only ninety pounds when she reached Nome and her normal weight is 120 pounds.

I still maintain that Ada Blackjack was a real heroine and that there is nothing to justify me in the faintest belief that she did not do for Lorne all that she was able to do.

I am writing this article because I feel that I owe it to the public and to a poor Eskimo woman who is being wronged and is helpless to defend herself.

Mr. Knight also granted a newspaper interview, in which he repeated his support of Ada Blackjack and his condemnation of Harold Noice. The Galles, the Maurers, and the Crawfords all wrote to Stefansson and to each other to offer their support of Ada. They considered it an outrage and an insult after what each of them had been through.

Death Is Blamed on Eskimo Woman.

Refusal of Marriage Held Cause of Faithlessness.

Ada Blackjack Accused.

Lorne Knight's Fate Could Have Been Prevented by Reputed Heroine, Rescuer Says.

But what of Ada? As the article was picked up by newspapers around the globe, there was no word from the accused.

*   *   *

Survivor of Arctic Trip Is in City, the *Los Angeles Times* stated on its front page, the morning after Ada had walked off the boat. "Last night," the article read, "efforts to obtain from Mrs. Blackjack a confirmation or denial of the charges made by Noice were met with a blunt refusal to talk."

The article was everywhere. They hadn't been on land long before Peggy Fletcher was told of Noice's allegations against Ada. It was so difficult to understand that in just six short months he could have changed his story so drastically. She couldn't imagine his reasons.

When she saw the article, she was even more mystified. It was badly written and unspeakably insulting. And it came just when Peggy was trying to teach Ada that not everyone was unkind or had a hidden motive and to convince Ada not to be suspicious of everyone she met. And now here was Noice—one of the few people Ada trusted, and the man she believed had saved her life—proving Peggy wrong.

Before Peggy told Ada about the articles, she asked Ada if she had had any trouble with Noice.

No, Ada said. She had written him to thank him for saving her life, but he did not answer her. Then, after a long pause, she said, "Well, I do not know what Mr. Noice can be saying about me—but whatever he does say I can't help—but he did come and save my life."

Peggy dreaded showing the article to Ada, but knew she must, and so she gave it to Ada to read when they were by themselves. Peggy would have shielded her from the news if she could, but reporters were already asking Ada for her reaction, and as a result Ada was confused and anxious.

Peggy sat watching Ada as she read. Ada made no sound except once, when she caught her breath sharply, and then she continued to read. After she had finished, she set the article aside and looked up at Peggy.

"Well, maybe white people could do more," she said after a few minutes, "maybe people would think I did not do enough, but I did all I knew how to do—maybe no one believe me—but I cannot help that. I did all I know how to do."

Whenever they set foot outside, reporters seemed to be everywhere, blasting Ada with questions about the missing pages of Lorne Knight's diary. Had she committed the crime? Did she remove them as Noice charged? Time and again, she repeated the same words she had said to Stefansson when she met with him in Seattle—she had not touched that diary of Knight's, except to shut it away in the box he used for storage. She had not removed any pages and she did not believe Knight had done so either. The diary, she told them, was intact when she gave it to Noice.

What about Lorne Knight? Had she left him to die? Had she herself grown fat while he was starving? Had she watched him waste away because she was too lazy to do anything? Or had she done it out of spite?

Ada tried to enjoy her time in Los Angeles and to push the article out of her mind. After searching for a hotel for Ada that would take "foreigners," Peggy Fletcher found the Hotel St. Marks, which was a grand building perched right on top of Venice Beach. Ada was anxious to see the ocean and to feel the sand beneath her feet, and Bennett was beside himself with excitement. They went for long walks on the sand and in the shallow edge of the water and saw all kinds of curiosities. There was a man eating fire while walking on glass with his bare feet. There was a mummy on display in a museum of curiosities. There were two small cows, which a man told them had been found in the mountains. And there was a merry-go-round, which Bennett rode while Ada watched. But her excitement was dampened by the stories in the newspaper, and she told Peggy that everything she did or saw now seemed empty.

Still, she tried to push it all to the back of her mind. She learned that she could get around on her own, as long as Peggy told her where she should go and how to get there. She was not as afraid as she had been when she first arrived in Seattle and had only walked around and around her hotel block for exercise, not wanting to get lost. Peggy had asked Ada if she could eat on one dollar a day, and Ada thought so. Ada missed her mother's cooking and the meals of seal and un- salted dry meat. But she was in California now and knew she must make do.

Ada wanted to stay on her own with Bennett, away from the re- porters who seemed to know where and how to find her. Peggy paid a week's rent and gave Ada $10 for her food allowance. Peggy would continue to stay across town with her friends, but she promised to check in regularly with Ada to see if she and Bennett needed anything. As Ada and Bennett hopped the streetcar for Venice, Peggy hoped that Ada would keep away from the kind of bad characters she oc- casionally seemed to attract.

In spite of her heartache over the Noice charges, Ada sat down in her hotel room on February 17 and wrote a letter to Mr. Stefansson, to thank him for the trip he had given her. "I'm sorry for I spent all these money for you, if it isn't for Bennetts health I wouldn't take this trip and spent your money. Mrs. Fletcher is paying for the rent of Hotel. She said its from you. So its very nice of you give me a present of this trip which I would never see this beautiful country. And I don't understand why Mr. Noice saying something against me. Although I been writing letter to him and thank him for saving my life. And never get answered no wonder he never answer my letter."

She continued to see Peggy, to take Bennett for walks on the beach, and to marvel at the sunshine and warmth. Bennett seemed stronger; the air and sun had done him good. To see him in good health was all Ada had ever wished for. But inside, she couldn't help brooding. She had trusted Noice. Why would he say lies about her? *That she could have averted the tragedy; that she refused to work or visit the traps; that she knew how to handle a rifle and was a good hunter, although she claimed she could not shoot. That she was well and fat while Lorne Knight was just a corpse.* This last accusation angered her the most of all. That anyone would say she was discovered well and fat when in fact she was thirty pounds lighter than her normal weight and so weak she could barely stand.

On February 26, Ada put on her new dress and took Bennett's hand and boarded the streetcar for downtown Los Angeles. She had learned to hate reporters, but decided now she must talk to them, to answer the charges, and to stand up for herself because no one else would. It was up to her to fix this, just as it had been up to her to take over when Lorne Knight became sick. If she could build a boat and learn to trap, teach herself to shoot, and stare a polar bear in the eye without flinching, she could tell her side of the story.

Downtown, Ada led Bennett directly to the newspaper office where she asked to see a reporter. "When I got to thinking about what they are saying about me," she told Peggy afterward, "my throat chokes and tears run from my eyes like water in the river when ice melts, and I turn my face away and look out car window so no one will be seeing me—and I think I will walk up to newspaper office and say a few words."

She said more than a few words and the *Los Angeles Times* printed all of them in three lengthy articles over five days. *Ada Blackjack Hits Back*, was the headline of the first one, splashed across the front page. Followed by *Death Vigil in Arctic Snows: Ada Blackjack Tells More of Polar Doom*. And *Ada Blackjack Refutes Noice: Woman Denies Starving Knight*.

It was the first time Ada had actually told her own story in her own words, and she made a considerable impression on the *Times* reporter.

"A little woman not five feet tall, with the high, broad cheekbones, the slanting brown eyes, and the rich blush of color of her race under her dusky skin . . . stood alone and uncertain on the shores of a vaster, drearier sea than the Arctic, the great ocean of uncertainty, ignorance and incredulity."

"Other allegations made by Noice need not be repeated," she told the reporter. "I don't care about that. What hurts me is that it should be said I grew fat on the food he might have had."

Her eyes filled as she talked, but her voice remained steady. She simply brushed aside the tears as she told the reporter of Knight's illness—and that he was left behind because he was ill with scurvy. She told of teaching herself how to trap so that she could get the food when Knight was too sick to rise from his bed, and of hunting gull eggs for him. She had chopped and hauled wood for the fire, even when she was sick herself.

I don't think I could have pulled through if it hadn't been for thoughts of my little boy at home. I had to live for him.

But that month was the death of Knight. He never got over it. Day by day he grew weaker. For the last two days he was unconscious. Before that, while he still had his mind and could talk, he thanked me for what I had done for him. He told me that if he ever lived to get back to his people, he would see that I was not forgotten. He told me, if he died, to take care of myself and try to live until the rescue party came.

I gave my diary and Knight's diary to Mr. Noice with my own hands. He says he found them on the floor of the tent. That is not true. I gave them to him. Would I have done that, if I had known they held words that could be used against me?

During the month while I was too sick to trap, Knight was sometimes angry with me. I suppose he thought I was shirking, that I ought to have got him fresh food. I couldn't. I needed fresh food myself, but I was too weak to get it.

I have written to Mr. Noice, asking for my diary back. He never answered.

That is all I have to tell, except that Knight's mother and father, who heard first what I am telling you now, believed me.

On Wrangel Island, Ada Blackjack was forced to be, as one of the articles pointed out, "doctor, nurse, companion, servant and huntswoman in one. Ada was woodsman, too."

Newspaper editorials took her side against Noice. "They found her broke in Nome and took her on a terrible adventure. I think she had a rotten deal both from the living and the dead," said one.

"She had 'guts' like a hero," read another. "Her physical stomach wasn't a bit more adapted to seal oil and blubber than theirs. But in Ada's heart there was a fire that isn't easily blown out. If Ada ever takes it into her head that she would like to see what the North Pole looks like she will wade up and look at the place—and without so much melodrama in the way of radio outfits, newspaper syndicates and farewell messages."

"For two months I was alone on the island," Ada said. "It was hard. But these accusations are harder still. There is no truth to them."

One of the articles concluded, "She will not be heard from again, if she can help it, she intimated. When summer comes, Ada and her little boy are going back where they belong, up North, back home."

A week after speaking to the newspaper, Ada was packed and ready to leave California. She had enjoyed her time in the sun and the sand, but was bitter now and felt it was time to leave. Peggy Fletcher accompanied Ada and Bennett to the train and hopped aboard to explain the Pullman cars to Ada and to ask the porter and the conductor to look after Ada and Bennett for her.

Ada told Peggy again how grateful she was to Stefansson for the trip. Peggy noted that there was something deeply sad about her since the Noice attack. Ada had been forced to face the memories she'd been avoiding, in order to save her reputation.

Before they parted, Ada inquired once more about her diary. Would Mr. Stefansson be returning it to her and when could she expect it? With Noice using her own diary against her to make his accusations, Ada was even more determined to have it back. When Peggy assured her that he would send it just as soon as he'd had it copied, Ada merely nodded. She hadn't trusted Stefansson before, just as she didn't trust most people. But after this trip, her opinion of him had changed.

*   *   *

Noice's treatment of Ada was shocking. Each of the four families—the Maurers, Crawfords, Knights, and Galles—felt the outrage deeply. Mrs. Galle spoke for all of them when she wrote to Stefansson to say she hoped that Noice would be stopped from committing any more unjust acts against innocent people. And Stefansson eagerly embraced the role of savior. He would straighten out Noice, he promised the families, and he would tell the truth about it all in his book.

While the Maurers, the Galles, and the Knights waited eagerly for its publication, the Crawfords were filled with dread. There would be no truth in the manuscript, they feared, and they braced themselves for the opening of old wounds and the beginning of new ones.

In his book, *The Last Voyage of the Karluk* (1916), Robert Bartlett had given a vivid description of his journey across the ice of Wrangel Island to Siberia. He had made the trek in March of 1914 and he knew, better than anyone, the near impossibility of ice conditions. Attempting the trip in January must have been hell. Bartlett wrote to the Maurers because he knew Fred from that earlier expedition. The Crawfords read his account, paying special attention to the chapters dealing with the Siberian crossing, and then sent it on to the Galles so that they could better understand what the boys had been up against.

It was hard not to fault the other families for their ignorance and apparent blind faith in Stefansson. Mrs. Crawford thought little of the rough-hewn Mr. Knight, with his simple, frank language and direct way of speaking; the religiously zealous Maurers, with their fervent adoration of Stefansson; and the naive and uninformed Galles. She preferred to correspond with Mrs. Anderson and others whom she felt understood her intellectually and emotionally. She had so little in common with these people, except the fact that their sons had died together.

Still, she tried to remember that the other families were not the enemy, and she wrote to Mr. Knight to acknowledge his words about a commemoration for the boys. She asked him to destroy her last letters, which were hastily and angrily written, and agreed with him that "In all matters, we the relatives of the boys should stand together and what you wish us to do in regard to a memorial for your brave son, both my husband and I will do. Lorne and Allan were true friends and we, their parents must be so too."

But she would not forgive Stefansson or make amends with him.

*   *   *

In March, with the accusations against Ada Blackjack made public, Frances Allison felt satisfied at last. Once he had done what she had insisted, she forgave her husband and they excitedly planned a belated honeymoon. They would spend a glorious two years in, of all places, the Arctic, living among the Eskimos on King William Island, off the northern coast of Alaska. It would be nice to have her husband to herself, away from outside distractions and anyone who might try to interfere in their relationship. Frances planned to study the native music, and Noice would write his observations of Eskimo life, while also recording their history and collecting relics from their past. Frances would be the first white woman ever to attempt to negotiate the Northwest Passage, as well as the first white woman ever to set foot on King William Island.

A crew of eight loaded the ship with supplies, including twenty thousand pounds of hard tack. They were going to travel from New York through the Panama Canal and eventually up to Vancouver, along the Canadian shore, to the Bering Strait, Coronation Gulf, past Victoria Land to the island. The schooner Noice had chosen for the trip had been renamed *Frances*, in honor of his bride. It was a happy time for Noice. Any misgivings he had harbored about slandering Ada faded as he saw the contentment of and approval from his wife. They were together again and things between them seemed better and happier than they had ever been.

And they were working on a new article for the papers—something more scandalous than anything yet printed. It dealt with Lorne Knight, Ada Blackjack, and Allan Crawford, and was certain to ensure that no one would ever think of any of the three as heroic again. They sent the piece to the editor of the *Toronto Star*, who refused to print it. He told Noice frankly that he could not imagine anyone publishing such garbage.

New Philadelphia

Dear Galle Family!

In your last letter I discovered that you can read German which makes me very happy.

I want to tell you something about our family life. We came to America in 1872. There were born 11 children of which 4 are living. If Fred were still alive, which we hope he is, then there would be 5 still alive.

My dear Mrs. Galle your beautiful letters made us feel good. It is hard for all our 4 families to lose our children in this way. It is hard on us at our age. My husband is 79 years and I am 74. Fred is the youngest and I cannot get him off my mind.

We must console ourselves and believe in God's grace although we cannot see each other.

Respectfully,
Mrs. David Maurer

Twenty

NEIGHBORS REPORTED THE case to the police. When they climbed the steps to the "poor rooms" on Seattle's Sixth Avenue and Columbia Street, they found child and mother sick and penniless. The woman seemed frightened and nervous, and the little boy's tonsils were inflamed and raw.

The news made the papers: *Ada Blackjack Is in Seattle Hospital in Destitute Condition.* It appeared just a few weeks after she had returned from Los Angeles. A woman from British Columbia wrote to the City Hospital in Seattle, where Ada and Bennett had been admitted. She had read a piece in the *Vancouver Sun* about Ada's desperate circumstances and enclosed a dollar for Ada, even though the woman had four children of her own to support. "I am very grieved," the letter said, "because I read sometime ago in the Manchester *Guardian Weekly*, a long account of your bravery during the expedition . . . and I thought your heroism and courage and Christian faith in God were just splendid, and never thought that you would ever be allowed to lack anything."

Stefansson asked A. J. T. Taylor to keep him updated on Ada's situation. Now that he had the rights to the diary and photographs, there was no need for fancy trips to California or new clothes, but he still wanted to keep Ada in his good graces. "I am afraid she is going to be somewhat of a nuisance to us in the future," warned Taylor, "unless she goes back to Nome and forgets that she is either a heroine or a villain."

*　*　*

Harold Noice had sent A. J. T. Taylor the Galle diary in a small tin box. No one had told Taylor that the box contained the journal pages, and so it sat unopened in his office for weeks until the Galle family continued to press for it, and Noice insisted he had turned it over. At that time, Taylor sorted through the box's contents and discovered twenty pages or so of handwritten text on separate pieces of paper cut to fit the size of the container. The writing was faded and seemed to be a kind of shorthand—abbreviations, brief phrases, and every now and then a full sentence. It must have served as a trigger for Galle's memory—notes he kept to use in his diary.

Stefansson deciphered it as best he could on a train ride to San Francisco, had copies made of the document for himself—including a typewritten copy—and then sent the original with the transcription to Mr. and Mrs. Galle from Adelaide, Australia, where he had embarked on a lecture tour. Galle's notes had helped fill in some of the gaps in Stefansson's book, which he had finished writing on a voyage from San Francisco to Hawaii. He included a special appendix at the end of the manuscript, dealing specifically with the Milton Galle papers.

Finally, after nearly a year of waiting for the diary fragment, the thin stack of pages arrived on Academy Street in New Braunfels, Texas. Even with the brevity of the content, one prominent fact emerged from the diary that disturbed his family—Milton clearly had reservations about journeying to Siberia. "Could I discard the feelings I have about our unwillingness on Milton's part to make the trip to Siberia," Mrs. Galle wrote to Stefansson, "I would be more at peace."

*　*　*

On August 6, 1924, an official pronouncement was made: The Canadian and British governments laid no claim to Wrangel Island. The Minister of the Interior stated clearly before the Canadian Parliament not only that the Dominion made "no claim to sovereignty over Wrangel Island," but also that "Mr. Stefansson was no longer in the pay of the Canadian Government."

The decision presented a problem for Stefansson. If the Canadians and the British wanted nothing to do with his claim to the island, what was he supposed to do with the colonists who were holding Wrangel for them? He would have to organize yet another expedition to transport them home. But perhaps the United States might want a chance at it. Perhaps they could be convinced to use it as a trading station and take over all responsibility for the place.

Just a few months earlier, he had spoken to Carl Lomen, willing, at last, to turn over complete possession of the island to him. "How would you like to take Wrangel Island off my hands, Carl?" was the way Stefansson presented his offer.

"I like the idea," Lomen answered. "But why give it up?"

"I can't afford the luxury any longer," was Stefansson's reply.

"Just how expensive would it be to me to take over your interest?"

"Well," Stefansson began, "there are thirteen persons on the island, one white man, Charles Wells, and twelve Eskimos. You would have to send a ship to visit them this summer, but I believe your portion of the fur-catch would more than repay you."

The financial aspects didn't concern Carl so much as the idea of adding a valuable island to the United States appealed to him. As Stefansson remarked with bitterness, so many people were blind to the island's potential.

Carl and Ralph Lomen purchased the title to Wrangel Island from Stefansson in May 1924 and then filed claim to it with the State Department in Washington, D.C. Carl agreed to take on responsibility for the removal of Charles Wells's party, and he and his brother contracted Captain Louis Lane to travel to the island in his ship *Herman*. Remembering his young friend and former neighbor Lorne Knight, Captain Lane agreed. For three weeks, the ship skirted the miles of ice surrounding Wrangel Island, and found it impenetrable.

When the ship broke a crankshaft, they were forced to turn back toward home. Thirty-eight miles to the east lay a small, hostile scrap of earth called Herald Island. As they crept past its shoreline, Lane and his crew could see the outline of what looked to be sleds tumbled across the beach. Hastily, Captain Lane gave orders to halt the ship, and set ashore with several of his men.

When they waded aground, they found themselves in a kind of graveyard, grim and barren, a wasteland of white and rock. Scattered across the windswept shore were human relics—pemmican tins, a rifle, knives, snow goggles, scraps of tent, and the sleds they had spotted.

And then someone held up a jawbone. And another, and another. When they discovered the fourth one, it was clear they had not found Allan Crawford, Fred Maurer, and Milton Galle. These human remains could, thought Lane, have belonged to four of the young men on Stefansson's 1913 Canadian Arctic Expedition, who became separated from the party after the ship was crushed in the ice. But there was no way to be certain until they took an inventory of the relics and collected them to be examined.

Captain Lane raised the American stars and stripes over that barren wasteland before returning to his ship, and soon they were back in Alaska, without Charles Wells and his Eskimo companions, but with the jawbones of four brave young men who had also lost their lives under Stefansson's command. The mystery of their deaths was at least partially cleared, but the mystery of what had happened to Crawford, Maurer, and Galle remained.

* * *

Relief, such as it was, came to those on Wrangel Island in the form of a Russian warship, able to break through the roughest, most impenetrable ice fields. The *Red October*, flying the Soviet flag, and armed with a six-pound cannon, headed for Wrangel Island in mid-August 1924. A company of Russian infantry sailed aboard her, with orders to seize all inhabitants and their belongings and establish, once and for all, ownership of the island in the name of the USSR.

There had been thirteen colonists in all when they had settled on Wrangel Island in September 1923. Now Charles Wells's party had increased to fourteen, with the birth of a baby girl. Since landing on the island, they had led a peaceful existence, occupying much of their time hunting and fishing and exploring the terrain.

To the Russian government, there had been relief at the official pronouncement by the British and Canadian governments that neither had an interest in Wrangel. On August 20, the *Red October* found the ice conditions more relenting than the *Herman* had, and anchored off Wrangel Island. Thinking it Stefansson's supply ship, Charles Wells and the Eskimos paddled out to meet the vessel in a skin boat. When Wells recognized the Russian flag, he hastily turned back, but the men aboard shouted for him to pull alongside the ship. The Eskimos in the skin boat were terrified of being shot, and, in spite of Wells, skimmed the umiak alongside the *Red October*.

Wells and his companions were assured that they would not be harmed, but they were immediately placed under arrest by the Soviet guards. On Wrangel Island, the Russian flag was raised, and $10,000 worth of furs was confiscated. After a month spent conducting scientific work on the island, the Russians sailed back to Vladivostok with their prisoners.

The news made headlines. "Soviet officials," wrote the *New York Evening Post*, "express keen satisfaction over the success of the expedition on the armed transport *Red October*, in planting the red flag on Wrangel Island, off Northern Siberia, taking formal possession. They believe this action will settle the status of the island, which has been in dispute for more than half a century."

While imprisoned, Charles Wells died of pneumonia, and at least one of the Eskimo children perished. The Eskimos who survived were deported to China, where they were detained at Sui Fen Ho and held until arrangements could be made to retrieve them and pay their expenses home. Eventually, they were brought back to Alaska through the efforts of the American Red Cross, who intervened on their behalf by transmitting a check to the Chinese for $1,600.

When the news reached New Braunfels, Alma Galle felt a new kind of exasperation and helplessness. The Russians would have removed any remaining signs or clues of her son's party. They might have destroyed evidence or documents or belongings simply to be rid of them, or they might have taken them as souvenirs.

Perhaps it was ridiculous to hold out hope, when the other families had long since given up. Perhaps she was foolish to have put such faith in every little glimmer, like the *Christian Science Monitor* article with its curious and suspicious date, or the psychic her sister Maggie consulted who had predicted Milton would be coming home. She supposed it was wasteful to study maps late into the night and read everything she could find to try to understand the currents of the sea surrounding Wrangel Island. But there had been a ship, the *Maud*, which had drifted between the island and Siberia. Her geographical map showed that the *Maud* might have taken the same path as Milton and the others when they set off on their trek. Perhaps someone aboard had seen something . . .

Harry Galle wrote to Captain Louis Lane, just to be certain that the men found on Herald Island were in fact members of the earlier expedition. Lane wrote back to confirm that they were.

*　　*　　*

On September 1, 1924, the first letter of commemoration arrived in New Braunfels. As agreed upon, each family exchanged a letter or note honoring the anniversary of the deaths of Crawford, Knight, Maurer, and Galle. Fred Maurer's parents wrote first: "It has been a year of anxiety, of hopes and fears—not only for our boys in the North, but for each other as well. May we hear from you as often as you feel like writing for it does help bear our great loss."

There was apparently great excitement in the Knight household because Stefansson had hired Joseph as his secretary, which meant their younger son would be traveling across the United States and Canada the following winter on Stefansson's Chautauqua tour, just as Milton Galle had done. They felt the experience would be a good one for him.

"We have never seen you but we have felt your sympathetic heart throbs and the scalding of your tears and we know that we are kindred in one great sorrow," the Knights' letter to the Galles began. "Let us be consoled in the fact that, they were four men of the quality seldom found, 100 per cent men, they were all equally brave and fearless in the discharge of their duty and they have left a record which bestows glory on them."

"Our thoughts have been with you all," wrote Professor and Mrs. Crawford, "and with the members of the other bereaved families throughout this day—the first anniversary of the day when the cruel news of the loss of our gallant boys came."

"We must all try to be as happy as we can under the circumstances and see love in everything and every body for our boys sake," read the letter from Delphine Maurer. "We must all go on and try to think of them as just 'being away,' for really that is all there is to it after all and some day we will join them."

For the first time, Alma had to admit to herself that they would probably never know just what had happened to Milton and the others. She and his father would most likely spend the rest of their lives wondering how and when and where Sohnie had died. There was no death date to commemorate, no burial place at which to mourn, no peace of mind for a mother who was haunted at night by the possibility of a son's painful, lingering death. Each time she visited the graves of her parents, she wished for a grave for Milton, on which to plant some flowers.

"It is not a 'Friendly Arctic' in which Wrangel Island lies," she wrote to friends, "and it may sound bitter . . . when I say I wish it had never been discovered."

*   *   *

On October 19, 1924, Noice and his attorney offered Stefansson a retraction to publish in his book about Wrangel Island. Noice was willing to admit that he had exaggerated certain facts. In exchange, he asked that Stefansson refrain from publishing certain charges and evidence against him.

Noice knew that Stefansson could and would ruin him if he didn't cooperate. Joseph Bernard, who had led the unsuccessful relief trip to the island in 1922, said that Stefansson claimed to have threatened Noice until he gave up the pages torn out of Knight's diary. And there were rumors that Stefansson and his friends at the Explorers' Club in New York had forced Noice's hand in writing the retraction with the threat of expulsion from the club. Whether they were bluffing or not, Noice was an easily influenced young man. His own lawyer advised Noice to throw himself on Stefansson's mercy and ask his forgiveness. It would be better for Noice, in the long run, than holding to the lies he had fabricated about Ada or even to the truths—such as the fact that the men had left the island because they were starving—that he had promoted. The attorney tried to convince Frances Noice, too, that it was the only course of action, but she refused to see the sense in it.

It was easier to give in by this point than to fight Stefansson any longer, and Noice was tired of fighting. He believed that Stefansson was jealous that he had gotten to the story first. Stefansson had certainly shown, with the *Karluk* escapade, that he had no qualms about exploiting the words of dead men. After their deaths, he had twisted the words of several late members of his past expedition, including one particular instance in which he was accused of creating a diary from thin air. Noice believed that if Stefansson was truly upset about something, it wasn't that Lorne Knight had been exploited. It was that someone else had done the exploiting—and reaped the benefits—first.

Others suspected this, too. Mae Belle Anderson remarked to Mrs. Crawford that, "In Noice's favour can be said that he has beaten Stefansson at his own game by methods which he learned from Stefansson himself. Again and again Stefansson has stolen material just as Noice has done this time."

Noice had idolized Stefansson—until he had served under him in 1916. But now there was nothing but deep resentment, hurt, humiliation, and fear.

Noice had told Frances certain things about Ada Blackjack and the men—things he knew weren't true, but then he hadn't expected her to mention them outside the marriage. When she insisted on publishing the "truth," Noice hadn't been able to tell her he had made it up.

But now he was prepared to make amends by admitting publicly and officially that Ada Blackjack was, in fact, a hero, and that he had created scandal out of thin air. Frances, of course, was disgusted, and left him, once and for all. There would be no more reconciliations between them.

Noice and Fanny parted ways in Brazil. She left him nothing except a return ticket, and he went back to New York, penniless and distraught. He had been working on a book about the Wrangel Island Expedition, and had destroyed the manuscript just to make Frances happy. But that wasn't enough to placate her, so he found himself with no moneymaking ventures up his sleeve, except a few motion picture films he had taken in the Arctic and on other travels. He shopped these around, but could find no takers.

Noice was now completely alone in every way. His wife had left him, his friends had deserted him, his colleagues had shunned him, and the promising career he had been building for himself was crumbling. Also gone were his integrity, pride, and self-respect.

After he returned from Brazil, he contacted Stefansson and asked for an interview. But at that interview, he went beyond simply repudiating the stories he had invented. He yielded to the pressure of Stefansson's influence and threats, and retracted the facts he sincerely believed to be true and which Stefansson disagreed with—namely, that the men were starving when they left Wrangel Island for Siberia.

"I am glad to take this opportunity of correcting some misjudgments," Noice began. He was teetering on the edge of a nervous breakdown, he said, brought on by the severe pain of his dislocated shoulder and the agonizing operation he had undergone to have the shoulder reset. He emphasized his "nervous condition," his "nervous prostration," the "nervous strain" he had been under at the time of reporting the Wrangel Island news. The nerves were apparently due to many factors—the pain of his shoulder, the anxiety over the outfitting and departure of the relief expedition, the threats made by the Russians, the pressure to reach Wrangel Island, and the shock of the tragedy he discovered once there.

He also felt he had a right to Knight's diary because he had found it, which, to him, meant that he could do exactly as he pleased with it, including selling it and altering its content.

Noice now said exactly what Stefansson wanted him to—that Maurer and Knight were not really inexperienced; there had been no shortage of food, which led to that final, fateful attempt to reach Siberia—never mind that Maurer's farewell letter to Delphine had clearly cited lack of food as their reason for leaving; and they had probably died a very fast and painless death, not like the different scenarios he had proposed earlier.

"My complete breakdown," he concluded, "followed soon after the publication of the original long and detailed newspaper story and its approach must have been the cause of what I later printed and which I was then convinced I was justified by Knight's and Ada Blackjack's diaries. I sincerely regret that any false impressions have been given and humbly apologize for my errors."

After the retraction was written, Noice signed his apology before witnesses—Stefansson, Isaiah Bowman, H. M. Brigham, and young Joseph Knight, working as Stefansson's secretary.

According to Stefansson, Noice urged him, of his own volition, to publish his retraction in the Wrangel Island book, so that the world could read the truth, once and for all. A triumphant Stefansson not only included the retraction in his manuscript, but spent a good part of the book discussing it.

With the Noice retraction, Stefansson expected that Professor and Mrs. Crawford would change their minds about refusing to contribute to his book in any way. He sent them the manuscript, hoping they would read it. If Noice hadn't painted Knight and Maurer, the two seasoned veterans, as being so inexperienced and incompetent, Stefansson reasoned, the Crawfords would not have been so upset about the fact that he had sent young Allan north with them. Now Stefansson expected to be forgiven.

But in their eyes, the Noice retraction changed nothing. It only served as proof of Stefansson's great and harmful influence on others. However, Professor and Mrs. Crawford did agree—reluctantly—to read the manuscript, if only to guard themselves and their son against any further misrepresentation.

In October 1924, Professor Crawford wrote to A. J. T. Taylor with his criticisms. There were many statements contained therein with which they did not agree—particularly those beginning "the relatives and myself are of the opinion . . ." or "Of course the relatives and myself are of the opinion . . ." The Crawfords resented the implication that they would ever—or had ever—agreed with Stefansson on anything, and wired their objection directly to Stefansson's publisher, the Macmillan Company, saying, "We now think it much wiser to specify by name the relatives to whom the author refers."

Stefansson thought their reaction pitiable. If only he had "as sympathetic cooperation from Mr. and Mrs. Crawford as I have from the other relatives I could make for Allan a place in Canadian history that would not only be his truly but would also be a solace to his parents."

He needed their permission to print Allan's last letters to them and to him. He felt the letters should be included in the book, but he was afraid of a lawsuit, should he publish without the parents' consent. Belle Anderson wholeheartedly supported Mrs. Crawford's wish not to contribute to the book in any way. "If Stefansson gets hold of a line of your son's letter for publication in his book," she wrote, "it means that you endorse the book. You may not think that, but everyone who reads the book will think so, and you join the other relatives in white-washing Stefansson and showing that it was pure accident that caused the death of the boys and not his mismanagement. I feel strongly that the letter of so honourable and gallant a lad as Allan Crawford deserves a more honourable and better place for publication than in any book written by Stefansson."

After the manuscript underwent some edits, the Crawfords were alerted that much of what they considered objectionable had been altered. Professor Crawford excused himself from reading the edited manuscript, as he did not "think it wise to do so." Furthermore, Professor Crawford wrote Mr. Taylor, "You claim that the manuscript has been re-written and objectionable matter eliminated. Does the objectionable matter eliminated include these statements which give the impression that the boys' salaries have been paid? While on this subject it is rather a coincidence that this Sunday just one year ago, you telephoned me to the effect that the debt owing to our late son would be paid 'about February.'"

Stefansson had asked each family to write a biographical sketch of the young man they had lost. Of course, the Crawfords refused, and so he found himself with bios of Knight, Maurer, and Galle, but nothing about Allan Crawford. He did not want to publish sketches of all the men but one, and so he would omit them.

He could resolve himself to this, but before the book was published, there was just one more missing piece that he needed to find.

*   *   *

In December 1924, Peggy Fletcher, setting out on a mission for her friend Stefansson, found Ada Blackjack living in a squalid little place in Seattle. There was just one room, with a partial kitchen jutting dismally off it. The high spirits and effervescence Peggy had witnessed in Ada on the trip to California were missing, and a definite gloom hung about her now. She seemed heartbroken and lonely, but she was glad to see Mrs. Fletcher, and so was Bennett.

To Peggy's surprise, there was a new baby, just two months old, on whom Ada obviously doted. His name, Ada said, was Billy, but Peggy didn't know if the father was Harvey or someone else. She noticed a man's coat hanging on the back of the door, and when she asked if the baby's father helped her out any, Ada said yes. "Is he still on the boat?" Peggy asked.

"Yes," Ada answered again.

But then she said no more. Peggy took the three of them outside for a walk, even though the temperature hovered near zero. Neither Ada nor Bennett had gloves, so Peggy stopped and bought them some, and also some toys for the children for Christmas. Ada was still anxious about her diary. She wanted very badly to have it back and asked Mrs. Fletcher repeatedly to please look into it for her. Ada exhibited none of her old enthusiasm or cheer, but Bennett, at least, seemed more fit and robust since the last time Peggy had seen him.

Stefansson had asked Peggy to get a statement from Ada about the missing pages in Knight's diary, but this time he wanted her words written down, in her own handwriting. Peggy took Ada and the children to her hotel for a hot lunch, and while they were there she asked Ada to write down her words. She tried to treat the matter casually because she knew Ada might resist otherwise. Ada wrote a few lines on a piece of hotel stationery: "I never show the Knights dairy since Mr. Noise got to dairy. I didn't tear the leaf out of it and I didn't read it."

Afterward, Peggy sent Ada and the children home in a taxi. Then she returned to her hotel room and wrote a letter to Stefansson about her visit. She included the note from Ada and sent it registered mail to Stefansson so that he could publish it in his book.

The next day, Peggy went to visit Ada again, and when the landlord rapped against Ada's door and announced that Mrs. Fletcher was there to see her, there was a shout from Bennett on the other side: "Oh! It's Mrs. Fletcher! It's Mrs. Fletcher!" Then there was the sound of running feet, and Ada throwing open the door with a smile on her face.

There was more that Stefansson needed to know, and Peggy had promised him she would do her best. She knew it was important that the entire Wrangel Island story was told, and that included Ada's viewpoint, but she knew, too, to be as natural as possible with Ada, so that she didn't trigger her usual suspicions. Peggy sat down with Bennett on her knee and told Ada there was some information Stefansson wondered about. Did the men take any specimens or rocks away with them from the island, that sort of thing. Ada didn't remember, but thought Knight might have brought some back from a trip to the interior of the island.

Peggy nodded and listened and bounced Bennett on her knee as she scribbled a few notes. Ada walked up and down, trying to quiet the baby, who wouldn't stop crying. She talked to Peggy over the noise as she remembered things.

Afterward, Peggy took her notes back to the hotel and sealed the envelope immediately. There could be no notary public or attorney present because Ada would only close her mouth and refuse to say a word, so this was the best way to get the information to Stefansson as accurately as possible.

Glorious was life
When standing at one's fishing hole
On the ice.
But did standing at the fishing hole bring me joy?
No! Ever was I so anxious
For my tiny little fish-hook
If it should not get a bite . . .

—NETSIT, *"Dead Man's Song"*
Eskimo poem

Twenty-one

ADA HAD SPENT MOST of her money, although she wasn't sure how. She knew there was money waiting for her in a bank somewhere in Nome—the rest of the money she had earned from Wrangel Island—but no one had told her how to get it. She'd had plenty to live on in Seattle, so much money at first that she wasn't worried about anything extra, but now she was unable to pay Bennett's board at school, so that he was living with her again, and she was struggling to keep her family fed. She had been searching for work, but because no one had a job for her, she finally approached the Bureau of Education for help. As decreed by the U.S. Government, the Bureau was the official guardian of the nation's Eskimos. Ada was trying to be careful with the money they gave her, to make it last as long as possible so that she wouldn't have to ask for more.

They enjoyed a festive Christmas, thanks to Mrs. Fletcher. But now it was January of 1925, and Ada was still living in one room with her two little boys and trying to figure out how to sustain them.

To add to her worries, Bennett's eyes were failing. His school clinic decided it was a syphilitic condition, no doubt inherited from one of his parents, which made the doctor there feel the boy was untreatable. Bennett was a naturally bright child, but if he was to succeed in school, he would need special training because his interest shifted quickly from one thing to another, and his health was never stable.

Then, in February, things grew even worse. Ada was walking down the street, carrying her baby, when she slipped off the curb and fell in front of an automobile. "After escaping the terrible fate of starvation in the bleak Arctic, Mrs. Ada Blackjack, Eskimo, nearly met death beneath an auto on Seattle streets yesterday," the papers reported.

She suffered only a sprained knee, but Billy sustained a wound to the scalp. The driver of the car rushed from behind the wheel to help her, taking her at once to the city hospital. After she and the baby were tended to, he drove them home.

One thing had become increasingly clear to Ada—she must leave Seattle. She had thought about it for some time and the accident was the final motivation to make her go. There was no work for her and no reason to stay. She wanted to get away from the newspapermen who still came around all the time, and from Harvey, who yelled at her. People were talking about her ever since Noice had printed his lies. She had spoken up for herself, but they seemed to believe the lies instead, and so Ada didn't feel welcome anymore.

She didn't tell anyone, not even her family, where she was going because she didn't want the newspapers to discover her destination— Spokane, Washington—and she didn't want Harvey to come after her. He had used her fame and notoriety for money, even though she had believed he loved her. He had treated her nicely at first, but when the public demand for her threatened to die down even a little, he accused her of following him from Nome to Seattle, shouting insults at her the way Blackjack used to do. They'd had a fierce argument, and she decided she didn't want to see or speak to him again.

She liked the idea of moving to Spokane because she didn't know anyone there. If she couldn't find work, she figured she could get some help from the Salvation Army. She bought the tickets to Spokane herself, and managed to draw $40 from the bank to take with her.

Once there, she and her children moved into a small room with a kitchen, which she had paid for in full for the week, and she bought groceries for them, leaving her with only 65 cents.

She didn't know the address of the man who was keeping her money for her in Nome, and so she wrote to Gertrude Andrus, one of Stefansson's colleagues in Seattle, to ask her for the information and to tell her not to mention to anyone where she was. If Gertrude could send her $10 or $20 from the money she had saved, Ada would be grateful.

She included her address and asked that Gertrude mail the letter and money to Mrs. Alscie W. Adwin. "I don't want this old name," she told her. "It isn't very nice to try to change my name but this Ada Blackjack name is going around too strong for me now. Anyway I shouldn't have this name for I was divorced from Blackjack and he was married to another woman and she is Mrs. Blackjack in Nome now . . . and why should I be call Mrs. Blackjack when there is another Mrs. Blackjack. Well I should change my name long ago but I never thought of any thing like this. I guess I couldn't very well get out of this name but I wish you would write and tell me what you think of it."

Ada found a woman to look after the children for her for $5.00 a week so that she could go out and look for work during the days. She was going to try her best to find a job without using the name she now hated so much.

*   *   *

In April 1925, Stefansson's book, *The Adventure of Wrangel Island,* was published with an introduction by John Knight. In the preface, Stefansson went so far as to call the senior Knight his coauthor, largely due to the contribution of Lorne's diary, on which a good part of the book was based.

The public had been inundated by press reports of the expedition for the past two years, and, consequently, the book sales were disappointing. But a great fuss was made in the papers about the Noice retraction, which was printed in full, and of the mutilated diary pages. Stefansson's charges against Noice were made clear in the book: He had purposely defaced Lorne Knight's diary; he had withheld and censored the last letter Knight wrote to his mother; he had " 'piratically appropriated' the papers of the dead men"; and he had viciously slandered Ada Blackjack.

Stefansson came across as a hero in the newspaper accounts, as he defended the dead men and discredited Noice's lies; Noice was described in the book as a "villain" and "scoundrel." After publication, no one wanted anything to do with him, although there was pity from the people who knew Stefansson best and who felt Noice, although foolish and reckless, had been badly used.

The book was barely out a few days when Noice read the latest headline: *Wife Goes to Reno on Noice Retraction.*

He had just turned thirty and he had moved out of the Villa Richard in Fort Lee, New Jersey, where he had been living with Frances since their marriage. Now, his address was a cramped apartment on West Seventy-sixth Street in New York, across from the Explorers Club. He was so proud of his membership there because you must be a person of note and some distinction to be invited to join. But he knew that this would be taken away from him, too, just as everything else had.

It was no surprise that Frances was headed to Reno to divorce him. He had been expecting it for some time, but it was another thing altogether to find out about it in the papers.

* * *

At the end of April 1925, after collecting her late husband's insurance payment, Delphine Jones Maurer married George A. Bretz of New Waterford, Ohio. To the parents of Fred Maurer, who still believed that their son might reappear some day, it was shocking but not surprising. They had never entirely warmed to Delphine. They knew that Fred had not wanted to marry her and had only done so because he thought it would keep her from killing herself and because he didn't want to seem a cad. But if she wanted to marry again so soon, they would be pleased for her and wish her the best of luck because there was nothing else they could do.

In June 1925, autographed copies of Stefansson's *The Adventure of Wrangel Island* were delivered to the families. The Knights alone were wholly proud of the book. There were a few sentences and wordings that the Galles wished had been altered, but they found the book interesting and felt grateful to have an official record of their son's last journey, especially one that the public could read. Alma pasted the last picture taken of Milton before setting sail for Wrangel Island—laughing and carefree on the deck of the *Silver Wave*—into one of the end papers and wrote his birth date below it.

The Maurers had looked forward to reading the book for some time. John Maurer had been in close touch with Stefansson during the writing of it and had passed along the family's many notes and suggestions, but he was surprised to find few of them appearing in the finished work. The family wasn't pleased with Stefansson's representation of events—his repeated suggestions that the four young men were incompetent and that they ventured to Siberia merely because they were homesick and wanted news from Stefansson, when Fred's letter to Delphine clearly emphasized the shortage of food.

Professor Crawford found the book insulting and condescending, and resented the depiction of his son and the other young men. He felt they came across as bumbling, inept, and clumsy, and was astounded at Stefansson's insinuation that the expedition had actually been the brainchild of Fred Maurer and Lorne Knight, as if his own interest had been only secondary. What was even worse, Stefansson stated frequently throughout the text that Crawford and the others had not left the island due to a shortage of food, but rather out of a desire to get news to Stefansson. To Professor and Mrs. Crawford, this was unforgivable.

After so much contemplation and struggle, the Crawfords decided to issue a statement, which was published in the *New York World* under the headline *Parents Blame Stefansson for Crawford's Death.*

For many months past we have read in silence statements in the press contributed or inspired by Mr. Vilhjalmur Stefansson "explaining" the tragedy of Wrangel Island. In some instances these statements have been contrary to facts, in others, a false impression has been conveyed by a more or less skillful use of partial truths for the purpose of deceiving the public and thereby, if possible, lightening the burden of culpability for the tragedy which Mr. Stefansson now bears.

In addition to making misleading statements Mr. Stefansson . . . has endeavoured to convince the public that their tragic end was a mere accident, that starvation could not have been its cause, although he himself has admitted that a supply for six months was all the food he advised them to take, and has stated in the London Spectator (August 18, 1923) that "their supplies probably gave out a year ago"!!

But it is in Frederick Maurer's farewell letter . . . that the most conclusive evidence is given that the fatal attempt to make the hazardous crossing to Siberia was made necessary through scarcity of food. Maurer's letter reads in part as follows:—

"The chief reason for our leaving is the shortage of food. There is not adequate food for all, there being only ten twenty-pound cases of hard bread and three pokes of seal oil to last until next summer."

That our son considered his party to be only the preliminary or advance party of a much larger expedition which Mr. Stefansson was to lead the following summer is shown by his letters written in 1921 to us and to friends. He had the utmost confidence that Mr. Stefansson would join him on Wrangel Island in July

1922. The faith of the boy in the man is infinitely pathetic—even up to the very end he was confident that Stefansson had kept faith with him.

It was this failure on the part of Mr. Stefansson to keep faith with the boys, and join them in 1922, together with the totally inadequate supplies with which he encouraged them to embark (in order to prove his theory that man can "live off the country" in the Arctic) that led to the needless suffering and death of our son and his companions.

Before the article was printed, the other parents received telegrams from the *New York World*, asking if they supported the Crawfords' statement. Even with their own objections to some of the material in Stefansson's book, the Maurers and the Galles preferred to stand by Stefansson. "The Maurer Family stands by Mr. Stefansson on the attitude he takes on the tragedy," John wired to the *World*.

After the statement was released—and newspapers across Canada and the United States picked up the story—the Galles and the Maurers distanced themselves from the Crawfords, and John Maurer asked Stefansson not to involve them in his quarrel with that family, with whom, as far as he was concerned, he wanted nothing more to do.

In June 1925, the Canadian House of Commons, prompted by the Crawfords' published statement and their charges against Stefansson, met to debate the Wrangel Island situation and to establish whether or not Allan Crawford had, in fact, died of negligence. The government wanted to determine its own responsibility in the matter as well.

One point seemed clear—if the government of Canada was responsible to anyone, it was to Crawford, who had been led to believe by Stefansson that he was acting in the service of Canada and Great Britain, when, in fact, he had been acting for Stefansson. The members of the House argued over Stefansson's actions and even his nationality. No one could determine if he was actually Canadian in the first place. A member of the Progressive Party commented that, "He is sometimes one and sometimes the other. Sometimes he is an American and sometimes he is a Canadian, just as it suits him or wherever he happens to be living."

But there was one matter upon which the members of the House seemed to agree—a memorial of some sort should be erected to honor Allan Crawford, the one Canadian member of the expedition and a young man "of exceptional attainment and personality and character." Prime Minister Mackenzie King and the leader of the opposition, Arthur Meighen, both concluded that a tribute should be made. "If there is aught remaining to be done," remarked Prime Minister King, "it is to acknowledge the great patriotism of this young lad who . . . showed exceptional courage and daring, and who, I feel, deserves at the hands of the country some expression of honour to his memory."

*　　*　　*

Whatever else was accomplished by the publication of Stefansson's book, Ada Blackjack's status as hero had been restored, and to the parents of her four companions, this was a triumph.

Yet it was as if she herself had disappeared. The Knights had lost touch with her, as had Inglis Fletcher and Stefansson, and no amount of searching could locate her. She seemed to have completely withdrawn from the world until July 1925, when the *Toronto Mail & Empire* reported that Ada Blackjack was returning home to Nome, Alaska. This news came from the Alaska division of the U.S. Bureau of Education.

But after that, there was no more news, and for two more years, no one heard anything of Ada Blackjack.

The next reports of her whereabouts surfaced in 1927. Ada was ill with tuberculosis and preparing to die. She had placed Bennett and Billy in the care of the Jesse Lee Home, a mission school near Seward, Alaska, on the southern coast, and now she was entering a hospital on Kodiak Island, in the Gulf of Alaska, some 250 miles from Anchorage. According to the article, Ada had contracted tuberculosis on Wrangel Island and did not have much longer to live.

Once again, she made the headlines, and greater details followed in subsequent articles. "Ada will die of tuberculosis," predicted the *Kansas City Journal* on August 1, 1927. "I know I have only a little time to live and I want the children to be safe and happy," she told them. Ada was not able to care for her sons anymore. Work was scarce, although she took what she could find. Bennett, at age nine, had contracted spinal meningitis, which left him deaf and blind in one eye. Ada was in and out of the hospital, and there was little she could do for him or for Billy, who was now three.

Most of the children at the Jesse Lee Home were orphans and the majority of these were native Alaskans. Many, like Billy and Bennett, were waiting for their parents to be cured of tuberculosis, which was prevalent in Eskimo communities and often was responsible for extinguishing entire villages. Some of the children never saw their parents again and there they remained.

The Home had begun in 1890 as a six-room house, which was attached to a government school. But in 1924, the Jesse Lee Home moved to Seward. Mountains, forests, and streams surrounded it and bears often wandered onto the grounds. It was reportedly a warm, idyllic place for children.

When Bennett and Billy arrived, the Home had two separate dormitories, one for boys and one for girls, and a schoolhouse. Each dormitory room contained ten or twelve beds and the children were housed according to age, so that Bennett and Billy lived separately. Still, they saw each other during the day while they worked outside growing food and tending the garden, and harvesting the salmon that lived in the streams.

Bennett was taught to read and write at the Home, and even learned to play music despite his hearing disability. He spoke rarely because his speech was difficult to understand, which made the other children tease him. He grew up tough and fierce and would frequently get into fights with the other boys. But he looked after his little brother; if anyone ever picked on Billy, Bennett came to the rescue. He also taught Billy sign language so that they could speak to one another.

When her fragile health allowed, Ada came to see them. She was thin and pale and often coughed up blood. Although she seemed like a stranger to Billy, the very sight of her brought joy to Bennett. He would instruct Billy to pay attention to her when she came to see them, otherwise she would feel sad, and he promised his brother that one day Ada would come for them, once she was better. But Billy didn't want to think of leaving, and to him, the housemother, Miss Ard, was the one who gave him the comfort and love that his absent mother could not.

For Ada, it was heartbreaking to be separated from her children, and to see the distance in Billy's eyes as he regarded her on her visits. When Ada came to tell them that her sister had died, Bennett began to cry but Billy could only pretend to be sad because he had no connection to his aunt.

The *Toronto Mail & Empire* proclaimed Ada the first Eskimo heroine in history, and observed that "Hardship of the sternest kind is the only kind of life Ada Blackjack has ever known, with the exception of the few months which she spent in the United States after her rescue from Wrangel, when Stefansson brought her down to civilization to help her rid her mind of the haunting thoughts of the two years spent on the Arctic island."

Stefansson read the newspaper reports along with everyone else. But instead of sympathy, he felt nothing but disgust for Ada. In his eyes, Ada Blackjack was one person who was beyond help, because no matter how much money she was given by him or by the Bureau of Education, she seemed unable to manage it and only seemed to lose it quickly. Now there were stories of tuberculosis, none of which he believed, and he decided to write her off as a lost cause and wash his hands of her for good. He had heard nothing of her for many months, and he hoped never to again.

PART VI

REMEMBRANCE

I thank God for living.

—ADA BLACKJACK

THE ADA BLACKJACK FUND
for
"The Heroine of the Arctic"
Tacoma, Washington
❄

June 1, 1928

Dear Friend:

Tomorrow may be too late!

Because it has been declared that Death is the price that Ada Blackjack must pay for her heroism.

Now she has been all but forgotten by the country she served, with the verdict of death ringing in her ears.

In recognition of her courage then—and her needs now, a small select group of American men and women are being asked to assist the Fund and form a Committee of One Hundred.

So, on behalf of an obscure and uncomplaining Eskimo woman and her children, we are asking you for your help.

The suffering that Ada Blackjack endured was too much—the Arctic cold that seared her lungs made her easy prey to the ravages of tuberculosis.

A few dollars from each will enable us to put a roof over Ada Blackjack's head, pay her present debts (due to her inability to earn), maintain her in some degree of comfort and keep the spectre of want from the door, help to clothe and educate her children. We will have the watchful and trustworthy assistance of Dr. Firestone, of the Alaska Bureau of Education, in the expenditure of any funds for her relief.

On Wrangel Island Ada Blackjack was true to her trust and steadfast in the face of Arctic dangers—shall we now restore to her home this Eskimo woman, with her Christian code of honor, her heroic struggle to live, and care for her children—in short make her remaining days a little more comfortable, a little less harsh?

Yours sincerely,
Burt E. Anderson
Treasurer, Ada Blackjack Fund

Twenty-two

LIFE HAD BEEN A STRUGGLE for Ada. Her physicians had predicted she would die from tuberculosis, but she had clung to life. She took the work she could find and labored until her cough returned. She was forced back to the hospital to recuperate, and her house in Nome was sold to pay her debts.

In May of 1928, during a time of record trading on Wall Street and just one month before Amelia Earhart became the first woman to fly across the Atlantic, Ada wed Ralph Traffers, who worked as mate on the motorship *Margnita*, which traveled a route between Juneau and Sitka. They divorced shortly afterward and later she married a man named George Johnson. When that marriage ended, Ada found herself once again unable to support herself. On December 8, 1928, the stock market had plunged twenty-two points. On October 24, 1929—better known as Black Thursday—the stock market crashed. Ada moved from Juneau to Kodiak to Seattle, where she lived for fourteen years. "I had a hard time in Seattle," she later recalled. "There was no money and I had to have surgery. Welfare told me to get out and go to work."

When her son Billy was nine, she was able to take the children away from the Jesse Lee Home and bring them to live with her. She herded reindeer and hunted and trapped to earn a living, and whenever Billy asked her to tell him about the Wrangel Island Expedition, she became angry.

"Never mind," she would say. "I don't want to talk about it."

But one day, when Billy was fifteen years old, Ada said softly, "When I was on the expedition and the others had gone away and I was with Knight taking care of him, he said he wanted to marry me if we ever got back." There is no evidence that Knight ever proposed to Ada, but it was what she remembered.

Often, when she finished with her work, she would sing to Billy. For years, she sang him one particular tune, which seemed to have no words. To Billy, it sounded like nonsense—"Ah nooga naga nooga"—and as he grew older, he became increasingly irritated by it. Eventually he asked his mother what the song meant.

"There is no translation," she told him. "There are no words for it in English. But it means 'I love you.' "

When Billy grew up and left home, Ada continued to take care of Bennett. Eventually, she moved to Anchorage, where she lived alone in a shack. She had few possessions, but her most prized was the Bible given to her by Lorne Knight. Memories haunted her and she still was led to tears when she remembered certain aspects of the expedition. As much as she tried to face the memories and to flee from them, she would never get over the death of Knight, the disappearance of the three other men, or the hardship she had endured both on Wrangel Island and back in civilization. She struggled for years to find work and earn a living, trying her hand at sewing, housekeeping, fishing, hunting, and berry picking. Stefansson had once promised her a share of royalties from his book, *The Adventure of Wrangel Island*, but she had never received anything.

*   *   *

Over the years, rumors of possible sightings of white men in the Arctic or in Siberia drifted in and out like the tide off Wrangel Island. Alma

Galle, in particular, followed up every lead because it had become clear to her some time ago that Stefansson was doing little to find her son.

So it was Alma who wrote to the Soviet Information Bureau to ask if they had found the boys or knew something of their whereabouts. And it was Alma who contacted the Travelogue Film Company, which was heading into the Arctic for four months. The members of the company did not know if they would journey as far as the Siberian coast, they told her, but promised to keep eyes and ears open for a trace of the lost men.

And, most important and intriguing of all, there was the Swenson Fur Trading Company. In the spring and summer of 1930, a report from the company gave the Galles, the Maurers, and the Crawfords one last, exciting glimmer of hope. Captain Olaf Swenson, who had rescued the *Karluk* men from Wrangel Island in 1914, made trips into the far North nearly every year, and now he contacted Thomas Maurer about another sighting. Some Eskimos mentioned they had seen an ice floe carrying a tent.

The Eskimos lived sixty miles from the mouth of the Kolyma River at Cape Baronoff in eastern Siberia, approximately 150 miles southwest of Wrangel Island. One of the local reindeer herders had been out on the ice, they said, about a mile and a half offshore at the edge of open water. He found what he described to be a tattered and broken tent drifting on an ice floe. He lifted a corner of the tent and beneath it found the legs and head of a man and the upper body of another man. Dropping the tent flap, he ran back to the beach and told everyone what he had seen.

Afterward, he refused to talk or say anything more than what he had initially reported, and the cake of ice continued its wayward path into the heart of the ocean. But days later, some wreckage washed ashore in the same spot. It appeared to be the rubble of a ship. A small vessel had been reported lost at sea in the area years ago, but it was hard to know if the men on the ice floe were from the same disaster. To Swenson, the herder's silence was suspicious, and he suspected the man had stolen something from the tent and now feared a reprimand by government officials, which was why he had stopped talking about it.

"It is sometimes very difficult to get the proper information from the natives," Olaf Swenson wrote to the Galles, "as some of them have a weakness for enlarging on facts, and as only one native saw this broken-down tent, and afterwards refusing to talk about it, it is hard to tell whether he really saw bodies under the canvas or not." Still, the movement of the currents led Swenson to believe that the skeletons belonged to the Crawford party. In any case, he promised to keep the families updated if he learned anything further.

As Helen Crawford remarked, "All this has revived the horror of the terrible early days of the tragedy."

* * *

"I always dread this time of the year," wrote Mrs. Crawford on September 1, 1930; "it brings back so vividly the unforgettable agony of those days seven years ago and I sometimes wonder if it is best to recall it as we do by exchanging letters on Sept. 1st."

Through the years, the consistency of the letters dwindled, depending on family illness or hardship, but at least one member of each family would remember. They carried on the tradition for ten years, perhaps longer, although those letters, if they existed at all, have disappeared. On September 1, 1934, Helen Crawford wrote the last surviving letter of the series.

"When I woke up this morning and remembered it was September 1st, eleven years since we lost our boys, my first thought was, 'What a wonderful healer time is!' Eleven years ago I did not believe I should ever again know a moment free from bitter pain. But time has somewhat dulled the pain. I have not heard from the Maurers for two years, but nevertheless I think I should send a message to them on this day."

*   *   *

Just a week before Mary Maurer died, a news report filtered over the radio announcing that Fred Maurer had reappeared in the North and had broadcast his arrival himself. Mary was due at a stitchery at the church, but stayed home instead, awaiting word from her son. There had been no official confirmation as of yet, and Mary was anxious. If Fred were alive, she was desperate to see him. She had been ill off and on for months, suffering from severe attacks of asthma, but she vowed to hang on until Fred reached her.

She died a week later, on February 4, 1926, of hypostatic pneumonia, which was caused by heart blockage triggered by the asthma. She was seventy-five years old and passed away at home, surrounded by family. Just the night before, she had enjoyed a cheerful evening with close friends and seemed to be in good spirits. The supposed news of Fred's survival had lifted her and filled her with a joy she did not think herself capable of anymore.

A devout member of the First Reformed Church and of the Ladies' Aid Society, Mary Maurer had thrown herself into work at the New Philadelphia auxiliary of the Union hospital. She had tried to busy herself with her family, her friends, her work, since she had first heard the news of Fred's disappearance.

Four children survived her and ten grandchildren. But until the moment of her death, she never gave up the hope that her baby, Fred, was alive somewhere, even though his brothers and sister had long since resigned themselves to the fact of his death. She promised everyone she knew that she would live long enough to see Fred come home again.

After Mary's death, there was no further news regarding Fred and the radio report, and this, coupled with his wife's passing, seemed to break the spirit of David Maurer. Those closest to him expected that he wouldn't last long without his wife, and almost immediately, his own health seemed to deteriorate. He was 81 when he followed Mary in death nine months later, on November 19. He also died at home.

Fred, in his last letter to his mother, had made it clear he blamed no one but himself for his choices in life. He had elected the career of explorer, fully aware of the dangers, and he alone had made the decision to go north again under Stefansson. Few people understood such a desire, given Maurer's tragic history with Wrangel Island, but his parents had done their best to support his need to return to that place.

*   *   *

"Some day the truth will come out," Mrs. Anderson assured Mrs. Crawford. "Allan Crawford belongs to history and history is bigger than your life or mine."

The House of Commons' ruling and the publication of the Crawfords' statement had brought some degree of satisfaction, but Helen Crawford was filled with a longing for justice. She would never forget or forgive what Stefansson had done to her son and to her family, and the bitter feeling would only deepen as the years passed.

In the summer of 1928, Professor and Mrs. Crawford, with Marjorie and Johnnie, took a vacation to Europe. They needed to get away from Canada and from the memories that lingered. The family had made a habit of summer vacations together, but in 1928 they decided to go somewhere where they could escape Stefansson and the mentions of Wrangel Island that still appeared in the papers now and then. So they settled on a European tour and sailed abroad.

Professor Crawford's mustache and hair had whitened since the death of his son, but this only made him appear more distinguished and elegant. He seemed a bit thinner, a bit more retiring, but as full of energy as he had always been. When he died suddenly and unexpectedly in Innsbruck, Austria, on July 17, it was a shock to everyone. Afterward, the doctors diagnosed a heart attack due to hardening of the arteries. The newspapers, as usual, picked up the story, and conjectured that it might have been heat stroke instead, but there had been no excessive heat, as far as Helen could remember.

Helen was completely and utterly lost. She had been so preoccupied with Allan's death that she had never foreseen or contemplated her husband's.

"My husband was not ill a day," she wrote Mrs. Galle. "He had not missed a meal nor a night's sleep on all our travels, nor did he complain of an ache or pain. We had no suspicion of heart trouble, nor did he himself. There is no doubt that Allan's death had its effect in shortening his father's life."

After burying her husband in Austria, Helen and the children returned to their empty house in Toronto on August 2. Marjorie was a senior at the University of Toronto and was engaged to be married in one week. It would be a quiet wedding.

The love of her daughter and her younger child, Johnnie, who was only fourteen, meant a great deal, but it was hard for Helen Crawford to feel anything but helplessness. "I feel at times I simply cannot go on living," Helen confided to Alma Galle, "but I know I must for my children."

* * *

In 1926, Joseph Knight, brother of Lorne and former secretary to Vilhjalmur Stefansson, married Ada Gertrude McGee; everyone who knew Joseph and the story of his brother and Ada Blackjack found it extremely ironic.

Joseph had completed his work with Stefansson after the end of Stefansson's lecture tour, and when he returned home to McMinnville, Oregon, he joined his father in business. There was an office in nearby Portland now and one in Hillsboro. John Knight ran the Portland office, and he engaged Joseph to oversee the McMinnville branch.

The Knights had managed to recover somewhat after Lorne's death. They were filled with a steadfast belief and faith in Mr. Stefansson, who they felt had been nothing but kind and generous to their family. They were surrounded by close friends and a warm, tight-knit community that continued to offer support. They needed that support again when Joseph and Ada's baby son, John Marion Knight, died at birth.

They needed it once more on October 2, 1930, when Joseph was involved in a violent automobile accident. He died of his injuries the following day. He was twenty-seven years old. John Knight was seventy, and Georgia was sixty-seven when they buried the last of their children.

Mr. Knight gave the responsibility of the Portland office to someone else and focused on McMinnville, the scene of so much of their former happiness—and sorrow—taking over the office that Joseph had run.

Chaplain Frank Wortman gave the eulogy at Joseph's funeral, and his words spoke to the loss of Lorne, too: "True, our brother has journeyed away from us. His dream ship, frail or staunch . . . has sailed to another shore. The clock of his days has stopped. Upon its dial, the motionless shadows mark eleven, with us the golden hour of recollection. Whatever may have been his accomplishments, we are his treasurers. It devolves upon us to cherish his good deeds, to forget his imperfections and to inscribe his name upon tablets of love and memory. As he was true to every one of us, let us be true to him. And so I say . . . 'Good-bye, good-bye until the hour of eleven shall regularly return.' Thou art I and I am thou, for thy name I have as a talisman upon my heart."

John Knight could not understand how so much tragedy could happen to one family. Every day, he had talked of Lorne and Allan, Milton and Fred, and relived with his wife the funny and touching stories from Lorne's boyhood days. He never expected that they would one day be doing the same for Joseph.

Mrs. Knight and Joseph's widow visited his grave two or three times a week, decorating it with colorful and fragrant flowers they grew themselves. But John Knight couldn't bring himself to go with them. All these years, he had wished for a final resting place where he could visit Lorne and talk to him and go to pay his respects, but now he knew he could not go to see Joseph because, as he wrote to the other families in his September 1 letter of commemoration for 1931, "I always

want to bring him home with me and my inability to do so, breaks
my heart."

He often sat at his desk and gazed at a picture of his two sons.
And then his gaze would shift to the photograph on his wall of Lorne,
Milton, Allan, Fred, and Ada Blackjack.

*   *   *

If Harry and Alma Galle had known anything of Stefansson's character
in 1921, they were certain they would have stopped Milton from going
north for him.

In 1928, Alma Galle was still writing letters to Stefansson, trying to
retrieve the money due her son. He still claimed debts and bankruptcy,
and pointed out that because the Stefansson Arctic Exploration and
Development Company had been incorporated, it meant he had no
more legal liability than any of the other stockholders.

"Since my paying you anything on the company's account is illegal,
and would involve me in legal difficulties with the creditors, too, you
must consider the enclosed $200. as a gift, prompted only by sym-
pathy, and a purely personal matter between us," he wrote her.

But it was not enough. Milton, she knew, was owed more for the
furs he had collected, and so she kept writing. In January 1929, she
still had not received a satisfactory answer to her requests. It had been
a year since she had last heard from Stefansson. "I can only say," she
wrote, "I wish the time was here that I should not feel it necessary to
approach the subject of financial affairs to you."

Again, she heard nothing.

She wrote November 1, 1932, to say, "However great this task of
writing about finances is, I feel I shall have to again remind you how
much we would be helped, should you be able to send what is still
left of Milton's money. Just why we have had to wait, when others
have long had their money and already 11 years have elapsed since
our boys left home, we cannot understand. Truly I believe you might

to some extent feel the Depression too, for it misses few if any people at all." She never heard from Stefansson again.

Times were hard for everyone in New Braunfels, and the Galles were no exception. There was little work for a house painter, but Harry had finally been able to secure a job in east Texas, some 380 miles from their home. Alma missed him while he was away, but she hoped that the new year—1933—would bring better luck for them.

Instead, Harry underwent a cataract operation that was unsuccessful, and he became completely blind in one eye. By 1933, he was blind in both eyes and unable to earn a living. Somehow, they managed to get by, and Elsie and Alfred both graduated from college at the University of Texas in Austin.

In December of 1933, there was, at last, a piece of good news. A letter had been found by Russian colonists on Wrangel Island—just a small scrap of paper that appeared to be quite old. It contained directions, and words of work that had been done, efforts that had been made, and faith in a leader who had never come. But there had been expectation, not only that this leader would join them, but that all of their hard work and effort would be rewarded some day. It was signed Milton Galle, and, while it wasn't the last letter his mother had been hoping for, it was a piece of him come home.

*   *   *

After the publication of *The Adventure of Wrangel Island* in 1925, Harold Noice seemed to disappear. Friends stopped hearing from him and even the Explorers Club eventually lost touch with him. But in 1939, a book by Noice entitled *Back of Beyond* was published by Putnam. It detailed an expedition to the Upper Amazon to photograph a remote native tribe named the Pogsas, whom the flyleaf described as "strange, completely primitive dwarfs of the deepest jungle."

It was an engaging page-turner, filled with sensational tales of cannibalism, hurricanes, poisoned darts, tribal rites, flesh-eating plants, hostile peoples, the bleached bones of a white man, and the fleeing for his life of the author. Noice was forty-three years old at the time of the book's publication, and it seemed that he had reemerged from the public humiliation and scandal of his earlier years with some success.

There was a radio serial running—"The Black Flame of the Amazon"—which was based on Noice's experiences in *Back of Beyond*. He contributed articles to the *American Anthropologist* and even directed a few short pictures in Hollywood.

But the Wrangel Island disgrace would never completely escape him.

On July 16, 1937, Stefansson and Carl Lomen toured the Federal Bureau of Investigation in Washington, D.C. Stefansson was in a hurry and asked the guide to show them only the most interesting points, as he needed to leave in half an hour. Stefansson found the tour fascinating, particularly the crime laboratory. He asked to speak to one of the handwriting experts and was introduced to the man in charge of the technical laboratory, a man named E. P. Coffey. Stefansson told Coffey that he possessed a diary of an Arctic explorer who had died in 1923, but that the document had been mutilated by another member of the expedition. Could he send this diary to the Bureau so that they could attempt to decipher the original writing?

After the tour, Stefansson and Lomen were brought to Director J. Edgar Hoover's office, where Stefansson and Hoover discussed the matter in detail. Stefansson had removed one of the leaves from the diary himself and sent it to Hamburg, where a specialist in the field of criminal falsifications of documents, Dr. Rudolf Kraul, Department Director of the Chemische Staats-Laboratorium, had been studying the document for a year, trying to decipher the blacked-out writing. Dr. Kraul had contacted Stefansson after reading *The Adventure of Wrangel Island*, volunteering his expertise.

Before Kraul, a team from Harvard's Fogg Museum had made their own attempt to restore the obliterated words. They worked with a sample page first, using similar paper to that in Knight's diary, which they gently sponged with ethylene dichloride, to dissolve surface pencil marks and allow the original impressions to appear. Afterward, the paper was sponged with a mixture of zinc oxide and ethylene dichloride, which reduced the shine, and then the paper was placed between two pieces of plate glass and photographed with the illumination of a microscopic lamp. They tried both optical and chemical methods, but the museum, like Kraul, had to admit defeat, and the most they had been able to restore was the time of day of the entry Stefansson had sent them.

J. Edgar Hoover was delighted to help, and asked that the manuscript be sent to him. It then took two years before Dr. Kraul finished his own examination of the material and returned it to Stefansson, who then forwarded the sample page and specimen photographs to Hoover. By October 1939, the Bureau had deciphered at least a dozen words. To do more, they told Stefansson, they would need the preceding page where they might find telling indentations from the original writing, and they would also perform a treatment with photographic plates. But E. P. Coffey made it clear to Stefansson that, while they would give him their technical assistance in deciphering the pages, the FBI would not undertake an official investigation into the matter. Coffey and Hoover knew of Stefansson's reputation and were well aware that "he is prone to use situations to his own advantage wherever possible."

The Fogg Museum was still in possession of Volume I of Knight's diary, which they promptly transferred to the Federal Bureau of Investigation. The original Volume II was still with the Knight family in McMinnville, and Stefansson asked them to send it to the Bureau for study. The Knights agreed readily, and forwarded the journal, with its loose binding and separated pages, to Washington.

The passages had been deleted with careful calculation. A rubber eraser and a soft pencil were the weapons. Knight had originally used an ordinary number two graphite pencil, and a 2b was employed to do the crossing out and marking over. Horizontal lines had been drawn to black out the impressions, but the indentations had remained, and from these Coffey and his team were able to restore the majority of the missing text. On December 21, 1939, Hoover sent Stefansson a summation of what was found.

Noice claimed that the diary contained evidence of immorality, but the FBI's investigation turned up nothing more than that Ada Blackjack seemed to fancy Allan Crawford and that Noice had destroyed passages with careful deliberation. Most of the blackouts involved the activities of Ada Blackjack and her refusal to work during the early weeks when she was suffering from homesickness and Arctic Hysteria. But many of the recovered sections seemed completely innocent, merely containing the words Crawford and Ada in the same sentence. It was clear that Noice had wanted to imply scandal where none existed. The entries revealed no immoral acts or relations between the men and their seamstress.

"Summarizing the evidence from the context and from the words restored," Hoover concluded in his letter, "it is apparent that the deletions are of a character which would occur if a person reading hastily through the diary and failing to observe in detail all of the entries, desires to create the impression of some sensational information being suppressed and hastily erases portions at places which because of the erasures will appear significant but which actually contain no more information than other portions which remain unchanged."

There would be, however, no going after Noice in the press, for the investigation had been conducted as a favor, and Stefansson was forbidden from discussing it publicly. He did ask for permission, however, to share Hoover's letter with the Knights, Crawfords, Maurers, and Galles.

Despite the brief triumph he felt over Noice's retraction and later over the recovery of the diary text, Stefansson had managed to sabotage his own reputation with the Wrangel Island affair. It was nearly impossible to involve the governments of two countries such as Britain and Canada in an international scandal and emerge unscathed. He was bankrupt and shunned by other polar explorers, but he continued to write and to lecture.

As the years passed, he began to deny that he had much at all to do with the Wrangel Island venture, claiming instead, as he had tried to imply in his book, that it was the brainchild of Lorne Knight and Fred Maurer, and that he had only helped them to realize their goal.

In the late 1940s, Elsie Galle's son, Jim Lawless, attended a lecture of Stefansson's at the New Mexico Military Institute, where Jim was a student. He was eager to speak to the man who was such a legend in his family. When he approached Stefansson afterward and introduced himself, telling him that he was the nephew of Milton Galle, Stefansson became very uncomfortable and, as quickly as he could, turned his back on the boy and walked away.

* * *

In 1935, author Max Miller spotted a lone figure walking down a beach in the Aleutian Islands. It was the figure of a woman, small and childlike, and she was carefully gathering driftwood. By the look of her strained face, the lines about her eyes and mouth, she appeared to be an Eskimo woman of forty, although her diminutive size made her seem more like a girl.

It was clear she was not looking for company, nor was she eager to talk to a stranger. She would have passed by him anonymously had Miller not recognized her. Twelve years had passed since her face had appeared almost daily in magazines and newspapers, but the figure was clearly that of Ada Blackjack. The world had lost touch with her. The press speculated in later years about what had happened to her. There were rumors—she was wasting away from tuberculosis; she was struck dead by a car; she sold her soul to Hollywood; she returned to the Arctic to die; she changed her identity; she vanished. Yet here she was.

When Miller spoke to her, she gave him the same cool gaze she had given to reporters all those years earlier when they had wanted her picture. She did not smile or make conversation. She merely waited patiently and politely while Miller spoke of Wrangel Island, her former Arctic home, and of the small colony of Russians that now occupied it.

After he was through, she shifted the gunnysack of driftwood beneath her arm and began to walk away. "I really will have to be going," she said. "I should have gathered this driftwood earlier."

Feb. 28, 1974

P.O. Box 215
Hanover, N.H. 03755

Dear Mr. Crosby:

Thank you for the call yesterday regarding Mrs. Ada Blackjack
Johnson. I talked to her son, Billy, last night, regarding your
call—and between us we can provide the following information:
Name: Mrs. Ada Johnson.
Address: 221 ½ West 12th St., Anchorage, Alaska 99501.
Born: May 10, 1898 (approximate) at Spruce Creek, a village site
    on Alaska's Seward Peninsula. The village no longer exists. She
    was born Ada Delutuk, a full-blooded Eskimo.
State of health: Fair.
Particular needs: Money, but much too proud to ask for it.
The son, Billy, as I mentioned, is recovering from a heart attack.
Nevertheless, he told me that you are welcome to contact him for
any additional information, and your kind inquiry was most wel-
come.

Sincerely,

Stanton H. Patty
Alaska Editor
The Seattle Times

Epilogue

WRANGEL ISLAND TODAY IS every bit as remote and barren as it was in 1921. The winds blow year round, sweeping across the frozen tundra, the mountainous interior, the dark gravel beaches, and the jagged cliffs. For much of the year, nature sleeps here, waking up long enough in summer to bloom through the snow. Daisies, poppies, and forget-me-nots shiver vibrantly beneath the midnight sun, while willows and birches flourish.

The harbors, the capes, the rivers, the mountain peaks, have all been named by now. The island has been used by Russia as a prison, a concentration camp for political prisoners, and a K.G.B. camp for training foreign agents.

A colony of Eskimos now resides there, living side by side with a herd of musk oxen and reindeer. Russia has created a wildlife refuge on the island, and polar bears still roam the vast tundra. There is an airstrip and a meteorological station—one of the largest in the North—and if you are lucky and it is a good year for ice travel and if the Russian government approves, for a hefty price you may be able to pay your way to the island for a visit. There are no hotels, of course, but the island holds much interest for historians, geologists, photographers, wildlife enthusiasts, botanists, and modern-day explorers.

There are rumors of a monument on its frozen shores, commemo-

rating the four lost men of Stefansson's Wrangel Island Expedition—
the three who vanished into the blinding white of the Arctic horizon,
and the young man who died waiting for them to return. But it is only
a rumor. No such monument exists.

Thousands of miles away in New Philadelphia, Ohio, in the hills
of Amish country, the Maurer house and tailor shop is now a parking
lot for the First United Methodist Church. Until her death in 2002,
Marian Reiss, Fred Maurer's niece, lived down the street from where
he grew up, and even in her nineties she remembered vividly what a
dashing man her uncle Fred was.

In 1925, the New Philadelphia Chamber of Commerce passed a
resolution to place a memorial drinking fountain honoring Maurer in
the public square. The drinking fountain, like his house, is gone, but
just a few blocks from his old address there is a memorial gravestone
in the Maurer family plot. The burnished gray marble is suitably traditional and refined, and the words etched into the large rectangular
block read simply:

IN MEMORIAM

FREDERICK W. MAURER

1893—LOST IN ARCTIC—1923

In McMinnville, Oregon, the memorial stone for Lorne Knight is
large and impressive. The rough-hewn boulder sits alone in the midst
of a public park, surrounded by sidewalk, trees, and grass.

The Knights had pressed for a memorial at their son's gravesite on
Wrangel Island, but there were too many obstacles standing in the way—
the expense of transportation, not to mention the threat of Russian interference. When their friends and neighbors discovered the difficulty
the Knights were having, they pitched in together to build a monument
for Lorne. It would not rest at the head of their son's grave, as they had
originally wanted, but it would be a place they could come to mourn him.

IN MEMORY OF

E. LORNE KNIGHT

1893-1923

STEFANSSON CANADIAN ARCTIC EXPEDITION

1915-1919

REACHED 80 DEG. 26 MIN. NORTH LATITUDE

PERISHED ON WRANGELL ISLAND 1923

ERECTED BY THE CITIZENS OF YAMHILL COUNTY

1932

That same year, *Pechuck: Lorne Knight's Adventures in the Arctic* was published by Dodd, Mead & Company. Written by Richard Gill Montgomery, *Pechuck* was based largely on the 1916–1919 diary Knight kept during his first expedition with Stefansson. It was written in the first person, in the boldly colorful, slangy style that was so typically Knight, and related, according to the flyleaf, the tale of "a true and unusual experience which came to an American boy."

"God did not always use angels among men to accomplish his ends," Mrs. Anderson wrote to Mrs. Crawford in 1923, just months after Allan Crawford and the others were declared missing. "V.S. certainly is no angel, but let us wait before we say that no good is going to come out of the Wrangel Island tragedy."

After a long and bitter struggle, several moving and impressive tributes were given to Allan Crawford. Because of his Canadian citizenship, he was the only member of the Wrangel Island Expedition to be officially honored by the Canadian government. The first tribute, a plaque, was hung in the entrance to the Public Archives building in Ottawa. A scholarship was set up in his name at the University of Toronto, just as Allan had requested in his last letter to his parents before leaving Wrangel Island for Siberia. Out of his own savings, estimated at $3,385, he had designated twenty-five dollars be given each year to a student taking the highest marks in chemistry and physics at the June tests for pass matriculation. The Allan Crawford Scholarship was established in 1924. The very first award was presented by University of Toronto President Sir Robert Falconer, to whom Stefansson had written in 1921 searching for a young Canadian to head his expedition.

In addition, a plaque commemorating Crawford was placed in the University of Toronto's Convocation Hall. It was erected by his fellow students and read, TO COMMEMORATE THE VALOUR AND PATRIOTISM OF ALLAN RUDYARD CRAWFORD, AN UNDERGRADUATE OF THIS UNIVERSITY WHO LOST HIS LIFE WHILE COMMANDER AND SCIENTIST OF THE WRANGEL ISLAND EXPEDITION, 1921–1923. And yet another plaque was hung in the auditorium of the University of Toronto Schools, which commemorated Crawford's SACRIFICE AND HEROISM, and pronounced him AS FULL OF VALOUR AS OF KINDNESS, PRINCELY IN BOTH.

The Public Archives plaque is no longer on display. When the new Archives building was erected, the plaque came down and was tucked away in an attic or a basement. But the Allan Crawford Prize in Chemistry and Physics—now valued at three hundred dollars—is still given yearly.

There is no memorial for Milton Galle, of New Braunfels, Texas. Because they never accepted the fact that he was dead, his family chose not to commemorate him in the family cemetery.

Long after Alfred and Elsie each married and had children, Alma Galle would talk about Sohnie living somewhere on the Siberian coast. Later, she gradually closed herself off from the memories. Milton's pictures were removed from mantelpieces and tabletops and no one spoke of him, especially in front of his mother. She seemed a sad woman in later life, people said, and they rarely saw her smile.

When the New Braunfels paper proposed running a series of articles on Milton after Stefansson's death in 1962, Alma thought she was at last ready to talk about her son again and to see the story in print.

She let the newspaper borrow Milton's photographs and diary, but after three of the articles appeared, she asked Elsie to make them stop the series. It was too painful for her to relive those memories and to endure a whole new generation of townspeople discussing the legend of Milton Galle. So Elsie went down to the newspaper office to retrieve the diary and pictures.

The next generation of Galles grew up knowing little about their famous ancestor. In 1996, when Elsie was a grandmother, she spent her last Christmas with her family, and for the first time in many years allowed herself to speak about her older brother Milton. Her grandson Bill had brought her an old dance card and pictures of her parents and brothers and he watched as her eyes filled with tears. "Why are you so interested in Milton?" she asked him, unable to understand how her beloved brother, long-dead, could be so important to someone who had never even met him.

The only aspect that survived Milton Galle, besides a fragment of his diary, was his prized Corona typewriter. But even that has disappeared over the years. In fact, nobody in his family today is even certain it was returned to them by Stefansson, as he had promised. In New Braunfels, Texas, no one outside of his distant family members has ever heard of Milton Galle. There is no more Chautauqua to look forward to each year in New Braunfels, no more broad, brown tents promising the world on the center square.

Train tracks still dissect the town, and Amtraks and carrier trains roar past the edge of Galle's backyard, where his house still stands, his initials still carved into the wood of the basement eaves.

* * *

The letter was dated June 28, 1950, and the return address was Seattle, Washington. "Dear Stefansson," it began, "I'm hoping this would reach you as I need your help very much. I am writing this for you had promise to pay so much a year or so you had only given me 300. at the time you got the story suppose to be 500. Please sent me 200 dollars as soon as you get this. If don't I will have to get a lawyer get it for me. As I had been sick for last two years with liver trouble." It was signed "formerly Ada Black Jack, now Ada Johnson."

It seemed her "pathetic case," as he termed it to Carl Lomen, was up again. Stefansson wrote to Ada to remind her that not only had she been paid off, he had paid her above and beyond what he owed her, citing all the gifts she had been given of clothes and toys for Bennett, and the additional money she had received from him and from Inglis Fletcher now and again when she had been down on her luck.

"These charities finally had to cease," he wrote her, "both because I could not spare the money and because, according to what my friends and yours told me who knew what you did with the money, you kept giving away to others what I gave you, instead of saving it up for your own use."

Stefansson never heard from her again. He died twelve years later at the age of eighty-two of a stroke.

Bennett Blackjack died in 1972 at the age of fifty-eight. The following year, Ada Blackjack, then seventy-four years old, broke the long silence of the past four decades and granted a newspaper interview for the first time since she had taken the streetcar to the newspaper office in downtown Los Angeles in 1924. It is the only first-person record of her activities in the forty-nine years since she returned from California.

"It is still awfully hard to talk about," she told the reporter in 1973 when he asked about Wrangel Island. But she had promised Billy, then vice president of the Alaska Federation of Natives in Seattle, that she would try her best to tell her story. You have an obligation to history, he told her, and she agreed.

She remembered the food running out and the announcement that Crawford and Knight would go for help. She remembered their return and the defeated look in Knight's eyes, and then the departure of Crawford, Galle, and Maurer. They were never seen again, "no trace at all," Ada said. "What happened, I don't know. Maybe they fell through the ice. Or they might have been killed by the Russians."

She remembered vividly the decline of Knight's health. "It was a bad time," she said. "I don't like to talk about it."

When she was able to speak again, she told of teaching herself to shoot and to hunt, of cooking soup from ducks for Knight when he was unable to swallow anything heartier. After Knight died, she wondered if she would die as well, but somehow she never gave up hope. "I think I would have died, too," she told the reporter. "It's hard to talk about what you feel when someone dies and you are alone."

Even at age seventy-four, the memories of those horrific months on Wrangel Island were as vivid and disturbing as they had been in 1923. Sometimes, she told the reporter, when she heard the howling of the sled dogs beneath the midnight sun, their noses turned to heaven, she knew they were singing a song for those who had been lost. To her, they sang for Crawford, Galle, Maurer, and Knight. For years, she had tried to forget, but there were reminders everywhere and her dreams were still interrupted, and sometimes in her head she heard Noice's words, telling the world that she could have done more.

Her son Billy called her brave, but Ada never thought of herself in that way. "Brave? I don't know about that," she would say. "But I would never give up hope while I'm still alive."

It was the last interview she ever granted.

In 1979, Ada visited with the nieces of Fred Maurer in Ohio. She stayed with them for three days and spent most of her time working a *Star Wars* puzzle. Ada loved solving puzzles, enjoying the way the pieces fit so neatly together, each having a place, and the feeling of satisfaction she had when it was finished. Maurer's nieces, Jeannette and Marian, were impressed by her graciousness, and the following year Jeannette visited Ada at the Palmer Pioneers' Nursing Home in Palmer, Alaska, where she had moved. Ada was longing for a taste of dried salmon, but when Jeannette couldn't find any she brought Ada some fresh fruit instead. She thought it tasted wonderful.

Not long afterward, Ada suffered a stroke that left her without speech. She also was diagnosed with cancer of the bladder. Then, on May 29, 1983, Ada Delutuk Blackjack Johnson died at age eighty-five at the Palmer Pioneers' Home, where no one knew she was once an Arctic hero.

On the day of her death, Ada's son Billy traveled from Seattle to visit her, his arms filled with flowers and gifts. But when he arrived at the nursing home, he was told she had died just hours before.

"Am I beautiful?" she asked him once.

"Yes you are," he had told her. "The most beautiful mother in the world."

For ten years, Billy had been campaigning to obtain official recognition for his mother's bravery in the Arctic. After Ada's death, he was determined that she should not be forgotten. "I consider my mother Ada Blackjack to be one of the most loving mothers in this world and one of the greatest heroines in the history of Arctic exploration," he said. "She survived against all odds. It's a wonderful story that should not be lost of . . . a mother fighting to survive to live so she could carry on with her son. Her story of survival in the Arctic will be a great chapter in the history of the Arctic and Alaska."

Only a handful of people attended the funeral of Ada Blackjack—Billy and his wife Janice, and a scattering of family members and friends. With Bennett buried at her head, there was only a makeshift aluminum marker to indicate Ada's grave. Ada herself had not wanted a stone or plaque. Without one, she figured, she might at last be granted the anonymity she had been seeking in the last years of her life.

But Billy Blackjack Johnson wanted his mother to be remembered after death. In his new hometown of Wilson, North Carolina, he ordered a large, rectangular plaque, which he and his wife transported across the country by plane. Now mounted on Ada's grave in Anchorage Memorial Park Cemetery, it reads simply: HEROINE—WRANGEL IS-LAND EXPEDITION.

But to Ada's son, it was not enough. Ada had been badly hurt by

Noice and badly used by Stefansson. Her life, since 1923, had been a constant fight to survive—grief, poverty, public accusation and humiliation, illness, and the nightmares that haunted her. But she alone had sustained herself and her boys, and when she was too ill to care for her sons, she had made sure they were sent to those who could. She alone had done the work to earn the money to bring them back to her so that they could once again live together as a family, and she alone had lived to tell the story of Wrangel Island.

"The final chapter," Billy Johnson wrote to the Alaska Legislature, "should read that the State of Alaska recognized Ada Blackjack as the heroine of the Wrangell Island expedition. It could read that the State of Alaska has a true native heroine that participated in the early exploration of the Arctic. The State of Alaska has within it the power to write a happy ending to such a sad happening."

One month after Ada's death, she was granted her happy ending. The Alaska Legislature officially honored her and recognized her on June 16, 1983, as a true and courageous hero, "a small token of remembrance for a woman whose bravery and heroic deeds have gone unnoticed for so many years." Representative John G. Fuller added, "I deeply regret that we were not able to serve Ada with this citation while she was alive."

Born in 1898 just east of Nome, Ada was selected to travel with the ill-fated expedition organized in 1921 by Vilhjalmur Stefansson to explore remote and uninhabited Wrangel Island. It was two years before the young woman was rescued from the island, the only member of the landing party to live through the ordeal. The fate of some members is unknown to this day.

What is known is that for month after lonely and terrifying month Ada Blackjack Johnson cared for an ill member of the crew, lived off the land, battled polar bears and somehow managed to survive until a rescue boat arrived nearly two years after she had arrived on the island.

Not many Alaskans remember this soft-spoken and vital woman. In the years following her heroic feat she was forgotten by most people who knew of her ordeal. The middle years of her life were not pleasant, although we are convinced she would have been the last to complain.

We urge Alaskans to become familiar with the story of Ada Blackjack Johnson who recently passed away in Palmer. From her story we can each gain an insight into the life and personal courage of a resident of our state who survived under unbearable circumstances only to be forgotten by her friends and neighbors.

It is our duty and obligation to honor Ada Blackjack Johnson for her astounding courage, her spiritual strength and her commitment to her fellow man.

If his mother had been alive to receive her memoriam, Billy knew she would have smiled in that slow and enigmatic way she had, head tilted to one side, brown eyes peering upward, saying simply—if she even spoke at all—"I am so grateful."

Acknowledgments

THANKS, FIRST AND FOREMOST, to my right hand, Jessica Gilroy. Without her keen eye, general all-around genius, and inherent sunniness, writing this book wouldn't have been nearly so enjoyable—or so (virtually) painless.

Special thanks as well to the brilliant, dedicated, and effervescent Lynn Thompson, of New Braunfels, Texas. Her persistence and generosity helped me discover Milton Galle.

Other thanks go to Bobbie Jo Dombey, for her dynamite research; Michael MacDonald of the National Archives of Canada, for his extraordinary professional support; and Earl Olmstead, Steve Vasbinder, and the Tusc-Kent Archives in Ohio, for hospitality, generosity, and expertise. Gratitude also to Charlotte Johnson Houtchens of the American University Library; Loretta Andress of the University of Alaska; Tahitia Orr of the Alaska State Library; Caroline Atuk-Derrick of the Elmer E. Rasmuson Library; Mary Boccaccio of the Joyner Library at East Carolina University; Becky Lombardo of the Sophienburg–New Braunfels Archives and Museum of History in New Braunfels, Texas; Matt Sneddon; the folks at StarLab in Bethesda, Maryland; Krista Fogelman and Todd Crawford, the world's best neighbors and cat sitters; and the amazing Lynne Haaland and her HiP Design team.

Thanks to the fine staff at Dartmouth College Library, particularly Joshua Shaw, Stanley W. Brown, and Sarah Hartwell, who were tremendously helpful and a genuine pleasure to work with.

I am beholden to the families of Ada Blackjack, Milton Galle, Fred Maurer, and Lorne Knight, who were so generous with their support and materials, and who quickly became my friends: Ada's wonderful son, Billy Blackjack Johnson, who fought so long and hard to have his mother's heroism recognized and who passed away just months before this book's publication, and his lovely wife, Janice, who welcomed me into their home and their memories; Milton Galle's nieces, Kathy Long and Mary Pat Hughes, and nephew Jim Lawless; Lorne Knight's cousin, Don Knight; the many members of Fred Maurer's generous family; and Vilhjalmur Stefansson's widow, Evelyn Stefansson Nef. Special thanks to Galle's great-nephew Bill Lawless, to whom I am forever indebted, and to Maurer's niece, the late Marian Reiss, who wanted so much to see this book in print and who supported this endeavor in any way she could.

I consider myself lucky to have a brilliant editor in Will Schwalbe, with whom I am blessed to be working again. A million thanks to him and to all of the amazing people at Hyperion—including the fabulous Kiera Hepford and the supremely gifted Alison Warner—who helped this book be born. Thanks as well to Theresa Craig for copyediting.

And to the best, most brilliant agent on this planet, John Ware, I send endless gratitude for his wisdom, guidance, humor, and compassion, and for taking a chance on me four years ago.

My friends, as always, were there for me, understanding my long silences and sporadic e-mails. Love and thanks to Joe Kraemer, for being there from the beginning—from Richmond, Indiana, where our hair was big and so were our dreams, to the here and now, where he is still my best man. To Angelo Surmelis for unconditional love, endless consultations, always "getting it," and for being my own Will Truman. To Beth Jennings-White—phenomenal woman and true friend—who has been with me ever since Señor Hollingsworth sat us next to each other in seventh grade Spanish class. To Valerie Frey, Jessica Hartz, and Melissa McKay, for fun, laughter, and understanding. And to Rachel Kay Brookmire and Ami Martin Wilber.

To the home front—John Hreno, whom I love more than words, and whose love and support and dinner making are indescribable. And George, Percy, and Satchmo, the feline literary trio. Once again, Percy stayed loyally glued to my side for each of those long hours, and Satchmo (brand-new to the literary life) learned very quickly to perch on the computer monitor so that he could paw each word as it came from my fingers. But the biggest scratch under the chin goes to the magnificent George, whose instinctive comic timing helped me make it through the darkness.

I am blessed with a big, crazy, loving family, too vast to be singled out by name. But I must give thanks to my aunts, Lynn Duval Clark and Paula Sturdivant, and Linda "Mom" Hreno, for special comfort, and to my cousins Lisa von Sprecken, Lisa Duval, Derek Duval, and Evan Sturdivant for stepping into the roles of sisters and brothers when I needed it most. Thanks, too, to my stepbrother, John Keller, and to my brother in spirit, Robert Hamilton. Thanks also to the universe for making Eleanor Marsh Hearon Niven my grandmother. Every inch of her feisty "5 foot 2 and eyes of blue" will be missed more than I can say.

Everyone has always envied me my mother, and with good reason. Penelope Niven manages to be inspiration, best friend, confidante, commiserator, savior, and angel all in one.

Lastly, I am blessed to have had Jack F. McJunkin Jr., as my father. He was a remarkable man, who gave more to this book than anyone else, and whom I will always miss, no matter how much he fills my heart. For you, Dad—this book and all those to follow.

Endnotes

Legend

- *BBJ*—Billy Blackjack Johnson
- *DART*—Dartmouth College Library
- *DN*—Don Knight
- *FG*—Fitzhugh Green Papers, Georgetown
- *IFP*—Inglis Fletcher Papers, East Carolina Manuscript Collection, East Carolina University
- *KL*—Kathy Long Private Collection
- *LAW*—Bill Lawless Private Collection
- *MR*—Marian Reiss Private Collection
- *NAC*—National Archives of Canada
- *NLS*—National Library of Scotland
- *TUSC*—Tusc-Kent Archives
- *UAA*—Archives and Manuscripts Department, Consortium Library, University of Alaska Anchorage

Primary Sources and Methodology

As cited in the endnotes, *Ada Blackjack* is based on the diaries, journals, letters, unpublished manuscripts, and papers written by the members of the 1921 Wrangel Island Expedition and their families. Ada Blackjack, Lorne Knight, and Milton Galle left diaries or diary fragments, and, in the case of the Knight and Galle journals, numerous versions exist, varying slightly in content. In these cases, I consulted all versions, but have only quoted from the original version of each, provided to me by the family of Milton Galle.

Ada Blackjack is also based on the personal papers of Vilhjalmur Stefansson, and other pertinent letters and journals, as well as on documents and public records in government and library archives.

In addition to the primary written sources, I conducted interviews and/or carried on extensive correspondence with the following sources:

- Billy Blackjack Johnson, son of Ada Blackjack
- Bill Lawless, great-nephew of Milton Galle
- Kathy Long, niece of Milton Galle
- Mary Pat Hughes, niece of Milton Galle
- Don Knight, cousin of Lorne Knight
- Marian Reiss, niece of Fred Maurer

I have also been in contact with numerous other family members, family friends, and acquaintances who had memories and information to share.

Government Documents

- Canadian House of Commons Debates, June 10, 1925, NAC
- FBI Freedom of Information/Privacy Acts Section; Vilhjalmur Stefansson, File: 100–7516 Section 1
- Hearings Before the General Board of the Navy, 1923, Vol. 2, Navy Department, Washington, DC

Major Unpublished Sources

In addition, I have relied on the following sources:

- Anderson, Rudolph Martin, Papers and Documents, Rudolph Martin Anderson Collection/Anderson-Allstrand Collection, NAC/R6390-0-1-E
- Blackjack, Ada, Diary, papers, and documents, Billy Blackjack Johnson Private Collection
- Blackjack, Ada, Papers and documents, UAA
- Fletcher, Inglis, Papers and documents, Joyner Library
- Galle, Milton, Diary, papers, and documents, Bill Lawless Private Collection
- Galle, Milton, Papers and documents, Kathy Long Private Collection
- Johnson, Billy Blackjack, *The Jesse Lee Home: Shelter from the Storm*, Billy Blackjack Johnson Private Collection
- Knight, Lorne, Diary, papers, and documents, Kathy Long Private Collection
- Knight, Lorne, Diary, papers, and documents, NAC, Lorne Knight Fonds, NAC/R6640-0-8-E
- Knight, Lorne, "Summary of Wrangel Island Expedition," NAC, William Laird McKinlay Fonds, NAC/R2289-0-X-E
- McKinlay, William L., Correspondence and Papers of William Laird McKinlay, NLS/DEP 357

- McKinlay, William L., First Draft of Manuscript *Karluk*, unpublished manuscript, William Laird McKinlay Fonds, NAC/R2289-0-X-E.
- McKinlay, William L., Second Draft of Manuscript *Karluk*, unpublished manuscript, William Laird McKinlay Fonds, NAC/R2289-0-X-E.
- Maurer, Fred, Lecture: "A Fight for Life in the Arctic." 1914, Rudolph Martin Anderson Collection/Anderson-Allstrand Collection, NAC/R6390-0-1-E
- Maurer, Fred, Papers and documents, Marian Reiss Private Collection
- Stefansson Collection, including all official documents of the Wrangel Island Expedition of 1921 as well as papers and documents of Vilhjalmur Stefansson, Ada Blackjack, Lorne Knight, Allan Crawford, Fred Maurer, Milton Galle, and Harold Noice, Dartmouth College Library

Magazine and Newspaper Clippings

In citing newspaper articles, many of which were contained in albums and private files, I have provided whatever data was available.

I. Secondary Sources Cited in Notes

- The Bible, King James Version. Nashville: Thomas Nelson Publishers, 1972.
- Gould, Joseph E., *The Chautauqua Movement*. Albany: State University of New York Press, 1961.
- Grun, Bernard, *The Timetables of History: A Horizontal Linkage of People and Events*. New York: Touchstone, 1946.
- Knight, Lorne, *Pechuck*. Caldwell, Idaho: The Caxton Printers, Ltd., 1948.
- Le Bourdais, D. M., *Stefansson: Ambassador of the North*. Montreal: Harvest House, 1963.
- Muir, John, *The Cruise of the Corwin*. San Francisco: Sierra Club Books, 1993.
- Niven, Jennifer, *The Ice Master*. New York: Hyperion, 2000.
- Noice, Harold, *Back of Beyond*. New York: G. P. Putnam's Sons, 1939.
- Noice, Harold, *With Stefansson in the Arctic*. New York: Dodd, Mead & Company, 1924.
- Norman, Howard, *Northern Tales*. New York: Pantheon, 1990.
- Petrone, Penny, *Northern Voices: Inuit Writing in English*. Toronto: University of Toronto Press, 1988.
- Pierce, R. V., M.D., *The People's Common Sense Medical Adviser*. Buffalo, New York: The World's Dispensary Medical Association, 1918.
- Stefansson, Vilhjalmur, *The Adventure of Wrangel Island*. New York: Macmillan, 1925.
- Stefansson, Vilhjalmur, *The Friendly Arctic*. New York: Macmillan, 1921.

II. Other Selected Secondary Sources

• Brower, Charles D., *Fifty Years Below Zero: A Lifetime of Adventure in the Far North*. Fairbanks: University of Alaska Press, 1994.
• Brown, Dale, *Wild Alaska*. New York: Time-Life Books, 1972.
• Carlyle, Thomas, *Heroes and Hero Worship*. Chicago: Donohue Brothers.
• Carpenter, Kenneth, *The History of Scurvy and Vitamin C*. Cambridge University Press, 1989.
• Case, Victoria and Robert Ormond, *We Called It Culture: The Story of Chautauqua*. Garden City, New York: Doubleday & Company, Inc., 1948.
• Daniel, Thomas M., *Captain of Death: The Story of Tuberculosis*. Boydell & Brewer, 1999.
• De Coccola, Raymond and Paul King, *The Incredible Eskimo: Life Among the Barren Land Eskimo*. Canada: Hancock House, 1989.
• Diubaldo, Richard J., *Stefansson and the Canadian Arctic*. Montreal: McGill-Queen's University Press, 1978.
• Feeney, Robert E., *Polar Journeys: The Role of Food and Nutrition in Early Exploration*. Fairbanks: University of Alaska Press and American Chemical Society, 1997.
• Harrison, Harry P. as told to Karl Detzer, *Culture Under Canvas: The Story of Tent Chautauqua*. New York: Hastings House, Publishers, 1958.
• Harvard Classics, *Pepita Jimenez, A Happy Boy, and Skipper Worse*. New York: P. F. Collier & Son, 1917.
• Harvie, David I., *Limeys: The True Story of One Man's War Against Ignorance, the Establishment and the Deadly Scurvy*. Sutton Publishing, 2002.
• Hess, Alfred, *Scurvy: Past and Present*. Academic Press, 1982.
• LeRoux, Odette, Marion E. Jackson, and Minnie Aodla Freeman, *Inuit Women Artists*. San Francisco: Chronicle Books, 1994.
• McClintock, Captain Francis, *The Voyage of the 'Fox.'* Könemann, 1998.
• Mountfield, David, *A History of Polar Exploration*. New York: The Dial Press, 1974.
• Murray, John, *Alaska*. Compass American Guides, 1997.
• Nelson, Richard K., *Hunters of the Northern Ice*. Chicago: University of Chicago Press, 1969.
• Nordenskiöld, Adolf Erik, *The Arctic Voyages of Adolf Erik Nordenskiöld*. London: Macmillan, 1879.
• Pálsson, Gísli, *Writing on Ice: The Ethnographic Notebooks of Vilhjalmur Stefansson*. Boston: University Press of New England, 2001.
• Rabelais, François, *Gargantua & Pantagruel*. New York: The Heritage Press, 1936.
• Rothman, Sheila M., *Living in the Shadow of Death: Tuberculosis and the Social Experience of Illness in American History*. Baltimore: Johns Hopkins University Press, 1995.

• Scott, Marian, *Chautauqua Caravan*. New York: D. Appleton-Century Company, Inc., 1939.
• Stefansson, Vilhjalmur, *Discovery: The Autobiography of Vilhjalmur Stefansson*. New York: McGraw-Hill Book Company, 1964.
• Stefansson, Vilhjalmur, *My Life with the Eskimo*. New York: Collier Books, 1971.
• Stephen, Leslie, *An Agnostic's Apology*. London: Smith, Elder, & Co., 1893.
• Swaney, Deanna, *The Arctic*. Oakland, California: Lonely Planet Publications, 1999.
• Willis, Clint, *Ice: Stories of Survival from Polar Exploration*. New York: Thunders' Mouth Press/Balliett & Fitzgerald Inc., 1999.
• Wright, Helen S., *The Great White North*. New York: Macmillan, 1910.

Endnotes

| ix | "As she looked . . ." | "The Lady in the Moon," as told to Inglis Fletcher by Ada Blackjack, February 11, 1924, IFP |

PREFACE

1	"Brave? I don't . . ."	The Sunday *Denver Post*, "Lone Survivor Ada Blackjack Recalls Arctic," January 14, 1973
2	"Real history is . . ."	Mae Belle Anderson to Helen Crawford, January 5, 1924, NAC
3	"I recall her . . ."	John Tetpon to Jennifer Niven, January 27, 2003

PART I

| 5 | "There, with only . . ." | *The World Magazine*, "Ada Blackjack, Heroine of Arctic Expedition, Remains Unhonored While She Lives," October 30, 1927 |

ONE

9	"habitually enigmatic . . ."	Stefansson, *The Adventure of Wrangel Island*, p. 341: "The Story of Ada Blackjack" by Inglis Fletcher
9	"Ada, look at . . ."	Inglis Fletcher to Stefansson, February 10, 1924, DART
9	She also knew . . .	www.polarbearsalive.org/facts5.htm

| 10 | "bone poor, almost . . ." | *Los Angeles Times*, "Death Vigil in Arctic Snows," February 28, 1924 |
| 12 | "Here was a . . ." | Fred Maurer, "A Fight for Life in the Arctic," Chautauqua lecture 1914, NAC |

TWO

13	"the most American . . ."	Joseph E. Gould, *The Chautauqua Movement*, p. 97
14	"Seven days filled . . ."	*Herald-Zeitung*, April 1, 1921
16	But the 1913 . . .	See Jennifer Niven's *The Ice Master* for more detail on this expedition.
17	"It seemed like . . ."	Fred Maurer, "A Fight for Life in the Arctic," p. 12, NAC
17	"Can you give . . ."	Fred Maurer telegram to Stefansson, 1921, DART
17	"Sorry no chance . . ."	Stefansson telegram to Fred Maurer, 1921, DART
18	"Why should any . . ."	Stefansson, *The Friendly Arctic*, p. 7
18	"The land up . . ."	*The Friendly Arctic*, p. 7
19	"In order to . . ."	*The Friendly Arctic*, p. 7
19	"Given a healthy . . ."	*Morning Oregonian*, undated newspaper article, LAW
19	"I think that . . ."	Hearings before the General Board of the Navy, 1923, Vol. 2, Navy Department, Washington, p. 5, DART
19	"In one way . . ."	William McKinlay, Stefansson bio, NLS
19	"The Arctic as . . ."	*The Friendly Arctic*, p. 8
20	"Famous Stefansson . . ."	Stefansson, "Chapter 78—The Chautauqua Years: 1921–1930," pp. 2-3, DART
20	"must have been . . ."	Lorne Knight, *Pechuck*, p. 1
21	"It's just as . . ."	*Pechuck*, p. 59
22	"Would you do . . ."	*Pechuck*, p. 289
23	"The explorer . . ."	*The Friendly Arctic*, p. 8
23	"Purpose—plus punch . . ."	Chautauqua Newsletter, March 18, 1921, LAW

26	"When the world . . ."	*The Friendly Arctic*, p. 6
27	"During your stay . . ."	Stefansson to Fred Maurer, February 23, 1921, DART
27	"Did you see . . ."	Stefansson to Fred Maurer, February 23, 1921, DART
29	"Ottawa, Ontario . . ."	Stefansson to Sir Robert Falconer, *The Adventure of Wrangel Island*

THREE

30	"I am planning . . ."	Stefansson to Sir Robert Falconer, March 13, 1921, *The Adventure of Wrangel Island*, pp. 417–418
31	"If you are . . ."	Allan Crawford to Stefansson, April 11, 1921, *The Adventure of Wrangel Island*, p. 79
32	"Although I have . . ."	Allan Crawford to Stefansson, April 11, 1921, *The Adventure of Wrangel Island*, p. 79
33	"Your qualifications look . . ."	Stefansson telegram to Allan Crawford, April 24, 1921, DART
34	"Stefansson is a . . ."	J. B. Harkin to W. W. Cory, March 2, 1921, NAC
34	"Of course you . . ."	Lorne Knight to Stefansson, May 8, 1921, DART
34	"Would you go . . ."	Stefansson telegram to Lorne Knight, June 6, 1921, DART
35	"I am not . . ."	Stefansson to Allan Crawford, June 11, 1921, *The Adventure of Wrangel Island*, p. 82
39	"Milton's knowledge . . ."	J. I. Knight to the Galles, April 25, 1925, LAW
40	"I am simply . . ."	Milton Galle to his parents, August 15, 1921, LAW
41	"Stef has chosen . . ."	Milton Galle to his parents, August 15, 1921, LAW
41	"To my thinking . . ."	Milton Galle to his mother, July 20, 1921, LAW
42	"to some fur . . ."	Stefansson to Orville Wright, August 24, 1922, DART
46	"But after meeting . . ."	Fred Maurer to his mother, September 5, 1921, DART

46	"Without an ac-tual . . ."	Stefansson to Mrs. Crawford, August 29, 1921, DART
47	"The polar regions . . ."	Stefansson to Delphine Maurer, October 15, 1921, DART
47	"Although we are . . ."	Fred Maurer to his mother, September 5, 1921, DART
48	"He has the . . ."	J. I. Knight to Stefansson, October 28, 1921, DART
49	"We are proud . . ."	J. I. Knight to Harry Galle, August 20, 1921, LAW
49	"not for me . . ."	Milton Galle to his parents, August 15, 1921, LAW
49	"We may have . . ."	Alma Galle to Stefansson, August 24, 1921, LAW
50	"Always remember . . ."	Stefansson to Allan Crawford, August 15, 1921, DART
51	"We will do . . ."	Allan Crawford to Stefansson, August 18, 1921, DART
51	"I guess this . . ."	Allan Crawford to Helen Crawford, August 18, 1921, DART
52	"The female sha-man . . ."	From *Northern Tales* by Howard Norman, copyright © 1990 by Howard Norman. Used by permission of Pantheon Books, a division of Random House, Inc. (pp. 180–182)

FOUR

54	"Past Point . . ."	Milton Galle to Stefansson, September 8, 1921, DART
56	"Our future lies . . ."	Miscellaneous photographs, LAW
56	"Bud—How's this . . ."	Miscellaneous photographs, KL
56	"There has been . . ."	Miscellaneous photographs, LAW
56	"We are having . . ."	Lorne Knight to Stefansson, September 4, 1921, DART
56	"A very simple . . ."	Stefansson to J. I. Knight, September 20, 1921, DART
60	Once Ada agreed . . .	My research has uncovered numerous opinions from various sources about Ada's possible activities as a prostitute. However, I have been unable to find any actual documentation or verifica-

tion of this, and any official documents that might have shed light on the matter no longer exist.

61	"All in all . . ."	Milton Galle to Stefansson, September 8, 1921, DART
62	"Some places get . . ."	Lorne Knight, "Summary of Wrangel Island Expedition," September 16, 1921, to August 26, 1922, p. 1, NAC
62	There were those . . .	Mae Belle Anderson to Helen Crawford, August 31, 1924, NAC
63	"I wish to . . ."	Milton Galle to Stefansson, September 8, 1921, DART
65	"the sickest mortals . . ."	Knight, "Summary of Wrangel Island Expedition," September 16, 1921, to August 26, 1922, p. 1, NAC
66	"Keep note of . . ."	Allan Crawford to Helen Crawford, September 15, 1921, DART
67	"in total disregard . . ."	Fred Maurer, "Adventures on an Arctic Whaler," TUSC/MR
67	"The old island . . ."	Fred Maurer to his mother, September 15, 1921, LAW

PART II

69	"A land more . . ."	John Muir, *The Cruise of the Corwin*, p. 134
70	"Associated Press . . ."	Associated Press article, unnamed newspaper clipping, September 28, 1921, LAW

FIVE

71	"I, Allan Rudyard . . ."	*The Adventure of Wrangel Island*, Wrangel Island Proclamation, illustration facing p. 119
76	"Sick Headache . . ."	*Common Sense Medical Advisor*, p. 329
76	"I shall not . . ."	*New York World*, "Parents Blame Stefansson for Crawford's Death," May 10, 1925
77	They got their . . .	*The Cruise of the Corwin*, p. 139
78	"We will watch . . ."	Lorne Knight's diary, September 29, 1921, KL
80	"Oh, Crawford . . ."	"Summary of Wrangel Island Expedition," November 7, 1921, NAC

80	"When the mail . . ."	"Summary of Wrangel Island Expedition," November 7, 1921, NAC
80	"Have tried coaxing . . ."	Lorne Knight's diary, October 1, 1921, KL
80	And then something . . .	Dr. Rudolph Martin Anderson later theorized that Crawford might have been poisoned by eating the liver of a polar bear, which had been known to cause similar sicknesses in others, including an Eskimo family he had heard of who had died from it.
82	They found Ada's . . .	"Summary of Wrangel Island Expedition," November 7, 1921, NAC
85	"This may all . . ."	Lorne Knight's diary, November 18–20, 1921, KL
86	"But if at . . ."	"Summary of Wrangel Island Expedition," November 23, 1921, NAC
88	"like an inverted . . ."	Lorne Knight's diary, November 27, 1921, KL
88	"She will not . . ."	Lorne Knight's diary, November 24, 1921, KL
88	"I'll bet I . . ."	Lorne Knight's diary, November 23, 1921, KL
88	"If there is . . ."	Lorne Knight's diary, November 25, 1921, KL
89	There was a . . .	Similar to Seasonal Affective Disorder (aka SAD)
89	"utterances of erotic . . ."	Stanislaus Novakovsky, *Ecology*, Vol. V, No. 2, p. 116
90	"as only a . . ."	Novakovsky, *Ecology*, Vol. V, No. 2, p. 124
91	"Special cable to the . . ."	*New York Times*, March 20, 1992

SIX

92	"I shall not . . ."	*New York Times*, September 28, 1921
93	"effected a renewal . . ."	*New York Times*, September 28, 1921
93	"Of what use . . ."	*New York Times*, March 22, 1922
93	"The Government . . ."	Le Bourdais, *Stefansson: Ambassador of the North*, p. 166

94	"Wrangel Island . . ."	*Washington Times*, *The National Daily*, "Wrangel Isle Land of Russia, U.S. Concludes," Tuesday, May 23, 1922
94	"like plutocrats"	"Summary of Wrangel Island Expedition," August 21, 1922, NAC
96	"What should I . . ."	Lorne Knight's diary, December 17, 1921, KL
99	"Now I will . . ."	"Summary of Wrangel Island Expedition," August 21, 1922, NAC
100	"I wonder what . . ."	"Summary of Wrangel Island Expedition," August 21, 1922, NAC
102	"I'll put C. up . . ."	"Summary of Wrangel Island Expedition," August 21, 1922, NAC
104	"Our names should . . ."	Lorne Knight's diary, June 13, 1922, KL
105	"Please urge upon . . ."	*The Adventure of Wrangel Island*, p. 136
108	"August 23, 1922 . . ."	Stefansson to John Maurer, August 23, 1922, DART

SEVEN

111	"jake"	"Summary of Wrangel Island Expedition," August 26, 1922, p. 11, NAC
111	"We will be . . ."	Ralph Lomen to Allan Crawford, August 19, 1922, DART
112	"Of course, we . . ."	J. I. Knight to Harry Galle, August 19, 1922, LAW
113	"We would greatly . . ."	J. I. Knight to Stefansson, August 31, 1922, DART
113	They had read . . .	Milton Galle was correct.
115	"If you are . . ."	Milton Galle diary, July 18, 1922, LAW
116	"Can you imagine . . ."	"Summary of Wrangel Island Expedition," August 26, 1922, p. 11, NAC
119	"Fear mishap has . . ."	J. T. Crawford to Stefansson, September 11, 1922, LAW
119	*"Teddy Bear . . ."*	Stefansson MSS 98, 14:5, Chapter 9, p. 5, DART
120	"deeply concerned"	*New York Times*, September 25, 1922
120	"If a native . . ."	*Denver Post*, December 24, 1923

120	"We had no . . ."	*The Adventure of Wrangel Island*, p. 142
120	"Is there nothing . . ."	J. T. Crawford to Stefansson, September 22, 1922, LAW
120	"There is . . ."	Stefansson to Helen Crawford, November 24, 1922, DART
120	"As I see . . ."	Stefansson to Delphine Maurer, October 3, 1922, DART
121	"How welcome any . . ."	Alma Galle to Stefansson, undated letter, LAW
121	"This means merely . . ."	Stefansson to Harry Galle, October 2, 1922, LAW
122	"They are safe . . ."	J. I. Knight to Harry Galle, September 21, 1922, LAW
122	"I shoot, no . . ."	Milton Galle's diary, July 23, 1922, LAW
123	"Coffee has taken . . ."	Milton Galle's diary, August 24, 1922, LAW
123	"At a dinner . . ."	Milton Galle's diary, September 13, 1922, LAW
124	"Let her blow . . ."	Lorne Knight's diary, September 12, 1922, KL
125	"Get the hell . . ."	Milton Galle's diary, September 25, 1922, LAW
126	"Coffee for you"	Milton Galle's diary, September 28, 1922, LAW
126	"demonstrate the . . ."	Lorne Knight's diary, September 22, 1922, KL
126	"mysterious dash"	Milton Galle's diary, September 25, 1922, LAW
127	"K keeps conversation . . ."	Milton Galle's diary, September 28, 1922, LAW
128	"I would have . . ."	Lorne Knight, *Pechuck*, pp. 182–183
130	"Now what can . . ."	Milton Galle's diary, September 18, 1922, LAW
131	"Dear Sister . . ."	Alma Galle to Maggie Galle, undated, LAW

EIGHT

133	"there hain't none . . ."	Lorne Knight's diary, October 5, 1922, KL
135	"There are so . . ."	Mae Belle Anderson to Helen Crawford, May 19, 1924, NAC

136	"If one can . . ."	Lorne Knight's diary, November 1, 1922, KL
137	"Game is *scarce* . . ."	Allan Crawford to Stefansson, January 7, 1923, LAW
137	"Of course I . . ."	Lorne Knight to Stefansson, January 4, 1923, LAW
137	"Crawford and I . . ."	Lorne Knight to Georgia Knight, January 4, 1923, LAW
138	"From my accrued . . ."	Allan Crawford to his family, January 7, 1923, LAW
139	"The going ahead . . ."	Lorne Knight's diary, January 10, 1923, KL
140	"One time . . ."	"Lady in the Moon," as told to Inglis Fletcher by Ada Blackjack, February 11, 1924, IFP
143	"poorest hands for . . ."	Lorne Knight's diary, January 12, 1923, KL
143	"weak as a . . ."	Lorne Knight's diary, February 8, 1923, KL
143	"I am nearly . . ."	Lorne Knight's diary, January 12, 1923, KL
143	"It will be . . ."	Lorne Knight's diary, January 12, 1923, KL
144	"We hoped to . . ."	Lorne Knight's diary, January 15, 1923, KL
144	"nice and warm . . ."	Lorne Knight's diary, January 18, 1923, KL
145	"Of all the . . ."	Lorne Knight's diary, January 19, 1923, KL
146	"it is essential . . ."	Lorne Knight's diary, January 21, 1923, KL
148	"Knight is troubled . . ."	Allan Crawford to Stefansson, January 28, 1923, *The Adventure of Wrangel Island*, p. 260
148	"The chief reason . . ."	Fred Maurer to Delphine Maurer, January 29, 1923, DART
148	"My dear Mother . . ."	Fred Maurer to his mother, January 29, 1923, LAW
149	"Why Galle leave?"	Ada Blackjack notebook calendar, DART
149	"I wonder what . . ."	Lorne Knight's diary, January 29, 1923, KL
150	"for as I . . ."	Lorne Knight's diary, January 29, 1923, KL

150	*"Come on bear"*	Lorne Knight's diary, February 2, 1923, KL
151	"blowing and drift-ing . . ."	Lorne Knight's diary, January 31, 1923, KL

PART III

153	"I must stay . . ."	"The Story of Ada Blackjack," p. 343, *The Adventure of Wrangel Island*
154	*"Sunday Times* (Lon-don) . . ."	*Sunday Times* (London), "Stefansson Quits; Gives Up Exploring; Will Devote His Future Telling About Possibilities in the 'Friendly Arctic,' " January 1923

NINE

155	"I'm all right . . ."	*Los Angeles Times*, "Death Vigil in Arctic Snows," February 28, 1924
156	"I guess we . . ."	*Los Angeles Times*, "Death Vigil in Arctic Snows," February 28, 1924
157	"Next came bloat-ing . . ."	Lorne Knight's diary, February 8, 1923, KL
158	Bad as all . . .	*New York Globe*, "How to Keep Well" by A. F. Currier, M.D., undated news clipping
159	"But on the . . ."	Lorne Knight's diary, February 6, 1923, KL
161	"When I say . . ."	Lorne Knight's diary, February 11, 1923, KL
161	"Thank fortune . . ."	Lorne Knight's diary, February 12, 1923, KL
162	"fresh raw meat . . ."	Lorne Knight's diary, February 13, 1923, KL
162	"Oh Yes! My . . ."	Lorne Knight's diary, February 25, 1923, KL
162	"trip hammer"	Lorne Knight's diary, February 16, 1923, KL
163	"full stomach of . . ."	Lorne Knight's diary, February 20, 1923, KL
165	"Troubled some last . . ."	Lorne Knight's diary, March 3, 1923, KL
165	"Cannot eat the . . ."	Lorne Knight's diary, March 11, 1923, KL

166	"as thin as . . ."	Lorne Knight's diary, March 21, 1923, KL
166	"Not that I . . ."	Lorne Knight's diary, March 23, 1923, KL
166	"as a conversational-ist . . ."	Lorne Knight's diary, March 3, 1923, KL
168	"March 1923 . . ."	Alma Galle to J. I. Knight, March, 1923, LAW

TEN

171	"It has caught . . ."	Ada Blackjack's diary, March, 28, 1923, UAA/BBJ
171	"But my eye is . . ."	Ada Blackjack's diary, April 2, 1923, UAA/BBJ
171	"If anything hap-pen . . ."	Ada Blackjack's diary, April 2, 1923, UAA/BBJ
172	"We look at . . ."	Ada Blackjack's diary, March 26, 1923, UAA/BBJ
174	"to cruel"	Ada Blackjack's diary, April 21, 1923, UAA/BBJ
174	"He never stop . . ."	Ada Blackjack's diary, April 21, 1923, UAA/BBJ
175	"This is the . . ."	Ada Blackjack's diary, April 21, 1923, UAA/BBJ
175	"If I be . . ."	Ada Blackjack's diary, April 21, 1923, UAA/BBJ
176	"If I happen . . ."	Ada Blackjack's diary, April 30, 1923, UAA/BBJ
177	"I will not . . ."	"The Story of Ada Blackjack," p. 339, *The Adventure of Wrangel Island*
177	"I thought to . . ."	"The Story of Ada Blackjack," p. 342, *The Adventure of Wrangel Island*
178	"Knight," she called . . .	Ada Blackjack's statement to E. R. Jordan, p. 3, DART
179	"when I shoot . . ."	"The Story of Ada Blackjack," p. 343, *The Adventure of Wrangel Island*
179	"I said to . . ."	"The Story of Ada Blackjack," p. 343, *The Adventure of Wrangel Island*
181	"The *Nation* . . ."	The *Nation*, "Wrangel Island," September 19, 1923

ELEVEN

182	"Who told you . . ."	Ada Blackjack's diary, May 7, 1923, UAA/BBJ
185	"Look what I . . ."	"The Story of Ada Blackjack," p. 331, *The Adventure of Wrangel Island*
187	"White ladies want . . ."	"The Story of Ada Blackjack," pp. 348–349, *The Adventure of Wrangel Island*
187	"Ada, Mr. Knight . . ."	"The Story of Ada Blackjack," p. 348, *The Adventure of Wrangel Island*
188	"Ada," Knight said . . .	"The Story of Ada Blackjack," p. 348, *The Adventure of Wrangel Island*
192	"June 17, 1923 . . ."	J. I. Knight to the Galles, June 17, 1923, LAW

TWELVE

194	"should confine its . . ."	*Vancouver Sun & Province*, "Joint Action on Wrangell," April 9, 1923
195	"the men on . . ."	Stefansson to Mr. Finnie, March 24, 1923, DART
195	"Illness is, of . . ."	Stefansson to J. I. Knight, January 8, 1923, DART
196	Stefansson estimated . . .	American Institute of Economic Research, Cost of Living Calculator, *http://www*.aier.org/cgi-bin/colcalculator.cgi
198	It was difficult . . .	*Los Angeles Times*, "Ending Years in the Arctic," October 19, 1921
199	"easy if only . . ."	*The Friendly Arctic*, p. 669
200	"challenging, calling . . ."	Harold Noice, *With Stefansson in the Arctic*, p. 17
201	"Seattle Boy Becomes . . ."	*With Stefansson in the Arctic*, p. 33
201	"Adventure!" Stefansson had . . .	*With Stefansson in the Arctic*, p. 31–32
201	Noice was sufficiently . . .	*With Stefansson in the Arctic*, p. 45
201	"if this man . . ."	*With Stefansson in the Arctic*, p. 32
201	"few 'human' traits . . ."	*With Stefansson in the Arctic*, p. 267
202	"June 10. This . . ."	Ada Blackjack's diary, June 10, 1923, UAA/BBJ

202	"white like paper"	"The Story of Ada Blackjack," p. 348, *The Adventure of Wrangel Island*
202	"Presented to Ada . . ."	Lorne Knight's Bible, presented to Ada Blackjack (Bible currently in possession of Billy Blackjack Johnson)
203	"Pretty good shooting . . ."	Ada Blackjack's diary, June 17, 1923, UAA/BBJ

PART IV

| 206 | "Here lies a . . ." | Words written on a piece of paper, folded within the pages of Lorne Knight's diary, NAC |

THIRTEEN

207	"Don't leave me . . ."	Ada Blackjack's statement to E. R. Jordan, p. 4, *Adventure of Wrangel Island*
207	"What is the . . ."	Ada Blackjack's statement to E. R. Jordan, p. 4, *Adventure of Wrangel Island*
208	"Dear Galle . . ."	*The Literary Digest*, December 8, 1923
209	"Wrangel, Island . . ."	Ada Blackjack's record of Lorne Knight's death, DART [Note: Knight apparently died either on June 22 or June 23, as Ada records both as his death date in separate places.]
212	"In case he . . ."	J. I. Knight to Harry Galle, July 10, 1923, LAW
213	"It is unthinkable . . ."	A. J. T. Taylor to Olive Wilcox, July 29, 1923, DART
213	"Must load . . ."	Harold Noice to Stefansson, July 27, 1923, DART
214	"Do not make . . ."	Harold Noice to Stefansson, July 28, 1923, DART
214	"The Siberian . . ."	Associated Press Dispatch, July 30, 1923
214	"Soviet officials are . . ."	*The Globe and Mail*, July 30, 1923
214	"equivalent to an . . ."	Canadian Press, *Mail*, July 30, 1923
214	"A critical time . . ."	A. J. T. Taylor to William Cory, July 29, 1923, DART
215	"Until we are . . ."	William Cory to A. J. T. Taylor, July 30, 1923, DART

215	By the last . . .	American Institute of Economic Research, Cost of Living Calculator, http://www.aier.org/cgi-bin/ colcalculator.cgi
215	"Siberian sending ship . . ."	Harold Noice to Stefansson, July 28, 1923, DART
216	"June 24th . . ."	*The Literary Digest*, December 8, 1923
216	"June 25th . . ."	*The Literary Digest*, December 8, 1923
216	"June 26th . . ."	*The Literary Digest*, December 8, 1923
216	"had a nice . . ."	Ada Blackjack's diary, June 26, 1923, UAA/BBJ
217	"June 28th . . ."	*The Literary Digest*, December 8, 1923
217	"July 1st . . ."	Ada Blackjack's diary, July 1, 1923, UAA/BBJ
218	"Fourth of July"	Ada Blackjack's diary, July 4, 1923, UAA/BBJ
218	"I am glad . . ."	"The Story of Ada Blackjack," p. 344, *The Adventure of Wrangel Island*
219	She purposely did . . .	"The Story of Ada Blackjack," p. 344, *The Adventure of Wrangel Island*
220	"It look like . . ."	Ada Blackjack's diary, July 21, 1923, UAA/BBJ
220	"July 23 . . ."	Ada Blackjack's diary, July 23, 1923, UAA/BBJ
221	"if the lord . . ."	Ada Blackjack's diary, July 28, 1923, UAA/BBJ
223	"McMinnville, Oreg . . ."	J. I. Knight to Harry Galle, August 8, 1923, LAW

FOURTEEN

224	"Everybody London . . ."	Stefansson to Harold Noice, August 1, 1923, DART
225	"adventurous patriots . . ."	*The Adventure of Wrangel Island*, pp. 162–163
225	Stefansson had . . .	The Stefansson Arctic Exploration and Development Company Limited Statement of Affairs as of 9 October, 1923, DART
227	"Christian fostering . . ."	*Los Angeles Sunday Times*, "Wrangell Isle Dash Is Begun," August 26, 1923

227	"I am leaving . . ."	*Los Angeles Sunday Times*, "Wrangell Isle Dash Is Begun," August 26, 1923
228	"So far we . . ."	Ralph Lomen (quoting Harold Noice) to A. J. T. Taylor, August 23, 1923, DART
228	"What's the matter . . ."	*Des Moines Register*, "Wrangell Isle Tragedy Story Told by Noice," September 5, 1923
229	"But whosoever . . ."	John 4:14
230	"How is it . . ."	John 4:9
230	"Whosoever drinketh . . ."	John 4:14
230	"But the hour . . ."	John 4:23 and 4:24
230	"Jesus saith unto . . ."	John 4:26
230	"But if ye . . ."	Lev. 26:14 and 26:16
231	"And if ye . . ."	Lev. 26:21 and 26:22
231	"Trust in the . . ."	Prov. 3:3, 3:4, 3:5, 3:6, and 3:7
231	"Thank living . . ."	Ada Blackjack's diary, August 1, 1923, UAA/BBJ
232	"the Lord Jesus . . ."	Ada Blackjack's diary, August 6, 1923, UAA/BBJ
232	"So it looks . . ."	Ada Blackjack's diary, August 8, 1923, UAA/BBJ
233	"saviour Jesus"	Ada Blackjack's diary, August 8, 1923, UAA/BBJ
233	The next morning . . .	Ada Blackjack's diary, August 12, 1923, UAA/BBJ
234	"and I thank . . ."	Ada Blackjack's diary, August 17, 1923, UAA/BBJ
235	"It seemed to . . ."	*Des Moines Register*, "Wrangell Isle Tragedy Story Told by Noice," September 5, 1923
235	"Prepare a special . . ."	Unnamed newspaper article, "Human Figure Disclosed on Wrangell Island Beach," September 4, 1923
236	Full speed astern . . .	*The Literary Digest*, December 8, 1923
236	"Were we in . . ."	*Des Moines Register*, "Eskimo Woman, Lone Survivor, Greets Noice," September 7, 1923
237	Noice watched her . . .	*The Literary Digest*, December 8, 1923
237	"Where is Crawford . . ."	*The Literary Digest*, December 8, 1923

237	"Why is not . . ."	"The Story of Ada Blackjack," p. 334, *The Adventure of Wrangel Island*
238	"I expected to . . ."	*The Literary Digest*, December 8, 1923
238	"There is no-body . . ."	*The Literary Digest*, December 8, 1923
238	"Knight, he died . . ."	*Twice-a-Week Spokesman Review*, "Woman Only Survivor of Wrangell Island Party," September 14, 1923
239	"She heard the . . ."	"Lady in the Moon," as told to Inglis Fletcher by Ada Blackjack, February 11, 1924, IFP

FIFTEEN

240	"I wonder if . . ."	*Toronto Star*, "Arctic Heroine Wins Where Strong Men Fail," September 7, 1923
241	"I had hard . . ."	*The Literary Digest*, December 8, 1923
241	"Knight—he dead . . ."	*The Literary Digest*, December 8, 1923
241	"After Knight die . . ."	*The Literary Digest*, December 8, 1923
242	"Such was the . . ."	*The Literary Digest*, December 8, 1923
242	"The white man's . . ."	Noice, *With Stefansson in the Arctic*, pp. 160–161
242	"I'm sorry I . . ."	*The Literary Digest*, December 8, 1923
244	"Nome, Alaska, Aug . . ."	*The Adventure of Wrangel Island*, p. 168
245	Ada was anxious . . .	Interview with John Tetpon, nephew of Ada Blackjack, January 27, 2003
245	The first female . . .	Bernard Grun, *The Timetables of History*
246	"It was no . . ."	Ada's statement to E. R. Jordan, p. 6, *Adventure of Wrangel Island*
246	"Crawford's death is . . ."	*Twin Falls News*, "Pays Tribute to American," September 2, 1923
246	"One good hunter . . ."	*New York Times*, "Wrangell Island Tragedy," September 3, 1923
246	"prevent, as far . . ."	*Adventure of Wrangel Island*, p. 360
247	"I knew even . . ."	*Adventure of Wrangel Island*, p. 360
247	"minimize the . . ."	Stefansson, telegram to D. M. Le Bourdais, September 5, 1923, DART
247	"We must keep . . ."	Stefansson to Harold Noice, September 12, 1923, DART

248	"Life looked so . . ."	*Toronto Star*, "Mother Had a Premonition She Would Not See Son Again," September 1, 1923
248	"He was her . . ."	*Toronto Star*, "Mother Had a Premonition She Would Not See Son Again," September 1, 1923
249	"Deepest sympathy . . ."	Stefansson, telegram to J. T. Crawford, undated, DART
249	"He was a . . ."	*Toronto Star*, "Mother Had a Premonition She Would Not See Son Again," September 1, 1923
250	"Deepest sympathy . . ."	Unnamed newspaper clipping, "Relief Expedition Says Maurer Dead," September 1, 1923, MR
251	"The Arctic has . . ."	*Seattle Daily Times*, "Seattle Man Hero of Arctic," September 2, 1923
251	"We deeply regret . . ."	A. J. T. Taylor and John Anderson, telegram to Harry and Alma Galle, September 3, 1923, LAW
251	"Deepest sympathy . . ."	J. T. Crawford, telegram to Harry and Alma Galle, September 3, 1923, LAW
253	"they died in . . ."	J. I. Knight to Harry and Alma Galle, September 3, 1923, LAW
253	"this does me . . ."	J. I. Knight to Harry and Alma Galle, September 3, 1923, LAW
254	"The ordeal is . . ."	J. I. Knight to Harry and Alma Galle, September 3, 1923, LAW
254	"It seems to . . ."	J. I. Knight to Stefansson, September 5, 1923, LAW
254	"as steel"	J. I. Knight to Stefansson, September 5, 1923, LAW
255	"How I wish . . ."	J. I. Knight to Stefansson, September 5, 1923, LAW

PART V

| 259 | "There was nothing . . ." | "Lady in the Moon," as told to Inglis Fletcher by Ada Blackjack, IFP |
| 260 | "*Montreal Standard* . . ." | *Montreal Standard*, "Mr. Stefansson Shows Results," September 9, 1923 |

SIXTEEN

262	"In view of . . ."	*Toronto Star*, "Stefansson Still Has Hopes That Allan Crawford's Alive," September 11, 1923
262	"Is Allan Crawford . . ."	*Toronto Star*, "Trip Wrangel Id. to Siberia 110 Miles, Required 17 Days," September 4, 1923
262	"The first thing . . ."	*Toronto Star*, "Should Not Give Up Hope of Finding Crawford Alive," September 4, 1923
263	"Maurer's family . . ."	*Toronto Star*, "Ask U.S. to Send Ship to Look for Crawford," September 10, 1923
264	"behalf of Milton . . ."	B. F. Nebergall to Hon. Charles Evans Hughes, September 6, 1923, LAW
264	"If you can . . ."	B. F. Nebergall to Hon. Morris Sheppard, September 6, 1923, LAW
264	"I wish to . . ."	Harry M. Wurzbach to B. F. Nebergall, September 10, 1923, LAW
264	"I am at . . ."	C. B. Hudspeth to Emil Heinen, September 11, 1923, LAW
264	"I shall be . . ."	Morris Sheppard to B. F. Nebergall, September 14, 1923, LAW
265	"all the love . . ."	J. I. Knight to Harry Galle, September 20, 1923, LAW
265	"No information . . ."	William Phillips, Acting Secretary of State, to Morris Sheppard, September 19, 1923, LAW
266	"He further stated . . ."	Kate George to Hon. Emil Heinen, September 19, 1923, LAW
266	"Certainly we cannot . . ."	Unnamed newspaper article, "Should Not Give Up Hope of Finding Crawford Alive," September 4, 1923
266	"It is hard . . ."	*Telegraph*, "University Is Opened: Tribute to A. Crawford," September 26, 1923
267	"Grotesque fallacy . . ."	*Saturday Night*, "The Un-Friendly Arctic," September 15, 1923
268	"Could a land . . ."	*The Varsity*, "Allan Crawford and 'The Friendly Arctic,'" September 28, 1923
268	"Wrangel Island is . . ."	*The Globe and Mail*, "Gallant Allan Crawford," September 3, 1923

268	"No one can . . ."	*Saturday Night*, "The Un-Friendly Arctic," September 15, 1923
268	"We have no . . ."	Unnamed and undated newspaper article, "Siberia Asked to Help Search for Crawford," LAW
269	"There have been . . ."	*Toronto Mail & Empire*, "Have Furled Flag On Wrangel Island," September 8, 1923
269	"Crawford crossed to . . ."	*Toronto Star*, "Stefansson Still Has Hope That Allan Crawford's Alive," September 11, 1923
269	"As to the . . ."	*Toronto Star*, "Shatters Faint Hope of Finding Men Still Alive," September 10, 1923
270	"So we must . . ."	John Maurer to Harry Galle, October 15, 1923, LAW
270	"Don't you know . . ."	Mae Belle Anderson to Helen Crawford, November 14, 1923, NAC
270	"I am sincerely . . ."	Delphine Maurer to Stefansson, October 24, 1923, DART
272	"Unfortunately you . . ."	Stefansson, telegram to J. I. Knight, October 22, 1923, DART
272	"The expedition did . . ."	Stefansson to J. I. Knight, October 23, 1923, DART
273	"I do not . . ."	J. I. Knight to Harry Galle, September 20, 1923, LAW
274	"They seemed to . . ."	J. I. Knight to Stefansson, October 12, 1923, DART
275	"There are hundreds . . ."	Harry Galle to Mr. Scarborough, September 25, 1923, LAW
276	"I blame Steffanson[sic] . . ."	Dora (last name unknown) to Harry and Alma Galle, September 25, 1923, LAW
276	"Evidently," Miss Wilcox . . .	Olive Wilcox to Alma Galle, October 11, 1923, LAW
278	"Other miscarriages . . ."	*London Times*, "Wrangel Island Tragedy," October 9, 1923
278	"It seems also . . ."	*London Times*, "Wrangel Island Tragedy," October 9, 1923
278	"The unaccountable . . ."	*London Times*, "Wrangel Island Tragedy," October 9, 1923
279	"The blow is . . ."	J. T. Crawford to Stefansson, November 28, 1923, DART
281	*Pathfinder of . . .*	*Pathfinder of Alaska*, "Russia and Wrangell Island," September 1, 1923

SEVENTEEN

282	"I wonder what . . ."	Mae Belle Anderson to Helen Crawford, November 8, 1923, NAC
282	To Ada, Seattle . . .	*The Adventure of Wrangel Island,* pp. 344–345
284	"prostituted it as . . ."	J. I. Knight to Harold Noice, November 1923, unsent letter, DART
284	"You are playing . . ."	J. I. Knight to Harold Noice, November 1923, unsent letter, DART
287	"For some years . . ."	Mae Belle Anderson to Helen Crawford, December 29, 1923, NAC
287	"He could have . . ."	Mae Belle Anderson to Helen Crawford, February 6, 1924, NAC
288	"I am glad . . ."	Mae Belle Anderson to Helen Crawford, November 4, 1923, NAC
288	"make out that . . ."	Mae Belle Anderson to Helen Crawford, November 8, 1923, NAC
288	"Let us devote . . ."	J. I. Knight to Helen Crawford, November 10, 1923, LAW
288	"They all bring . . ."	J. I. Knight to the Crawfords, Galles and Maurers, January 31, 1924, LAW
288	"To commemorate . . ."	J. I. Knight to Helen Crawford, November 10, 1923, LAW
289	"gather flowers and . . ."	J. I. Knight to Helen Crawford, December 5, 1923, LAW
290	"We regret that . . ."	Alma Galle to Stefansson, December 29, 1923, DART
292	"closed up like . . ."	J. I. Knight to Stefansson, December 3, 1923, DART
294	"Why did Noice . . ."	J. I. Knight to Stefansson, December 3, 1923, DART
296	"This is a . . ."	J. I. Knight to the Galles, December 17, 1923, LAW
297	"Well, I must . . ."	J. I. Knight to the Galles, December 17, 1923, LAW
298	"Noice saved my . . ."	J. I. Knight to Stefansson, December 17, 1923, LAW
299	"could teach some . . ."	J. I. Knight to Stefansson, December 17, 1923, LAW
299	"nearer to us . . ."	J. I. Knight to Stefansson, December 17, 1923, LAW
300	"What a lot . . ."	J. I. Knight to Stefansson, December 17, 1923, LAW

300	"she was the . . ."	J. I. Knight to the Galles, December 17, 1923, LAW
301	"Damn. That makes . . ."	J. I. Knight to the Galles, December 17, 1923, LAW
301	"You are all . . ."	J. I. and Georgia Knight to Ada Blackjack, December 18, 1923, LAW
304	"We hereby designate . . ."	September 1 agreement between families, January 1, 1924, LAW
305	He offered her . . .	H. G. Jones, "Ada Blackjack and the Wrangel Island Tragedy," *Terre Incognitae*, Volume 31, 1999
305	"I will tell . . ."	*The Adventure of Wrangel Island*, p. 373
306	"January 1924 . . ."	Alma Galle to Ada Blackjack, January 1924 (undated), rough draft, LAW
307	"Seattle, Jan. 30 . . ."	Ada Blackjack to Alma Galle, January 30, 1924, LAW

EIGHTEEN

309	"her statements . . ."	Statement by John Allison, p. 6, DART
309	"Knowing my sister . . ."	Statement by John Allison, p. 6, DART
310	"I sensed . . ."	Statement by John Allison, p. 8, DART
311	"too much trouble . . ."	Inglis Fletcher to Stefansson, February 6, 1924, DART
313	"like an animal"	Nan Allan to Inglis Fletcher, February 11, 1924, DART
314	"You must shoot . . ."	Inglis Fletcher to Stefansson, February 8, 1924, DART
314	"Well, I don't . . ."	Inglis Fletcher to Stefansson, March 8, 1924, DART
315	"just sit still . . ."	Inglis Fletcher to Stefansson, February 8, 1924, DART
315	"I have been . . ."	Inglis Fletcher to Stefansson, February 8, 1924, DART
315	"Do you think . . ."	Inglis Fletcher to Stefansson, February 8, 1924, DART
315	"It is like . . ."	Inglis Fletcher to Stefansson, February 8, 1924, DART
316	"halfbreed"	*The Adventure of Wrangel Island*, p. 346
316	"Were there many . . ."	*The Adventure of Wrangel Island*, p. 346

316	"it always makes . . ."	*The Adventure of Wrangel Island*, p. 346
316	"Too many questions . . ."	Inglis Fletcher to Stefansson, February 12, 1924, DART
318	"If I have . . ."	Inglis Fletcher to Stefansson, February 10, 1924, DART
319	"When thinking of . . ."	Alma Galle to Stefansson, February 16, 1924, DART
319	"I am more . . ."	Alma Galle to Ada Roach, n.d., LAW
319	"The truth is . . ."	H. H. Langton, *The Canadian Historical Review of the Adventure of Wrangel Island*, NAC
320	" 'done for' from . . ."	Mae Belle Anderson to Helen Crawford, March 11, 1924, NAC
320	"If I would . . ."	William McKinlay on the Wrangel Island Expedition, NAC
320	"Mr. Knight thinks . . ."	Mae Belle Anderson to Helen Crawford, February 16, 1924, NAC
321	"Stefansson could not . . ."	Mae Belle Anderson to Helen Crawford, June 20, 1924, NAC
321	"Now that a . . ."	Alma Galle to Stefansson, October 21, 1924, DART
322	"Oh, Oh!"	Inglis Fletcher to Stefansson, February 10, 1924, DART
323	"If my mother . . ."	Inglis Fletcher to Stefansson, February 10, 1924, DART
323	"I do not . . ."	Inglis Fletcher to Stefansson, February 10, 1924, DART
323	"Are they for . . ."	Inglis Fletcher to Stefansson, February 10, 1924, DART
323	"Please tell him . . ."	Inglis Fletcher to Stefansson, February 10, 1924, DART
324	"The New York . . ."	*New York World*, "Spurned Eskimo Woman Is Blamed for Arctic Death," February 11, 1924

NINETEEN

326	"Spurned Eskimo . . ."	*New York World*, February 11, 1924
326	"I thought you . . ."	*The Adventure of Wrangel Island*, p. 372
327	"The hills look . . ."	Inglis Fletcher to Stefansson, February 12, 1924, DART

327	"Here is my . . ."	Inglis Fletcher to Stefansson, February 12, 1924, DART
328	"Now the old . . ."	"Lady in the Moon," as told to Inglis Fletcher by Ada Blackjack, February 11, 1924, IFP
329	"During the six . . ."	*The Adventure of Wrangel Island*, pp. 375-377
331	"Last night . . ."	*Los Angeles Times*, "Survivor of Arctic Trip Is in City," February 13, 1924
331	"Well, I do . . ."	Inglis Fletcher to Stefansson, February 18, 1924, DART
331	"Well, maybe white . . ."	*The Adventure of Wrangel Island*, p. 349
333	"I'm sorry for . . ."	Ada Blackjack to Stefansson, February 17, 1924, DART
333	"That she could . . ."	*New York World*, "Spurned Eskimo Woman Is Blamed for Arctic Death," February 11, 1924
334	"When I got . . ."	*The Adventure of Wrangel Island*, p. 349
334	"A little woman . . ."	*Los Angeles Times*, "Ada Blackjack Hits Back," February 27, 1924
334	"Other allegations . . ."	*Los Angeles Times*, "Ada Blackjack Hits Back," February 27, 1924
335	"I don't think . . ."	*Los Angeles Times*, "Ada Blackjack Hits Back," February 27, 1924
335	"doctor, nurse . . ."	*Los Angeles Times*, "Death Vigil in Arctic Snows," February 28, 1924
336	"They found her . . ."	Unnamed, undated newspaper article, "Ada the Eskimo" (Stef MSS 196.97: Fletcher, Inglis (2) 1922-25), DART
336	"She had 'guts' . . ."	Unnamed, undated newspaper article, "In a Biological Sense" (Stef MSS 196: 97: Fletcher, Inglis (2) 1922-25), DART
336	"For two months . . ."	Unnamed, undated newspaper article, "Ada Blackjack Refutes Noice," by Consolidated Press (Stef MSS 196:97: Fletcher, Inglis (2) 1922-25), DART
336	"She will not . . ."	*Los Angeles Times*, "Death Vigil in Arctic Snows," February 28, 1924
338	"In all matters . . ."	J. I. Knight to Stefansson, December 3, 1923, DART
340	"New Philadelphia . . ."	Mary Maurer to the Galles, August 10, 1924, LAW (translated from German by Jessica Gilroy)

TWENTY

341	"Ada Blackjack is . . ."	Unnamed, undated newspaper article, LAW
341	"I am very . . ."	*Anchorage Times*, "Only Survivor of Arctic Expedition Dies in Obscurity," June 5, 1983
341	"I am afraid . . ."	A. J. T. Taylor to Stefansson, March 29, 1924, DART
342	"Could I discard . . ."	Alma Galle to Stefansson, October 21, 1924, DART
343	"no claim to . . ."	*London Times*, "Wrangel Island," April 9, 1924
343	"How would you . . ."	*ASIA*, "Staking Wrangel Island," by D. M. Le Bourdais, April 1925
344	And then someone . . .	The four jawbones did, in fact, belong to members of Stefansson's Canadian Arctic Expedition: First Mate Sandy Anderson; Second Mate Charles Barker; and seamen John Brady and Edmund Lawrence Golightly (alias Archie King).
345	"Soviet officials . . ."	*New York Evening Post*, "Soviet to Lease Wrangel," September 20, 1924
346	Perhaps it was . . .	An intriguing letter from Alma's sister Maggie, dated May 10, 1925 (LAW), stated that she and her husband had been to the Majestic Theatre at their home in Austin to see a psychic and mind reader who was passing through town. "He's alive. He's not dead," the psychic said when asked about Milton Galle, "—two men left—four men were on the island. He is wearing a uniform now." She told them he had been captured in Siberia and was not being held prisoner but was being kept quiet due to governmental reasons.
346	"It has been . . ."	David and Mary Maurer and family to Harry and Alma Galle and family, August 28, 1924, LAW
347	"We have never . . ."	J. I. and Georgia Knight to friends, September 1, 1924, LAW
347	"Our thoughts have . . ."	The Crawfords to the Galles, September 1, 1924, LAW

347	"We must all . . ."	Delphine Maurer to Alma Galle, September 3, 1924, LAW
348	"It is not . . ."	Alma Galle to Mr. and Mrs. Robb, undated, LAW
348	Noice knew that . . .	Mae Belle Anderson to Helen Crawford, April 21, 1924, NAC
349	"In Noice's favour . . ."	Mae Belle Anderson to Helen Crawford, January 20, 1924, NAC
350	"I am glad . . ."	Harold Noice's retraction to Stefansson, October 19, 1924, LAW
350	"My complete . . ."	Harold Noice's retraction to Stefansson, October 19, 1924, LAW
351	"the relatives and . . ."	J. T. Crawford to A. J. T. Taylor, October 13, 1924, DART, and J. T. Crawford telegram to Macmillan Co., undated, DART
351	"We now think . . ."	J. T. and Helen Crawford to the Macmillan Co., October 16, 1924, DART
351	"as sympathetic . . ."	Stefansson to A. J. T. Taylor, November 20, 1924, DART
352	"If Stefansson gets . . ."	Mae Belle Anderson to Helen Crawford, April 26, 1924, NAC
352	"think it wise . . ."	J. T. Crawford to A. J. T. Taylor, December 19, 1924, DART
352	"You claim that . . ."	J. T. Crawford to A. J. T. Taylor, December 14, 1924, DART
353	"Is he still . . ."	Inglis Fletcher to Stefansson, December 20, 1924, DART
353	"I never show . . ."	Ada Blackjack to Stefansson, December 20, 1924, DART
354	"Oh! It's . . ."	Inglis Fletcher to Stefansson, December 21, 1924, DART
355	"Glorious was life . . ."	Netsit, *Northern Voices*, "Dead Man's Song," pp. 34–35

TWENTY-ONE

357	"After escaping the . . ."	Mae Belle Anderson to Helen Crawford, February 25, 1925, NAC
358	"I don't want . . ."	Ada Blackjack to Gertrude Andrus, April 13, 1925, DART
358	"It isn't very . . ."	Ada Blackjack to Gertrude Andrus, April 16, 1925, DART

359	" 'piratically appropriated' . . ."	*New York World*, "Stefansson Says No-ice Admits Slurring Wrangel Island Heroes," April 20, 1925
359	"Wife Goes to . . ."	*New York Evening Post*, "Wife Goes to Reno on Noice Retraction," April 20, 1925
361	"For many months . . ."	*New York World*, "Parents Blame Stefansson for Crawford's Death," May 10, 1925
362	"The Maurer Family . . ."	John Maurer to Stefansson, May 3, 1925, LAW
362	"He is sometimes . . ."	Canadian House of Commons Debates, June 10, 1925, NAC
363	"of exceptional . . ."	Canadian House of Commons Debates, June 10, 1925, NAC
363	"If there is . . ."	Canadian House of Commons Debates, June 10, 1925, NAC
364	"Ada will die . . ."	*Kansas City Journal*, "Arctic Heroine Going Back to Die on Island," August 1, 1927
365	"Hardship of the . . ."	*Toronto Mail & Empire*, "Ada Blackjack Goes North to Die," November 1, 1927
365	Stefansson read the . . .	Stefansson to Carl Lomen, July 6, 1950, IFP

PART VI

| 367 | "I thank God . . ." | Ada Blackjack's diary, July 23, 1923, UAA/BBJ |
| 368 | "THE ADA BLACKJACK . . ." | Burt E. Anderson to Commander Fitz-hugh Green, June 1, 1928, FG |

TWENTY-TWO

369	"I had a . . ."	Sunday *Denver Post*, "Lone Survivor Ada Blackjack Recalls Arctic," January 14, 1973
370	"Never mind . . ."	Interview with Billy Blackjack Johnson, January 25, 2003
370	"When I was . . ."	Interview with Billy Blackjack Johnson, January 25, 2003

370	"Ah nooga naga . . ."	Interview with Billy Blackjack Johnson, January 25, 2003
372	"It is sometimes . . ."	Olaf Swenson to the Galles, July 1, 1930, LAW
372	"All this has . . ."	Helen Crawford to Alma Galle, March 27, 1930, LAW
372	"I always dread . . ."	Helen Crawford to Harry and Alma Galle, September 1, 1930, LAW
372	"When I woke . . ."	Helen Crawford to Alma Galle, September 1, 1934, LAW
374	"Some day the . . ."	Mae Belle Anderson to Helen Crawford, February 9, 1927, NAC
375	"My husband was . . ."	Helen Crawford to Alma Galle, September 1, 1928, LAW
375	"I feel at . . ."	Helen Crawford to Alma Galle, September 1, 1928, LAW
376	"True, our brother . . ."	McMinnville *Elk*, "McMinnville Elks Mourn Death of Joseph I. Knight," October 25, 1930, LAW
376	"I always want . . ."	J. I. Knight to friends, September 8, 1924, LAW
377	"Since my paying . . ."	Stefansson to Alma Galle, January 14, 1928, LAW
377	"I can only . . ."	Alma Galle to Stefansson, January 20, 1929, LAW
377	"However great this . . ."	Alma Galle to Stefansson, November 1, 1932, LAW
378	"strange, completely . . ."	Harold Noice, *Back of Beyond*, 1939
380	"he is prone . . ."	E. P. Coffey to Mr. Ladd, October 11, 1939 (FBI Freedom of Information/Privacy Acts Section; Vilhjalmur Stefansson, File: 100-7516 Section 1)
381	"Summarizing the . . ."	J. Edgar Hoover to Stefansson, December 21, 1939 (Freedom of Information/Privacy Acts Section; Vilhjalmur Stefansson, File: 100-7516 Section 1)
382	In the late . . .	Interview with Bill Lawless, April 2002 and again October 10, 2002, LAW
383	"I really will . . ."	*Literary Digest*, July 13, 1935, p. 29
384	"Feb. 28, 1974 . . ."	Stanton H. Patty to William S. Crosby, February 28, 1974, DART

EPILOGUE

387	"In memory of . . ."	Don Knight, cousin of E. Lorne Knight, DN
387	"a true and . . ."	Lorne Knight, *Pechuck*, 1932, flyleaf
387	"God did not . . ."	Mae Belle Anderson to Helen Crawford, December 14, 1923, NAC
388	"To commemorate . . ."	*Toronto Star*, "Fellow Students Honor Late Allan Crawford," June 1, 1924
388	"sacrifice and heroism . . ."	*Toronto Star*, "University Schools Memorial," June 18, 1924
388	Long after Alfred . . .	Interview with Don Tolle, March 2002
389	"Why are you . . ."	Interview with Bill Lawless, October 30, 2002, LAW
389	"Dear Stefansson . . ."	Ada Blackjack Johnson to Stefansson, June 28, 1950, IFP
390	"formerly Ada . . ."	Ada Blackjack Johnson to Stefansson, June 28, 1950, IFP
390	"pathetic case"	Stefansson to Carl Lomen, July 6, 1950, IFP
390	"These charities . . ."	Stefansson to Ada Blackjack, July 6, 1950, IFP
390	"It is still . . ."	Sunday *Denver Post*, "Lone Survivor Ada Blackjack Recalls Arctic," January 14, 1973
390	But she had . . .	Sunday *Denver Post*, "Lone Survivor Ada Blackjack Recalls Arctic," January 14, 1973
390	"no trace at . . ."	Sunday *Denver Post*, "Lone Survivor Ada Blackjack Recalls Arctic," January 14, 1973
391	"It was a . . ."	Sunday *Denver Post*, "Lone Survivor Ada Blackjack Recalls Arctic," January 14, 1973
391	"I think I . . ."	Sunday *Denver Post*, "Lone Survivor Ada Blackjack Recalls Arctic," January 14, 1973
391	"Brave? I don't . . ."	Sunday *Denver Post*, "Lone Survivor Ada Blackjack Recalls Arctic," January 14, 1973
392	"Am I beautiful . . ."	Interview with Billy Blackjack Johnson, January 25, 2003

392   "I consider my . . ."   CIRI Newsletter, "Look Back in History: Ada Blackjack Johnson—Arctic Heroine"

393   "The final chapter . . ."   Billy Blackjack Johnson letter, 1973, UAA/BBJ

393   "a small token . . ."   Rep. John G. Fuller to Billy Blackjack Johnson, August 26, 1983, BBJ

393   "Born in 1898 . . ."   The Alaska Legislature, In Memoriam: Ada Blackjack Johnson, June 16, 1983, UAA/BBJ

394   "I am so . . ."   Billy Blackjack Johnson to Rep. Frank R. Ferguson, September 13, 1983, UAA/BBJ

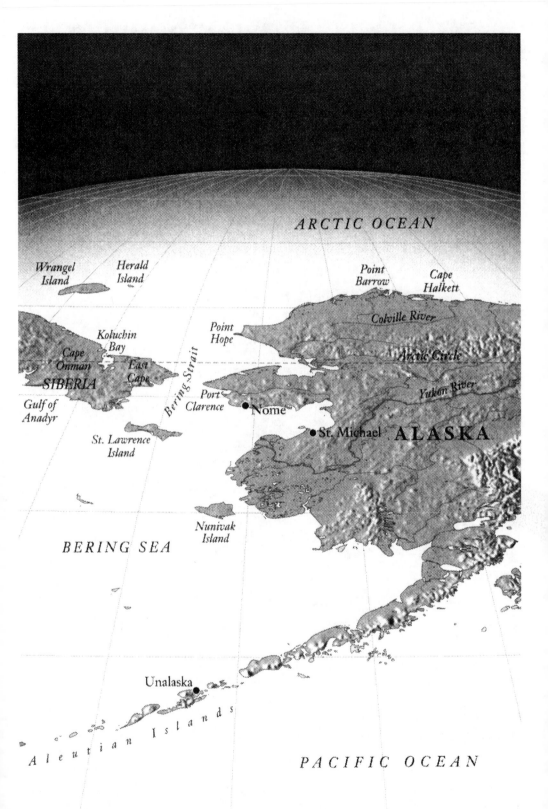

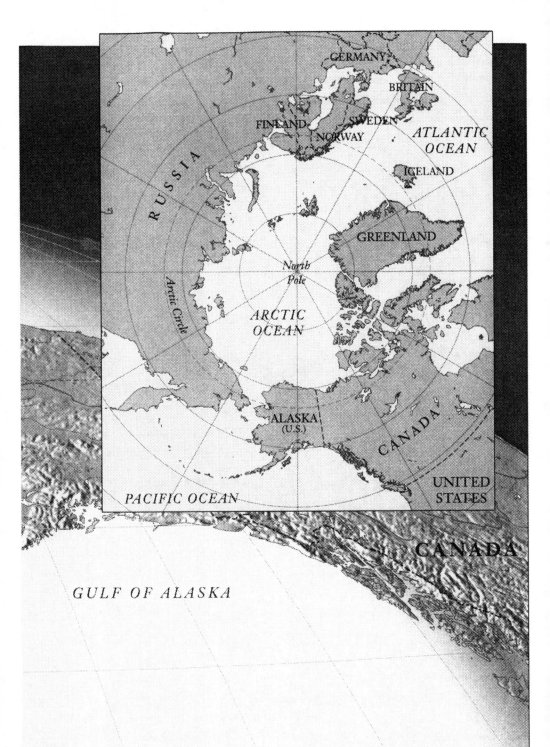

GERMANY

BRITAIN

FINLAND SWEDEN
NORWAY

ATLANTIC
OCEAN

RUSSIA

ICELAND

GREENLAND

North
Pole

Arctic Circle

ARCTIC
OCEAN

ALASKA
(U.S.)

CANADA

UNITED
STATES

PACIFIC OCEAN

CANADA

GULF OF ALASKA

CPSIA information can be obtained at www.ICGtesting.com
Printed in the USA
LVOW11*1327060216

474006LV00006B/7/P

9 780786 868636